Life on
the Mississippi

Mark Twain

Life on
the Mississippi

WITH AN INTRODUCTION BY
Jonathan Raban

PAPERBACK CLASSICS

GUY CARDWELL
WROTE THE NOTES AND SELECTED THE
TEXT FOR THIS VOLUME

Contents

INTRODUCTION

by Jonathan Raban

Later in life, Twain would claim *Life on the Mississippi* as his own favorite among his books, but in the winter of 1882, when he was struggling to finish it against a deadline, it was his millstone and his albatross. From his desk in Hartford he plagued his friends with weary bulletins: "The spur and burden of the contract are intolerable to me. I can endure the irritation of it no longer . . ."; "I never had such a fight over a book in my life before . . ."; ". . . this wretched God-damned book."

Yet, when he put his signature to that accursed contract, the job of writing a book on the Mississippi must have seemed a breeze. The guts of the project were already to hand, in the seven articles, totalling 35,000 words, which he had published in the *Atlantic Monthly* in 1875, under the title of "Old Times on the Mississippi." The articles had come to Twain in a single fluent burst of work, while he paused in the writing of *The Adventures of Tom Sawyer*, and their portrait of the artist as a young river pilot had already earned him a round of invigorating critical applause. All he had to do now was to capitalize on their success and expand the series to book length.

The *Atlantic Monthly* pieces were suffused with the roseate style of *Tom Sawyer*. The "white town drowsing in the sunshine of a summer's morning" in "Old Times" is set in the same key and the same tempo as "The sun rose upon a tranquil world, and beamed down upon the peaceful village like a benediction" in *Tom Sawyer*. Both the magazine series and the boys' book represent the river as an idyllic playground. In both, Twain re-created his own youth and wrote of a lost age when America itself was still young.

In fact, only thirteen years intervened between May 1861, when Twain, aged 25, made his last trip on the river as a pilot, and October 1874, when he sat down to write "Old Times"; it might as well have been a century. War had changed the world beyond recognition or repair. Before the war, the Mississippi had been the arterial mainstream of mid-century American life; after the blockade of Memphis in 1861, the river was broken in two, its trade killed for the duration. It was the end of the culture of the steamboat and the river town. When peace eventually came, the railroads took most of the traffic that had once gone by water. Twain at 38 was able to look back at his own young manhood as if it were ancient history; his memories—both in *Tom Sawyer* and in "Old Times"—have the hauntedness, the glowing remoteness, of those of a man in his nonage.

Between the New England *now* of his writing and the Missouri *then* of his fiction and reminiscence lay a personal as well as a national cataclysm. When the war put an end to his career as a river pilot (a career in which he was by all accounts extremely happy), he enlisted in the Marion Rangers, a band of Confederate guerrillas based in Missouri—a state that remained loyal to the Union despite the secessionist stand made by its governor. The next few weeks were spent in hiding or on the run. Then Twain, in the company of his brother Orion, who had been appointed Secretary to the Nevada Territory, fled West—first to the gold-diggings, then to the San Francisco newspapers, where he quickly established himself as a famously droll columnist. In *Life on the Mississippi* he vilifies the Confederate South in a tone of wise, and seemingly age-old, contempt; it's worth remembering that he began the Civil War as a Rebel volunteer, and spent the rest of it in a state of what amounted to internal exile.

He emerged in 1865 with a new name, a new profession, and a new political view of the world. The young humorist Mark Twain was an entirely different kind of animal from the young pilot Samuel Clemens; and Mark Train would commit himself to so befogging and mythologizing the past of Samuel Clemens that it would turn into the best and most glorious of the mature writer's inventions. The "Old Times" pieces were fiction—a fiction made credible, in every sentence, with autobiographical fact. From the makeshift and muddy raw material of western life in the 1840's they created a golden age of innocence and harmony as pure, and as unreachable, as that pastoral world of nymphs and swains on which the poets of the Jacobean court used to dote.

It was a fiction that could not be indefinitely sustained. Even before he finished the *Atlantic Monthly* series, there were signs that Twain was beginning to scrape the bottom of that particular barrel. Article 7 (Chapters XVI–XVII of *Life on the Mississippi*), with its steamboat-race statistics and its limp anecdotal ending, is not a patch on Twain's portrait of his boyhood and his apprenticeship as a cub pilot under Horace Bixby. To make a whole book out of the river, he needed to construct a bang-up-to-date modern (even modern*ist*) frame in which to hang his idealized picture of the past. He would pit the antebellum Golden Age against the postbellum Gilded Age.

In April 1882, he went back to the river. It was a triumphal, grandee's return. Twain took with him Charles Osgood (his literary agent and the manager of his publishing house) and Roswell Phelps, who was signed on as a stenographer to take down the great writer's small talk. He at least toyed with the idea of taking on an assumed name; as C. L. Samuel of New York—a rich Jewish East Coaster—he might eavesdrop, like Huck Finn, on people speaking of his younger self as if he were dead.

The Twain party arrived at St. Louis, rode down the river to New Orleans, then up the river again to Minneapolis. A month after setting out, Twain was back in Hartford, where he quickly found that the book, far from being an easy assignment, was the most mulish and immoveable project that he had faced in his entire writing life.

Reading *Life on the Mississippi*, it is not the river one sees first but the writer's desk—a desk littered with magazines, books, brochures, writing pads. There is the stack of seven-year-old issues of the *Atlantic Monthly*; a pile of recently acquired guidebooks, bland and boosterish then as now; several American travelogues by British authors—Frances Trollope, Captain Marryat, Captain Basil Hall; a copy of *A Tramp Abroad*, published two years before, from which some overspill material (like "A Dying Man's Confession") might be filched for the Mississippi book. Most important of all, there is the half-finished manuscript of *Huckleberry Finn*.

Few books expose the halting progress of their own authorship so plainly as this one does. You catch the rhythm of Twain's working days from it—the bad ones along with the good ones. A day of plodding journalism will be succeeded by a day of happy inspiration; sometimes Twain nods over the work, then, suddenly, he quickens and takes wing. When his energy flags, he goes back to the books and papers on the desk, searching for a quotation that will fit, or for an idea that will move the manuscript along for another thousand words.

Chapter XXXVIII, "The House Beautiful," provides a nice example of Twain at work, doodling and improvising his way around the river. It begins with a steamboat run, quotes Dickens on steamboats, then, triggered by little more than the mention of Dickens's name, launches into a brilliant Dickensian pastiche. Twain, diverted into thoughts of Dickens's animated London interiors (or so I surmise), begins to apply Dickens's patent brand of telegrammatic syntax to a childhood memory of his own—his childhood visits to the farmhouse owned by his uncle and aunt, John and Patsy Quarles, in Florida, Missouri. The result is a wonderful exercise in rapt memoriousness. A whole society is brought to life in an epic inventory of its household effects. It is at once the cleverest imitation of Dickens ever written and a magnificent original in its own right. Later, when he returned to *Huckleberry Finn* (and all the internal evidence suggests that the passage in *Life on the Mississippi* came first), Twain used this chapter as a quarry from which to extract material to furnish the Grangerford house. The second time around, Huck does the seeing, and gets it poignantly wrong.

The chapter loops its way back to steamboat architecture and, a page later, Twain—on what is evidently a dull morning—is down to one of his regular ploys-of-last-resort and quoting Mrs. Trollope. Both the rollercoaster motion and the essential literariness of the method are typical of *Life on the Mississippi*. Like the river itself, the book is labyrinthine, a succession of meanders, chutes, and cutoffs; it turns digression into a structural principle, as Twain wanders downstream, then up, branching off at will into recollections, swoops of fancy, lectures, fictions, facts, guided tours, meditations, and sly parodies.

It is a palimpsest, with one style of writing laid slantwise on top of another, and it is a book obsessed with the meaning and consequence of writing. When Twain blames the Civil War on the South's fatal weakness for the romantic prose of Sir Walter Scott, he is joking, but only just. *Life on the Mississippi* is profoundly charged with the insight that, in Wittgenstein's happy formulation, the world we live in is the words we use, and that the United States in the late nineteenth century was living in a language that had become corrupt and stale. The book begins in newspaperese—a slather of routine statistical journalism, as if the great river might be netted in a mesh of facts and figures; it ends in a tongue-in-cheek pastiche of varnished guidebook prose, full of tired lyricism and spurious Indian legends. En route, Twain keeps up a continuous—and often very funny—attack on the language of romantic cliché.

Twain's real opponent is not Scott, or Poe (who is mocked and imitated in Chapter XXXI), or the New Orleans *Times-Democrat* journalist who is given a dressing-down in Chapter XLV, but himself. He suffered from what he labels "the artificial-flower complaint," and his own prose (in *Innocents Abroad,* in *Tom Sawyer,* and in the "Old Times" pieces) had strong Confederate leanings. The passage he quotes from the New Orleans journalist ("On Saturday, early in the morning, the beauty of the place graced our cabin . . .") sounds very like the kind of sentence in his early work to which Twain himself might, with hindsight, have posted a rejection slip.

He had already created, in manuscript, the clear and powerful voice of Huckleberry Finn: a voice without literary precedent. *Life on the Mississippi* counts the cost of that creation. It shows Twain in the act of wrestling with the demons of the language—battling, in parody and pastiche, toward a new way of rendering the world in writing. Style after style is tried out on the river, and found wanting. All Twain's literary ancestors, from his journalist-brother Orion to Dickens, are mimicked, some in homage, some in excoriation. This is a far more anarchic book than has generally been acknowledged.

Its emotional and stylistic heart resides in Chapters LIII to LVI, where Twain goes back to his old home in Hannibal. The tone throughout is conventionally fond ("this tranquil refuge of my childhood . . .”). It is the required tone of a man revisiting his past and finding it at once sweetly evocative and changed almost beyond recognition. It is a cunning mask. For the memories that the town brings to mind are violently at war with the style in which they are recalled. Fondly, at leisure, Twain dwells on the story of his schoolmate who was taunted to his death by Twain and his playfellows, on the tramp who burned himself to death in the town jail, on the man who fancied himself a serial murderer, on the woman driven insane by another childish prank, and on the town's chief tourist attraction, the pickled body of a fourteen-year-old girl. He laments the passing of the slaughterhouse and discovers Tom Sawyer's sweetheart Becky Thatcher (for it is surely she) in the person of a raddled and promiscuous crone. Every page is littered with the town dead; the unmathematical reader will rapidly lose count of the corpses that form the main punctuation points in Twain's story of his homecoming.

It is an extraordinary performance. Manner and matter are played against each other, tenor and descant, in a brilliant and unsettling black comedy. Here, as almost everywhere else in the book, Twain is working on the edge of parody. The model in these chapters is Washington Irving's "Rip Van Winkle," and the connection between Irving's story and Twain's reworking of it is precise and suggestive. Van Winkle slept through the American Revolution; Twain has, as it were, slept through the American Civil War. Wakened at last, he is a very old man indeed—far, far older than the 46-year-old who made the literal return to Hannibal.

He might have called the book *Death on the Mississippi*. When he came to pick up the threads of the "Old Times" series, in Chapter XVIII, he built the book up to its first climax—the story of his brother Henry's death in an explosion aboard the steamboat *Pennsylvania*. The scene of the "death house" in Memphis ("Two long rows of prostrate forms—more than forty, in all—and every face and head a shapeless wad of loose raw cotton.") is the last we see of the antebellum Mississippi, and the bodies of the people killed in the explosion, viewed as in an improvised field hospital, foreshadow the bodies of those about to be killed in the Civil War.

Thereafter, Twain can't keep his pen away from the subject.

He jokes about it. He spins out morbid gothic tales. He records it as a matter of important fact, and, when he reaches the last page of the book, he drags death in by its heels, in a facetious metaphor:

> A dead man could get up a better legend than this one. I don't mean a fresh man either; I mean a man that's been dead weeks and weeks.

As he wrote to his wife, Livy, when he was on the river in May 1882:

> That world which I knew in its blossoming youth is old and bowed and melancholy, now; its soft cheeks are leathery and wrinkled, the fire is gone out in its eyes, and the spring from its step. It will be dust and ashes when I come again. I have been clasping hands with the moribund . . .

In the same letter, he called his return to the past "this hideous trip," and when he settled down to write his book, he wrote compulsively of dead people, dead cities (like the town of Napoleon, Arkansas, washed away by the river), a dead civilization. The brightest, funniest moments in the book are shot through with a kind of jaunty necrophilia.

It is the conceit, and necessary premise, of the "modernist" writer to believe that he or she has somehow survived into an era without precedent, beyond history—that the world in effect died sometime between the time he or she was born and the time in which he or she is writing. No one in the late twentieth century has subscribed more fervently to this belief than Twain did in the late nineteenth. The Civil War was his Holocaust and his nuclear bomb. *Life on the Mississippi* shows him dealing with that predicament in a typically modernist way—in pastiche, in parody, in writing (as John Barth described Borges) "postscripts to the corpus of literature." It is a strange, untidy, uncomfortable, and secretive book, and it is no wonder that Twain, having sweated blood to make it work, should have been so proud of it long after its publication.

Life on the Mississippi

The "Body of the Nation"

But the basin of the Mississippi is the BODY OF THE NATION. All the other parts are but members, important in themselves, yet more important in their relations to this. Exclusive of the Lake basin and of 300,000 square miles in Texas and New Mexico, which in many aspects form a part of it, this basin contains about 1,250,000 square miles. In extent it is the second great valley of the world, being exceeded only by that of the Amazon. The valley of the frozen Obi approaches it in extent; that of the La Plata comes next in space, and probably in habitable capacity, having about $^8/_9$ of its area; then comes that of the Yenisei, with about $^7/_9$; the Lena, Amoor, Hoang-ho, Yang-tse-kiang, and Nile, $^5/_9$; the Ganges, less than $^1/_2$; the Indus, less than $^1/_3$; the Euphrates, $^1/_5$; the Rhine, $^1/_{15}$. It exceeds in extent the whole of Europe, exclusive of Russia, Norway, and Sweden. *It would contain Austria four times, Germany or Spain five times, France six times, the British Islands or Italy ten times.* Conceptions formed from the river-basins of Western Europe are rudely shocked when we consider the extent of the valley of the Mississippi; nor are those formed from the sterile basins of the great rivers of Siberia, the lofty plateaus of Central Asia, or the mighty sweep of the swampy Amazon more adequate. Latitude, elevation, and rainfall all combine to render every part of the Mississippi Valley capable of supporting a dense population. *As a dwelling-place for civilized man it is by far the first upon our globe.* —EDITOR'S TABLE, *Harper's Magazine, February, 1863.*

Contents.

I.

The River and Its History

THE MISSISSIPPI is well worth reading about. It is not a commonplace river, but on the contrary is in all ways remarkable. Considering the Missouri its main branch, it is the longest river in the world—four thousand three hundred miles. It seems safe to say that it is also the crookedest river in the world, since in one part of its journey it uses up one thousand three hundred miles to cover the same ground that the crow would fly over in six hundred and seventy-five. It discharges three times as much water as the St. Lawrence, twenty-five times as much as the Rhine, and three hundred and thirty-eight times as much as the Thames. No other river has so vast a drainage-basin: it draws its water supply from twenty-eight States and Territories; from Delaware, on the Atlantic seaboard, and from all the country between that and Idaho on the Pacific slope—a spread of forty-five degrees of longitude. The Mississippi receives and carries to the Gulf water from fifty-four subordinate rivers that are navigable by steamboats, and from some hundreds that are navigable by flats and keels. The area of its drainage-basin is as great as the combined areas of England, Wales, Scotland, Ireland, France, Spain, Portugal, Germany, Austria, Italy, and Turkey; and almost all this wide region is fertile; the Mississippi valley, proper, is exceptionally so.

It is a remarkable river in this: that instead of widening toward its mouth, it grows narrower; grows narrower and deeper. From the junction of the Ohio to a point half way down to the sea, the width averages a mile in high water: thence to the sea the width steadily diminishes, until, at the "Passes," above the mouth, it is but little over half a mile. At the junction of the Ohio the Mississippi's depth is eighty-seven feet; the depth increases gradually, reaching one hundred and twenty-nine just above the mouth.

The difference in rise and fall is also remarkable—not in the upper, but in the lower river. The rise is tolerably uniform down to Natchez (three hundred and sixty miles above the mouth)—about fifty feet. But at Bayou La Fourche the river rises only twenty-four feet; at New Orleans only fifteen, and just above the mouth only two and one half.

An article in the New Orleans "Times-Democrat," based upon reports of able engineers, states that the river annually empties four hundred and six million tons of mud into the Gulf of Mexico—which brings to mind Captain Marryat's rude name for the Mississippi—"the Great Sewer." This mud, solidified, would make a mass a mile square and two hundred and forty-one feet high.

The mud deposit gradually extends the land—but only gradually; it has extended it not quite a third of a mile in the two hundred years which have elapsed since the river took its place in history. The belief of the scientific people is, that the mouth used to be at Baton Rouge, where the hills cease, and that the two hundred miles of land between there and the Gulf was built by the river. This gives us the age of that piece of country, without any trouble at all—one hundred and twenty thousand years. Yet it is much the youthfulest batch of country that lies around there anywhere.

The Mississippi is remarkable in still another way—its disposition to make prodigious jumps by cutting through narrow necks of land, and thus straightening and shortening itself. More than once it has shortened itself thirty miles at a single jump! These cut-offs have had curious effects: they have thrown several river towns out into the rural districts, and built up sand bars and forests in front of them. The town of Delta used to be three miles below Vicksburg: a recent cut-off has radically changed the position, and Delta is now *two miles above* Vicksburg.

Both of these river towns have been retired to the country by that cut-off. A cut-off plays havoc with boundary lines and jurisdictions: for instance, a man is living in the State of Mississippi to-day, a cut-off occurs to-night, and to-morrow the man finds himself and his land over on the other side of the river, within the boundaries and subject to the laws of the State of Louisiana! Such a thing, happening in the upper river in the old times, could have transferred a slave from Missouri to Illinois and made a free man of him.

The Mississippi does not alter its locality by cut-offs alone:

it is always changing its habitat *bodily*—is always moving bodily *sidewise*. At Hard Times, La., the river is two miles west of the region it used to occupy. As a result, the original *site* of that settlement is not now in Louisiana at all, but on the other side of the river, in the State of Mississippi. *Nearly the whole of that one thousand three hundred miles of old Mississippi River which La Salle floated down in his canoes, two hundred years ago, is good solid dry ground now.* The river lies to the right of it, in places, and to the left of it in other places.

Although the Mississippi's mud builds land but slowly, down at the mouth, where the Gulf's billows interfere with its work, it builds fast enough in better protected regions higher up: for instance, Prophet's Island contained one thousand five hundred acres of land thirty years ago; since then the river has added seven hundred acres to it.

But enough of these examples of the mighty stream's eccentricities for the present—I will give a few more of them further along in the book.

Let us drop the Mississippi's physical history, and say a word about its historical history—so to speak. We can glance briefly at its slumbrous first epoch in a couple of short chapters; at its second and wider-awake epoch in a couple more; at its flushest and widest-awake epoch in a good many succeeding chapters; and then talk about its comparatively tranquil present epoch in what shall be left of the book.

The world and the books are so accustomed to use, and over-use, the word "new" in connection with our country, that we early get and permanently retain the impression that there is nothing old about it. We do of course know that there are several comparatively old dates in American history, but the mere figures convey to our minds no just idea, no distinct realization, of the stretch of time which they represent. To say that De Soto, the first white man who ever saw the Mississippi River, saw it in 1542, is a remark which states a fact without interpreting it: it is something like giving the dimensions of a sunset by astronomical measurements, and cataloguing the colors by their scientific names;—as a result, you get the bald fact of the sunset, but you don't see the sunset. It would have been better to paint a picture of it.

The date 1542, standing by itself, means little or nothing to us; but when one groups a few neighboring historical dates and facts around it, he adds perspective and color, and then realizes that this is one of the American dates which is quite respectable for age.

For instance, when the Mississippi was first seen by a white man, less than a quarter of a century had elapsed since Francis I.'s defeat at Pavia; the death of Raphael; the death of Bayard, *sans peur et sans reproche*; the driving out of the Knights-Hospitallers from Rhodes by the Turks; and the placarding of the Ninety-Five Propositions,—the act which began the Reformation. When De Soto took his glimpse of the river, Ignatius Loyola was an obscure name; the order of the Jesuits was not yet a year old; Michael Angelo's paint was not yet dry on the Last Judgment in the Sistine Chapel; Mary Queen of Scots was not yet born, but would be before the year closed. Catherine de Medici was a child; Elizabeth of England was not yet in her teens; Calvin, Benvenuto Cellini, and the Emperor Charles V. were at the top of their fame, and each was manufacturing history after his own peculiar fashion; Margaret of Navarre was writing the "Heptameron" and some religious books,—the first survives, the others are forgotten, wit and indelicacy being sometimes better literature-preservers than holiness; lax court morals and the absurd chivalry business were in full feather, and the joust and the tournament were the frequent pastime of titled fine gentlemen who could fight better than they could spell, while religion was the passion of their ladies, and the classifying their offspring into children of full rank and children by brevet their pastime. In fact, all around, religion was in a peculiarly blooming condition: the Council of Trent was being called; the Spanish Inquisition was roasting, and racking, and burning, with a free hand; elsewhere on the continent the nations were being persuaded to holy living by the sword and fire; in England, Henry VIII. had suppressed the monasteries, burnt Fisher and another bishop or two, and was getting his English reformation and his harem effectively started. When De Soto stood on the banks of the Mississippi, it was still two years before Luther's death; eleven years before the burning of Servetus; thirty years before the St. Bartholomew slaughter; Rabelais was not yet published; "Don Quixote" was not yet written; Shakspeare was not yet born; a hundred long years must still elapse before Englishmen would hear the name of Oliver Cromwell.

Unquestionably the discovery of the Mississippi is a datable fact which considerably mellows and modifies the shiny newness of our country, and gives her a most respectable outside-aspect of rustiness and antiquity.

De Soto merely glimpsed the river, then died and was buried in it by his priests and soldiers. One would expect the priests and the soldiers to multiply the river's dimensions by ten—the Spanish custom of the day—and thus move other adventurers to go at once and explore it. On the contrary, their narratives when they reached home, did not excite that amount of curiosity. The Mississippi was left unvisited by whites during a term of years which seems incredible in our energetic days. One may "sense" the interval to his mind, after a fashion, by dividing it up in this way: After De Soto glimpsed the river, a fraction short of a quarter of a century elapsed, and then Shakspeare was born; lived a trifle more than half a century, then died; and when he had been in his grave considerably more than half a century, the *second* white man saw the Mississippi. In our day we don't allow a hundred and thirty years to elapse between glimpses of a marvel. If somebody should discover a creek in the county next to the one that the North Pole is in, Europe and America would start fifteen costly expeditions thither: one to explore the creek, and the other fourteen to hunt for each other.

For more than a hundred and fifty years there had been white settlements on our Atlantic coasts. These people were in intimate communication with the Indians: in the south the Spaniards were robbing, slaughtering, enslaving and converting them; higher up, the English were trading beads and blankets to them for a consideration, and throwing in civilization and whiskey, "for lagniappe;"[1] and in Canada the French were schooling them in a rudimentary way, missionarying among them, and drawing whole populations of them at a time to Quebec, and later to Montreal, to buy furs of them. Necessarily, then, these various clusters of whites must have heard of the great river of the far west; and indeed, they

[1]See page 273.

did hear of it vaguely,—so vaguely and indefinitely, that its course, proportions, and locality were hardly even guessable. The mere mysteriousness of the matter ought to have fired curiosity and compelled exploration; but this did not occur. Apparently nobody happened to want such a river, nobody needed it, nobody was curious about it; so, for a century and a half the Mississippi remained out of the market and undisturbed. When De Soto found it, he was not hunting for a river, and had no present occasion for one; consequently he did not value it or even take any particular notice of it.

But at last La Salle the Frenchman conceived the idea of seeking out that river and exploring it. It always happens that when a man seizes upon a neglected and important idea, people inflamed with the same notion crop up all around. It happened so in this instance.

Naturally the question suggests itself, Why did these people want the river now when nobody had wanted it in the five preceding generations? Apparently it was because at this late day they thought they had discovered a way to make it useful; for it had come to be believed that the Mississippi emptied into the Gulf of California, and therefore afforded a short cut from Canada to China. Previously the supposition had been that it emptied into the Atlantic, or Sea of Virginia.

II.

The River and Its Explorers

L A SALLE himself sued for certain high privileges, and they were graciously accorded him by Louis XIV. of inflated memory. Chief among them was the privilege to explore, far and wide, and build forts, and stake out continents, and hand the same over to the king, and pay the expenses himself; receiving, in return, some little advantages of one sort or another; among them the monopoly of buffalo hides. He spent several years and about all of his money, in making perilous and painful trips between Montreal and a fort which he had built on the Illinois, before he at last succeeded in getting his expedition in such a shape that he could strike for the Mississippi.

And meantime other parties had had better fortune. In 1673 Joliet the merchant, and Marquette the priest, crossed the country and reached the banks of the Mississippi. They went by way of the Great Lakes; and from Green Bay, in canoes, by way of Fox River and the Wisconsin. Marquette had solemnly contracted, on the feast of the Immaculate Conception, that if the Virgin would permit him to discover the great river, he would name it Conception, in her honor. He kept his word. In that day, all explorers travelled with an outfit of priests. De Soto had twenty-four with him. La Salle had several, also. The expeditions were often out of meat, and scant of clothes, but they always had the furniture and other requisites for the mass; they were always prepared, as one of the quaint chroniclers of the time phrased it, to "explain hell to the salvages."

On the 17th of June, 1673, the canoes of Joliet and Marquette and their five subordinates reached the junction of the Wisconsin with the Mississippi. Mr. Parkman says: "Before them a wide and rapid current coursed athwart their way, by the foot of lofty heights wrapped thick in forests." He continues: "Turning southward, they paddled down the stream, through a solitude unrelieved by the faintest trace of man."

A big cat-fish collided with Marquette's canoe, and startled him; and reasonably enough, for he had been warned by the Indians that he was on a foolhardy journey, and even a fatal one, for the river contained a demon "whose roar could be heard at a great distance, and who would engulf them in the abyss where he dwelt." I have seen a Mississippi cat-fish that was more than six feet long, and weighed two hundred and fifty pounds; and if Marquette's fish was the fellow to that one, he had a fair right to think the river's roaring demon was come.

"At length the buffalo began to appear, grazing in herds on the great prairies which then bordered the river; and Marquette describes the fierce and stupid look of the old bulls as they stared at the intruders through the tangled mane which nearly blinded them."

The voyagers moved cautiously: "Landed at night and made a fire to cook their evening meal; then extinguished it, embarked again, paddled some way farther, and anchored in the stream, keeping a man on the watch till morning."

They did this day after day and night after night; and at the end of two weeks they had not seen a human being. The river was an awful solitude, then. And it is now, over most of its stretch.

But at the close of the fortnight they one day came upon the footprints of men in the mud of the western bank—a Robinson Crusoe experience which carries an electric shiver with it yet, when one stumbles on it in print. They had been warned that the river Indians were as ferocious and pitiless as the river demon, and destroyed all comers without waiting for provocation; but no matter, Joliet and Marquette struck into the country to hunt up the proprietors of the tracks. They found them, by and by, and were hospitably received and well treated—if to be received by an Indian chief who has taken off his last rag in order to appear at his level best is to be received hospitably; and if to be treated abundantly to fish, porridge, and other game, including dog, and have these things forked into one's mouth by the ungloved fingers of Indians is to be well treated. In the morning the chief and six hundred of his tribesmen escorted the Frenchmen to the river and bade them a friendly farewell.

On the rocks above the present city of Alton they found

some rude and fantastic Indian paintings, which they describe. A short distance below "a torrent of yellow mud rushed furiously athwart the calm blue current of the Mississippi, boiling and surging and sweeping in its course logs, branches, and uprooted trees." This was the mouth of the Missouri, "that savage river," which "descending from its mad career through a vast unknown of barbarism, poured its turbid floods into the bosom of its gentle sister."

By and by they passed the mouth of the Ohio; they passed canebrakes; they fought mosquitoes; they floated along, day after day, through the deep silence and loneliness of the river, drowsing in the scant shade of makeshift awnings, and broiling with the heat; they encountered and exchanged civilities with another party of Indians; and at last they reached the mouth of the Arkansas (about a month out from their starting-point), where a tribe of war-whooping savages swarmed out to meet and murder them; but they appealed to the Virgin for help; so in place of a fight there was a feast, and plenty of pleasant palaver and fol-de-rol.

They had proved to their satisfaction, that the Mississippi did not empty into the Gulf of California, or into the Atlantic. They believed it emptied into the Gulf of Mexico. They turned back, now, and carried their great news to Canada.

But belief is not proof. It was reserved for La Salle to furnish the proof. He was provokingly delayed, by one misfortune after another, but at last got his expedition under way at the end of the year 1681. In the dead of winter he and Henri de Tonty, son of Lorenzo Tonty, who invented the tontine, his lieutenant, started down the Illinois, with a following of eighteen Indians brought from New England, and twenty-three Frenchmen. They moved in procession down the surface of the frozen river, on foot, and dragging their canoes after them on sledges.

At Peoria Lake they struck open water, and paddled thence to the Mississippi and turned their prows southward. They ploughed through the fields of floating ice, past the mouth of the Missouri; past the mouth of the Ohio, by and by; "and, gliding by the wastes of bordering swamp, landed on the 24th of February near the Third Chickasaw Bluffs," where they halted and built Fort Prudhomme.

"Again," says Mr. Parkman, "they embarked; and with every stage of their adventurous progress, the mystery of this vast new world was more and more unveiled. More and more they entered the realms of spring. The hazy sunlight, the warm and drowsy air, the tender foliage, the opening flowers, betokened the reviving life of nature."

Day by day they floated down the great bends, in the shadow of the dense forests, and in time arrived at the mouth of the Arkansas. First, they were greeted by the natives of this locality as Marquette had before been greeted by them—with the booming of the war drum and the flourish of arms. The Virgin composed the difficulty in Marquette's case; the pipe of peace did the same office for La Salle. The white man and the red man struck hands and entertained each other during three days. Then, to the admiration of the savages, La Salle set up a cross with the arms of France on it, and took possession of the whole country for the king—the cool fashion of the time—while the priest piously consecrated the robbery with a hymn. The priest explained the mysteries of the faith "by signs," for the saving of the savages; thus compensating them with possible possessions in Heaven for the certain ones on earth which they had just been robbed of. And also, by signs, La Salle drew from these simple children of the forest acknowledgments of fealty to Louis the Putrid, over the water. Nobody smiled at these colossal ironies.

These performances took place on the site of the future town of Napoleon, Arkansas, and there the first confiscation-cross was raised on the banks of the great river. Marquette's and Joliet's voyage of discovery ended at the same spot—the site of the future town of Napoleon. When De Soto took his fleeting glimpse of the river, away back in the dim early days, he took it from that same spot—the site of the future town of Napoleon, Arkansas. Therefore, three out of the four memorable events connected with the discovery and exploration of the mighty river occurred, by accident, in one and the same place. It is a most curious distinction, when one comes to look at it and think about it. France stole that vast country on that spot, the future Napoleon; and by and by Napoleon himself was to give the country back again!—make restitution, not to the owners, but to their white American heirs.

The voyagers journeyed on, touching here and there; "passed the sites, since become historic, of Vicksburg and Grand Gulf;" and visited an imposing Indian monarch in the Teche country, whose capital city was a substantial one of sun-baked bricks mixed with straw—better houses than many that exist there now. The chief's house contained an audience room forty feet square; and there he received Tonty in State, surrounded by sixty old men clothed in white cloaks. There was a temple in the town, with a mud wall about it ornamented with skulls of enemies sacrificed to the sun.

The voyagers visited the Natchez Indians, near the site of the present city of that name, where they found a "religious and political despotism, a privileged class descended from the sun, a temple and a sacred fire." It must have been like getting home again; it was home with an advantage, in fact, for it lacked Louis XIV.

A few more days swept swiftly by, and La Salle stood in the shadow of his confiscating cross, at the meeting of the waters from Delaware, and from Itaska, and from the mountain ranges close upon the Pacific, with the waters of the Gulf of Mexico, his task finished, his prodigy achieved. Mr. Parkman, in closing his fascinating narrative, thus sums up:

> "On that day, the realm of France received on parchment a stupendous accession. The fertile plains of Texas; the vast basin of the Mississippi, from its frozen northern springs to the sultry borders of the Gulf; from the woody ridges of the Alleghanies to the bare peaks of the Rocky Mountains—a region of savannas and forests, sun-cracked deserts and grassy prairies, watered by a thousand rivers, ranged by a thousand warlike tribes, passed beneath the sceptre of the Sultan of Versailles; and all by virtue of a feeble human voice, inaudible at half a mile."

III.

Frescoes from the Past

APPARENTLY the river was ready for business, now. But no, the distribution of a population along its banks was as calm and deliberate and time-devouring a process as the discovery and exploration had been.

Seventy years elapsed, after the exploration, before the river's borders had a white population worth considering; and nearly fifty more before the river had a commerce. Between La Salle's opening of the river and the time when it may be said to have become the vehicle of anything like a regular and active commerce, seven sovereigns had occupied the throne of England, America had become an independent nation, Louis XIV. and Louis XV. had rotted and died, the French monarchy had gone down in the red tempest of the revolution, and Napoleon was a name that was beginning to be talked about. Truly, there were snails in those days.

The river's earliest commerce was in great barges—keelboats, broadhorns. They floated and sailed from the upper rivers to New Orleans, changed cargoes there, and were tediously warped and poled back by hand. A voyage down and back sometimes occupied nine months. In time this commerce increased until it gave employment to hordes of rough and hardy men; rude, uneducated, brave, suffering terrific hardships with sailor-like stoicism; heavy drinkers, coarse frolickers in moral sties like the Natchez-under-the-hill of that day, heavy fighters, reckless fellows, every one, elephantinely jolly, foul-witted, profane; prodigal of their money, bankrupt at the end of the trip, fond of barbaric finery, prodigious braggarts; yet, in the main, honest, trustworthy, faithful to promises and duty, and often picturesquely magnanimous.

By and by the steamboat intruded. Then, for fifteen or twenty years, these men continued to run their keelboats down-stream, and the steamers did all of the up-stream business, the keelboatmen selling their boats in New Orleans, and returning home as deck passengers in the steamers.

But after a while the steamboats so increased in number and

in speed that they were able to absorb the entire commerce; and then keelboating died a permanent death. The keelboatman became a deck hand, or a mate, or a pilot on the steamer; and when steamer-berths were not open to him, he took a berth on a Pittsburgh coal-flat, or on a pine-raft constructed in the forests up toward the sources of the Mississippi.

In the heyday of the steamboating prosperity, the river from end to end was flaked with coal-fleets and timber rafts, all managed by hand, and employing hosts of the rough characters whom I have been trying to describe. I remember the annual processions of mighty rafts that used to glide by Hannibal when I was a boy,—an acre or so of white, sweet-smelling boards in each raft, a crew of two dozen men or more, three or four wigwams scattered about the raft's vast level space for storm-quarters,—and I remember the rude ways and the tremendous talk of their big crews, the ex-keelboatmen and their admiringly patterning successors; for we used to swim out a quarter or third of a mile and get on these rafts and have a ride.

By way of illustrating keelboat talk and manners, and that now-departed and hardly-remembered raft-life, I will throw in, in this place, a chapter from a book which I have been working at, by fits and starts, during the past five or six years, and may possibly finish in the course of five or six more. The book is a story which details some passages in the life of an ignorant village boy, Huck Finn, son of the town drunkard of my time out west, there. He has run away from his persecuting father, and from a persecuting good widow who wishes to make a nice, truth-telling, respectable boy of him; and with him a slave of the widow's has also escaped. They have found a fragment of a lumber raft (it is high water and dead summer time), and are floating down the river by night, and hiding in the willows by day,—bound for Cairo,—whence the negro will seek freedom in the heart of the free States. But in a fog, they pass Cairo without knowing it. By and by they begin to suspect the truth, and Huck Finn is persuaded to end the dismal suspense by swimming down to a huge raft which they have seen in the distance ahead of them, creeping aboard under cover of the darkness, and gathering the needed information by eavesdropping:—

But you know a young person can't wait very well when he is impatient to find a thing out. We talked it over, and by and by Jim said it was such a black night, now, that it would n't be no risk to swim down to the big raft and crawl aboard and listen,—they would talk about Cairo, because they would be calculating to go ashore there for a spree, maybe, or anyway they would send boats ashore to buy whiskey or fresh meat or something. Jim had a wonderful level head, for a nigger: he could most always start a good plan when you wanted one.

I stood up and shook my rags off and jumped into the river, and struck out for the raft's light. By and by, when I got down nearly to her, I eased up and went slow and cautious. But everything was all right—nobody at the sweeps. So I swum down along the raft till I was most abreast the camp fire in the middle, then I crawled aboard and inched along and got in amongst some bundles of shingles on the weather side of the fire. There was thirteen men there—they was the watch on deck of course. And a mighty rough-looking lot, too. They had a jug, and tin cups, and they kept the jug moving. One man was singing—roaring, you may say; and it was n't a nice song—for a parlor anyway. He roared through his nose, and strung out the last word of every line very long. When he was done they all fetched a kind of Injun war-whoop, and then another was sung. It begun:—

> "There was a woman in our towdn,
>   In our towdn did dwed'l (dwell,)
> She loved her husband dear-i-lee,
>   But another man twyste as wed'l.
>
> Singing too, riloo, riloo, riloo,
>   Ri-too, riloo, rilay - - - e,
> She loved her husband dear-i-lee,
>   But another man twyste as wed'l."

And so on—fourteen verses. It was kind of poor, and when he was going to start on the next verse one of them said it was the tune the old cow died on; and another one said, "Oh, give us a rest." And another one told him to take a walk. They made fun of him till he got mad and jumped up and begun to cuss the crowd, and said he could lam any thief in the lot.

They was all about to make a break for him, but the biggest man there jumped up and says: —

"Set whar you are, gentlemen. Leave him to me; he 's my meat."

Then he jumped up in the air three times and cracked his heels together every time. He flung off a buckskin coat that was all hung with fringes, and says, "You lay thar tell the chawin-up 's done;" and flung his hat down, which was all over ribbons, and says, "You lay thar tell his sufferins is over."

Then he jumped up in the air and cracked his heels together again and shouted out: —

"Whoo-oop! I 'm the old original iron-jawed, brass-mounted, copper-bellied corpse-maker from the wilds of Arkansaw!—Look at me! I 'm the man they call Sudden Death and General Desolation! Sired by a hurricane, dam 'd by an earthquake, half-brother to the cholera, nearly related to the small-pox on the mother's side! Look at me! I take nineteen alligators and a bar'l of whiskey for breakfast when I 'm in robust health, and a bushel of rattlesnakes and a dead body when I 'm ailing! I split the everlasting rocks with my glance, and I squench the thunder when I speak! Whoo-oop! Stand back and give me room according to my strength! Blood 's my natural drink, and the wails of the dying is music to my ear! Cast your eye on me, gentlemen!—and lay low and hold your breath, for I 'm bout to turn myself loose!"

All the time he was getting this off, he was shaking his head and looking fierce, and kind of swelling around in a little circle, tucking up his wrist-bands, and now and then straightening up and beating his breast with his fist, saying, "Look at me, gentlemen!" When he got through, he jumped up and cracked his heels together three times, and let off a roaring "whoo-oop! I 'm the bloodiest son of a wildcat that lives!"

Then the man that had started the row tilted his old

slouch hat down over his right eye; then he bent stooping forward, with his back sagged and his south end sticking out far, and his fists a-shoving out and drawing in in front of him, and so went around in a little circle about three times, swelling himself up and breathing hard. Then he straightened, and jumped up and cracked his heels together three times before he lit again (that made them cheer), and he begun to shout like this:—

"Whoo-oop! bow your neck and spread, for the kingdom of sorrow 's a-coming! Hold me down to the earth, for I feel my powers a-working! whoo-oop! I 'm a child of sin, *don't* let me get a start! Smoked glass, here, for all! Don't attempt to look at me with the naked eye, gentlemen! When I 'm playful I use the meridians of longitude and parallels of latitude for a seine, and drag the Atlantic Ocean for whales! I scratch my head with the lightning and purr myself to sleep with the thunder! When I 'm cold, I bile the Gulf of Mexico and bathe in it; when I 'm hot I fan myself with an equinoctial storm; when I 'm thirsty I reach up and suck a cloud dry like a sponge; when I range the earth hungry, famine follows in my tracks! Whoo-oop! Bow your neck and spread! I put my hand on the sun's face and make it night in the earth; I bite a piece out of the moon and hurry the seasons; I shake myself and crumble the mountains! Contemplate me through leather— *don't* use the naked eye! I 'm the man with a petrified heart and biler-iron bowels! The massacre of isolated communities is the pastime of my idle moments, the destruction of nationalities the serious business of my life! The boundless vastness of the great American desert is my enclosed property, and I bury my dead on my own premises!" He jumped up and cracked his heels together three times before he lit (they cheered him again), and as he come down he shouted out: "Whoo-oop! bow your neck and spread, for the pet child of calamity 's a-coming!"

Then the other one went to swelling around and blowing again—the first one—the one they called Bob; next, the Child of Calamity chipped in again, bigger than ever; then they both got at it at the same time, swelling round and round each other and punching their fists most into each other's faces, and whooping and jawing like Injuns; then Bob called the Child names, and the Child called him names back again: next, Bob called him a heap rougher names and the Child come back at him with the very worst kind of language; next, Bob knocked the Child's hat off, and the Child picked it up and kicked Bob's ribbony hat about six foot; Bob went and got it and said never mind, this war n't going to be the last of this thing, because he was a man that never forgot and never forgive, and so the Child better look out, for there was a time a-coming, just as sure as he was a living man, that he would have to answer to him with the best blood in his body. The Child said no man was willinger than he was for that time to come, and he would give Bob fair warning, *now*, never to cross his path again, for he could never rest till he had waded in his blood, for such was his nature, though he was sparing him now on account of his family, if he had one.

Both of them was edging away in different directions, growling and shaking their heads and going on about what they was going to do; but a little black-whiskered chap skipped up and says:—

"Come back here, you couple of chicken-livered cowards, and I 'll thrash the two of ye!"

And he done it, too. He snatched them, he jerked them this way and that, he booted them around, he knocked them sprawling faster than they could get up. Why, it war n't two minutes till they begged like dogs—and how the other lot did yell and laugh and clap their hands all the way through, and shout "Sail in, Corpse-Maker!" "Hi! at him again, Child of Calamity!" "Bully for you, little Davy!" Well, it was a perfect pow-wow for a while. Bob and the Child had red noses and black eyes when they got through. Little Davy made them own up that they was sneaks and cowards and not fit to eat with a dog or drink with a nigger; then Bob and the Child shook hands with each other, very solemn, and said they had always respected each other and was willing to let bygones be bygones. So then they washed their faces in the river; and just then there was a loud order to stand by for a crossing, and some of them went forward to man the sweeps there, and the rest went aft to handle the after-sweeps.

I laid still and waited for fifteen minutes, and had a smoke out of a pipe that one of them left in reach; then the crossing was finished, and they stumped back and had a drink around and went to talking and singing again. Next they got out an old fiddle, and one played, and another patted juba, and the rest turned themselves loose on a regular old-fashioned keel-boat break-down. They couldn't keep that up very long without getting winded, so by and by they settled around the jug again.

They sung "jolly, jolly raftsman's the life for me," with a rousing chorus, and then they got to talking about differences betwixt hogs, and their different kind of habits; and next about women and their different ways; and next about the best ways to put out houses that was afire; and next about what ought to be done with the Injuns; and next about what a king had to do, and how much he got; and next about how to make cats fight; and next about what to do when a man has fits; and next about differences betwixt clear-water rivers and muddy-water ones. The man they called Ed said the muddy Mississippi water was wholesomer to drink than the clear water of the Ohio; he said if you let a pint of this yaller Mississippi water settle, you would have about a half to three quarters of an inch of mud in the bottom, according to the stage of the river, and then it war n't no better then Ohio water—what you wanted to do was to keep it stirred up—and when the river was low, keep mud on hand to put in and thicken the water up the way it ought to be.

The Child of Calamity said that was so; he said there was nutritiousness in the mud, and a man that drunk Mississippi water could grow corn in his stomach if he wanted to. He says:—

"You look at the graveyards; that tells the tale. Trees won't grow worth shucks in a Cincinnati graveyard, but in a Sent Louis graveyard they grow upwards of eight hundred foot high. It 's all on account of the water the people drunk before they laid up. A Cincinnati corpse don't richen a soil any."

And they talked about how Ohio water did n't like to mix with Mississippi water. Ed said if you take the Mississippi on a rise when the Ohio is low, you'll find a wide band of clear water all the way down the east side of the Mississippi for a hundred mile or more, and the minute you get out a quarter of a mile from shore and pass the line, it is all thick and yaller the rest of the way across. Then they talked about how to keep tobacco from getting mouldy, and from that they went into ghosts and told about a lot that other folks had seen; but Ed says:—

"Why don't you tell something that you 've seen yourselves? Now let me have a say. Five years ago I was on a raft as big as this, and right along here it was a bright moonshiny night, and I was on watch and boss of the stabboard oar forrard, and one of my pards was a man named Dick Allbright, and he come along to where I was sitting, forrard—gaping and stretching, he was—and stooped down on the edge of the raft and washed his face in the river, and come and set down by me and got out his pipe, and had just got it filled, when he looks up and says,—

" 'Why looky-here,' he says, 'ain't that Buck Miller's place, over yander in the bend?'

" 'Yes,' says I, 'it is—why?' He laid his pipe down and leant his head on his hand, and says,—

" 'I thought we 'd be furder down.' I says,—

" 'I thought it too, when I went off watch'—we was standing six hours on and six off—'but the boys told me,' I says, 'that the raft didn't seem to hardly move, for the last hour,'—says I, 'though she 's a slipping along all right, now,' says I. He give a kind of a groan, and says,—

" 'I 've seed a raft act so before, along here,' he says, ' 'pears to me the current has most quit above the head of this bend durin' the last two years,' he says.

"Well, he raised up two or three times, and looked away off and around on the water. That started me at it, too. A body is always doing what he sees somebody else doing, though there may n't be no sense in it. Pretty soon I see a black something floating on the water away off to stabboard and quartering behind us. I see he was looking at it, too. I says,—

" 'What 's that?' He says, sort of pettish,—

" 'Tain't nothing but an old empty bar'l.'

" 'An empty bar'l!' says I, 'why,' says I, 'a spy-glass is a fool to *your* eyes. How can you tell it 's an empty bar'l?' He says,—

" 'I don't know; I reckon it ain't a bar'l, but I thought it might be,' says he.

" 'Yes,' I says, 'so it might be, and it might be anything else, too; a body can't tell nothing about it, such a distance as that,' I says.

"We had n't nothing else to do, so we kept on watching it. By and by I says,—

" 'Why looky-here, Dick Allbright, that thing 's a-gaining on us, I believe.'

"He never said nothing. The thing gained and gained, and I judged it must be a dog that was about tired out. Well, we swung down into the crossing, and the thing floated across the bright streak of the moonshine, and, by George, it *was* a bar'l. Says I,—

" 'Dick Allbright, what made you think that thing was a bar'l, when it was a half a mile off,' says I. Says he,—

" 'I don't know.' Says I,—

" 'You tell me, Dick Allbright.' He says,—

" 'Well, I knowed it was a bar'l; I 've seen it before; lots has seen it; they says it 's a hanted bar'l.'

"I called the rest of the watch, and they come and stood there, and I told them what Dick said. It floated right along abreast, now, and did n't gain any more. It was about twenty foot off. Some was for having it aboard, but the rest did n't want to. Dick Allbright said rafts that had fooled with it had got bad luck by it. The captain of the watch said he did n't believe in it. He said he reckoned the bar'l gained on us because it was in a little better current than what we was. He said it would leave by and by.

"So then we went to talking about other things, and we had a song, and then a breakdown; and after that the captain of the watch called for another song; but it was clouding up, now, and the bar'l stuck right thar in the same place, and the song did n't seem to have much warm-up to it, somehow, and so they did n't finish it, and there war n't any cheers, but it sort of dropped flat, and nobody said anything for a minute. Then everybody tried to talk at once, and one chap got off a joke, but it war n't no use, they did n't laugh, and even the chap that made the joke did n't laugh at it, which ain't usual. We all just settled down glum, and watched the bar'l, and was oneasy and oncomfortable. Well, sir, it shut down black and still, and then the wind begin to moan around, and next the lightning begin to play and the thunder to grumble. And pretty soon there was a regular storm, and in the middle of it a man that was running aft stumbled and fell and sprained his ankle so that he had to lay up. This made the boys shake their heads. And every time the lightning come, there was that bar'l with the blue lights winking around it. We was always on the look-out for it. But by and by, towards dawn, she was gone. When the day come we could n't see her anywhere, and we war n't sorry, neither.

"But next night about half-past nine, when there was songs and high jinks going on, here she comes again, and took her old roost on the stabboard side. There war n't no more high jinks. Everybody got solemn; nobody talked; you could n't get anybody to do anything but set around moody and look at the bar'l. It begun to cloud up again. When the watch changed, the off watch stayed up, 'stead of turning in. The storm ripped and roared around all night, and in the middle of it another man tripped and sprained his ankle, and had to knock off. The bar'l left towards day, and nobody see it go.

"Everybody was sober and down in the mouth all day. I don't mean the kind of sober that comes of leaving liquor alone,—not that. They was quiet, but they all drunk more than usual,—not together,—but each man sidled off and took it private, by himself.

"After dark the off watch did n't turn in; nobody sung, nobody talked; the boys did n't scatter around, neither; they sort of huddled together, forrard; and for two hours they set there, perfectly still, looking steady in the one direction, and heaving a sigh once in a while. And then, here comes the bar'l again. She took up her old place. She staid there all night; nobody turned in. The storm come on again, after midnight. It got awful dark; the rain poured down; hail, too; the thunder boomed and roared and bellowed; the wind blowed a hurricane; and the lightning spread over everything in big sheets of glare, and showed the whole raft as plain as day; and the river lashed up white as milk as far as you could see for miles, and there was that bar'l jiggering along, same as ever. The captain ordered the watch to man the after sweeps for a crossing, and nobody would go,—no more sprained ankles for them, they said. They would n't even *walk* aft. Well then, just then the sky split wide open, with a crash, and the lightning killed two men of the after watch, and crippled two more. Crippled them how, says you? Why, *sprained their ankles!*

"The bar'l left in the dark betwixt lightnings, towards dawn. Well, not a body eat a bite at breakfast that morning. After that the men loafed around, in twos and threes, and talked low together. But none of them herded with Dick Allbright. They all give him the cold shake. If he come around where any of the men was, they split up and sidled away. They would n't man the sweeps with him. The captain had all the skiffs hauled up on the raft, alongside of his wigwam, and would n't let the dead men be took ashore to be planted; he did n't believe a man that got ashore would come back; and he was right.

"After night come, you could see pretty plain that there was going to be trouble if that bar'l come again; there was such a muttering going on. A good many wanted to kill Dick Allbright, because he'd seen the bar'l on other trips, and that had an ugly look. Some wanted to put him ashore. Some said, let's all go ashore in a pile, if the bar'l comes again.

"This kind of whispers was still going on, the men being bunched together forrard watching for the bar'l, when, lo and behold you, here she comes again. Down she comes, slow and steady, and settles into her old tracks. You could a heard a pin drop. Then up comes the captain, and says:—

" 'Boys, don't be a pack of children and fools; I don't want this bar'l to be dogging us all the way to Orleans, and *you* don't; well, then, how 's the best way to stop it?

Burn it up,—that 's the way. I'm going to fetch it aboard,'
he says. And before anybody could say a word, in he went.

"He swum to it, and as he come pushing it to the raft,
the men spread to one side. But the old man got it aboard
and busted in the head, and there was a baby in it! Yes sir,
a stark naked baby. It was Dick Allbright's baby; he owned
up and said so.

" 'Yes,' he says, a-leaning over it, 'yes, it is my own la-
mented darling, my poor lost Charles William Allbright deceased,' says he,—for he could curl his tongue around the
bulliest words in the language when he was a mind to, and
lay them before you without a jint started, anywheres. Yes,
he said he used to live up at the head of this bend, and one
night he choked his child, which was crying, not intending
to kill it,—which was prob'ly a lie,—and then he was
scared, and buried it in a bar'l, before his wife got home,
and off he went, and struck the northern trail and went to
rafting; and this was the third year that the bar'l had chased
him. He said the bad luck always begun light, and lasted
till four men was killed, and then the bar'l did n't come any
more after that. He said if the men would stand it one
more night,—and was a-going on like that,—but the men
had got enough. They started to get out a boat to take him
ashore and lynch him, but he grabbed the little child all of
a sudden and jumped overboard with it hugged up to his
breast and shedding tears, and we never see him again in
this life, poor old suffering soul, nor Charles William neither."

"*Who* was shedding tears?" says Bob; "was it Allbright
or the baby?"

"Why, Allbright, of course; didn't I tell you the baby
was dead? Been dead three years—how could it cry?"

"Well, never mind how it could cry—how could it *keep*
all that time?" says Davy. "You answer me that."

"I don't know how it done it," says Ed. "It done it
though—that 's all I know about it."

"Say—what did they do with the bar'l?" says the Child
of Calamity.

"Why, they hove it overboard, and it sunk like a chunk
of lead."

"Edward, did the child look like it was choked?" says one.

"Did it have its hair parted?" says another.

"What was the brand on that bar'l, Eddy?" says a fellow they called Bill.

"Have you got the papers for them statistics, Edmund?" says Jimmy.

"Say, Edwin, was you one of the men that was killed by the lightning?" says Davy.

"Him? O, no, he was both of 'em," says Bob. Then they all haw-hawed.

"Say, Edward, don't you reckon you 'd better take a pill? You look bad—don't you feel pale?" says the Child of Calamity.

"O, come, now, Eddy," says Jimmy, "show up; you must a kept part of that bar'l to prove the thing by. Show us the bunghole— *do*—and we'll all believe you."

"Say, boys," says Bill, "less divide it up. Thar 's thirteen of us. I can swaller a thirteenth of the yarn, if you can worry down the rest."

Ed got up mad and said they could all go to some place which he ripped out pretty savage, and then walked off aft cussing to himself, and they yelling and jeering at him, and roaring and laughing so you could hear them a mile.

"Boys, we 'll split a watermelon on that," says the Child of Calamity; and he come rummaging around in the dark amongst the shingle bundles where I was, and put his hand on me. I was warm and soft and naked; so he says "Ouch!" and jumped back.

"Fetch a lantern or a chunk of fire here, boys—there 's a snake here as big as a cow!"

So they run there with a lantern and crowded up and looked in on me.

"Come out of that, you beggar!" says one.

"Who are you?" says another.

"What are you after here? Speak up prompt, or overboard you go."

"Snake him out, boys. Snatch him out by the heels."

I began to beg, and crept out amongst them trembling.

They looked me over, wondering, and the Child of Calamity says: —

"A cussed thief! Lend a hand and less heave him overboard!"

"No," says Big Bob, "less get out the paint-pot and paint him a sky blue all over from head to heel, and *then* heave him over!"

"Good! that 's it. Go for the paint, Jimmy."

When the paint come, and Bob took the brush and was just going to begin, the others laughing and rubbing their hands, I begun to cry, and that sort of worked on Davy, and he says: —

" 'Vast there! He 's nothing but a cub. I 'll paint the man that tetches him!"

So I looked around on them, and some of them grumbled and growled, and Bob put down the paint, and the others did n't take it up.

"Come here to the fire, and less see what you 're up to here," says Davy. "Now set down there and give an account of yourself. How long have you been aboard here?"

"Not over a quarter of a minute, sir," says I.

"How did you get dry so quick?"

"I don't know, sir. I 'm always that way, mostly."

"Oh, you are, are you? What 's your name?"

I war n't going to tell my name. I did n't know what to say, so I just says:

"Charles William Allbright, sir."

Then they roared—the whole crowd; and I was mighty glad I said that, because maybe laughing would get them in a better humor.

When they got done laughing, Davy says: —

"It won't hardly do, Charles William. You could n't have growed this much in five year, and you was a baby when you come out of the bar'l, you know, and dead at that. Come, now, tell a straight story, and nobody 'll hurt you, if you ain't up to anything wrong. What *is* your name?"

"Aleck Hopkins, sir. Aleck James Hopkins."

"Well, Aleck, where did you come from, here?"

"From a trading scow. She lays up the bend yonder. I was born on her. Pap has traded up and down here all his life; and he told me to swim off here, because when you went by he said he would like to get some of you to speak to a Mr. Jonas Turner, in Cairo, and tell him—"

"Oh, come!"

"Yes, sir, it 's as true as the world; Pap he says—"

"Oh, your grandmother!"

They all laughed, and I tried again to talk, but they broke in on me and stopped me.

"Now, looky-here," says Davy; "you 're scared, and so you talk wild. Honest, now, do you live in a scow, or is it a lie?"

"Yes, sir, in a trading scow. She lays up at the head of the bend. But I war n't born in her. It 's our first trip."

"Now you 're talking! What did you come aboard here, for? To steal?"

"No, sir, I did n't.—It was only to get a ride on the raft. All boys does that."

"Well, I know that. But what did you hide for?"

"Sometimes they drive the boys off."

"So they do. They might steal. Looky-here; if we let you off this time, will you keep out of these kind of scrapes hereafter?"

" 'Deed I will, boss. You try me."

"All right, then. You ain't but little ways from shore. Overboard with you, and don't you make a fool of yourself another time this way.—Blast it, boy, some raftsmen would rawhide you till you were black and blue!"

I did n't wait to kiss good-bye, but went overboard and broke for shore. When Jim come along by and by, the big raft was away out of sight around the point. I swum out and got aboard, and was mighty glad to see home again.

The boy did not get the information he was after, but his adventure has furnished the glimpse of the departed raftsman and keelboatman which I desire to offer in this place.

I now come to a phase of the Mississippi River life of the flush times of steamboating, which seems to me to warrant full examination—the marvellous science of piloting, as displayed there. I believe there has been nothing like it elsewhere in the world.

IV.

The Boys' Ambition

WHEN I WAS a boy, there was but one permanent ambition among my comrades in our village[1] on the west bank of the Mississippi River. That was, to be a steamboatman. We had transient ambitions of other sorts, but they were only transient. When a circus came and went, it left us all burning to become clowns; the first negro minstrel show that came to our section left us all suffering to try that kind of life; now and then we had a hope that if we lived and were good, God would permit us to be pirates. These ambitions faded out, each in its turn; but the ambition to be a steamboatman always remained.

Once a day a cheap, gaudy packet arrived upward from St. Louis, and another downward from Keokuk. Before these events, the day was glorious with expectancy; after them, the day was a dead and empty thing. Not only the boys, but the whole village, felt this. After all these years I can picture that old time to myself now, just as it was then: the white town drowsing in the sunshine of a summer's morning; the streets empty, or pretty nearly so; one or two clerks sitting in front of the Water Street stores, with their splint-bottomed chairs tilted back against the wall, chins on breasts, hats slouched over their faces, asleep—with shingle-shavings enough around to show what broke them down; a sow and a litter of pigs loafing along the sidewalk, doing a good business in watermelon rinds and seeds; two or three lonely little freight piles scattered about the "levee;" a pile of "skids" on the slope of the stone-paved wharf, and the fragrant town drunkard asleep in the shadow of them; two or three wood flats at the head of the wharf, but nobody to listen to the peaceful lapping of the wavelets against them; the great Mississippi, the majestic, the magnificent Mississippi, rolling its mile-wide tide along, shining in the sun; the dense forest away on the other side; the "point" above the town, and the "point" be-

[1] Hannibal, Missouri.

37

low, bounding the river-glimpse and turning it into a sort of sea, and withal a very still and brilliant and lonely one. Presently a film of dark smoke appears above one of those remote "points;" instantly a negro drayman, famous for his quick eye and prodigious voice, lifts up the cry, "S-t-e-a-m-boat a-comin'!" and the scene changes! The town drunkard stirs, the clerks wake up, a furious clatter of drays follows, every house and store pours out a human contribution, and all in a twinkling the dead town is alive and moving. Drays, carts, men, boys, all go hurrying from many quarters to a common centre, the wharf. Assembled there, the people fasten their eyes upon the coming boat as upon a wonder they are seeing for the first time. And the boat *is* rather a handsome sight, too. She is long and sharp and trim and pretty; she has two tall, fancy-topped chimneys, with a gilded device of some kind swung between them; a fanciful pilot-house, all glass and "gingerbread," perched on top of the "texas" deck behind them; the paddle-boxes are gorgeous with a picture or with gilded rays above the boat's name; the boiler deck, the hurricane deck, and the texas deck are fenced and ornamented with clean white railings; there is a flag gallantly flying from the jack-staff; the furnace doors are open and the fires glaring bravely; the upper decks are black with passengers; the captain stands by the big bell, calm, imposing, the envy of all; great volumes of the blackest smoke are rolling and tumbling out of the chimneys—a husbanded grandeur created with a bit of pitch pine just before arriving at a town; the crew are grouped on the forecastle; the broad stage is run far out over the port bow, and an envied deck-hand stands picturesquely on the end of it with a coil of rope in his hand; the pent steam is screaming through the gauge-cocks; the captain lifts his hand, a bell rings, the wheels stop; then they turn back, churning the water to foam, and the steamer is at rest. Then such a scramble as there is to get aboard, and to get ashore, and to take in freight and to discharge freight, all at one and the same time; and such a yelling and cursing as the mates facilitate it all with! Ten minutes later the steamer is under way again, with no flag on the jack-staff and no black smoke issuing from the chimneys. After ten more minutes the town is dead again, and the town drunkard asleep by the skids once more.

My father was a justice of the peace, and I supposed he possessed the power of life and death over all men and could hang anybody that offended him. This was distinction enough for me as a general thing; but the desire to be a steamboatman kept intruding, nevertheless. I first wanted to be a cabin-boy, so that I could come out with a white apron on and shake a table-cloth over the side, where all my old comrades could see me; later I thought I would rather be the deck-hand who stood on the end of the stage-plank with the coil of rope in his hand, because he was particularly conspicuous. But these were only day-dreams,—they were too heavenly to be contemplated as real possibilities. By and by one of our boys went away. He was not heard of for a long time. At last he turned up as apprentice engineer or "striker" on a steamboat. This thing shook the bottom out of all my Sunday-school teachings. That boy had been notoriously worldly, and I just the reverse; yet he was exalted to this eminence, and I left in obscurity and misery. There was nothing generous about this fellow in his greatness. He would always manage to have a rusty bolt to scrub while his boat tarried at our town, and he would sit on the inside guard and scrub it, where we could all see him and envy him and loathe him. And whenever his boat was laid up he would come home and swell around the town in his blackest and greasiest clothes, so that nobody could help remembering that he was a steamboatman; and he used all sorts of steamboat technicalities in his talk, as if he were so used to them that he forgot common people could not understand them. He would speak of the "labboard" side of a horse in an easy, natural way that would make one wish he was dead. And he was always talking about "St. Looy" like an old citizen; he would refer casually to occasions when he "was coming down Fourth Street," or when he was "passing by the Planter's House," or when there was a fire and he took a turn on the brakes of "the old Big Missouri;" and then he would go on and lie about how many towns the size of ours were burned down there that day. Two or three of the boys had long been persons of consideration among us because they had been to St. Louis once and had a vague general knowledge of its wonders, but the day of their glory was over now. They lapsed into a humble silence, and learned to disappear when the ruthless "cub"-engineer approached. This fellow had money, too, and hair oil. Also an ignorant silver watch and a showy brass watch chain. He wore a leather belt and used no suspenders. If ever a youth was cordially admired and hated by his comrades, this one was. No girl could withstand his charms. He "cut out" every boy in the village. When his boat blew up at last, it diffused a tranquil contentment among us such as we had not known for months. But when he came home the next week, alive, renowned, and appeared in church all battered up and bandaged, a shining hero, stared at and wondered over by everybody, it seemed to us that the partiality of Providence for an undeserving reptile had reached a point where it was open to criticism.

This creature's career could produce but one result, and it speedily followed. Boy after boy managed to get on the river. The minister's son became an engineer. The doctor's and the post-master's sons became "mud clerks;" the wholesale liquor dealer's son became a bar-keeper on a boat; four sons of the chief merchant, and two sons of the county judge, became pilots. Pilot was the grandest position of all. The pilot, even in those days of trivial wages, had a princely salary—from a hundred and fifty to two hundred and fifty dollars a month, and no board to pay. Two months of his wages would pay a preacher's salary for a year. Now some of us were left disconsolate. We could not get on the river—at least our parents would not let us.

So by and by I ran away. I said I never would come home again till I was a pilot and could come in glory. But somehow I could not manage it. I went meekly aboard a few of the boats that lay packed together like sardines at the long St. Louis wharf, and very humbly inquired for the pilots, but got only a cold shoulder and short words from mates and clerks. I had to make the best of this sort of treatment for the time being, but I had comforting day-dreams of a future when I should be a great and honored pilot, with plenty of money, and could kill some of these mates and clerks and pay for them.

V.

I Want to Be a Cub-Pilot

MONTHS AFTERWARD the hope within me struggled to a reluctant death, and I found myself without an ambition. But I was ashamed to go home. I was in Cincinnati, and I set to work to map out a new career. I had been reading about the recent exploration of the river Amazon by an expedition sent out by our government. It was said that the expedition, owing to difficulties, had not thoroughly explored a part of the country lying about the head-waters, some four thousand miles from the mouth of the river. It was only about fifteen hundred miles from Cincinnati to New Orleans, where I could doubtless get a ship. I had thirty dollars left; I would go and complete the exploration of the Amazon. This was all the thought I gave to the subject. I never was great in matters of detail. I packed my valise, and took passage on an ancient tub called the "Paul Jones," for New Orleans. For the sum of sixteen dollars I had the scarred and tarnished splendors of "her" main saloon principally to myself, for she was not a creature to attract the eye of wiser travellers.

When we presently got under way and went poking down the broad Ohio, I became a new being, and the subject of my own admiration. I was a traveller! A word never had tasted so good in my mouth before. I had an exultant sense of being bound for mysterious lands and distant climes which I never have felt in so uplifting a degree since. I was in such a glorified condition that all ignoble feelings departed out of me, and I was able to look down and pity the untravelled with a compassion that had hardly a trace of contempt in it. Still, when we stopped at villages and wood-yards, I could not help lolling carelessly upon the railings of the boiler deck to enjoy the envy of the country boys on the bank. If they did not seem to discover me, I presently sneezed to attract their attention, or moved to a position where they could not help seeing me. And as soon as I knew they saw me I gaped and stretched, and gave other signs of being mightily bored with travelling.

I kept my hat off all the time, and stayed where the wind and the sun could strike me, because I wanted to get the bronzed and weather-beaten look of an old traveller. Before the second day was half gone, I experienced a joy which filled me with the purest gratitude; for I saw that the skin had begun to blister and peel off my face and neck. I wished that the boys and girls at home could see me now.

We reached Louisville in time—at least the neighborhood of it. We stuck hard and fast on the rocks in the middle of the river, and lay there four days. I was now beginning to feel a strong sense of being a part of the boat's family, a sort of infant son to the captain and younger brother to the officers. There is no estimating the pride I took in this grandeur, or the affection that began to swell and grow in me for those people. I could not know how the lordly steamboatman scorns that sort of presumption in a mere landsman. I particularly longed to acquire the least trifle of notice from the big stormy mate, and I was on the alert for an opportunity to do him a service to that end. It came at last. The riotous powwow of setting a spar was going on down on the forecastle, and I went down there and stood around in the way—or mostly skipping out of it—till the mate suddenly roared a general order for somebody to bring him a capstan bar. I sprang to his side and said: "Tell me where it is—I 'll fetch it!"

If a rag-picker had offered to do a diplomatic service for the Emperor of Russia, the monarch could not have been more astounded than the mate was. He even stopped swearing. He stood and stared down at me. It took him ten seconds to scrape his disjointed remains together again. Then he said impressively: "Well, if this don't beat hell!" and turned to his work with the air of a man who had been confronted with a problem too abstruse for solution.

I crept away, and courted solitude for the rest of the day. I did not go to dinner; I stayed away from supper until everybody else had finished. I did not feel so much like a member of the boat's family now as before. However, my spirits returned, in instalments, as we pursued our way down the river. I was sorry I hated the mate so, because it was not in (young) human nature not to admire him. He was huge and muscular, his face was bearded and whiskered all over; he had a red woman and a blue woman tattooed on his right arm,—one on each side of a blue anchor with a red rope to it; and in the matter of profanity he was sublime. When he was getting out cargo at a landing, I was always where I could see and hear. He felt all the majesty of his great position, and made the world feel it, too. When he gave even the simplest order, he discharged it like a blast of lightning, and sent a long, reverberating peal of profanity thundering after it. I could not help contrasting the way in which the average landsman would give an order, with the mate's way of doing it. If the landsman should wish the gang-plank moved a foot farther forward, he would probably say: "James, or William, one of you push that plank forward, please;" but put the mate in his place, and he would roar out: "Here, now, start that gang-plank for'ard! Lively, now! *What* 're you about! Snatch it! *snatch* it! There! there! Aft again! aft again! Don't you hear me? Dash it to dash! are you going to *sleep* over it! '*Vast* heaving. 'Vast heaving, I tell you! Going to heave it clear astern? WHERE 're you going with that barrel! *for'ard* with it 'fore I make you swallow it, you dash-dash-dash-*dashed* split between a tired mud-turtle and a crippled hearse-horse!"

I wished I could talk like that.

When the soreness of my adventure with the mate had somewhat worn off, I began timidly to make up to the humblest official connected with the boat—the night watchman. He snubbed my advances at first, but I presently ventured to offer him a new chalk pipe, and that softened him. So he allowed me to sit with him by the big bell on the hurricane deck, and in time he melted into conversation. He could not well have helped it, I hung with such homage on his words and so plainly showed that I felt honored by his notice. He told me the names of dim capes and shadowy islands as we glided by them in the solemnity of the night, under the winking stars, and by and by got to talking about himself. He seemed over-sentimental for a man whose salary was six dollars a week—or rather he might have seemed so to an older person than I. But I drank in his words hungrily, and with a faith that might have moved mountains if it had been applied judiciously. What was it to me that he was soiled and seedy and fragrant with gin? What was it to me that his grammar was bad, his construction worse, and his profanity so void of art that it was an element of weakness rather than strength in his conversation? He was a wronged man, a man who had seen trouble, and that was enough for me. As he mellowed into his plaintive history his tears dripped upon the lantern in his lap, and I cried, too, from sympathy. He said he was the son of an English nobleman—either an earl or an alderman, he could not remember which, but believed was both; his father, the nobleman, loved him, but his mother hated him from the cradle; and so while he was still a little boy he was sent to "one of them old, ancient colleges"—he couldn't remember which; and by and by his father died and his mother seized the property and "shook" him, as he phrased it. After his mother shook him, members of the nobility with whom he was acquainted used their influence to get him the position of "lob-lolly-boy in a ship;" and from that point my watchman threw off all trammels of date and locality and branched out into a narrative that bristled all along with incredible adventures; a narrative that was so reeking with bloodshed and so crammed with hair-breadth escapes and the most engaging and unconscious personal villanies, that I sat speechless, enjoying, shuddering, wondering, worshipping.

It was a sore blight to find out afterwards that he was a low, vulgar, ignorant, sentimental, half-witted humbug, an untravelled native of the wilds of Illinois, who had absorbed wildcat literature and appropriated its marvels, until in time he had woven odds and ends of the mess into this yarn, and then gone on telling it to fledglings like me, until he had come to believe it himself.

VI.

A Cub-Pilot's Experience

WHAT WITH LYING on the rocks four days at Louisville, and some other delays, the poor old "Paul Jones" fooled away about two weeks in making the voyage from Cincinnati to New Orleans. This gave me a chance to get acquainted with one of the pilots, and he taught me how to steer the boat, and thus made the fascination of river life more potent than ever for me.

It also gave me a chance to get acquainted with a youth who had taken deck passage—more 's the pity; for he easily borrowed six dollars of me on a promise to return to the boat and pay it back to me the day after we should arrive. But he probably died or forgot, for he never came. It was doubtless the former, since he had said his parents were wealthy, and he only travelled deck passage because it was cooler.[1]

I soon discovered two things. One was that a vessel would not be likely to sail for the mouth of the Amazon under ten or twelve years; and the other was that the nine or ten dollars still left in my pocket would not suffice for so imposing an exploration as I had planned, even if I could afford to wait for a ship. Therefore it followed that I must contrive a new career. The "Paul Jones" was now bound for St. Louis. I planned a siege against my pilot, and at the end of three hard days he surrendered. He agreed to teach me the Mississippi River from New Orleans to St. Louis for five hundred dollars, payable out of the first wages I should receive after graduating. I entered upon the small enterprise of "learning" twelve or thirteen hundred miles of the great Mississippi River with the easy confidence of my time of life. If I had really known what I was about to require of my faculties, I should not have had the courage to begin. I supposed that all a pilot had to do was to keep his boat in the river, and I did not consider that that could be much of a trick, since it was so wide.

The boat backed out from New Orleans at four in the af-

[1] "Deck" passage— *i.e.*, steerage passage.

ternoon, and it was "our watch" until eight. Mr. Bixby, my chief, "straightened her up," plowed her along past the sterns of the other boats that lay at the Levee, and then said, "Here, take her; shave those steamships as close as you 'd peel an apple." I took the wheel, and my heart-beat fluttered up into the hundreds; for it seemed to me that we were about to scrape the side off every ship in the line, we were so close. I held my breath and began to claw the boat away from the danger; and I had my own opinion of the pilot who had known no better than to get us into such peril, but I was too wise to express it. In half a minute I had a wide margin of safety intervening between the "Paul Jones" and the ships; and within ten seconds more I was set aside in disgrace, and Mr. Bixby was going into danger again and flaying me alive with abuse of my cowardice. I was stung, but I was obliged to admire the easy confidence with which my chief loafed from side to side of his wheel, and trimmed the ships so closely that disaster seemed ceaselessly imminent. When he had cooled a little he told me that the easy water was close ashore and the current outside, and therefore we must hug the bank, up-stream, to get the benefit of the former, and stay well out, down-stream, to take advantage of the latter. In my own mind I resolved to be a down-stream pilot and leave the up-streaming to people dead to prudence.

Now and then Mr. Bixby called my attention to certain things. Said he, "This is Six-Mile Point." I assented. It was pleasant enough information, but I could not see the bearing of it. I was not conscious that it was a matter of any interest to me. Another time he said, "This is Nine-Mile Point." Later he said, "This is Twelve-Mile Point." They were all about level with the water's edge; they all looked about alike to me; they were monotonously unpicturesque. I hoped Mr. Bixby would change the subject. But no; he would crowd up around a point, hugging the shore with affection, and then say: "The slack water ends here, abreast this bunch of China-trees; now we cross over." So he crossed over. He gave me the wheel once or twice, but I had no luck. I either came near chipping off the edge of a sugar plantation, or I yawed too far from shore, and so dropped back into disgrace again and got abused.

The watch was ended at last, and we took supper and went to bed. At midnight the glare of a lantern shone in my eyes, and the night watchman said:—

"Come! turn out!"

And then he left. I could not understand this extraordinary procedure; so I presently gave up trying to, and dozed off to sleep. Pretty soon the watchman was back again, and this time he was gruff. I was annoyed. I said:

"What do you want to come bothering around here in the middle of the night for? Now as like as not I 'll not get to sleep again to-night."

The watchman said:—

"Well, if this an't good, I 'm blest."

The "off-watch" was just turning in, and I heard some brutal laughter from them, and such remarks as "Hello, watchman! an't the new cub turned out yet? He 's delicate, likely. Give him some sugar in a rag and send for the chambermaid to sing rock-a-by-baby to him."

About this time Mr. Bixby appeared on the scene. Something like a minute later I was climbing the pilot-house steps with some of my clothes on and the rest in my arms. Mr. Bixby was close behind, commenting. Here was something fresh—this thing of getting up in the middle of the night to go to work. It was a detail in piloting that had never occurred to me at all. I knew that boats ran all night, but somehow I had never happened to reflect that somebody had to get up out of a warm bed to run them. I began to fear that piloting was not quite so romantic as I had imagined it was; there was something very real and work-like about this new phase of it.

It was a rather dingy night, although a fair number of stars were out. The big mate was at the wheel, and he had the old tub pointed at a star and was holding her straight up the middle of the river. The shores on either hand were not much more than half a mile apart, but they seemed wonderfully far away and ever so vague and indistinct. The mate said:—

"We 've got to land at Jones's plantation, sir."

The vengeful spirit in me exulted. I said to myself, I wish you joy of your job, Mr. Bixby; you 'll have a good time finding Mr. Jones's plantation such a night as this; and I hope you never *will* find it as long as you live.

Mr. Bixby said to the mate:—

"Upper end of the plantation, or the lower?"

"Upper."

"I can't do it. The stumps there are out of water at this stage. It 's no great distance to the lower, and you 'll have to get along with that."

"All right, sir. If Jones don't like it he 'll have to lump it, I reckon."

And then the mate left. My exultation began to cool and my wonder to come up. Here was a man who not only proposed to find this plantation on such a night, but to find either end of it you preferred. I dreadfully wanted to ask a question, but I was carrying about as many short answers as my cargo-room would admit of, so I held my peace. All I desired to ask Mr. Bixby was the simple question whether he was ass enough to really imagine he was going to find that plantation on a night when all plantations were exactly alike and all the same color. But I held in. I used to have fine inspirations of prudence in those days.

Mr. Bixby made for the shore and soon was scraping it, just the same as if it had been daylight. And not only that, but singing—

"Father in heaven, the day is declining," etc.

It seemed to me that I had put my life in the keeping of a peculiarly reckless outcast. Presently he turned on me and said:—

"What's the name of the first point above New Orleans?"

I was gratified to be able to answer promptly, and I did. I said I did n't know.

"Don't *know*?"

This manner jolted me. I was down at the foot again, in a moment. But I had to say just what I had said before.

"Well, you 're a smart one," said Mr. Bixby. "What 's the name of the *next* point?"

Once more I did n't know.

"Well, this beats anything. Tell me the name of *any* point or place I told you."

I studied a while and decided that I could n't.

"Look here! What do you start out from, above Twelve-Mile Point, to cross over?"

"I—I—don't know."

"You—you—don't know?" mimicking my drawling manner of speech. "What *do* you know?"

"I—I—nothing, for certain."

"By the great Cæsar's ghost, I believe you! You 're the stupidest dunderhead I ever saw or ever heard of, so help me Moses! The idea of *you* being a pilot—*you*! Why, you don't know enough to pilot a cow down a lane."

Oh, but his wrath was up! He was a nervous man, and he shuffled from one side of his wheel to the other as if the floor was hot. He would boil a while to himself, and then overflow and scald me again.

"Look here! What do you suppose I told you the names of those points for?"

I tremblingly considered a moment, and then the devil of temptation provoked me to say:—

"Well—to—to—be entertaining, I thought."

This was a red rag to the bull. He raged and stormed so (he was crossing the river at the time) that I judge it made him blind, because he ran over the steering-oar of a trading-scow. Of course the traders sent up a volley of red-hot profanity. Never was a man so grateful as Mr. Bixby was: because he was brim full, and here were subjects who would *talk back*. He threw open a window, thrust his head out, and such an irruption followed as I never had heard before. The fainter and farther away the scowmen's curses drifted, the higher Mr. Bixby lifted his voice and the weightier his adjectives grew. When he closed the window he was empty. You could have drawn a seine through his system and not caught curses enough to disturb your mother with. Presently he said to me in the gentlest way:—

"My boy, you must get a little memorandum-book, and every time I tell you a thing, put it down right away. There 's only one way to be a pilot, and that is to get this entire river by heart. You have to know it just like A B C."

That was a dismal revelation to me; for my memory was never loaded with anything but blank cartridges. However, I did not feel discouraged long. I judged that it was best to make some allowances, for doubtless Mr. Bixby was "stretch-ing." Presently he pulled a rope and struck a few strokes on the big bell. The stars were all gone now, and the night was as black as ink. I could hear the wheels churn along the bank, but I was not entirely certain that I could see the shore. The voice of the invisible watchman called up from the hurricane deck:—

"What 's this, sir?"

"Jones's plantation."

I said to myself, I wish I might venture to offer a small bet that it is n't. But I did not chirp. I only waited to see. Mr. Bixby handled the engine bells, and in due time the boat's nose came to the land, a torch glowed from the forecastle, a man skipped ashore, a darky's voice on the bank said, "Gimme de k'yarpet-bag, Mars' Jones," and the next moment we were standing up the river again, all serene. I reflected deeply a while, and then said,—but not aloud,—Well, the finding of that plantation was the luckiest accident that ever happened; but it could n't happen again in a hundred years. And I fully believed it *was* an accident, too.

By the time we had gone seven or eight hundred miles up the river, I had learned to be a tolerably plucky upstream steersman, in daylight, and before we reached St. Louis I had made a trifle of progress in night-work, but only a trifle. I had a note-book that fairly bristled with the names of towns, "points," bars, islands, bends, reaches, etc.; but the informa-tion was to be found only in the note-book—none of it was in my head. It made my heart ache to think I had only got half of the river set down; for as our watch was four hours off and four hours on, day and night, there was a long four-hour gap in my book for every time I had slept since the voyage began.

My chief was presently hired to go on a big New Orleans boat, and I packed my satchel and went with him. She was a grand affair. When I stood in her pilot-house I was so far above the water that I seemed perched on a mountain; and her decks stretched so far away, fore and aft, below me, that I wondered how I could ever have considered the little "Paul Jones" a large craft. There were other differences, too. The "Paul Jones's" pilot-house was a cheap, dingy, battered rattletrap, cramped for room: but here was a sumptuous glass temple; room enough to have a dance in; showy red and gold window-curtains; an imposing sofa; leather cushions and a back to the high bench where visiting pilots sit, to spin yarns and "look at the river;" bright, fanciful "cuspadores" instead of a broad wooden box filled with sawdust; nice new oil-cloth on the floor; a hospitable big stove for winter; a wheel as high as my head, costly with inlaid work; a wire tiller-rope; bright brass knobs for the bells; and a tidy, white-aproned, black "texas-tender," to bring up tarts and ices and coffee during mid-watch, day and night. Now this was "something like;" and so I began to take heart once more to believe that piloting was a romantic sort of occupation after all. The moment we were under way I began to prowl about the great steamer and fill myself with joy. She was as clean and as dainty as a drawing-room; when I looked down her long, gilded saloon, it was like gazing through a splendid tunnel; she had an oil-picture, by some gifted sign-painter, on every state-room door; she glittered with no end of prism-fringed chandeliers; the clerk's office was elegant, the bar was marvellous, and the bar-keeper had been barbered and upholstered at incredible cost. The boiler deck (*i.e.*, the second story of the boat, so to speak), was as spacious as a church, it seemed to me; so with the forecastle; and there was no pitiful handful of deck-hands, firemen, and roust-abouts down there, but a whole battalion of men. The fires were fiercely glaring from a long row of furnaces, and over them were eight huge boilers! This was unutterable pomp. The mighty engines—but enough of this. I had never felt so fine before. And when I found that the regiment of natty servants respectfully "sir'd" me, my satisfaction was complete.

VII.

A Daring Deed

WHEN I RETURNED to the pilot-house St. Louis was gone and I was lost. Here was a piece of river which was all down in my book, but I could make neither head nor tail of it: you understand, it was turned around. I had seen it when coming up-stream, but I had never faced about to see how it looked when it was behind me. My heart broke again, for it was plain that I had got to learn this troublesome river *both ways*.

The pilot-house was full of pilots, going down to "look at the river." What is called the "upper river" (the two hundred miles between St. Louis and Cairo, where the Ohio comes in) was low; and the Mississippi changes its channel so constantly that the pilots used to always find it necessary to run down to Cairo to take a fresh look, when their boats were to lie in port a week; that is, when the water was at a low stage. A deal of this "looking at the river" was done by poor fellows who seldom had a berth, and whose only hope of getting one lay in their being always freshly posted and therefore ready to drop into the shoes of some reputable pilot, for a single trip, on account of such pilot's sudden illness, or some other necessity. And a good many of them constantly ran up and down inspecting the river, not because they ever really hoped to get a berth, but because (they being guests of the boat) it was cheaper to "look at the river" than stay ashore and pay board. In time these fellows grew dainty in their tastes, and only infested boats that had an established reputation for setting good tables. All visiting pilots were useful, for they were always ready and willing, winter or summer, night or day, to go out in the yawl and help buoy the channel or assist the boat's pilots in any way they could. They were likewise welcome because all pilots are tireless talkers, when gathered together, and as they talk only about the river they are always understood and are always interesting. Your true pilot cares nothing about anything on earth but the river, and his pride in his occupation surpasses the pride of kings.

We had a fine company of these river-inspectors along, this trip. There were eight or ten; and there was abundance of room for them in our great pilot-house. Two or three of them wore polished silk hats, elaborate shirt-fronts, diamond breastpins, kid gloves, and patent-leather boots. They were choice in their English, and bore themselves with a dignity proper to men of solid means and prodigious reputation as pilots. The others were more or less loosely clad, and wore upon their heads tall felt cones that were suggestive of the days of the Commonwealth.

I was a cipher in this august company, and felt subdued, not to say torpid. I was not even of sufficient consequence to assist at the wheel when it was necessary to put the tiller hard down in a hurry; the guest that stood nearest did that when occasion required—and this was pretty much all the time, because of the crookedness of the channel and the scant water. I stood in a corner; and the talk I listened to took the hope all out of me. One visitor said to another:—

"Jim, how did you run Plum Point, coming up?"

"It was in the night, there, and I ran it the way one of the boys on the 'Diana' told me; started out about fifty yards above the wood pile on the false point, and held on the cabin under Plum Point till I raised the reef—quarter less twain—then straightened up for the middle bar till I got well abreast the old one-limbed cotton-wood in the bend, then got my stern on the cotton-wood and head on the low place above the point, and came through a-booming—nine and a half."

"Pretty square crossing, an't it?"

"Yes, but the upper bar 's working down fast."

Another pilot spoke up and said:—

"I had better water than that, and ran it lower down; started out from the false point—mark twain—raised the second reef abreast the big snag in the bend, and had quarter less twain."

One of the gorgeous ones remarked:—

"I don't want to find fault with your leadsmen, but that 's a good deal of water for Plum Point, it seems to me."

There was an approving nod all around as this quiet snub dropped on the boaster and "settled" him. And so they went on talk-talk-talking. Meantime, the thing that was running in my mind was, "Now if my ears hear aright, I have not only to get the names of all the towns and islands and bends, and so on, by heart, but I must even get up a warm personal acquaintanceship with every old snag and one-limbed cotton-wood and obscure wood pile that ornaments the banks of this river for twelve hundred miles; and more than that, I must actually know where these things are in the dark, unless these guests are gifted with eyes that can pierce through two miles of solid blackness; I wish the piloting business was in Jericho and I had never thought of it."

At dusk Mr. Bixby tapped the big bell three times (the signal to land), and the captain emerged from his drawing-room in the forward end of the texas, and looked up inquiringly. Mr. Bixby said:—

"We will lay up here all night, captain."

"Very well, sir."

That was all. The boat came to shore and was tied up for the night. It seemed to me a fine thing that the pilot could do as he pleased, without asking so grand a captain's permission. I took my supper and went immediately to bed, discouraged by my day's observations and experiences. My late voyage's note-booking was but a confusion of meaningless names. It had tangled me all up in a knot every time I had looked at it in the daytime. I now hoped for respite in sleep; but no, it revelled all through my head till sunrise again, a frantic and tireless nightmare.

Next morning I felt pretty rusty and low-spirited. We went booming along, taking a good many chances, for we were anxious to "get out of the river" (as getting out to Cairo was called) before night should overtake us. But Mr. Bixby's partner, the other pilot, presently grounded the boat, and we lost so much time getting her off that it was plain the darkness would overtake us a good long way above the mouth. This was a great misfortune, especially to certain of our visiting pilots, whose boats would have to wait for their return, no matter how long that might be. It sobered the pilot-house talk a good deal. Coming up-stream, pilots did not mind low water or any kind of dark-ness; nothing stopped them but fog. But down-stream work was different; a boat was too nearly helpless, with a

stiff current pushing behind her; so it was not customary to
run down-stream at night in low water.

There seemed to be one small hope, however: if we could
get through the intricate and dangerous Hat Island crossing
before night, we could venture the rest, for we would have
plainer sailing and better water. But it would be insanity to
attempt Hat Island at night. So there was a deal of looking at
watches all the rest of the day, and a constant ciphering upon
the speed we were making; Hat Island was the eternal subject; sometimes hope was high and sometimes we were delayed in a bad crossing, and down it went again. For hours
all hands lay under the burden of this suppressed excitement;
it was even communicated to me, and I got to feeling so so-
licitous about Hat Island, and under such an awful pressure
of responsibility, that I wished I might have five minutes on
shore to draw a good, full, relieving breath, and start over
again. We were standing no regular watches. Each of our pilots ran such portions of the river as he had run when coming
up-stream, because of his greater familiarity with it; but both
remained in the pilot-house constantly.

An hour before sunset, Mr. Bixby took the wheel and Mr.
W—— stepped aside. For the next thirty minutes every man
held his watch in his hand and was restless, silent, and uneasy.
At last somebody said, with a doomful sigh,—

"Well yonder 's Hat Island—and we can't make it."

All the watches closed with a snap, everybody sighed and
muttered something about its being "too bad, too bad—ah,
if we could *only* have got here half an hour sooner!" and the
place was thick with the atmosphere of disappointment. Some
started to go out, but loitered, hearing no bell-tap to land.
The sun dipped behind the horizon, the boat went on. Inquiring looks passed from one guest to another; and one who
had his hand on the door-knob and had turned it, waited,
then presently took away his hand and let the knob turn back
again. We bore steadily down the bend. More looks were exchanged, and nods of surprised admiration—but no words.
Insensibly the men drew together behind Mr. Bixby, as the
sky darkened and one or two dim stars came out. The dead
silence and sense of waiting became oppressive. Mr. Bixby
pulled the cord, and two deep, mellow notes from the big

bell floated off on the night. Then a pause, and one more note was struck. The watchman's voice followed, from the hurricane deck:—

"Labboard lead, there! Stabboard lead!"

The cries of the leadsmen began to rise out of the distance, and were gruffly repeated by the word-passers on the hurricane deck.

"M-a-r-k three! . . . . M-a-r-k three! . . . . Quarter-less-three! . . . . Half twain! . . . . Quarter twain! . . . . M-a-r-k twain! . . . . Quarter-less"—

Mr. Bixby pulled two bell-ropes, and was answered by faint jinglings far below in the engine room, and our speed slackened. The steam began to whistle through the gauge-cocks. The cries of the leadsmen went on—and it is a weird sound, always, in the night. Every pilot in the lot was watching now, with fixed eyes, and talking under his breath. Nobody was calm and easy but Mr. Bixby. He would put his wheel down and stand on a spoke, and as the steamer swung into her (to me) utterly invisible marks—for we seemed to be in the midst of a wide and gloomy sea—he would meet and fasten her there. Out of the murmur of half-audible talk, one caught a coherent sentence now and then—such as:

"There; she 's over the first reef all right!"

After a pause, another subdued voice:—

"Her stern 's coming down just *exactly* right, by *George!*"

"Now she 's in the marks; over she goes!"

Somebody else muttered:—

"Oh, it was done beautiful— *beautiful!*"

Now the engines were stopped altogether, and we drifted with the current. Not that I could see the boat drift, for I could not, the stars being all gone by this time. This drifting was the dismalest work; it held one's heart still. Presently I discovered a blacker gloom than that which surrounded us. It was the head of the island. We were closing right down upon it. We entered its deeper shadow, and so imminent seemed the peril that I was likely to suffocate; and I had the strongest impulse to do *something,* anything, to save the vessel. But still Mr. Bixby stood by his wheel, silent, intent as a cat, and all the pilots stood shoulder to shoulder at his back.

"She 'll not make it!" somebody whispered.

The water grew shoaler and shoaler, by the leadsman's cries, till it was down to—

"Eight-and-a-half! . . . . E-i-g-h-t feet! . . . . E-i-g-h-t feet! . . . . Seven-and"—

Mr. Bixby said warningly through his speaking tube to the engineer:—

"Stand by, now!"

"Aye-aye, sir!"

"Seven-and-a-half! Seven feet! *Six*-and"—

We touched bottom! Instantly Mr. Bixby set a lot of bells ringing, shouted through the tube, "*Now*, let her have it— every ounce you 've got!" then to his partner, "Put her hard down! snatch her! snatch her!" The boat rasped and ground her way through the sand, hung upon the apex of disaster a single tremendous instant, and then over she went! And such a shout as went up at Mr. Bixby's back never loosened the roof of a pilot-house before!

There was no more trouble after that. Mr. Bixby was a hero that night; and it was some little time, too, before his exploit ceased to be talked about by river men.

Fully to realize the marvellous precision required in laying the great steamer in her marks in that murky waste of water, one should know that not only must she pick her intricate way through snags and blind reefs, and then shave the head of the island so closely as to brush the overhanging foliage with her stern, but at one place she must pass almost within arm's reach of a sunken and invisible wreck that would snatch the hull timbers from under her if she should strike it, and destroy a quarter of a million dollars' worth of steamboat and cargo in five minutes, and maybe a hundred and fifty human lives into the bargain.

The last remark I heard that night was a compliment to Mr. Bixby, uttered in soliloquy and with unction by one of our guests. He said:—

"By the Shadow of Death, but he 's a lightning pilot!"

VIII.

Perplexing Lessons

AT THE END of what seemed a tedious while, I had managed to pack my head full of islands, towns, bars,
"points," and bends; and a curiously inanimate mass of lumber it was, too. However, inasmuch as I could shut my eyes
and reel off a good long string of these names without leaving
out more than ten miles of river in every fifty, I began to feel
that I could take a boat down to New Orleans if I could make
her skip those little gaps. But of course my complacency
could hardly get start enough to lift my nose a trifle into the
air, before Mr. Bixby would think of something to fetch it
down again. One day he turned on me suddenly with this
settler:—

"What is the shape of Walnut Bend?"

He might as well have asked me my grandmother's opinion
of protoplasm. I reflected respectfully, and then said I did n't
know it had any particular shape. My gunpowdery chief went
off with a bang, of course, and then went on loading and
firing until he was out of adjectives.

I had learned long ago that he only carried just so many
rounds of ammunition, and was sure to subside into a very
placable and even remorseful old smooth-bore as soon as they
were all gone. That word "old" is merely affectionate; he was
not more than thirty-four. I waited. By and by he said,—

"My boy, you 've got to know the *shape* of the river perfectly. It is all there is left to steer by on a very dark night.
Everything else is blotted out and gone. But mind you, it has
n't the same shape in the night that it has in the day-time."

"How on earth am I ever going to learn it, then?"

"How do you follow a hall at home in the dark? Because
you know the shape of it. You can't see it."

"Do you mean to say that I 've got to know all the million
trifling variations of shape in the banks of this interminable
river as well as I know the shape of the front hall at home?"

"On my honor, you 've got to know them *better* than any
man ever did know the shapes of the halls in his own house."

"I wish I was dead!"

"Now I don't want to discourage you, but"—

"Well, pile it on me; I might as well have it now as another time."

"You see, this has got to be learned; there is n't any getting around it. A clear starlight night throws such heavy shadows that if you did n't know the shape of a shore perfectly you would claw away from every bunch of timber, because you would take the black shadow of it for a solid cape; and you see you would be getting scared to death every fifteen minutes by the watch. You would be fifty yards from shore all the time when you ought to be within fifty feet of it. You can't see a snag in one of those shadows, but you know exactly where it is, and the shape of the river tells you when you are coming to it. Then there 's your pitch-dark night; the river is a very different shape on a pitch-dark night from what it is on a starlight night. All shores seem to be straight lines, then, and mighty dim ones, too; and you 'd *run* them for straight lines only you know better. You boldly drive your boat right into what seems to be a solid, straight wall (you knowing very well that in reality there is a curve there), and that wall falls back and makes way for you. Then there 's your gray mist. You take a night when there 's one of these grisly, drizzly, gray mists, and then there is n't *any* particular shape to a shore. A gray mist would tangle the head of the oldest man that ever lived. Well, then, different kinds of *moonlight* change the shape of the river in different ways. You see"—

"Oh, don't say any more, please! Have I got to learn the shape of the river according to all these five hundred thousand different ways? If I tried to carry all that cargo in my head it would make me stoop-shouldered."

"*No!* you only learn *the* shape of the river; and you learn it with such absolute certainty that you can always steer by the shape that 's *in your head*, and never mind the one that 's before your eyes."

"Very well, I'll try it; but after I have learned it can I depend on it? Will it keep the same form and not go fooling around?"

Before Mr. Bixby could answer, Mr. W——— came in to take the watch, and he said,—

"Bixby, you 'll have to look out for President's Island and all that country clear away up above the Old Hen and Chickens. The banks are caving and the shape of the shores changing like everything. Why, you would n't know the point above 40. You can go up inside the old sycamore snag, now."[1]

So that question was answered. Here were leagues of shore changing shape. My spirits were down in the mud again. Two things seemed pretty apparent to me. One was, that in order to be a pilot a man had got to learn more than any one man ought to be allowed to know; and the other was, that he must learn it all over again in a different way every twenty-four hours.

That night we had the watch until twelve. Now it was an ancient river custom for the two pilots to chat a bit when the watch changed. While the relieving pilot put on his gloves and lit his cigar, his partner, the retiring pilot, would say something like this:—

"I judge the upper bar is making down a little at Hale's Point; had quarter twain with the lower lead and mark twain[2] with the other."

"Yes, I thought it was making down a little, last trip. Meet any boats?"

"Met one abreast the head of 21, but she was away over hugging the bar, and I could n't make her out entirely. I took her for the 'Sunny South'—had n't any skylights forward of the chimneys."

And so on. And as the relieving pilot took the wheel his partner[3] would mention that we were in such-and-such a bend, and say we were abreast of such-and-such a man's wood-yard or plantation. This was courtesy; I supposed it was *necessity*. But Mr. W—— came on watch full twelve minutes late on this particular night,—a tremendous breach of etiquette; in fact, it is the unpardonable sin among pilots. So Mr. Bixby gave him no greeting whatever, but simply surren-

---

[1] It may not be necessary, but still it can do no harm to explain that "inside" means between the snag and the shore.—M. T.

[2] Two fathoms. Quarter twain is $2\frac{1}{4}$ fathoms, $13\frac{1}{2}$ feet. Mark three is three fathoms.

[3] "Partner" is technical for "the other pilot."

dered the wheel and marched out of the pilot-house without a word. I was appalled; it was a villanous night for blackness, we were in a particularly wide and blind part of the river, where there was no shape or substance to anything, and it seemed incredible that Mr. Bixby should have left that poor fellow to kill the boat trying to find out where he was. But I resolved that I would stand by him any way. He should find that he was not wholly friendless. So I stood around, and waited to be asked where we were. But Mr. W—— plunged on serenely through the solid firmament of black cats that stood for an atmosphere, and never opened his mouth. Here is a proud devil, thought I; here is a limb of Satan that would rather send us all to destruction than put himself under obligations to me, because I am not yet one of the salt of the earth and privileged to snub captains and lord it over everything dead and alive in a steamboat. I presently climbed up on the bench; I did not think it was safe to go to sleep while this lunatic was on watch.

However, I must have gone to sleep in the course of time, because the next thing I was aware of was the fact that day was breaking, Mr. W—— gone, and Mr. Bixby at the wheel again. So it was four o'clock and all well—but me; I felt like a skinful of dry bones and all of them trying to ache at once.

Mr. Bixby asked me what I had stayed up there for. I confessed that it was to do Mr. W—— a benevolence,—tell him where he was. It took five minutes for the entire preposterousness of the thing to filter into Mr. Bixby's system, and then I judge it filled him nearly up to the chin; because he paid me a compliment—and not much of a one either. He said,—

"Well, taking you by-and-large, you do seem to be more different kinds of an ass than any creature I ever saw before. What did you suppose he wanted to know for?"

I said I thought it might be a convenience to him.

"Convenience! D-nation! Did n't I tell you that a man 's got to know the river in the night the same as he 'd know his own front hall?"

"Well, I can follow the front hall in the dark if I know it *is* the front hall; but suppose you set me down in the middle of it in the dark and not tell me which hall it is; how am *I* to know?"

"Well, you 've *got* to, on the river!"

"All right. Then I 'm glad I never said anything to Mr. W——"

"I should say so. Why, he 'd have slammed you through the window and utterly ruined a hundred dollars' worth of window-sash and stuff."

I was glad this damage had been saved, for it would have made me unpopular with the owners. They always hated anybody who had the name of being careless, and injuring things.

I went to work now to learn the shape of the river; and of all the eluding and ungraspable objects that ever I tried to get mind or hands on, that was the chief. I would fasten my eyes upon a sharp, wooded point that projected far into the river some miles ahead of me, and go to laboriously photographing its shape upon my brain; and just as I was beginning to succeed to my satisfaction, we would draw up toward it and the exasperating thing would begin to melt away and fold back into the bank! If there had been a conspicuous dead tree standing upon the very point of the cape, I would find that tree inconspicuously merged into the general forest, and occupying the middle of a straight shore, when I got abreast of it! No prominent hill would stick to its shape long enough for me to make up my mind what its form really was, but it was as dissolving and changeful as if it had been a mountain of butter in the hottest corner of the tropics. Nothing ever had the same shape when I was coming down-stream that it had borne when I went up. I mentioned these little difficulties to Mr. Bixby. He said, —

"That 's the very main virtue of the thing. If the shapes did n't change every three seconds they would n't be of any use. Take this place where we are now, for instance. As long as that hill over yonder is only one hill, I can boom right along the way I 'm going; but the moment it splits at the top and forms a V, I know I 've got to scratch to starboard in a hurry, or I 'll bang this boat's brains out against a rock; and then the moment one of the prongs of the V swings behind the other, I 've got to waltz to larboard again, or I 'll have a misunderstanding with a snag that would snatch the keelson out of this steamboat as neatly as if it were a sliver in your hand. If that hill did n't change its shape on bad nights there would be an awful steamboat grave-yard around here inside of a year."

It was plain that I had got to learn the shape of the river in all the different ways that could be thought of,—upside down, wrong end first, inside out, fore-and-aft, and "thortships,"—and then know what to do on gray nights when it had n't any shape at all. So I set about it. In the course of time I began to get the best of this knotty lesson, and my self-complacency moved to the front once more. Mr. Bixby was all fixed, and ready to start it to the rear again. He opened on me after this fashion:—

"How much water did we have in the middle crossing at Hole-in-the-Wall, trip before last?"

I considered this an outrage. I said:—

"Every trip, down and up, the leadsmen are singing through that tangled place for three quarters of an hour on a stretch. How do you reckon I can remember such a mess as that?"

"My boy, you 've got to remember it. You 've got to remember the exact spot and the exact marks the boat lay in when we had the shoalest water, in every one of the five hundred shoal places between St. Louis and New Orleans; and you must n't get the shoal soundings and marks of one trip mixed up with the shoal soundings and marks of another, either, for they 're not often twice alike. You must keep them separate."

When I came to myself again, I said,—

"When I get so that I can do that, I 'll be able to raise the dead, and then I won't have to pilot a steamboat to make a living. I want to retire from this business. I want a slushbucket and a brush; I 'm only fit for a roustabout. I have n't got brains enough to be a pilot; and if I had I would n't have strength enough to carry them around, unless I went on crutches."

"Now drop that! When I say I 'll learn[1] a man the river, I mean it. And you can depend on it, I'll learn him or kill him."

[1] "Teach" is not in the river vocabulary.

IX.

Continued Perplexities

THERE WAS no use in arguing with a person like this. I promptly put such a strain on my memory that by and by even the shoal water and the countless crossing-marks began to stay with me. But the result was just the same. I never could more than get one knotty thing learned before another presented itself. Now I had often seen pilots gazing at the water and pretending to read it as if it were a book; but it was a book that told me nothing. A time came at last, however, when Mr. Bixby seemed to think me far enough advanced to bear a lesson on water-reading. So he began:—

"Do you see that long slanting line on the face of the water? Now, that 's a reef. Moreover, it 's a bluff reef. There is a solid sand-bar under it that is nearly as straight up and down as the side of a house. There is plenty of water close up to it, but mighty little on top of it. If you were to hit it you would knock the boat's brains out. Do you see where the line fringes out at the upper end and begins to fade away?"

"Yes, sir."

"Well, that is a low place; that is the head of the reef. You can climb over there, and not hurt anything. Cross over, now, and follow along close under the reef—easy water there—not much current."

I followed the reef along till I approached the fringed end. Then Mr. Bixby said,—

"Now get ready. Wait till I give the word. She won't want to mount the reef: a boat hates shoal water. Stand by—wait—*wait*—keep her well in hand. *Now* cramp her down! Snatch her! snatch her!"

He seized the other side of the wheel and helped to spin it around until it was hard down, and then we held it so. The boat resisted, and refused to answer for a while, and next she came surging to starboard, mounted the reef, and sent a long, angry ridge of water foaming away from her bows.

"Now watch her; watch her like a cat, or she 'll get away from you. When she fights strong and the tiller slips a little, in a jerky, greasy sort of way, let up on her a trifle; it is the way she tells you at night that the water is too shoal; but keep edging her up, little by little, toward the point. You are well up on the bar, now; there is a bar under every point, because the water that comes down around it forms an eddy and allows the sediment to sink. Do you see those fine lines on the face of the water that branch out like the ribs of a fan? Well, those are little reefs; you want to just miss the ends of them, but run them pretty close. Now look out—look out! Don't you crowd that slick, greasy-looking place; there ain't nine feet there; she won't stand it. She begins to smell it; look sharp, I tell you! Oh blazes, there you go! Stop the starboard wheel! Quick! Ship up to back! Set her back!"

The engine bells jingled and the engines answered promptly, shooting white columns of steam far aloft out of the 'scape pipes, but it was too late. The boat had "smelt" the bar in good earnest; the foamy ridges that radiated from her bows suddenly disappeared, a great dead swell came rolling forward and swept ahead of her, she careened far over to larboard, and went tearing away toward the other shore as if she were about scared to death. We were a good mile from where we ought to have been, when we finally got the upper hand of her again.

During the afternoon watch the next day, Mr. Bixby asked me if I knew how to run the next few miles. I said:—

"Go inside the first snag above the point, outside the next one, start out from the lower end of Higgins's wood-yard, make a square crossing and"—

"That 's all right. I 'll be back before you close up on the next point."

But he was n't. He was still below when I rounded it and entered upon a piece of river which I had some misgivings about. I did not know that he was hiding behind a chimney to see how I would perform. I went gayly along, getting prouder and prouder, for he had never left the boat in my sole charge such a length of time before. I even got to "setting" her and letting the wheel go, entirely, while I vaingloriously turned my back and inspected the stern marks and hummed a tune, a sort of easy indifference which I had prodigiously admired in Bixby and other great pilots. Once I inspected rather long, and when I faced to the front again my heart flew into my mouth so suddenly that if I had n't clapped my teeth together I should have lost it. One of those frightful bluff reefs was stretching its deadly length right across our bows! My head was gone in a moment; I did not know which end I stood on; I gasped and could not get my breath; I spun the wheel down with such rapidity that it wove itself together like a spider's web; the boat answered and turned square away from the reef, but the reef followed her! I fled, and still it followed still it kept—right across my bows! I never looked to see where I was going, I only fled. The awful crash was imminent—why did n't that villain come! If I committed the crime of ringing a bell, I might get thrown overboard. But better that than kill the boat. So in blind desperation I started such a rattling "shivaree" down below as never had astounded an engineer in this world before, I fancy. Amidst the frenzy of the bells the engines began to back and fill in a furious way, and my reason forsook its throne—we were about to crash into the woods on the other side of the river. Just then Mr. Bixby stepped calmly into view on the hurricane deck. My soul went out to him in gratitude. My distress vanished; I would have felt safe on the brink of Niagara, with Mr. Bixby on the hurricane deck. He blandly and sweetly took his tooth-pick out of his mouth between his fingers, as if it were a cigar,—we were just in the act of climbing an overhanging big tree, and the passengers were scudding astern like rats,— and lifted up these commands to me ever so gently:—

"Stop the starboard. Stop the larboard. Set her back on both."

The boat hesitated, halted, pressed her nose among the boughs a critical instant, then reluctantly began to back away.

"Stop the larboard. Come ahead on it. Stop the starboard. Come ahead on it. Point her for the bar."

I sailed away as serenely as a summer's morning. Mr. Bixby came in and said, with mock simplicity,—

"When you have a hail, my boy, you ought to tap the big bell three times before you land, so that the engineers can get ready."

I blushed under the sarcasm, and said I had n't had any hail.

"Ah! Then it was for wood, I suppose. The officer of the watch will tell you when he wants to wood up."

I went on consuming, and said I was n't after wood.

"Indeed? Why, what could you want over here in the bend, then? Did you ever know of a boat following a bend upstream at this stage of the river?"

"No, sir,—and *I* was n't trying to follow it. I was getting away from a bluff reef."

"No, it was n't a bluff reef; there is n't one within three miles of where you were."

"But I saw it. It was as bluff as that one yonder."

"Just about. Run over it!"

"Do you give it as an order?"

"Yes. Run over it."

"If I don't, I wish I may die."

"All right; I am taking the responsibility."

I was just as anxious to kill the boat, now, as I had been to save her before. I impressed my orders upon my memory, to be used at the inquest, and made a straight break for the reef. As it disappeared under our bows I held my breath; but we slid over it like oil.

"Now don't you see the difference? It was n't anything but a *wind* reef. The wind does that."

"So I see. But it is exactly like a bluff reef. How am I ever going to tell them apart?"

"I can't tell you. It is an instinct. By and by you will just naturally *know* one from the other, but you never will be able to explain why or how you know them apart."

It turned out to be true. The face of the water, in time, became a wonderful book—a book that was a dead language to the uneducated passenger, but which told its mind to me without reserve, delivering its most cherished secrets as clearly as if it uttered them with a voice. And it was not a book to be read once and thrown aside, for it had a new story to tell every day. Throughout the long twelve hundred miles there was never a page that was void of interest, never one that you could leave unread without loss, never one that you would want to skip, thinking you could find higher enjoyment in some other thing. There never was so wonderful a book written by man; never one whose interest was so absorbing, so unflagging, so sparklingly renewed with every re-perusal. The passenger who could not read it was charmed with a peculiar sort of faint dimple on its surface (on the rare occasions when he did not overlook it altogether); but to the pilot that was an *italicized* passage; indeed, it was more than that, it was a legend of the largest capitals, with a string of shouting exclamation points at the end of it; for it meant that a wreck or a rock was buried there that could tear the life out of the strongest vessel that ever floated. It is the faintest and simplest expression the water ever makes, and the most hideous to a pilot's eye. In truth, the passenger who could not read this book saw nothing but all manner of pretty pictures in it, painted by the sun and shaded by the clouds, whereas to the trained eye these were not pictures at all, but the grimmest and most dead-earnest of reading-matter.

Now when I had mastered the language of this water and had come to know every trifling feature that bordered the great river as familiarly as I knew the letters of the alphabet, I had made a valuable acquisition. But I had lost something, too. I had lost something which could never be restored to me while I lived. All the grace, the beauty, the poetry had gone out of the majestic river! I still keep in mind a certain wonderful sunset which I witnessed when steamboating was new to me. A broad expanse of the river was turned to blood; in the middle distance the red hue brightened into gold, through which a solitary log came floating, black and conspicuous; in one place a long, slanting mark lay sparkling upon the water; in another the surface was broken by boiling, tumbling rings, that were as many-tinted as an opal; where the ruddy flush was faintest, was a smooth spot that was covered with graceful circles and radiating lines, ever so delicately traced; the shore on our left was densely wooded, and the sombre shadow that fell from this forest was broken in one place by a long, ruffled trail that shone like silver; and high above the forest wall a clean-stemmed dead tree waved a single leafy bough that glowed like a flame in the unobstructed splendor that was flowing from the sun. There were graceful curves, reflected images, woody heights, soft distances; and over the whole scene, far and near, the dissolving lights drifted steadily, enriching it, every passing moment, with new marvels of coloring.

I stood like one bewitched. I drank it in, in a speechless rapture. The world was new to me, and I had never seen anything like this at home. But as I have said, a day came when I began to cease from noting the glories and the charms which the moon and the sun and the twilight wrought upon the river's face; another day came when I ceased altogether to note them. Then, if that sunset scene had been repeated, I should have looked upon it without rapture, and should have commented upon it, inwardly, after this fashion: This sun means that we are going to have wind to-morrow; that floating log means that the river is rising, small thanks to it; that slanting mark on the water refers to a bluff reef which is going to kill somebody's steamboat one of these nights, if it keeps on stretching out like that; those tumbling "boils" show a dissolving bar and a changing channel there; the lines and circles in the slick water over yonder are a warning that that troublesome place is shoaling up dangerously; that silver streak in the shadow of the forest is the "break" from a new snag, and he has located himself in the very best place he could have found to fish for steamboats; that tall dead tree, with a single living branch, is not going to last long, and then how is a body ever going to get through this blind place at night without the friendly old landmark?

No, the romance and the beauty were all gone from the river. All the value any feature of it had for me now was the amount of usefulness it could furnish toward compassing the safe piloting of a steamboat. Since those days, I have pitied doctors from my heart. What does the lovely flush in a beauty's cheek mean to a doctor but a "break" that ripples above some deadly disease? Are not all her visible charms sown thick with what are to him the signs and symbols of hidden decay? Does he ever see her beauty at all, or does n't he simply view her professionally, and comment upon her unwholesome condition all to himself? And does n't he sometimes wonder whether he has gained most or lost most by learning his trade?

X.

Completing My Education

WHOSOEVER HAS DONE me the courtesy to read my chapters which have preceded this may possibly wonder that I deal so minutely with piloting as a science. It was the prime purpose of those chapters; and I am not quite done yet. I wish to show, in the most patient and painstaking way, what a wonderful science it is. Ship channels are buoyed and lighted, and therefore it is a comparatively easy undertaking to learn to run them; clear-water rivers, with gravel bottoms, change their channels very gradually, and therefore one needs to learn them but once; but piloting becomes another matter when you apply it to vast streams like the Mississippi and the Missouri, whose alluvial banks cave and change constantly, whose snags are always hunting up new quarters, whose sandbars are never at rest, whose channels are forever dodging and shirking, and whose obstructions must be confronted in all nights and all weathers without the aid of a single light-house or a single buoy; for there is neither light nor buoy to be found anywhere in all this three or four thousand miles of villanous river.[1] I feel justified in enlarging upon this great science for the reason that I feel sure no one has ever yet written a paragraph about it who had piloted a steamboat himself, and so had a practical knowledge of the subject. If the theme were hackneyed, I should be obliged to deal gently with the reader; but since it is wholly new, I have felt at liberty to take up a considerable degree of room with it.

When I had learned the name and position of every visible feature of the river; when I had so mastered its shape that I could shut my eyes and trace it from St. Louis to New Orleans; when I had learned to read the face of the water as one would cull the news from the morning paper; and finally, when I had trained my dull memory to treasure up an endless array of soundings and crossing-marks, and keep fast hold of them, I judged that my education was complete: so I got to

[1] True at the time referred to; not true now (1882).

tilting my cap to the side of my head, and wearing a tooth-pick in my mouth at the wheel. Mr. Bixby had his eye on these airs. One day he said, —

"What is the height of that bank yonder, at Burgess's?"

"How can I tell, sir? It is three quarters of a mile away."

"Very poor eye—very poor. Take the glass."

I took the glass, and presently said, —

"I can't tell. I suppose that that bank is about a foot and a half high."

"Foot and a half! That 's a six-foot bank. How high was the bank along here last trip?"

"I don't know; I never noticed."

"You did n't? Well, you must always do it hereafter."

"Why?"

"Because you 'll have to know a good many things that it tells you. For one thing, it tells you the stage of the river—tells you whether there 's more water or less in the river along here than there was last trip."

"The leads tell me that." I rather thought I had the advantage of him there.

"Yes, but suppose the leads lie? The bank would tell you so, and then you 'd stir those leadsmen up a bit. There was a ten-foot bank here last trip, and there is only a six-foot bank now. What does that signify?"

"That the river is four feet higher than it was last trip."

"Very good. Is the river rising or falling?"

"Rising."

"No it ain't."

"I guess I am right, sir. Yonder is some drift-wood floating down the stream."

"A rise *starts* the drift-wood, but then it keeps on floating a while after the river is done rising. Now the bank will tell you about this. Wait till you come to a place where it shelves a little. Now here; do you see this narrow belt of fine sedi-ment? That was deposited while the water was higher. You see the drift-wood begins to strand, too. The bank helps in other ways. Do you see that stump on the false point?"

"Ay, ay, sir."

"Well, the water is just up to the roots of it. You must make a note of that."

"Why?"

"Because that means that there 's seven feet in the chute of 103."

"But 103 is a long way up the river yet."

"That 's where the benefit of the bank comes in. There is water enough in 103 *now*, yet there may not be by the time we get there; but the bank will keep us posted all along. You don't run close chutes on a falling river, up-stream, and there are precious few of them that you are allowed to run at all down-stream. There 's a law of the United States against it. The river may be rising by the time we get to 103, and in that case we 'll run it. We are drawing—how much?"

"Six feet aft,—six and a half forward."

"Well, you do seem to know something."

"But what I particularly want to know is, if I have got to keep up an everlasting measuring of the banks of this river, twelve hundred miles, month in and month out?"

"Of course!"

My emotions were too deep for words for a while. Presently I said,—

"And how about these chutes? Are there many of them?"

"I should say so. I fancy we shan't run any of the river this trip as you 've ever seen it run before—so to speak. If the river begins to rise again, we 'll go up behind bars that you 've always seen standing out of the river, high and dry like the roof of a house; we 'll cut across low places that you 've never noticed at all, right through the middle of bars that cover three hundred acres of river; we 'll creep through cracks where you 've always thought was solid land; we 'll dart through the woods and leave twenty-five miles of river off to one side; we 'll see the hind-side of every island between New Orleans and Cairo."

"Then I 've got to go to work and learn just as much more river as I already know."

"Just about twice as much more, as near as you can come at it."

"Well, one lives to find out. I think I was a fool when I went into this business."

"Yes, that is true. And you are yet. But you 'll not be when you 've learned it."

"Ah, I never can learn it."

"I will see that you *do*."

By and by I ventured again:—

"Have I got to learn all this thing just as I know the rest of the river—shapes and all—and so I can run it at night?"

"Yes. And you 've got to have good fair marks from one end of the river to the other, that will help the bank tell you when there is water enough in each of these countless places,—like that stump, you know. When the river first begins to rise, you can run half a dozen of the deepest of them; when it rises a foot more you can run another dozen; the next foot will add a couple of dozen, and so on: so you see you have to know your banks and marks to a dead moral certainty, and never get them mixed; for when you start through one of those cracks, there 's no backing out again, as there is in the big river; you 've got to go through, or stay there six months if you get caught on a falling river. There are about fifty of these cracks which you can't run at all except when the river is brim full and over the banks."

"This new lesson is a cheerful prospect."

"Cheerful enough. And mind what I 've just told you; when you start into one of those places you 've got to go through. They are too narrow to turn around in, too crooked to back out of, and the shoal water is always *up at the head*; never elsewhere. And the head of them is always likely to be filling up, little by little, so that the marks you reckon their depth by, this season, may not answer for next."

"Learn a new set, then, every year?"

"Exactly. Cramp her up to the bar! What are you standing up through the middle of the river for?"

The next few months showed me strange things. On the same day that we held the conversation above narrated, we met a great rise coming down the river. The whole vast face of the stream was black with drifting dead logs, broken boughs, and great trees that had caved in and been washed away. It required the nicest steering to pick one's way through this rushing raft, even in the day-time, when crossing from point to point; and at night the difficulty was mightily increased; every now and then a huge log, lying deep in the water, would suddenly appear right under our bows, coming head-on; no use to try to avoid it then; we could only stop the engines, and one wheel would walk over that log from one end to the other, keeping up a thundering racket and careening the boat in a way that was very uncomfortable to passengers. Now and then we would hit one of these sunken logs a rattling bang, dead in the centre, with a full head of steam, and it would stun the boat as if she had hit a continent. Sometimes this log would lodge, and stay right across our nose, and back the Mississippi up before it; we would have to do a little craw-fishing, then, to get away from the obstruction. We often hit *white* logs, in the dark, for we could not see them till we were right on them; but a black log is a pretty distinct object at night. A white snag is an ugly customer when the daylight is gone.

Of course, on the great rise, down came a swarm of prodigious timber-rafts from the head waters of the Mississippi, coal barges from Pittsburgh, little trading scows from everywhere, and broad-horns from "Posey County," Indiana, freighted with "fruit and furniture"—the usual term for describing it, though in plain English the freight thus aggrandized was hoop-poles and pumpkins. Pilots bore a mortal hatred to these craft; and it was returned with usury. The law required all such helpless traders to keep a light burning, but it was a law that was often broken. All of a sudden, on a murky night, a light would hop up, right under our bows, almost, and an agonized voice, with the backwoods "whang" to it, would wail out:—

"Whar 'n the —— you goin' to! Cain't you see nothin', you dash-dashed aig-suckin', sheep-stealin', one-eyed son of a stuffed monkey!"

Then for an instant, as we whistled by, the red glare from our furnaces would reveal the scow and the form of the gesticulating orator as if under a lightning-flash, and in that instant our firemen and deck-hands would send and receive a tempest of missiles and profanity, one of our wheels would walk off with the crashing fragments of a steering-oar, and down the dead blackness would shut again. And that flatboatman would be sure to go into New Orleans and sue our boat, swearing stoutly that he had a light burning all the time, when in truth his gang had the lantern down below to sing and lie and drink and gamble by, and no watch on deck. Once, at night, in one of those forest-bordered crevices (behind an island) which steamboatmen intensely describe with the phrase "as dark as the inside of a cow," we should have eaten up a Posey County family, fruit, furniture, and all, but that they happened to be fiddling down below and we just caught the sound of the music in time to sheer off, doing no serious damage, unfortunately, but coming so near it that we had good hopes for a moment. These people brought up their lantern, then, of course; and as we backed and filled to get away, the precious family stood in the light of it—both sexes and various ages—and cursed us till everything turned blue. Once a coal-boatman sent a bullet through our pilot-house, when we borrowed a steering-oar of him in a very narrow place.

XI.

The River Rises

DURING THIS BIG RISE these small-fry craft were an intolerable nuisance. We were running chute after chute,—a new world to me,—and if there was a particularly cramped place in a chute, we would be pretty sure to meet a broad-horn there; and if he failed to be there, we would find him in a still worse locality, namely, the head of the chute, on the shoal water. And then there would be no end of profane cordialities exchanged.

Sometimes, in the big river, when we would be feeling our way cautiously along through a fog, the deep hush would suddenly be broken by yells and a clamor of tin pans, and all in an instant a log raft would appear vaguely through the webby veil, close upon us; and then we did not wait to swap knives, but snatched our engine bells out by the roots and piled on all the steam we had, to scramble out of the way! One does n't hit a rock or a solid log raft with a steamboat when he can get excused.

You will hardly believe it, but many steamboat clerks always carried a large assortment of religious tracts with them in those old departed steamboating days. Indeed they did. Twenty times a day we would be cramping up around a bar, while a string of these small-fry rascals were drifting down into the head of the bend away above and beyond us a couple of miles. Now a skiff would dart away from one of them, and come fighting its laborious way across the desert of water. It would "ease all," in the shadow of our forecastle, and the panting oarsmen would shout, "Gimmee a pa-a-per!" as the skiff drifted swiftly astern. The clerk would throw over a file of New Orleans journals. If these were picked up *without comment*, you might notice that now a dozen other skiffs had been drifting down upon us without saying anything. You understand, they had been waiting to see how No. 1 was going to fare. No. 1 making no comment, all the rest would bend to their oars and come on, now; and as fast as they came the clerk would heave over neat bundles of religious tracts, tied to shingles. The amount of hard swearing which twelve packages of religious literature will command when impartially divided up among twelve raftsmen's crews, who have pulled a heavy skiff two miles on a hot day to get them, is simply incredible.

As I have said, the big rise brought a new world under my vision. By the time the river was over its banks we had forsaken our old paths and were hourly climbing over bars that had stood ten feet out of water before; we were shaving stumpy shores, like that at the foot of Madrid Bend, which I had always seen avoided before; we were clattering through chutes like that of 82, where the opening at the foot was an unbroken wall of timber till our nose was almost at the very spot. Some of these chutes were utter solitudes. The dense, untouched forest overhung both banks of the crooked little crack, and one could believe that human creatures had never intruded there before. The swinging grape-vines, the grassy nooks and vistas glimpsed as we swept by, the flowering creepers waving their red blossoms from the tops of dead trunks, and all the spendthrift richness of the forest foliage, were wasted and thrown away there. The chutes were lovely places to steer in; they were deep, except at the head; the current was gentle; under the "points" the water was absolutely dead, and the invisible banks so bluff that where the tender willow thickets projected you could bury your boat's broadside in them as you tore along, and then you seemed fairly to fly.

Behind other islands we found wretched little farms, and wretcheder little log-cabins; there were crazy rail fences sticking a foot or two above the water, with one or two jeans-clad, chills-racked, yellow-faced male miserables roosting on the top-rail, elbows on knees, jaws in hands, grinding tobacco and discharging the result at floating chips through crevices left by lost teeth; while the rest of the family and the few farm-animals were huddled together in an empty wood-flat riding at her moorings close at hand. In this flatboat the family would have to cook and eat and sleep for a lesser or greater number of days (or possibly weeks), until the river should fall two or three feet and let them get back to their log-cabin and their chills again—chills being a merciful provision of an all-wise Providence to enable them to take exercise without exertion. And this sort of watery camping out was a thing which these people were rather liable to be treated to a couple of times a year: by the December rise out of the Ohio, and the June rise out of the Mississippi. And yet these were kindly dispensations, for they at least enabled the poor things to rise from the dead now and then, and look upon life when a steamboat went by. They appreciated the blessing, too, for they spread their mouths and eyes wide open and made the most of these occasions. Now what *could* these banished creatures find to do to keep from dying of the blues during the low-water season!

Once, in one of these lovely island chutes, we found our course completely bridged by a great fallen tree. This will serve to show how narrow some of the chutes were. The passengers had an hour's recreation in a virgin wilderness, while the boat-hands chopped the bridge away; for there was no such thing as turning back, you comprehend.

From Cairo to Baton Rouge, when the river is over its banks, you have no particular trouble in the night, for the thousand-mile wall of dense forest that guards the two banks all the way is only gapped with a farm or wood-yard opening at intervals, and so you can't "get out of the river" much easier than you could get out of a fenced lane; but from Baton Rouge to New Orleans it is a different matter. The river is more than a mile wide, and very deep—as much as two hundred feet, in places. Both banks, for a good deal over a hundred miles, are shorn of their timber and bordered by continuous sugar plantations, with only here and there a scattering sapling or row of ornamental China-trees. The timber is shorn off clear to the rear of the plantations, from two to four miles. When the first frost threatens to come, the planters snatch off their crops in a hurry. When they have finished grinding the cane, they form the refuse of the stalks (which they call *bagasse*) into great piles and set fire to them, though in other sugar countries the bagasse is used for fuel in the furnaces of the sugar mills. Now the piles of damp bagasse burn slowly, and smoke like Satan's own kitchen.

An embankment ten or fifteen feet high guards both banks of the Mississippi all the way down that lower end of the

river, and this embankment is set back from the edge of the
shore from ten to perhaps a hundred feet, according to circumstances; say thirty or forty feet, as a general thing. Fill
that whole region with an impenetrable gloom of smoke from
a hundred miles of burning bagasse piles, when the river is
over the banks, and turn a steamboat loose along there at
midnight and see how she will feel. And see how you will
feel, too! You find yourself away out in the midst of a vague
dim sea that is shoreless, that fades out and loses itself in the
murky distances; for you cannot discern the thin rib of embankment, and you are always imagining you see a straggling
tree when you don't. The plantations themselves are trans-
formed by the smoke, and look like a part of the sea. All
through your watch you are tortured with the exquisite misery of uncertainty. You hope you are keeping in the river, but
you do not know. All that you are sure about is that you are
likely to be within six feet of the bank *and* destruction, when
you think you are a good half-mile from shore. And you are
sure, also, that if you chance suddenly to fetch up against the
embankment and topple your chimneys overboard, you will
have the small comfort of knowing that it is about what you
were expecting to do. One of the great Vicksburg packets
darted out into a sugar plantation one night, at such a time,
and had to stay there a week. But there was no novelty about
it; it had often been done before.

I thought I had finished this chapter, but I wish to add a
curious thing, while it is in my mind. It is only relevant in
that it is connected with piloting. There used to be an excellent pilot on the river, a Mr. X., who was a somnambulist. It
was said that if his mind was troubled about a bad piece of
river, he was pretty sure to get up and walk in his sleep and
do strange things. He was once fellow-pilot for a trip or two
with George Ealer, on a great New Orleans passenger packet.
During a considerable part of the first trip George was uneasy, but got over it by and by, as X. seemed content to stay
in his bed when asleep. Late one night the boat was approaching Helena, Arkansas; the water was low, and the
crossing above the town in a very blind and tangled condition. X. had seen the crossing since Ealer had, and as the
night was particularly drizzly, sullen, and dark, Ealer was con-

sidering whether he had not better have X. called to assist in running the place, when the door opened and X. walked in. Now on very dark nights, light is a deadly enemy to piloting; you are aware that if you stand in a lighted room, on such a night, you cannot see things in the street to any purpose; but if you put out the lights and stand in the gloom you can make out objects in the street pretty well. So, on very dark nights, pilots do not smoke; they allow no fire in the pilot-house stove if there is a crack which can allow the least ray to escape; they order the furnaces to be curtained with huge tarpaulins and the sky-lights to be closely blinded. Then no light whatever issues from the boat. The undefinable shape that now entered the pilot-house had Mr. X.'s voice. This said,—

"Let me take her, George; I 've seen this place since you have, and it is so crooked that I reckon I can run it myself easier than I could tell you how to do it."

"It is kind of you, and I swear *I* am willing. I have n't got another drop of perspiration left in me. I have been spinning around and around the wheel like a squirrel. It is so dark I can't tell which way she is swinging till she is coming around like a whirligig."

So Ealer took a seat on the bench, panting and breathless. The black phantom assumed the wheel without saying anything, steadied the waltzing steamer with a turn or two, and then stood at ease, coaxing her a little to this side and then to that, as gently and as sweetly as if the time had been noonday. When Ealer observed this marvel of steering, he wished he had not confessed! He stared, and wondered, and finally said,—

"Well, I thought I knew how to steer a steamboat, but that was another mistake of mine."

X. said nothing, but went serenely on with his work. He rang for the leads; he rang to slow down the steam; he worked the boat carefully and neatly into invisible marks, then stood at the centre of the wheel and peered blandly out into the blackness, fore and aft, to verify his position; as the leads shoaled more and more, he stopped the engines entirely, and the dead silence and suspense of "drifting" followed; when the shoalest water was struck, he cracked on the steam, carried her handsomely over, and then began to work her warily into the next system of shoal marks; the same patient, heedful use of leads and engines followed, the boat slipped through without touching bottom, and entered upon the third and last intricacy of the crossing; imperceptibly she moved through the gloom, crept by inches into her marks, drifted tediously till the shoalest water was cried, and then, under a tremendous head of steam, went swinging over the reef and away into deep water and safety!

Ealer let his long-pent breath pour out in a great, relieving sigh, and said: —

"That 's the sweetest piece of piloting that was ever done on the Mississippi River! I would n't believed it could be done, if I had n't seen it."

There was no reply, and he added: —

"Just hold her five minutes longer, partner, and let me run down and get a cup of coffee."

A minute later Ealer was biting into a pie, down in the "texas," and comforting himself with coffee. Just then the night watchman happened in, and was about to happen out again, when he noticed Ealer and exclaimed, —

"Who is at the wheel, sir?"

"X."

"Dart for the pilot-house, quicker than lightning!"

The next moment both men were flying up the pilot-house companion-way, three steps at a jump! Nobody there! The great steamer was whistling down the middle of the river at her own sweet will! The watchman shot out of the place again; Ealer seized the wheel, set an engine back with power, and held his breath while the boat reluctantly swung away from a "towhead" which she was about to knock into the middle of the Gulf of Mexico!

By and by the watchman came back and said, —

"Did n't that lunatic tell you he was asleep, when he first came up here?"

"No."

"Well, he was. I found him walking along on top of the railings, just as unconcerned as another man would walk a pavement; and I put him to bed; now just this minute there he was again, away astern, going through that sort of tight-rope deviltry the same as before."

"Well, I think I 'll stay by, next time he has one of those fits. But I hope he 'll have them often. You just ought to have seen him take this boat through Helena crossing. *I* never saw anything so gaudy before. And if he can do such gold-leaf, kid-glove, diamond-breastpin piloting when he is sound asleep, what *could n't* he do if he was dead!"

XII.

Sounding

WHEN THE RIVER is very low, and one's steamboat is "drawing all the water" there is in the channel,—or a few inches more, as was often the case in the old times,—one must be painfully circumspect in his piloting. We used to have to "sound" a number of particularly bad places almost every trip when the river was at a very low stage.

Sounding is done in this way. The boat ties up at the shore, just above the shoal crossing; the pilot not on watch takes his "cub" or steersman and a picked crew of men (sometimes an officer also), and goes out in the yawl—provided the boat has not that rare and sumptuous luxury, a regularly-devised "sounding-boat"—and proceeds to hunt for the best water, the pilot on duty watching his movements through a spyglass, meantime, and in some instances assisting by signals of the boat's whistle, signifying "try higher up" or "try lower down;" for the surface of the water, like an oil-painting, is more expressive and intelligible when inspected from a little distance than very close at hand. The whistle signals are seldom necessary, however; never, perhaps, except when the wind confuses the significant ripples upon the water's surface. When the yawl has reached the shoal place, the speed is slackened, the pilot begins to sound the depth with a pole ten or twelve feet long, and the steersman at the tiller obeys the order to "hold her up to starboard;" or "let her fall off to larboard;"[1] or "steady—steady as you go."

When the measurements indicate that the yawl is approaching the shoalest part of the reef, the command is given to "ease all!" Then the men stop rowing and the yawl drifts with the current. The next order is, "Stand by with the buoy!" The moment the shallowest point is reached, the pilot delivers the order, "Let go the buoy!" and over she goes. If the pilot is not satisfied, he sounds the place again; if he finds better

---

[1]The term "larboard" is never used at sea, now, to signify the left hand; but was always used on the river in my time.

water higher up or lower down, he removes the buoy to that place. Being finally satisfied, he gives the order, and all the men stand their oars straight up in the air, in line; a blast from the boat's whistle indicates that the signal has been seen; then the men "give way" on their oars and lay the yawl alongside the buoy; the steamer comes creeping carefully down, is pointed straight at the buoy, husbands her power for the coming struggle, and presently, at the critical moment, turns on all her steam and goes grinding and wallowing over the buoy and the sand, and gains the deep water beyond. Or maybe she does n't; maybe she "strikes and swings." Then she has to while away several hours (or days) sparring herself off.

Sometimes a buoy is not laid at all, but the yawl goes ahead, hunting the best water, and the steamer follows along in its wake. Often there is a deal of fun and excitement about sounding, especially if it is a glorious summer day, or a blustering night. But in winter the cold and the peril take most of the fun out of it.

A buoy is nothing but a board four or five feet long, with one end turned up; it is a reversed school-house bench, with one of the supports left and the other removed. It is anchored on the shoalest part of the reef by a rope with a heavy stone made fast to the end of it. But for the resistance of the turned-up end of the reversed bench, the current would pull the buoy under water. At night, a paper lantern with a candle in it is fastened on top of the buoy, and this can be seen a mile or more, a little glimmering spark in the waste of blackness.

Nothing delights a cub so much as an opportunity to go out sounding. There is such an air of adventure about it; often there is danger; it is so gaudy and man-of-war-like to sit up in the stern-sheets and steer a swift yawl; there is something fine about the exultant spring of the boat when an experienced old sailor crew throw their souls into the oars; it is lovely to see the white foam stream away from the bows; there is music in the rush of the water; it is deliciously exhilarating, in summer, to go speeding over the breezy expanses of the river when the world of wavelets is dancing in the sun. It is such grandeur, too, to the cub, to get a chance to give an order; for often the pilot will simply say, "Let her go about!" and leave the rest to the cub, who instantly cries, in his sternest tone of command, "Ease starboard! Strong on the larboard! Starboard give way! With a will, men!" The cub enjoys sounding for the further reason that the eyes of the passengers are watching all the yawl's movements with absorbing interest if the time be daylight; and if it be night he knows that those same wondering eyes are fastened upon the yawl's lantern as it glides out into the gloom and dims away in the remote distance.

One trip a pretty girl of sixteen spent her time in our pilot-house with her uncle and aunt, every day and all day long. I fell in love with her. So did Mr. Thornburg's cub, Tom G——. Tom and I had been bosom friends until this time; but now a coolness began to arise. I told the girl a good many of my river adventures, and made myself out a good deal of a hero; Tom tried to make himself appear to be a hero, too, and succeeded to some extent, but then he always had a way of embroidering. However, virtue is its own reward, so I was a barely perceptible trifle ahead in the contest. About this time something happened which promised handsomely for me: the pilots decided to sound the crossing at the head of 21. This would occur about nine or ten o'clock at night, when the passengers would be still up; it would be Mr. Thornburg's watch, therefore my chief would have to do the sounding. We had a perfect love of a sounding-boat—long, trim, graceful, and as fleet as a greyhound; her thwarts were cushioned; she carried twelve oarsmen; one of the mates was always sent in her to transmit orders to her crew, for ours was a steamer where no end of "style" was put on.

We tied up at the shore above 21, and got ready. It was a foul night, and the river was so wide, there, that a landsman's uneducated eyes could discern no opposite shore through such a gloom. The passengers were alert and interested; everything was satisfactory. As I hurried through the engine-room, picturesquely gotten up in storm toggery, I met Tom, and could not forbear delivering myself of a mean speech:—

"Ain't you glad *you* don't have to go out sounding?"

Tom was passing on, but he quickly turned, and said,—

"Now just for that, you can go and get the sounding-pole

yourself. I was going after it, but I 'd see you in Halifax, now, before I 'd do it."

"Who wants you to get it? *I* don't. It 's in the sounding-boat."

"It ain't, either. It 's been new-painted; and it 's been up on the ladies cabin guards two days, drying."

I flew back, and shortly arrived among the crowd of watching and wondering ladies just in time to hear the command:

"Give way, men!"

I looked over, and there was the gallant sounding-boat booming away, the unprincipled Tom presiding at the tiller, and my chief sitting by him with the sounding-pole which I had been sent on a fool's errand to fetch. Then that young girl said to me,—

"Oh, how awful to have to go out in that little boat on such a night! Do you think there is any danger?"

I would rather have been stabbed. I went off, full of venom, to help in the pilot-house. By and by the boat's lantern disappeared, and after an interval a wee spark glimmered upon the face of the water a mile away. Mr. Thornburg blew the whistle, in acknowledgment, backed the steamer out, and made for it. We flew along for a while, then slackened steam and went cautiously gliding toward the spark. Presently Mr. Thornburg exclaimed,—

"Hello, the buoy-lantern's out!"

He stopped the engines. A moment or two later he said,—

"Why, there it is again!"

So he came ahead on the engines once more, and rang for the leads. Gradually the water shoaled up, and then began to deepen again! Mr. Thornburg muttered:—

"Well, I don't understand this. I believe that buoy has drifted off the reef. Seems to be a little too far to the left. No matter, it is safest to run over it, anyhow."

So, in that solid world of darkness we went creeping down on the light. Just as our bows were in the act of plowing over it, Mr. Thornburg seized the bell-ropes, rang a startling peal, and exclaimed,—

"My soul, it 's the sounding-boat!"

A sudden chorus of wild alarms burst out far below—a

pause—and then a sound of grinding and crashing followed. Mr. Thornburg exclaimed,—

"There! the paddle-wheel has ground the sounding-boat to lucifer matches! Run! See who is killed!"

I was on the main deck in the twinkling of an eye. My chief and the third mate and nearly all the men were safe. They had discovered their danger when it was too late to pull out of the way; then, when the great guards overshadowed them a moment later, they were prepared and knew what to do; at my chief's order they sprang at the right instant, seized the guard, and were hauled aboard. The next moment the sounding-yawl swept aft to the wheel and was struck and splintered to atoms. Two of the men and the cub Tom, were missing— a fact which spread like wild-fire over the boat. The passengers came flocking to the forward gangway, ladies and all, anxious-eyed, white-faced, and talked in awed voices of the dreadful thing. And often and again I heard them say, "Poor fellows! poor boy, poor boy!"

By this time the boat's yawl was manned and away, to search for the missing. Now a faint call was heard, off to the left. The yawl had disappeared in the other direction. Half the people rushed to one side to encourage the swimmer with their shouts; the other half rushed the other way to shriek to the yawl to turn about. By the callings, the swimmer was approaching, but some said the sound showed failing strength. The crowd massed themselves against the boiler-deck railings, leaning over and staring into the gloom; and every faint and fainter cry wrung from them such words as "Ah, poor fellow, poor fellow! is there *no* way to save him?"

But still the cries held out, and drew nearer, and presently the voice said pluckily,—

"I can make it! Stand by with a rope!"

What a rousing cheer they gave him! The chief mate took his stand in the glare of a torch-basket, a coil of rope in his hand, and his men grouped about him. The next moment the swimmer's face appeared in the circle of light, and in another one the owner of it was hauled aboard, limp and drenched, while cheer on cheer went up. It was that devil Tom.

The yawl crew searched everywhere, but found no sign of

the two men. They probably failed to catch the guard, tumbled back, and were struck by the wheel and killed. Tom had never jumped for the guard at all, but had plunged head-first into the river and dived under the wheel. It was nothing; I could have done it easy enough, and I said so; but everybody went on just the same, making a wonderful to-do over that ass, as if he had done something great. That girl could n't seem to have enough of that pitiful "hero" the rest of the trip; but little I cared; I loathed her, any way.

The way we came to mistake the sounding-boat's lantern for the buoy-light was this. My chief said that after laying the buoy he fell away and watched it till it seemed to be secure; then he took up a position a hundred yards below it and a little to one side of the steamer's course, headed the sounding-boat up-stream, and waited. Having to wait some time, he and the officer got to talking; he looked up when he judged that the steamer was about on the reef; saw that the buoy was gone, but supposed that the steamer had already run over it; he went on with his talk; he noticed that the steamer was getting very close down on him, but that was the correct thing; it was her business to shave him closely, for convenience in taking him aboard; he was expecting her to sheer off, until the last moment; then it flashed upon him that she was trying to run him down, mistaking his lantern for the buoy-light; so he sang out, "Stand by to spring for the guard, men!" and the next instant the jump was made.

XIII.

A Pilot's Needs

B UT I AM WANDERING from what I was intending to do, that is, make plainer than perhaps appears in the previous chapters, some of the peculiar requirements of the science of piloting. First of all, there is one faculty which a pilot must incessantly cultivate until he has brought it to absolute perfection. Nothing short of perfection will do. That faculty is memory. He cannot stop with merely thinking a thing is so and so; he must *know* it; for this is eminently one of the "exact" sciences. With what scorn a pilot was looked upon, in the old times, if he ever ventured to deal in that feeble phrase "I think," instead of the vigorous one "I know!" One cannot easily realize what a tremendous thing it is to know every trivial detail of twelve hundred miles of river and know it with absolute exactness. If you will take the longest street in New York, and travel up and down it, conning its features patiently until you know every house and window and door and lamp-post and big and little sign by heart, and know them so accurately that you can instantly name the one you are abreast of when you are set down at random in that street in the middle of an inky black night, you will then have a tolerable notion of the amount and the exactness of a pilot's knowledge who carries the Mississippi River in his head. And then if you will go on until you know every street crossing, the character, size, and position of the crossing-stones, and the varying depth of mud in each of those numberless places, you will have some idea of what the pilot must know in order to keep a Mississippi steamer out of trouble. Next, if you will take half of the signs in that long street, and *change their places* once a month, and still manage to know their new positions accurately on dark nights, and keep up with these repeated changes without making any mistakes, you will understand what is required of a pilot's peerless memory by the fickle Mississippi.

I think a pilot's memory is about the most wonderful thing in the world. To know the Old and New Testaments by heart, and be able to recite them glibly, forward or backward, or begin at random anywhere in the book and recite both ways and never trip or make a mistake, is no extravagant mass of knowledge, and no marvellous facility, compared to a pilot's massed knowledge of the Mississippi and his marvellous facility in the handling of it. I make this comparison deliberately, and believe I am not expanding the truth when I do it. Many will think my figure too strong, but pilots will not.

And how easily and comfortably the pilot's memory does its work; how placidly effortless is its way; how *unconsciously* it lays up its vast stores, hour by hour, day by day, and never loses or mislays a single valuable package of them all! Take an instance. Let a leadsman cry, "Half twain! half twain! half twain! half twain! half twain!" until it becomes as monotonous as the ticking of a clock; let conversation be going on all the time, and the pilot be doing his share of the talking, and no longer consciously listening to the leadsman; and in the midst of this endless string of half twains let a single "quarter twain!" be interjected, without emphasis, and then the half twain cry go on again, just as before: two or three weeks later that pilot can describe with precision the boat's position in the river when that quarter twain was uttered, and give you such a lot of head-marks, stern-marks, and side-marks to guide you, that you ought to be able to take the boat there and put her in that same spot again yourself! The cry of "quarter twain" did not really take his mind from his talk, but his trained faculties instantly photographed the bearings, noted the change of depth, and laid up the important details for future reference without requiring any assistance from *him* in the matter. If you were walking and talking with a friend, and another friend at your side kept up a monotonous repetition of the vowel sound A, for a couple of blocks, and then in the midst interjected an R, thus, A, A, A, A, A, R, A, A, A, etc., and gave the R no emphasis, you would not be able to state, two or three weeks afterward, that the R had been put in, nor be able to tell what objects you were passing at the moment it was done. But you could if your memory had been patiently and laboriously trained to do that sort of thing mechanically.

Give a man a tolerably fair memory to start with, and piloting will develop it into a very colossus of capability. But *only in the matters it is daily drilled in.* A time would come when the man's faculties could not help noticing landmarks and soundings, and his memory could not help holding on to them with the grip of a vice; but if you asked that same man at noon what he had had for breakfast, it would be ten chances to one that he could not tell you. Astonishing things can be done with the human memory if you will devote it faithfully to one particular line of business.

At the time that wages soared so high on the Missouri River, my chief, Mr. Bixby, went up there and learned more than a thousand miles of that stream with an ease and rapidity that were astonishing. When he had seen each division *once* in the daytime and *once* at night, his education was so nearly complete that he took out a "daylight" license; a few trips later he took out a full license, and went to piloting day and night,—and he ranked A 1, too.

Mr. Bixby placed me as steersman for a while under a pilot whose feats of memory were a constant marvel to me. However, his memory was born in him, I think, not built. For instance, somebody would mention a name. Instantly Mr. Brown would break in:—

"Oh, I knew *him.* Sallow-faced, red-headed fellow, with a little scar on the side of his throat, like a splinter under the flesh. He was only in the Southern trade six months. That was thirteen years ago. I made a trip with him. There was five feet in the upper river then; the 'Henry Blake' grounded at the foot of Tower Island drawing four and a half; the 'George Elliott' unshipped her rudder on the wreck of the 'Sunflower' "—

"Why, the 'Sunflower' did n't sink until"—

"*I* know when she sunk; it was three years before that, on the 2d of December; Asa Hardy was captain of her, and his brother John was first clerk; and it was his first trip in her, too; Tom Jones told me these things a week afterward in New Orleans; he was first mate of the 'Sunflower.' Captain Hardy stuck a nail in his foot the 6th of July of the next year, and died of the lockjaw on the 15th. His brother John died two years after,—3d of March,—erysipelas. I never saw either of the Hardys,—they were Alleghany River men,—but people who knew them told me all these things. And they said Captain Hardy wore yarn socks winter and summer just the same, and his first wife's name was Jane Shook,—she was from New England,—and his second one died in a lunatic asylum. It was in the blood. She was from Lexington, Kentucky. Name was Horton before she was married."

And so on, by the hour, the man's tongue would go. He could *not* forget any thing. It was simply impossible. The most trivial details remained as distinct and luminous in his head, after they had lain there for years, as the most memorable events. His was not simply a pilot's memory; its grasp was universal. If he were talking about a trifling letter he had received seven years before, he was pretty sure to deliver you the entire screed from memory. And then without observing that he was departing from the true line of his talk, he was more than likely to hurl in a long-drawn parenthetical biography of the writer of that letter; and you were lucky indeed if he did not take up that writer's relatives, one by one, and give you their biographies, too.

Such a memory as that is a great misfortune. To it, all occurrences are of the same size. Its possessor cannot distinguish an interesting circumstance from an uninteresting one. As a talker, he is bound to clog his narrative with tiresome details and make himself an insufferable bore. Moreover, he cannot stick to his subject. He picks up every little grain of memory he discerns in his way, and so is led aside. Mr. Brown would start out with the honest intention of telling you a vastly funny anecdote about a dog. He would be "so full of laugh" that he could hardly begin; then his memory would start with the dog's breed and personal appearance; drift into a history of his owner; of his owner's family, with descriptions of weddings and burials that had occurred in it, together with recitals of congratulatory verses and obituary poetry provoked by the same; then this memory would recollect that one of these events occurred during the celebrated "hard winter" of such and such a year, and a minute description of that winter would follow, along with the names of people who were frozen to death, and statistics showing the high figures which pork and hay went up to. Pork and hay would suggest corn and fodder; corn and fodder would sug-

gest cows and horses; cows and horses would suggest the circus and certain celebrated bare-back riders; the transition
from the circus to the menagerie was easy and natural; from
the elephant to equatorial Africa was but a step; then of
course the heathen savages would suggest religion; and at the
end of three or four hours' tedious jaw, the watch would
change, and Brown would go out of the pilot-house muttering extracts from sermons he had heard years before about
the efficacy of prayer as a means of grace. And the original
first mention would be all you had learned about that dog,
after all this waiting and hungering.

A pilot must have a memory; but there are two higher
qualities which he must also have. He must have good and
quick judgment and decision, and a cool, calm courage that
no peril can shake. Give a man the merest trifle of pluck to
start with, and by the time he has become a pilot he cannot
be unmanned by any danger a steamboat can get into; but
one cannot quite say the same for judgment. Judgment is a
matter of brains, and a man must *start* with a good stock of
that article or he will never succeed as a pilot.

The growth of courage in the pilot-house is steady all the
time, but it does not reach a high and satisfactory condition
until some time after the young pilot has been "standing his
own watch," alone and under the staggering weight of all the
responsibilities connected with the position. When an apprentice has become pretty thoroughly acquainted with the river,
he goes clattering along so fearlessly with his steamboat,
night or day, that he presently begins to imagine that it is *his*
courage that animates him; but the first time the pilot steps
out and leaves him to his own devices he finds out it was the
other man's. He discovers that the article has been left out of
his own cargo altogether. The whole river is bristling with
exigencies in a moment; he is not prepared for them; he does
not know how to meet them; all his knowledge forsakes him;
and within fifteen minutes he is as white as a sheet and scared
almost to death. Therefore pilots wisely train these cubs by
various strategic tricks to look danger in the face a little more
calmly. A favorite way of theirs is to play a friendly swindle
upon the candidate.

Mr. Bixby served me in this fashion once, and for years

afterward I used to blush even in my sleep when I thought of it. I had become a good steersman; so good, indeed, that I had all the work to do on our watch, night and day; Mr. Bixby seldom made a suggestion to me; all he ever did was to take the wheel on particularly bad nights or in particularly bad crossings, land the boat when she needed to be landed, play gentleman of leisure nine tenths of the watch, and collect the wages. The lower river was about bank-full, and if anybody had questioned my ability to run any crossing between Cairo and New Orleans without help or instruction, I should have felt irreparably hurt. The idea of being afraid of any crossing in the lot, in the *day-time*, was a thing too preposterous for contemplation. Well, one matchless summer's day I was bowling down the bend above island 66, brimful of self-conceit and carrying my nose as high as a giraffe's, when Mr. Bixby said,—

"I am going below a while. I suppose you know the next crossing?"

This was almost an affront. It was about the plainest and simplest crossing in the whole river. One could n't come to any harm, whether he ran it right or not; and as for depth, there never had been any bottom there. I knew all this, perfectly well.

"Know how to *run* it? Why, I can run it with my eyes shut."

"How much water is there in it?"

"Well, that is an odd question. I could n't get bottom there with a church steeple."

"You think so, do you?"

The very tone of the question shook my confidence. That was what Mr. Bixby was expecting. He left, without saying anything more. I began to imagine all sorts of things. Mr. Bixby, unknown to me, of course, sent somebody down to the forecastle with some mysterious instructions to the leadsmen, another messenger was sent to whisper among the officers, and then Mr. Bixby went into hiding behind a smokestack where he could observe results. Presently the captain stepped out on the hurricane deck; next the chief mate appeared; then a clerk. Every moment or two a straggler was added to my audience; and before I got to the head of the island I had fifteen or twenty people assembled down there under my nose. I began to wonder what the trouble was. As I started across, the captain glanced aloft at me and said, with a sham uneasiness in his voice,—

"Where is Mr. Bixby?"

"Gone below, sir."

But that did the business for me. My imagination began to construct dangers out of nothing, and they multiplied faster than I could keep the run of them. All at once I imagined I saw shoal water ahead! The wave of coward agony that surged through me then came near dislocating every joint in me. All my confidence in that crossing vanished. I seized the bell-rope; dropped it, ashamed; seized it again; dropped it once more; clutched it tremblingly once again, and pulled it so feebly that I could hardly hear the stroke myself. Captain and mate sang out instantly, and both together,—

"Starboard lead there! and quick about it!"

This was another shock. I began to climb the wheel like a squirrel; but I would hardly get the boat started to port before I would see new dangers on that side, and away I would spin to the other; only to find perils accumulating to starboard, and be crazy to get to port again. Then came the leadsman's sepulchral cry:—

"D-e-e-p four!"

Deep four in a bottomless crossing! The terror of it took my breath away.

"M-a-r-k three! . . . M-a-r-k three . . . Quarter less three! . . . Half twain!"

This was frightful! I seized the bell-ropes and stopped the engines.

"Quarter twain! Quarter twain! *Mark* twain!"

I was helpless. I did not know what in the world to do. I was quaking from head to foot, and I could have hung my hat on my eyes, they stuck out so far.

"Quarter *less* twain! Nine and a *half*!"

We were *drawing* nine! My hands were in a nerveless flutter. I could not ring a bell intelligibly with them. I flew to the speaking-tube and shouted to the engineer,—

"Oh, Ben, if you love me, *back* her! Quick, Ben! Oh, back the immortal *soul* out of her!"

I heard the door close gently. I looked around, and there stood Mr. Bixby, smiling a bland, sweet smile. Then the audience on the hurricane deck sent up a thundergust of humiliating laughter. I saw it all, now, and I felt meaner than the meanest man in human history. I laid in the lead, set the boat in her marks, came ahead on the engines, and said:—

"It was a fine trick to play on an orphan, *was n't* it? I suppose I 'll never hear the last of how I was ass enough to heave the lead at the head of 66."

"Well, no, you won't, maybe. In fact I hope you won't; for I want you to learn something by that experience. Did n't you *know* there was no bottom in that crossing?"

"Yes, sir, I did."

"Very well, then. You should n't have allowed me or anybody else to shake your confidence in that knowledge. Try to remember that. And another thing: when you get into a dangerous place, don't turn coward. That is n't going to help matters any."

It was a good enough lesson, but pretty hardly learned. Yet about the hardest part of it was that for months I so often had to hear a phrase which I had conceived a particular distaste for. It was, "Oh, Ben, if you love me, back her!"

XIV.

Rank and Dignity of Piloting

IN MY PRECEDING CHAPTERS I have tried, by going into the minutiæ of the science of piloting, to carry the reader step by step to a comprehension of what the science consists of; and at the same time I have tried to show him that it is a very curious and wonderful science, too, and very worthy of his attention. If I have seemed to love my subject, it is no surprising thing, for I loved the profession far better than any I have followed since, and I took a measureless pride in it. The reason is plain: a pilot, in those days, was the only unfettered and entirely independent human being that lived in the earth. Kings are but the hampered servants of parliament and people; parliaments sit in chains forged by their constituency; the editor of a newspaper cannot be independent, but must work with one hand tied behind him by party and patrons, and be content to utter only half or two thirds of his mind; no clergyman is a free man and may speak the whole truth, regardless of his parish's opinions; writers of all kinds are manacled servants of the public. We write frankly and fearlessly, but then we "modify" before we print. In truth, every man and woman and child has a master, and worries and frets in servitude; but in the day I write of, the Mississippi pilot had *none*. The captain could stand upon the hurricane deck, in the pomp of a very brief authority, and give him five or six orders while the vessel backed into the stream, and then that skipper's reign was over. The moment that the boat was under way in the river, she was under the sole and unquestioned control of the pilot. He could do with her exactly as he pleased, run her when and whither he chose, and tie her up to the bank whenever his judgment said that that course was best. His movements were entirely free; he consulted no one, he received commands from nobody, he promptly resented even the merest suggestions. Indeed, the law of the United States forbade him to listen to commands or suggestions, rightly considering that the pilot necessarily knew better how to handle the boat than anybody could tell him. So here was the novelty of a king without a keeper, an absolute monarch who was absolute in sober truth and not by a fiction of words. I have seen a boy of eighteen taking a great steamer serenely into what seemed almost certain destruction, and the aged captain standing mutely by, filled with apprehension but powerless to interfere. His interference, in that particular instance, might have been an excellent thing, but to permit it would have been to establish a most pernicious precedent. It will easily be guessed, considering the pilot's boundless authority, that he was a great personage in the old steamboating days. He was treated with marked courtesy by the captain and with marked deference by all the officers and servants; and this deferential spirit was quickly communicated to the passengers, too. I think pilots were about the only people I ever knew who failed to show, in some degree, embarrassment in the presence of travelling foreign princes. But then, people in one's own grade of life are not usually embarrassing objects.

By long habit, pilots came to put all their wishes in the form of commands. It "gravels" me, to this day, to put my will in the weak shape of a request, instead of launching it in the crisp language of an order.

In those old days, to load a steamboat at St. Louis, take her to New Orleans and back, and discharge cargo, consumed about twenty-five days, on an average. Seven or eight of these days the boat spent at the wharves of St. Louis and New Orleans, and every soul on board was hard at work, except the two pilots; *they* did nothing but play gentleman up town, and receive the same wages for it as if they had been on duty. The moment the boat touched the wharf at either city, they were ashore; and they were not likely to be seen again till the last bell was ringing and everything in readiness for another voyage.

When a captain got hold of a pilot of particularly high reputation, he took pains to keep him. When wages were four hundred dollars a month on the Upper Mississippi, I have known a captain to keep such a pilot in idleness, under full pay, three months at a time, while the river was frozen up. And one must remember that in those cheap times four hundred dollars was a salary of almost inconceivable splendor. Few men on shore got such pay as that, and when they did they were mightily looked up to. When pilots from either end of the river wandered into our small Missouri village, they were sought by the best and the fairest, and treated with exalted respect. Lying in port under wages was a thing which many pilots greatly enjoyed and appreciated; especially if they belonged in the Missouri River in the heyday of that trade (Kansas times), and got nine hundred dollars a trip, which was equivalent to about eighteen hundred dollars a month. Here is a conversation of that day. A chap out of the Illinois River, with a little stern-wheel tub, accosts a couple of ornate and gilded Missouri River pilots:—

"Gentlemen, I 've got a pretty good trip for the up-country, and shall want you about a month. How much will it be?"

"Eighteen hundred dollars apiece."

"Heavens and earth! You take my boat, let me have your wages, and I 'll divide!"

I will remark, in passing, that Mississippi steamboatmen were important in landsmen's eyes (and in their own, too, in a degree) according to the dignity of the boat they were on. For instance, it was a proud thing to be of the crew of such stately craft as the "Aleck Scott" or the "Grand Turk." Negro firemen, deck hands, and barbers belonging to those boats were distinguished personages in their grade of life, and they were well aware of that fact, too. A stalwart darkey once gave offence at a negro ball in New Orleans by putting on a good many airs. Finally one of the managers bustled up to him and said,—

"Who *is* you, any way? Who *is* you? dat 's what *I* wants to know!"

The offender was not disconcerted in the least, but swelled himself up and threw that into his voice which showed that he knew he was not putting on all those airs on a stinted capital.

"Who *is* I? Who *is* I? I let you know mighty quick who I is! I want you niggers to understan' dat I fires de middle do'[1] on de 'Aleck Scott!' "

That was sufficient.

The barber of the "Grand Turk" was a spruce young negro,

[1] Door.

who aired his importance with balmy complacency, and was greatly courted by the circle in which he moved. The young colored population of New Orleans were much given to flirting, at twilight, on the banquettes of the back streets. Somebody saw and heard something like the following, one evening, in one of those localities. A middle-aged negro woman projected her head through a broken pane and shouted (very willing that the neighbors should hear and envy), "You Mary Ann, come in de house dis minute! Stannin' out dah foolin' 'long wid dat low trash, an' heah's de barber off 'n de 'Gran' Turk' wants to conwerse wid you!"

My reference, a moment ago, to the fact that a pilot's peculiar official position placed him out of the reach of criticism or command, brings Stephen W—— naturally to my mind. He was a gifted pilot, a good fellow, a tireless talker, and had both wit and humor in him. He had a most irreverent independence, too, and was deliciously easy-going and comfortable in the presence of age, official dignity, and even the most august wealth. He always had work, he never saved a penny, he was a most persuasive borrower, he was in debt to every pilot on the river, and to the majority of the captains. He could throw a sort of splendor around a bit of harum-scarum, devil-may-care piloting, that made it almost fascinating—but not to everybody. He made a trip with good old Captain Y ——once, and was "relieved" from duty when the boat got to New Orleans. Somebody expressed surprise at the discharge. Captain Y—— shuddered at the mere mention of Stephen. Then his poor, thin old voice piped out something like this:—

"Why, bless me! I would n't have such a wild creature on my boat for the world—not for the whole world! He swears, he sings, he whistles, he yells—I never saw such an Injun to yell. All times of the night—it never made any difference to him. He would just yell that way, not for anything in particular, but merely on account of a kind of devilish comfort he got out of it. I never could get into a sound sleep but he would fetch me out of bed, all in a cold sweat, with one of those dreadful war-whoops. A queer being,—very queer being; no respect for anything or anybody. Sometimes he called me 'Johnny.' And he kept a fiddle, and a cat. He played execrably. This seemed to distress the cat, and so the cat would howl. Nobody could sleep where that man—and his family—was. And reckless? There never was anything like it. Now you may believe it or not, but as sure as I am sitting here, he brought my boat a-tilting down through those awful snags at Chicot under a rattling head of steam, and the wind a-blowing like the very nation, at that! My officers will tell you so. They saw it. And, sir, while he was a-tearing right down through those snags, and I a-shaking in my shoes and praying, I wish I may never speak again if he did n't pucker up his mouth and go to *whistling*! Yes, sir; whistling 'Buffalo gals, can't you come out to-night, can't you come out to-night, can't you come out to-night;' and doing it as calmly as if we were attending a funeral and were n't related to the corpse. And when I remonstrated with him about it, he smiled down on me as if I was his child, and told me to run in the house and try to be good, and not be meddling with my superiors!"[1]

Once a pretty mean captain caught Stephen in New Orleans out of work and as usual out of money. He laid steady siege to Stephen, who was in a very "close place," and finally persuaded him to hire with him at one hundred and twenty-five dollars per month, just half wages, the captain agreeing not to divulge the secret and so bring down the contempt of all the guild upon the poor fellow. But the boat was not more than a day out of New Orleans before Stephen discovered that the captain was boasting of his exploit, and that all the officers had been told. Stephen winced, but said nothing. About the middle of the afternoon the captain stepped out on the hurricane deck, cast his eye around, and looked a good deal surprised. He glanced inquiringly aloft at Stephen, but Stephen was whistling placidly, and attending to business. The captain stood around a while in evident discomfort, and once or twice seemed about to make a suggestion; but the etiquette of the river taught him to avoid that sort of rashness, and so he managed to hold his peace. He chafed and puzzled a few min-

[1]Considering a captain's ostentatious but hollow chieftainship, and a pilot's real authority, there was something impudently apt and happy about that way of phrasing it.

utes longer, then retired to his apartments. But soon he was out again, and apparently more perplexed than ever. Presently he ventured to remark, with deference,—

"Pretty good stage of the river now, ain't it, sir?"

"Well, I should say so! Bank-full *is* a pretty liberal stage."

"Seems to be a good deal of current here."

"Good deal don't describe it! It 's worse than a millrace."

"Is n't it easier in toward shore than it is out here in the middle?"

"Yes, I reckon it is; but a body can't be too careful with a steamboat. It 's pretty safe out here; can't strike any bottom here, you can depend on that."

The captain departed, looking rueful enough. At this rate, he would probably die of old age before his boat got to St. Louis. Next day he appeared on deck and again found Stephen faithfully standing up the middle of the river, fighting the whole vast force of the Mississippi, and whistling the same placid tune. This thing was becoming serious. In by the shore was a slower boat clipping along in the easy water and gaining steadily; she began to make for an island chute; Stephen stuck to the middle of the river. Speech was *wrung* from the captain. He said,—

"Mr. W——, don't that chute cut off a good deal of distance?"

"I think it does, but I don't know."

"Don't know! Well, is n't there water enough in it now to go through?"

"I expect there is, but I am not certain."

"Upon my word this is odd! Why, those pilots on that boat yonder are going to try it. Do you mean to say that you don't know as much as they do?"

"*They!* Why, *they* are two-hundred-and-fifty-dollar pilots! But don't you be uneasy; I know as much as any man can afford to know for a hundred and twenty-five!"

The captain surrendered.

Five minutes later Stephen was bowling through the chute and showing the rival boat a two-hundred-and-fifty-dollar pair of heels.

XV.

The Pilots' Monopoly

O NE DAY, on board the "Aleck Scott," my chief, Mr.
Bixby, was crawling carefully through a close place at
Cat Island, both leads going, and everybody holding his
breath. The captain, a nervous, apprehensive man, kept still
as long as he could, but finally broke down and shouted from
the hurricane deck,—

"For gracious' sake, give her steam, Mr. Bixby! give her
steam! She 'll never raise the reef on this headway!"

For all the effect that was produced upon Mr. Bixby, one
would have supposed that no remark had been made. But five
minutes later, when the danger was past and the leads laid in,
he burst instantly into a consuming fury, and gave the captain
the most admirable cursing I ever listened to. No bloodshed
ensued; but that was because the captain's cause was weak;
for ordinarily he was not a man to take correction quietly.

Having now set forth in detail the nature of the science of
piloting, and likewise described the rank which the pilot held
among the fraternity of steamboatmen, this seems a fitting
place to say a few words about an organization which the
pilots once formed for the protection of their guild. It was
curious and noteworthy in this, that it was perhaps the compactest, the completest, and the strongest commercial organization ever formed among men.

For a long time wages had been two hundred and fifty dollars a month; but curiously enough, as steamboats multiplied
and business increased, the wages began to fall little by little.
It was easy to discover the reason of this. Too many pilots
were being "made." It was nice to have a "cub," a steersman,
to do all the hard work for a couple of years, gratis, while his
master sat on a high bench and smoked; all pilots and captains had sons or nephews who wanted to be pilots. By and
by it came to pass that nearly every pilot on the river had a
steersman. When a steersman had made an amount of progress that was satisfactory to any two pilots in the trade, they
could get a pilot's license for him by signing an application

directed to the United States Inspector. Nothing further was needed; usually no questions were asked, no proofs of capacity required.

Very well, this growing swarm of new pilots presently began to undermine the wages, in order to get berths. Too late—apparently—the knights of the tiller perceived their mistake. Plainly, something had to be done, and quickly; but what was to be the needful thing? A close organization. Nothing else would answer. To compass this seemed an impossibility; so it was talked, and talked, and then dropped. It was too likely to ruin whoever ventured to move in the matter. But at last about a dozen of the boldest—and some of them the best—pilots on the river launched themselves into the enterprise and took all the chances. They got a special charter from the legislature, with large powers, under the name of the Pilots' Benevolent Association; elected their officers, completed their organization, contributed capital, put "association" wages up to two hundred and fifty dollars at once—and then retired to their homes, for they were promptly discharged from employment. But there were two or three unnoticed trifles in their by-laws which had the seeds of propagation in them. For instance, all idle members of the association, in good standing, were entitled to a pension of twenty-five dollars per month. This began to bring in one straggler after another from the ranks of the new-fledged pilots, in the dull (summer) season. Better have twenty-five dollars than starve; the initiation fee was only twelve dollars, and no dues required from the unemployed.

Also, the widows of deceased members in good standing could draw twenty-five dollars per month, and a certain sum for each of their children. Also, the said deceased would be buried at the association's expense. These things resurrected all the superannuated and forgotten pilots in the Mississippi Valley. They came from farms, they came from interior villages, they came from everywhere. They came on crutches, on drays, in ambulances,—any way, so they got there. They paid in their twelve dollars, and straightway began to draw out twenty-five dollars a month and calculate their burial bills.

By and by, all the useless, helpless pilots, and a dozen first-class ones, were in the association, and nine tenths of the best pilots out of it and laughing at it. It was the laughing-stock of the whole river. Everybody joked about the by-law requiring members to pay ten per cent of their wages, every month, into the treasury for the support of the association, whereas all the members were outcast and tabooed, and no one would employ them. Everybody was derisively grateful to the association for taking all the worthless pilots out of the way and leaving the whole field to the excellent and the deserving; and everybody was not only jocularly grateful for that, but for a result which naturally followed, namely, the gradual advance of wages as the busy season approached. Wages had gone up from the low figure of one hundred dollars a month to one hundred and twenty-five, and in some cases to one hundred and fifty; and it was great fun to enlarge upon the fact that this charming thing had been accomplished by a body of men not one of whom received a particle of benefit from it. Some of the jokers used to call at the association rooms and have a good time chaffing the members and offering them the charity of taking them as steersmen for a trip, so that they could see what the forgotten river looked like. However, the association was content; or at least it gave no sign to the contrary. Now and then it captured a pilot who was "out of luck," and added him to its list; and these later additions were very valuable, for they were good pilots; the incompetent ones had all been absorbed before. As business freshened, wages climbed gradually up to two hundred and fifty dollars—the association figure—and became firmly fixed there; and still without benefiting a member of that body, for no member was hired. The hilarity at the association's expense burst all bounds, now. There was no end to the fun which that poor martyr had to put up with.

However, it is a long lane that has no turning. Winter approached, business doubled and trebled, and an avalanche of Missouri, Illinois, and Upper Mississippi River boats came pouring down to take a chance in the New Orleans trade. All of a sudden, pilots were in great demand, and were correspondingly scarce. The time for revenge was come. It was a bitter pill to have to accept association pilots at last, yet captains and owners agreed that there was no other way. But none of these outcasts offered! So there was a still bitterer pill to be swallowed: they must be sought out and asked for their services. Captain—— was the first man who found it necessary to take the dose, and he had been the loudest derider of the organization. He hunted up one of the best of the association pilots and said,—

"Well, you boys have rather got the best of us for a little while, so I 'll give in with as good a grace as I can. I 've come to hire you; get your trunk aboard right away. I want to leave at twelve o'clock."

"I don't know about that. Who is your other pilot?"

"I 've got I. S——. Why?"

"I can't go with him. He don't belong to the association."

"What!"

"It 's so."

"Do you mean to tell me that you won't turn a wheel with one of the very best and oldest pilots on the river because he don't belong to your association?"

"Yes, I do."

"Well, if this is n't putting on airs! I supposed I was doing you a benevolence; but I begin to think that I am the party that wants a favor done. Are you acting under a law of the concern?"

"Yes."

"Show it to me."

So they stepped into the association rooms, and the secretary soon satisfied the captain, who said,—

"Well, what am I to do? I have hired Mr. S—— for the entire season."

"I will provide for you," said the secretary. "I will detail a pilot to go with you, and he shall be on board at twelve o'clock."

"But if I discharge S——, he will come on me for the whole season's wages."

"Of course that is a matter between you and Mr. S——, captain. We cannot meddle in your private affairs."

The captain stormed, but to no purpose. In the end he had to discharge S——, pay him about a thousand dollars, and take an association pilot in his place. The laugh was beginning to turn the other way, now. Every day, thenceforward, a new victim fell; every day some outraged captain discharged a non-association pet, with tears and profanity, and installed a hated association man in his berth. In a very little while, idle non-associationists began to be pretty plenty, brisk as business was, and much as their services were desired. The laugh was shifting to the other side of their mouths most palpably. These victims, together with the captains and owners, presently ceased to laugh altogether, and began to rage about the revenge they would take when the passing business "spurt" was over.

Soon all the laughers that were left were the owners and crews of boats that had two non-association pilots. But their triumph was not very long-lived. For this reason: It was a rigid rule of the association that its members should never, under any circumstances whatever, give information about the channel to any "outsider." By this time about half the boats had none but association pilots, and the other half had none but outsiders. At the first glance one would suppose that when it came to forbidding information about the river these two parties could play equally at that game; but this was not so. At every good-sized town from one end of the river to the other, there was a "wharf-boat" to land at, instead of a wharf or a pier. Freight was stored in it for transportation; waiting passengers slept in its cabins. Upon each of these wharf-boats the association's officers placed a strong box, fastened with a peculiar lock which was used in no other service but one—the United States mail service. It was the letter-bag lock, a sacred governmental thing. By dint of much beseeching the government had been persuaded to allow the association to use this lock. Every association man carried a key which would open these boxes. That key, or rather a peculiar way of holding it in the hand when its owner was asked for river information by a stranger,—for the success of the St. Louis and New Orleans association had now bred tolerably thriving branches in a dozen neighboring steamboat trades,—was the association man's sign and diploma of membership; and if the stranger did not respond by producing a similar key and holding it in a certain manner duly prescribed, his question was politely ignored. From the association's secretary each member received a package of more or less gorgeous blanks, printed like a bill-head, on handsome paper, properly ruled in columns; a bill-head worded something like this:—

STEAMER GREAT REPUBLIC.
JOHN SMITH, MASTER.
Pilots, John Jones and Thomas Brown.

CROSSINGS.	SOUNDINGS.	MARKS.	REMARKS.

These blanks were filled up, day by day, as the voyage progressed, and deposited in the several wharf-boat boxes. For instance, as soon as the first crossing, out from St. Louis, was completed, the items would be entered upon the blank, under the appropriate headings, thus:—

"St. Louis. Nine and a half (feet). Stern on court-house, head on dead cottonwood above wood-yard, until you raise the first reef, then pull up square." Then under head of Remarks: "Go just outside the wrecks; this is important. New snag just where you straighten down; go above it."

The pilot who deposited that blank in the Cairo box (after adding to it the details of every crossing all the way down from St. Louis) took out and read half a dozen fresh reports (from upward-bound steamers) concerning the river between Cairo and Memphis, posted himself thoroughly, returned them to the box, and went back aboard his boat again so armed against accident that he could not possibly get his boat into trouble without bringing the most ingenious carelessness to his aid.

Imagine the benefits of so admirable a system in a piece of river twelve or thirteen hundred miles long, whose channel was shifting every day! The pilot who had formerly been obliged to put up with seeing a shoal place once or possibly twice a month, had a hundred sharp eyes to watch it for him, now, and bushels of intelligent brains to tell him how to run it. His information about it was seldom twenty-four hours old. If the reports in the last box chanced to leave any misgivings on his mind concerning a treacherous crossing, he had his remedy; he blew his steam-whistle in a peculiar way as soon as he saw a boat approaching; the signal was answered in a peculiar way if that boat's pilots were association men;

and then the two steamers ranged alongside and all uncertainties were swept away by fresh information furnished to the inquirer by word of mouth and in minute detail.

The first thing a pilot did when he reached New Orleans or St. Louis was to take his final and elaborate report to the association parlors and hang it up there, — *after* which he was free to visit his family. In these parlors a crowd was always gathered together, discussing changes in the channel, and the moment there was a fresh arrival, everybody stopped talking till this witness had told the newest news and settled the latest uncertainty. Other craftsmen can "sink the shop," sometimes, and interest themselves in other matters. Not so with a pilot; he must devote himself wholly to his profession and talk of nothing else; for it would be small gain to be perfect one day and imperfect the next. He has no time or words to waste if he would keep "posted."

But the outsiders had a hard time of it. No particular place to meet and exchange information, no wharf-boat reports, none but chance and unsatisfactory ways of getting news. The consequence was that a man sometimes had to run five hundred miles of river on information that was a week or ten days old. At a fair stage of the river that might have answered; but when the dead low water came it was destructive.

Now came another perfectly logical result. The outsiders began to ground steamboats, sink them, and get into all sorts of trouble, whereas accidents seemed to keep entirely away from the association men. Wherefore even the owners and captains of boats furnished exclusively with outsiders, and previously considered to be wholly independent of the association and free to comfort themselves with brag and laughter, began to feel pretty uncomfortable. Still, they made a show of keeping up the brag, until one black day when every captain of the lot was formally ordered to immediately discharge his outsiders and take association pilots in their stead. And who was it that had the dashing presumption to do that? Alas, it came from a power behind the throne that was greater than the throne itself. It was the underwriters!

It was no time to "swap knives." Every outsider had to take his trunk ashore at once. Of course it was supposed that there was collusion between the association and the underwriters, but this was not so. The latter had come to comprehend the excellence of the "report" system of the association and the safety it secured, and so they had made their decision among themselves and upon plain business principles.

There was weeping and wailing and gnashing of teeth in the camp of the outsiders now. But no matter, there was but one course for them to pursue, and they pursued it. They came forward in couples and groups, and proffered their twelve dollars and asked for membership. They were surprised to learn that several new by-laws had been long ago added. For instance, the initiation fee had been raised to fifty dollars; that sum must be tendered, and also ten per cent of the wages which the applicant had received each and every month since the founding of the association. In many cases this amounted to three or four hundred dollars. Still, the association would not entertain the application until the money was present. Even then a single adverse vote killed the application. Every member had to vote yes or no in person and before witnesses; so it took weeks to decide a candidacy, because many pilots were so long absent on voyages. However, the repentant sinners scraped their savings together, and one by one, by our tedious voting process, they were added to the fold. A time came, at last, when only about ten remained outside. They said they would starve before they would apply. They remained idle a long while, because of course nobody could venture to employ them.

By and by the association published the fact that upon a certain date the wages would be raised to five hundred dollars per month. All the branch associations had grown strong, now, and the Red River one had advanced wages to seven hundred dollars a month. Reluctantly the ten outsiders yielded, in view of these things, and made application. There was *another* new by-law, by this time, which required them to pay dues not only on all the wages they had received since the association was born, but also on what they would have received if they had continued at work up to the time of their application, instead of going off to pout in idleness. It turned out to be a difficult matter to elect them, but it was accomplished at last. The most virulent sinner of this batch had stayed out and allowed "dues" to accumulate against him so long that he had to send in six hundred and twenty-five dollars with his application.

The association had a good bank account now, and was very strong. There was no longer an outsider. A by-law was added forbidding the reception of any more cubs or apprentices for five years; after which time a limited number would be taken, not by individuals, but by the association, upon these terms: the applicant must not be less than eighteen years old, and of respectable family and good character; he must pass an examination as to education, pay a thousand dollars in advance for the privilege of becoming an apprentice, and must remain under the commands of the association until a great part of the membership (more than half, I think) should be willing to sign his application for a pilot's license.

All previously-articled apprentices were now taken away from their masters and adopted by the association. The president and secretary detailed them for service on one boat or another, as they chose, and changed them from boat to boat according to certain rules. If a pilot could show that he was in infirm health and needed assistance, one of the cubs would be ordered to go with him.

The widow and orphan list grew, but so did the association's financial resources. The association attended its own funerals in state, and paid for them. When occasion demanded, it sent members down the river upon searches for the bodies of brethren lost by steamboat accidents; a search of this kind sometimes cost a thousand dollars.

The association procured a charter and went into the insurance business, also. It not only insured the lives of its members, but took risks on steamboats.

The organization seemed indestructible. It was the tightest monopoly in the world. By the United States law, no man could become a pilot unless two duly licensed pilots signed his application; and now there was nobody outside of the association competent to sign. Consequently the making of pilots was at an end. Every year some would die and others become incapacitated by age and infirmity; there would be no new ones to take their places. In time, the association could put wages up to any figure it chose; and as long as it should be wise enough not to carry the thing too far and provoke the national government into amending the licensing system, steamboat owners would have to submit, since there would be no help for it.

The owners and captains were the only obstruction that lay between the association and absolute power; and at last this one was removed. Incredible as it may seem, the owners and captains deliberately did it themselves. When the pilots' association announced, months beforehand, that on the first day of September, 1861, wages would be advanced to five hundred dollars per month, the owners and captains instantly put freights up a few cents, and explained to the farmers along the river the necessity of it, by calling their attention to the burdensome rate of wages about to be established. It was a rather slender argument, but the farmers did not seem to detect it. It looked reasonable to them that to add five cents freight on a bushel of corn was justifiable under the circumstances, overlooking the fact that this advance on a cargo of forty thousand sacks was a good deal more than necessary to cover the new wages.

So, straightway the captains and owners got up an association of their own, and proposed to put captains' wages up to five hundred dollars, too, and move for another advance in freights. It was a novel idea, but of course an effect which had been produced once could be produced again. The new association decreed (for this was before all the outsiders had been taken into the pilots' association) that if any captain employed a non-association pilot, he should be forced to discharge him, and also pay a fine of five hundred dollars. Several of these heavy fines were paid before the captains' organization grew strong enough to exercise full authority over its membership; but that all ceased, presently. The captains tried to get the pilots to decree that no member of their corporation should serve under a non-association captain; but this proposition was declined. The pilots saw that they would be backed up by the captains and the underwriters anyhow, and so they wisely refrained from entering into entangling alliances.

As I have remarked, the pilots' association was now the compactest monopoly in the world, perhaps, and seemed simply indestructible. And yet the days of its glory were numbered. First, the new railroad stretching up through Mississippi, Tennessee, and Kentucky, to Northern railway centres, began to divert the passenger travel from the steamers; next the war came and almost entirely annihilated the steamboating industry during several years, leaving most of the pilots idle, and the cost of living advancing all the time; then the treasurer of the St. Louis association put his hand into the till and walked off with every dollar of the ample fund; and finally, the railroads intruding everywhere, there was little for steamers to do, when the war was over, but carry freights; so straightway some genius from the Atlantic coast introduced the plan of towing a dozen steamer cargoes down to New Orleans at the tail of a vulgar little tug-boat; and behold, in the twinkling of an eye, as it were, the association and the noble science of piloting were things of the dead and pathetic past!

XVI.

Racing Days

IT WAS ALWAYS the custom for the boats to leave New Orleans between four and five o'clock in the afternoon. From three o'clock onward they would be burning rosin and pitch pine (the sign of preparation), and so one had the picturesque spectacle of a rank, some two or three miles long, of tall, ascending columns of coal-black smoke; a colonnade which supported a sable roof of the same smoke blended together and spreading abroad over the city. Every outward-bound boat had its flag flying at the jack-staff, and sometimes a duplicate on the verge staff astern. Two or three miles of mates were commanding and swearing with more than usual emphasis; countless processions of freight barrels and boxes were spinning athwart the levee and flying aboard the stage-planks; belated passengers were dodging and skipping among these frantic things, hoping to reach the forecastle companion way alive, but having their doubts about it; women with reticules and bandboxes were trying to keep up with husbands freighted with carpet-sacks and crying babies, and making a failure of it by losing their heads in the whirl and roar and general distraction; drays and baggage-vans were clattering hither and thither in a wild hurry, every now and then getting blocked and jammed together, and then during ten seconds one could not see them for the profanity, except vaguely and dimly; every windlass connected with every fore-hatch, from one end of that long array of steamboats to the other, was keeping up a deafening whiz and whir, lowering freight into the hold, and the half-naked crews of perspiring negroes that worked them were roaring such songs as "De Las' Sack! De Las' Sack!"—inspired to unimaginable exaltation by the chaos of turmoil and racket that was driving everybody else mad. By this time the hurricane and boiler decks of the steamers would be packed and black with passengers. The "last bells" would begin to clang, all down the line, and then the powwow seemed to double; in a moment or two the final warning came,—a simultaneous din of Chinese gongs, with

the cry, "All dat ain't goin', please to git asho'!"—and behold, the powwow quadrupled! People came swarming
ashore, overturning excited stragglers that were trying to
swarm aboard. One more moment later a long array of stage-
planks was being hauled in, each with its customary latest passenger clinging to the end of it with teeth, nails, and everything else, and the customary latest procrastinator making a
wild spring shoreward over his head.

Now a number of the boats slide backward into the stream,
leaving wide gaps in the serried rank of steamers. Citizens
crowd the decks of boats that are not to go, in order to see
the sight. Steamer after steamer straightens herself up, gathers
all her strength, and presently comes swinging by, under a
tremendous head of steam, with flag flying, black smoke rolling, and her entire crew of firemen and deck-hands (usually
swarthy negroes) massed together on the forecastle, the best
"voice" in the lot towering from the midst (being mounted
on the capstan), waving his hat or a flag, and all roaring a
mighty chorus, while the parting cannons boom and the mul-
titudinous spectators swing their hats and huzza! Steamer after steamer falls into line, and the stately procession goes
winging its flight up the river.

In the old times, whenever two fast boats started out on a
race, with a big crowd of people looking on, it was inspiring
to hear the crews sing, especially if the time were night-fall,
and the forecastle lit up with the red glare of the torch-
baskets. Racing was royal fun. The public always had an idea
that racing was dangerous; whereas the opposite was the
case—that is, after the laws were passed which restricted each
boat to just so many pounds of steam to the square inch. No
engineer was ever sleepy or careless when his heart was in a
race. He was constantly on the alert, trying gauge-cocks and
watching things. The dangerous place was on slow, plodding
boats, where the engineers drowsed around and allowed chips
to get into the "doctor" and shut off the water supply from
the boilers.

In the "flush times" of steamboating, a race between two
notoriously fleet steamers was an event of vast importance.
The date was set for it several weeks in advance, and from
that time forward, the whole Mississippi Valley was in a state

of consuming excitement. Politics and the weather were dropped, and people talked only of the coming race. As the time approached, the two steamers "stripped" and got ready. Every incumbrance that added weight, or exposed a resisting surface to wind or water, was removed, if the boat could possibly do without it. The "spars," and sometimes even their supporting derricks, were sent ashore, and no means left to set the boat afloat in case she got aground. When the "Eclipse" and the "A.L. Shotwell" ran their great race many years ago, it was said that pains were taken to scrape the gilding off the fanciful device which hung between the "Eclipse's" chimneys, and that for that one trip the captain left off his kid gloves and had his head shaved. But I always doubted these things.

If the boat was known to make her best speed when drawing five and a half feet forward and five feet aft, she was carefully loaded to that exact figure—she would n't enter a dose of homœopathic pills on her manifest after that. Hardly any passengers were taken, because they not only add weight but they never will "trim boat." They always run to the side when there is anything to see, whereas a conscientious and experienced steamboatman would stick to the centre of the boat and part his hair in the middle with a spirit level.

No way-freights and no way-passengers were allowed, for the racers would stop only at the largest towns, and then it would be only "touch and go." Coal flats and wood flats were contracted for beforehand, and these were kept ready to hitch on to the flying steamers at a moment's warning. Double crews were carried, so that all work could be quickly done.

The chosen date being come, and all things in readiness, the two great steamers back into the stream, and lie there jockeying a moment, and apparently watching each other's slightest movement, like sentient creatures; flags drooping, the pent steam shrieking through safety-valves, the black smoke rolling and tumbling from the chimneys and darkening all the air. People, people everywhere; the shores, the house-tops, the steamboats, the ships, are packed with them, and you know that the borders of the broad Mississippi are going to be fringed with humanity thence northward twelve hundred miles, to welcome these racers.

Presently tall columns of steam burst from the 'scape-pipes

of both steamers, two guns boom a good-by, two red-shirted heroes mounted on capstans wave their small flags above the massed crews on the forecastles, two plaintive solos linger on the air a few waiting seconds, two mighty choruses burst forth—and here they come! Brass bands bray Hail Columbia, huzza after huzza thunders from the shores, and the stately creatures go whistling by like the wind.

Those boats will never halt a moment between New Orleans and St. Louis, except for a second or two at large towns, or to hitch thirty-cord wood-boats alongside. You should be on board when they take a couple of those wood-boats in tow and turn a swarm of men into each; by the time you have wiped your glasses and put them on, you will be wondering what has become of that wood.

Two nicely matched steamers will stay in sight of each other day after day. They might even stay side by side, but for the fact that pilots are not all alike, and the smartest pilots will win the race. If one of the boats has a "lightning" pilot, whose "partner" is a trifle his inferior, you can tell which one is on watch by noting whether that boat has gained ground or lost some during each four-hour stretch. The shrewdest pilot can delay a boat if he has not a fine genius for steering. Steering is a very high art. One must not keep a rudder dragging across a boat's stern if he wants to get up the river fast.

There is a great difference in boats, of course. For a long time I was on a boat that was so slow we used to forget what year it was we left port in. But of course this was at rare intervals. Ferry-boats used to lose valuable trips because their passengers grew old and died, waiting for us to get by. This was at still rarer intervals. I had the documents for these occurrences, but through carelessness they have been mislaid. This boat, the "John J. Roe," was so slow that when she finally sunk in Madrid Bend, it was five years before the owners heard of it. That was always a confusing fact to me, but it is according to the record, any way. She was dismally slow; still, we often had pretty exciting times racing with islands, and rafts, and such things. One trip, however, we did rather well. We went to St. Louis in sixteen days. But even at this rattling gait I think we changed watches three times in Fort Adams reach, which is five miles long. A "reach" is a piece of straight river, and of course the current drives through such a place in a pretty lively way.

That trip we went to Grand Gulf, from New Orleans, in four days (three hundred and forty miles); the "Eclipse" and "Shotwell" did it in one. We were nine days out, in the chute of 63 (seven hundred miles); the "Eclipse" and "Shotwell" went there in two days. Something over a generation ago, a boat called the "J. M. White" went from New Orleans to Cairo in three days, six hours, and forty-four minutes. In 1853 the "Eclipse" made the same trip in three days, three hours, and twenty minutes.[1] In 1870 the "R. E. Lee" did it in three days and *one* hour. This last is called the fastest trip on record. I will try to show that it was not. For this reason: the distance between New Orleans and Cairo, when the "J. M. White" ran it, was about eleven hundred and six miles; consequently her average speed was a trifle over fourteen miles per hour. In the "Eclipse's" day the distance between the two ports had become reduced to one thousand and eighty miles; consequently her average speed was a shade under fourteen and three eighths miles per hour. In the "R. E. Lee's" time the distance had diminished to about one thousand and thirty miles; consequently her average was about fourteen and one eighth miles per hour. Therefore the "Eclipse's" was conspicuously the fastest time that has ever been made.

THE RECORD OF SOME FAMOUS TRIPS.

[*From Commodore Rollingpin's Almanac.*]

FAST TIME ON THE WESTERN WATERS.

FROM NEW ORLEANS TO NATCHEZ—268 MILES.

		D.	H.	M.			H.	M.
1814.	Orleans made the run in	6	6	40	1844.	Sultana . . .made the run in	19	45
1814.	Comet " "		5	10	1851.	Magnolia " "	19	50
1815.	Enterprise " "	4	11	20	1853.	A. L. Shotwell " "	19	49
1817.	Washington " "	4			1853.	Southern Belle " "	20	3
1817.	Shelby " "	3	20		1853.	Princess (No. 4) " "	20	26
1819.	Paragon " "	3	8		1853.	Eclipse " "	19	47
1828.	Tecumseh " "	3	1	20	1855.	Princess (New) " "	18	53
1834.	Tuscarora " "	1	21		1855.	Natchez (New) " "	17	30
1838.	Natchez " "	1	17		1856.	Princess (New) " "	17	30
1840.	Ed. Shippen " "	1	8		1870.	Natchez " "	17	17
1842.	Belle of the West "	1	18		1870.	R. E. Lee " "	17	11

[1]Time disputed. Some authorities add 1 hour and 16 minutes to this.

Time Tables—*Continued*

FROM NEW ORLEANS TO CAIRO—1,024 MILES.

		D.	H.	M.			D.	H.	M.
1844.	J. M. White made the run in	3	6	44	1869.	Dexter . . made the run in	3	6	20
1852.	Reindeer " "	3	12	45	1870.	Natchez " "	3	4	34
1853.	Eclipse " "	3	4	4	1870.	R. E. Lee " "	3	1	
1853.	A. L. Shotwell " "	3	3	40					

FROM NEW ORLEANS TO LOUISVILLE—1,440 MILES.

		D.	H.	M.			D.	H.	M.
1815.	Enterprise made the run in	25	2	40	1840.	Ed. Shippen made the run in	5	14	
1817.	Washington " "	25			1842.	Belle of the West "	6	14	
1817.	Shelby " "	20	4	20	1843.	Duke of Orleans "	5	23	
1819.	Paragon " "	18	10		1844.	Sultana " "	5	12	
1828.	Tecumseh " "	8	4		1849.	Bostona " "	5	8	
1834.	Tuscarora " "	7	16		1851.	Belle Key " "	4	23	
1837.	Gen. Brown " "	6	22		1852.	Reindeer " "	4	20	45
1837.	Randolph " "	6	22		1852.	Eclipse " "	4	19	
1837.	Empress " "	6	17		1853.	A. L. Shotwell "	4	10	20
1837.	Sultana " "	6	15		1853.	Eclipse " "	4	9	30

FROM NEW ORLEANS TO DONALDSVILLE—78 MILES.

		H.	M.			H.	M.
1852.	A. L. Shotwell made the run in	5	42	1860.	Atlantic . . . made the run in	5	11
1852.	Eclipse " "	5	42	1860.	Gen. Quitman " "	5	6
1854.	Sultana " "	5	12	1865.	Ruth " "	4	43
1856.	Princess " "	4	51	1870.	R. E. Lee " "	4	59

FROM NEW ORLEANS TO ST. LOUIS—1,218 MILES.

		D.	H.	M.			D.	H.	M.
1844.	J. M. White made the run in	3	23	9	1870.	Natchez . . made the run in	3	21	58
1849.	Missouri " "	4	19		1870.	R. E. Lee " "	3	18	14
1869.	Dexter " "	4	9						

FROM LOUISVILLE TO CINCINNATI—141 MILES.

		D.	H.	M.			D.	H.	M.
1819.	Gen. Pike made the run in	1	16		1843.	Congress made the run in		12	20
1819.	Paragon " "	1	14	20	1846.	Ben Franklin (No. 6) "		11	45
1822.	Wheeling Packet "	1	10		1852.	Alleghaney " "		10	38
1837.	Moselle "		12		1852.	Pittsburgh " "		10	23
1843.	Duke of Orleans "		12		1853.	Telegraph No. 3 "		9	52

FROM LOUISVILLE TO ST. LOUIS—750 MILES.

		D.	H.	M.			D.	H.	M.
1843.	Congress made the run in	2	1		1854.	Northerner made the run in	1	22	30
1854.	Pike " "	1	23		1855.	Southerner " "	1	19	

FROM CINCINNATI TO PITTSBURGH—490 MILES.

		D.	H.				D.	H.
1850.	Telegraph No. 2 made the run in	1	17	1852.	Pittsburgh made the run in	1	15
1851.	Buckeye State " "	1	16				

FROM ST. LOUIS TO ALTON—30 MILES.

		H.	M.			H.	M.
1853.	Altona . . . made the run in	1	35	1876.	War Eagle . . made the run in	1	37
1876.	Golden Eagle " "	1	37				

Time Tables—*Continued*

MISCELLANEOUS RUNS.

In June, 1859, the St. Louis and Keokuk Packet, City of Louisiana, made the run from St. Louis to Keokuk (214 miles) in 16 hours and 20 minutes, the best time on record.

In 1868 the steamer Hawkeye State, of the Northern Line Packet Company, made the run from St. Louis to St. Paul (800 miles) in 2 days and 20 hours. Never was beaten.

In 1853 the steamer Polar Star made the run from St. Louis to St. Joseph, on the Missouri River, in 64 hours. In July, 1856, the steamer Jas. H. Lucas, Andy Wineland, Master, made the same run in 60 hours and 57 minutes. The distance between the ports is 600 miles, and when the difficulties of navigating the turbulent Missouri are taken into consideration, the performance of the Lucas deserves especial mention.

The time made by the R. E. Lee from New Orleans to St. Louis in 1870, in her famous race with the Natchez, is the best on record, and, inasmuch as the race created a national interest, we give below her time table from port to port.

Left New Orleans, Thursday, June 30th, 1870, at 4 o'clock and 55 minutes, p.m.; reached

	D.	H.	M.		D.	H.	M.
Carrollton			27¹/₂	Vicksburg	1		38
Harry Hills	1		00¹/₂	Milliken's Bend	1	2	37
Red Church	1		39	Bailey's	1	3	48
Bonnet Carre	2		38	Lake Providence	1	5	47
College Point	3		50¹/₂	Greenville	1	10	55
Donaldsonville	4		59	Napoleon	1	16	22
Plaquemine	7		05¹/₂	White River	1	16	56
Baton Rouge	8		25	Australia	1	19	
Bayou Sara	10		26	Helena	1	23	25
Red River	12		56	Half Mile Below St. Francis	2		
Stamps	13		56	Memphis	2	6	9
Bryaro	15		51¹/₂	Foot of Island 37	2	9	
Hinderson's	16		29	Foot of Island 26	2	13	30
Natchez	17		11	Tow-head, Island 14	2	17	23
Cole's Creek	19		21	New Madrid	2	19	50
Waterproof	18		53	Dry Bar No. 10	2	20	37
Rodney	20		45	Foot of Island 8	2	21	25
St. Joseph	21		02	Upper Tow-head—Lucas Bend	3		
Grand Gulf	22		06	Cairo	3	1	
Hard Times	22		18	St. Louis	3	18	14
Half Mile Below Warrenton		1					

The Lee landed at St. Louis at 11:25 A.M., on July 4th, 1870—six hours and thirty-six minutes ahead of the Natchez. The officers of the Natchez claimed seven hours and one minute stoppage on account of fog and repairing machinery. The R. E. Lee was commanded by Captain John W. Cannon, and the Natchez was in charge of that veteran Southern boatman, Captain Thomas P. Leathers.

XVII.

Cut-Offs and Stephen

THESE DRY DETAILS are of importance in one particular.
They give me an opportunity of introducing one of the
Mississippi's oddest peculiarities,—that of shortening its
length from time to time. If you will throw a long, pliant
apple-paring over your shoulder, it will pretty fairly shape itself into an average section of the Mississippi River; that is,
the nine or ten hundred miles stretching from Cairo, Illinois,
southward to New Orleans, the same being wonderfully
crooked, with a brief straight bit here and there at wide intervals. The two-hundred-mile stretch from Cairo northward to
St. Louis is by no means so crooked, that being a rocky country which the river cannot cut much.

The water cuts the alluvial banks of the "lower" river into
deep horseshoe curves; so deep, indeed, that in some places if
you were to get ashore at one extremity of the horseshoe and
walk across the neck, half or three quarters of a mile, you
could sit down and rest a couple of hours while your steamer
was coming around the long elbow, at a speed of ten miles
an hour, to take you aboard again. When the river is rising
fast, some scoundrel whose plantation is back in the country,
and therefore of inferior value, has only to watch his chance,
cut a little gutter across the narrow neck of land some dark
night, and turn the water into it, and in a wonderfully short
time a miracle has happened: to wit, the whole Mississippi
has taken possession of that little ditch, and placed the coun-
tryman's plantation on its bank (quadrupling its value), and
that other party's formerly valuable plantation finds itself
away out yonder on a big island; the old water-course around
it will soon shoal up, boats cannot approach within ten miles
of it, and down goes its value to a fourth of its former worth.
Watches are kept on those narrow necks, at needful times,
and if a man happens to be caught cutting a ditch across
them, the chances are all against his ever having another opportunity to cut a ditch.

Pray observe some of the effects of this ditching business.

Once there was a neck opposite Port Hudson, Louisiana, which was only half a mile across, in its narrowest place. You could walk across there in fifteen minutes; but if you made the journey around the cape on a raft, you travelled thirty-five miles to accomplish the same thing. In 1722 the river darted through that neck, deserted its old bed, and thus shortened itself thirty-five miles. In the same way it shortened itself twenty-five miles at Black Hawk Point in 1699. Below Red River Landing, Raccourci cut-off was made (forty or fifty years ago, I think). This shortened the river twenty-eight miles. In our day, if you travel by river from the southern-most of these three cut-offs to the northernmost, you go only seventy miles. To do the same thing a hundred and seventy-six years ago, one had to go a hundred and fifty-eight miles!—a shortening of eighty-eight miles in that trifling distance. At some forgotten time in the past, cut-offs were made above Vidalia, Louisiana; at island 92; at island 84; and at Hale's Point. These shortened the river, in the aggregate, seventy-seven miles.

Since my own day on the Mississippi, cut-offs have been made at Hurricane Island; at island 100; at Napoleon, Arkansas; at Walnut Bend; and at Council Bend. These shortened the river, in the aggregate, sixty-seven miles. In my own time a cut-off was made at American Bend, which shortened the river ten miles or more.

Therefore, the Mississippi between Cairo and New Orleans was twelve hundred and fifteen miles long one hundred and seventy-six years ago. It was eleven hundred and eighty after the cutoff of 1722. It was one thousand and forty after the American Bend cut-off. It has lost sixty-seven miles since. Consequently its length is only nine hundred and seventy-three miles at present.

Now, if I wanted to be one of those ponderous scientific people, and "let on" to prove what had occurred in the remote past by what had occurred in a given time in the recent past, or what will occur in the far future by what has occurred in late years, what an opportunity is here! Geology never had such a chance, nor such exact data to argue from! Nor "development of species," either! Glacial epochs are great things, but they are vague—vague. Please observe:—

In the space of one hundred and seventy-six years the Lower Mississippi has shortened itself two hundred and forty-two miles. That is an average of a trifle over one mile and a third per year. Therefore, any calm person, who is not blind or idiotic, can see that in the Old Oölitic Silurian Period, just a million years ago next November, the Lower Mississippi River was upwards of one million three hundred thousand miles long, and stuck out over the Gulf of Mexico like a fishing-rod. And by the same token any person can see that seven hundred and forty-two years from now the Lower Mississippi will be only a mile and three quarters long, and Cairo and New Orleans will have joined their streets together, and be plodding comfortably along under a single mayor and a mutual board of aldermen. There is something fascinating about science. One gets such wholesale returns of conjecture out of such a trifling investment of fact.

When the water begins to flow through one of those ditches I have been speaking of, it is time for the people thereabouts to move. The water cleaves the banks away like a knife. By the time the ditch has become twelve or fifteen feet wide, the calamity is as good as accomplished, for no power on earth can stop it now. When the width has reached a hundred yards, the banks begin to peel off in slices half an acre wide. The current flowing around the bend travelled formerly only five miles an hour; now it is tremendously increased by the shortening of the distance. I was on board the first boat that tried to go through the cut-off at American Bend, but we did not get through. It was toward midnight, and a wild night it was—thunder, lightning, and torrents of rain. It was estimated that the current in the cut-off was making about fifteen or twenty miles an hour; twelve or thirteen was the best our boat could do, even in tolerably slack water, therefore perhaps we were foolish to try the cut-off. However, Mr. Brown was ambitious, and he kept on trying. The eddy running up the bank, under the "point," was about as swift as the current out in the middle; so we would go flying up the shore like a lightning express train, get on a big head of steam, and "stand by for a surge" when we struck the current that was whirling by the point. But all our preparations were useless. The instant the current hit us it spun us around like a top, the water deluged the forecastle, and the boat careened so far over that one could hardly keep his feet. The next instant we were away down the river, clawing with might and main to keep out of the woods. We tried the experiment four times. I stood on the forecastle companion way to see. It was astonishing to observe how suddenly the boat would spin around and turn tail the moment she emerged from the eddy and the current struck her nose. The sounding concussion and the quivering would have been about the same if she had come full speed against a sand-bank. Under the lightning flashes one could see the plantation cabins and the goodly acres tumble into the river; and the crash they made was not a bad effort at thunder. Once, when we spun around, we only missed a house about twenty feet, that had a light burning in the window; and in the same instant that house went overboard. Nobody could stay on our forecastle; the water swept across it in a torrent every time we plunged athwart the current. At the end of our fourth effort we brought up in the woods two miles below the cut-off; all the country there was overflowed, of course. A day or two later the cut-off was three quarters of a mile wide, and boats passed up through it without much difficulty, and so saved ten miles.

The old Raccourci cut-off reduced the river's length twenty-eight miles. There used to be a tradition connected with it. It was said that a boat came along there in the night and went around the enormous elbow the usual way, the pilots not knowing that the cut-off had been made. It was a grisly, hideous night, and all shapes were vague and distorted. The old bend had already begun to fill up, and the boat got to running away from mysterious reefs, and occasionally hitting one. The perplexed pilots fell to swearing, and finally uttered the entirely unnecessary wish that they might never get out of that place. As always happens in such cases, that particular prayer was answered, and the others neglected. So to this day that phantom steamer is still butting around in that deserted river, trying to find her way out. More than one grave watchman has sworn to me that on drizzly, dismal nights, he has glanced fearfully down that forgotten river as he passed the head of the island, and seen the faint glow of the spectre steamer's lights drifting through the distant gloom, and heard the muffled cough of her 'scape-pipes and the plaintive cry of her leads-men.

In the absence of further statistics, I beg to close this chapter with one more reminiscence of "Stephen."

Most of the captains and pilots held Stephen's note for borrowed sums, ranging from two hundred and fifty dollars upward. Stephen never paid one of these notes, but he was very prompt and very zealous about renewing them every twelve month.

Of course there came a time, at last, when Stephen could no longer borrow of his ancient creditors; so he was obliged to lie in wait for new men who did not know him. Such a victim was good-hearted, simple-natured young Yates (I use a fictitious name, but the real name began, as this one does, with a Y). Young Yates graduated as a pilot, got a berth, and when the month was ended and he stepped up to the clerk's office and received his two hundred and fifty dollars in crisp new bills, Stephen was there! His silvery tongue began to wag, and in a very little while Yates's two hundred and fifty dollars had changed hands. The fact was soon known at pilot headquarters, and the amusement and satisfaction of the old creditors were large and generous. But innocent Yates never suspected that Stephen's promise to pay promptly at the end of the week was a worthless one. Yates called for his money at the stipulated time; Stephen sweetened him up and put him off a week. He called then, according to agreement, and came away sugar-coated again, but suffering under another postponement. So the thing went on. Yates haunted Stephen week after week, to no purpose, and at last gave it up. And then straightway Stephen began to haunt Yates! Wherever Yates appeared, there was the inevitable Stephen. And not only there, but beaming with affection and gushing with apologies for not being able to pay. By and by, whenever poor Yates saw him coming, he would turn and fly, and drag his company with him, if he had company; but it was of no use; his debtor would run him down and corner him. Panting and red-faced, Stephen would come, with outstretched hands and eager eyes, invade the conversation, shake both of Yates's arms loose in their sockets, and begin: —

"My, what a race I 've had! I saw you did n't see me, and

so I clapped on all steam for fear I 'd miss you entirely. And here you are! there, just stand so, and let me look at you! Just the same old noble countenance." [To Yates's friend:] "Just look at him! *Look* at him! Ain't it just *good* to look at him! *Ain't* it now? Ain't he just a picture! *Some* call him a picture; *I* call him a panorama! That 's what he is—an entire panorama. And now I 'm reminded! How I do wish I could have seen you an hour earlier! For twenty-four hours I 've been saving up that two hundred and fifty dollars for you; been looking for you everywhere. I waited at the Planter's from six yesterday evening till two o'clock this morning, without rest or food; my wife says, 'Where have you been all night?' I said, 'This debt lies heavy on my mind.' She says, 'In all my days I never saw a man take a debt to heart the way you do.' I said, 'It 's my nature; how can *I* change it?' She says, 'Well, do go to bed and get some rest.' I said, 'Not till that poor, noble young man has got his money.' So I set up all night, and this morning out I shot, and the first man I struck told me you had shipped on the 'Grank Turk' and gone to New Orleans. Well, sir, I had to lean up against a building and cry. So help me goodness, I could n't help it. The man that owned the place come out cleaning up with a rag, and said he did n't like to have people cry against his building, and then it seemed to me that the whole world had turned against me, and it was n't any use to live any more; and coming along an hour ago, suffering no man knows what agony, I met Jim Wilson and paid him the two hundred and fifty dollars on account; and to think that here you are, now, and I have n't got a cent! But as sure as I am standing here on this ground on this particular brick,—there, I 've scratched a mark on the brick to remember it by,—I 'll borrow that money and pay it over to you at twelve o'clock sharp, to-morrow! Now, stand so; let me look at you just once more."

And so on. Yates's life became a burden to him. He could not escape his debtor and his debtor's awful sufferings on account of not being able to pay. He dreaded to show himself in the street, lest he should find Stephen lying in wait for him at the corner.

Bogart's billiard saloon was a great resort for pilots in those days. They met there about as much to exchange river news as to play. One morning Yates was there; Stephen was there, too, but kept out of sight. But by and by, when about all the pilots had arrived who were in town, Stephen suddenly appeared in the midst, and rushed for Yates as for a long-lost brother.

"*Oh*, I am so glad to see you! Oh my soul, the sight of you is such a comfort to my eyes! Gentlemen, I owe all of you money; among you I owe probably forty thousand dollars. I want to pay it; I intend to pay it—every last cent of it. You all know, without my telling you, what sorrow it has cost me to remain so long under such deep obligations to such patient and generous friends; but the sharpest pang I suffer—by far the sharpest—is from the debt I owe to this noble young man here; and I have come to this place this morning especially to make the announcement that I have at last found a method whereby I can pay off all my debts! And most especially I wanted *him* to be here when I announced it. Yes, my faithful friend,—my benefactor, I 've found the method! I 've found the method to pay off *all* my debts, and you 'll get your money!" Hope dawned in Yates's eye; then Stephen, beaming benignantly, and placing his hand upon Yates's head, added, "I am going to pay them off in alphabetical order!"

Then he turned and disappeared. The full significance of Stephen's "method" did not dawn upon the perplexed and musing crowd for some two minutes; and then Yates murmured with a sigh:—

"Well, the Y's stand a gaudy chance. He won't get any further than the C's in *this* world, and I reckon that after a good deal of eternity has wasted away in the next one, I 'll still be referred to up there as 'that poor, ragged pilot that came here from St. Louis in the early days!' "

XVIII.

I Take a Few Extra Lessons

D URING THE TWO or two and a half years of my apprenticeship, I served under many pilots, and had experience
of many kinds of steamboatmen and many varieties of steamboats; for it was not always convenient for Mr. Bixby to have
me with him, and in such cases he sent me with somebody
else. I am to this day profiting somewhat by that experience;
for in that brief, sharp schooling, I got personally and familiarly acquainted with about all the different types of human
nature that are to be found in fiction, biography, or history.
The fact is daily borne in upon me, that the average shore-
employment requires as much as forty years to equip a man
with this sort of an education. When I say I am still profiting
by this thing, I do not mean that it has constituted me a
judge of men—no, it has not done that; for judges of men
are born, not made. My profit is various in kind and degree;
but the feature of it which I value most is the zest which that
early experience has given to my later reading. When I find a
well-drawn character in fiction or biography, I generally take
a warm personal interest in him, for the reason that I have
known him before—met him on the river.

The figure that comes before me oftenest, out of the shadows of that vanished time, is that of Brown, of the steamer
"Pennsylvania"—the man referred to in a former chapter,
whose memory was so good and tiresome. He was a middle-
aged, long, slim, bony, smooth-shaven, horse-faced, ignorant,
stingy, malicious, snarling, fault-hunting, mote-magnifying
tyrant. I early got the habit of coming on watch with dread
at my heart. No matter how good a time I might have been
having with the off-watch below, and no matter how high
my spirits might be when I started aloft, my soul became lead
in my body the moment I approached the pilot-house.

I still remember the first time I ever entered the presence of
that man. The boat had backed out from St. Louis and was
"straightening down;" I ascended to the pilot-house in high
feather, and very proud to be semi-officially a member of the

executive family of so fast and famous a boat. Brown was at the wheel. I paused in the middle of the room, all fixed to make my bow, but Brown did not look around. I thought he took a furtive glance at me out of the corner of his eye, but as not even this notice was repeated, I judged I had been mistaken. By this time he was picking his way among some dangerous "breaks" abreast the wood-yards; therefore it would not be proper to interrupt him; so I stepped softly to the high bench and took a seat.

There was silence for ten minutes; then my new boss turned and inspected me deliberately and painstakingly from head to heel for about—as it seemed to me—a quarter of an hour. After which he removed his countenance and I saw it no more for some seconds; then it came around once more, and this question greeted me:—

"Are you Horace Bigsby's cub?"

"Yes, sir."

After this there was a pause and another inspection. Then:

"What's your name?"

I told him. He repeated it after me. It was probably the only thing he ever forgot; for although I was with him many months he never addressed himself to me in any other way than "Here!" and then his command followed.

"Where was you born?"

"In Florida, Missouri."

A pause. Then:—

"Dern sight better staid there!"

By means of a dozen or so of pretty direct questions, he pumped my family history out of me.

The leads were going now, in the first crossing. This interrupted the inquest. When the leads had been laid in, he resumed:—

"How long you been on the river?"

I told him. After a pause:—

"Where 'd you get them shoes?"

I gave him the information.

"Hold up your foot!"

I did so. He stepped back, examined the shoe minutely and contemptuously, scratching his head thoughtfully, tilting his high sugar-loaf hat well forward to facilitate the operation, then ejaculated, "Well, I 'll be dod derned!" and returned to his wheel.

What occasion there was to be dod derned about it is a thing which is still as much of a mystery to me now as it was then. It must have been all of fifteen minutes—fifteen minutes of dull, homesick silence—before that long horse-face swung round upon me again—and then, what a change! It was as red as fire, and every muscle in it was working. Now came this shriek:

"Here!—You going to set there all day?"

I lit in the middle of the floor, shot there by the electric suddenness of the surprise. As soon as I could get my voice I said, apologetically:—"I have had no orders, sir." "You 've had no *orders*! My, what a fine bird we are! We must have *orders*! Our father was a *gentleman*—owned slaves—and *we 've* been to *school*. Yes, *we* are a gentleman, *too*, and got to have *orders*! ORDERS, is it? ORDERS is what you want! Dod dern my skin, *I 'll* learn you to swell yourself up and blow around *here* about your dod-derned *orders*! G' way from the wheel!" (I had approached it without knowing it.)

I moved back a step or two, and stood as in a dream, all my senses stupefied by this frantic assault.

"What you standing there for? Take that ice-pitcher down to the texas-tender—come, move along, and don't you be all day about it!"

The moment I got back to the pilot-house, Brown said:—

"Here! What was you doing down there all this time?"

"I could n't find the texas-tender; I had to go all the way to the pantry."

"Derned likely story! Fill up the stove."

I proceeded to do so. He watched me like a cat. Presently he shouted:—

"Put down that shovel! Derndest numskull I ever saw—ain't even got sense enough to load up a stove."

All through the watch this sort of thing went on. Yes, and the subsequent watches were much like it, during a stretch of months. As I have said, I soon got the habit of coming on duty with dread. The moment I was in the presence, even in the darkest night, I could feel those yellow eyes upon me, and knew their owner was watching for a pretext to spit out some venom on me. Preliminarily he would say:—

"Here! Take the wheel."

Two minutes later:—

"*Where* in the nation you going to? Pull her down! pull her down!"

After another moment:—

"Say! You going to hold her all day? Let her go—meet her! meet her!"

Then he would jump from the bench, snatch the wheel from me, and meet her himself, pouring out wrath upon me all the time.

George Ritchie was the other pilot's cub. He was having good times now; for his boss, George Ealer, was as kind-hearted as Brown was n't. Ritchie had steered for Brown the season before; consequently he knew exactly how to entertain himself and plague me, all by the one operation. Whenever I took the wheel for a moment on Ealer's watch, Ritchie would sit back on the bench and play Brown, with continual ejaculations of "Snatch her! snatch her! Derndest mud-cat I ever saw!" "Here! Where you going *now*? Going to run over that snag?" "Pull her *down*! Don't you hear me? Pull her *down*!" "There she goes! *Just* as I expected! I *told* you not to cramp that reef. G' way from the wheel!"

So I always had a rough time of it, no matter whose watch it was; and sometimes it seemed to me that Ritchie's good-natured badgering was pretty nearly as aggravating as Brown's dead-earnest nagging.

I often wanted to kill Brown, but this would not answer. A cub had to take everything his boss gave, in the way of vigorous comment and criticism; and we all believed that there was a United States law making it a penitentiary offence to strike or threaten a pilot who was on duty. However, I could *imagine* myself killing Brown; there was no law against that; and that was the thing I used always to do the moment I was abed. Instead of going over my river in my mind as was my duty, I threw business aside for pleasure, and killed Brown. I killed Brown every night for months; not in old,

stale, commonplace ways, but in new and picturesque ones,—
ways that were sometimes surprising for freshness of design
and ghastliness of situation and environment.

Brown was *always* watching for a pretext to find fault; and
if he could find no plausible pretext, he would invent one. He
would scold you for shaving a shore, and for not shaving it;
for hugging a bar, and for not hugging it; for "pulling down"
when not invited, and for *not* pulling down when not invited;
for firing up without orders, and for waiting *for* orders. In a
word, it was his invariable rule to find fault with *everything*
you did; and another invariable rule of his was to throw all
his remarks (to you) into the form of an insult.

One day we were approaching New Madrid, bound down
and heavily laden. Brown was at one side of the wheel, steering; I was at the other, standing by to "pull down" or "shove
up." He cast a furtive glance at me every now and then. I had
long ago learned what that meant; viz., he was trying to invent a trap for me. I wondered what shape it was going to
take. By and by he stepped back from the wheel and said in
his usual snarly way:—

"Here!—See if you 've got gumption enough to round
her to."

This was simply *bound* to be a success; nothing could pre-
vent it; for he had never allowed me to round the boat to
before; consequently, no matter how I might do the thing,
he could find free fault with it. He stood back there with his
greedy eye on me, and the result was what might have been
foreseen: I lost my head in a quarter of a minute, and did n't
know what I was about; I started too early to bring the boat
around, but detected a green gleam of joy in Brown's eye,
and corrected my mistake; I started around once more while
too high up, but corrected myself again in time; I made other
false moves, and still managed to save myself; but at last I
grew so confused and anxious that I tumbled into the very
worst blunder of all—I got too far *down* before beginning to
fetch the boat around. Brown's chance was come.

His face turned red with passion; he made one bound,
hurled me across the house with a sweep of his arm, spun the
wheel down, and began to pour out a stream of vituperation
upon me which lasted till he was out of breath. In the course

of this speech he called me all the different kinds of hard names he could think of, and once or twice I thought he was even going to swear—but he had never done that, and he did n't this time. "Dod dern" was the nearest he ventured to the luxury of swearing, for he had been brought up with a wholesome respect for future fire and brimstone.

That was an uncomfortable hour; for there was a big audience on the hurricane deck. When I went to bed that night, I killed Brown in seventeen different ways—all of them new.

XIX.

Brown and I Exchange Compliments

TWO TRIPS LATER, I got into serious trouble. Brown was steering; I was "pulling down." My younger brother appeared on the hurricane deck, and shouted to Brown to stop at some landing or other a mile or so below. Brown gave no intimation that he had heard anything. But that was his way: he never condescended to take notice of an under clerk. The wind was blowing; Brown was deaf (although he always pretended he was n't), and I very much doubted if he had heard the order. If I had had two heads, I would have spoken; but as I had only one, it seemed judicious to take care of it; so I kept still.

Presently, sure enough, we went sailing by that plantation. Captain Klinefelter appeared on the deck, and said:—

"Let her come around, sir, let her come around. Did n't Henry tell you to land here?"

"*No*, sir!"

"I sent him up to do it."

"He *did* come up; and that 's all the good it done, the dodderned fool. He never said anything."

"Did n't *you* hear him?" asked the captain of me.

Of course I did n't want to be mixed up in this business, but there was no way to avoid it; so I said:—

"Yes, sir."

I knew what Brown's next remark would be, before he uttered it; it was:—

"Shut your mouth! you never heard anything of the kind."

I closed my mouth according to instructions. An hour later, Henry entered the pilot-house, unaware of what had been going on. He was a thoroughly inoffensive boy, and I was sorry to see him come, for I knew Brown would have no pity on him. Brown began, straightway:—

"Here! why did n't you tell me we 'd got to land at that plantation?"

"I did tell you, Mr. Brown."

"It 's a lie!"

I said:—

"You lie, yourself. He did tell you."

Brown glared at me in unaffected surprise; and for as much as a moment he was entirely speechless; then he shouted to me:—

"I 'll attend to your case in a half a minute!" then to Henry, "And you leave the pilot-house; out with you!"

It was pilot law, and must be obeyed. The boy started out, and even had his foot on the upper step outside the door, when Brown, with a sudden access of fury, picked up a ten-pound lump of coal and sprang after him; but I was between, with a heavy stool, and I hit Brown a good honest blow which stretched him out.

I had committed the crime of crimes,—I had lifted my hand against a pilot on duty! I supposed I was booked for the penitentiary sure, and could n't be booked any surer if I went on and squared my long account with this person while I had the chance; consequently I stuck to him and pounded him with my fists a considerable time,—I do not know how long, the pleasure of it probably made it seem longer than it really was;—but in the end he struggled free and jumped up and sprang to the wheel: a very natural solicitude, for, all this time, here was this steamboat tearing down the river at the rate of fifteen miles an hour and nobody at the helm! However, Eagle Bend was two miles wide at this bank-full stage, and correspondingly long and deep; and the boat was steering herself straight down the middle and taking no chances. Still, that was only luck—a body *might* have found her charging into the woods.

Perceiving, at a glance, that the "Pennsylvania" was in no danger, Brown gathered up the big spy-glass, war-club fashion, and ordered me out of the pilot-house with more than Comanche bluster. But I was not afraid of him now; so, instead of going, I tarried, and criticised his grammar; I reformed his ferocious speeches for him, and put them into good English, calling his attention to the advantage of pure English over the bastard dialect of the Pennsylvanian collieries whence he was extracted. He could have done his part to admiration in a cross-fire of mere vituperation, of course; but he was not equipped for this species of controversy; so he presently laid aside his glass and took the wheel, muttering and shaking his head; and I retired to the bench. The racket had brought everybody to the hurricane deck, and I trembled when I saw the old captain looking up from the midst of the crowd. I said to myself, "Now I *am* done for!"—For although, as a rule, he was so fatherly and indulgent toward the boat's family, and so patient of minor shortcomings, he could be stern enough when the fault was worth it.

I tried to imagine what he *would* do to a cub pilot who had been guilty of such a crime as mine, committed on a boat guard-deep with costly freight and alive with passengers. Our watch was nearly ended. I thought I would go and hide somewhere till I got a chance to slide ashore. So I slipped out of the pilot-house, and down the steps, and around to the texas door,—and was in the act of gliding within, when the captain confronted me! I dropped my head, and he stood over me in silence a moment or two, then said impressively,—

"Follow me."

I dropped into his wake; he led the way to his parlor in the forward end of the texas. We were alone, now. He closed the after door; then moved slowly to the forward one and closed that. He sat down; I stood before him. He looked at me some little time, then said,—

"So you have been fighting Mr. Brown?"

I answered meekly:—

"Yes, sir."

"Do you know that that is a very serious matter?"

"Yes, sir."

"Are you aware that this boat was ploughing down the river fully five minutes with no one at the wheel?"

"Yes, sir."

"Did you strike him first?"

"Yes, sir."

"What with?"

"A stool, sir."

"Hard?"

"Middling, sir."

"Did it knock him down?"

"He—he fell, sir."

"Did you follow it up? Did you do anything further?"

"Yes, sir."

"What did you do?"

"Pounded him, sir."

"Pounded him?"

"Yes, sir."

"Did you pound him much?—that is, severely?"

"One might call it that, sir, maybe."

"I 'm deucéd glad of it! Hark ye, never mention that I said that. You have been guilty of a great crime; and don't you ever be guilty of it again, on this boat. *But*—lay for him ashore! Give him a good sound thrashing, do you hear? I 'll pay the expenses. Now go—and mind you, not a word of this to anybody. Clear out with you!—you 've been guilty of a great crime, you whelp!"

I slid out, happy with the sense of a close shave and a mighty deliverance; and I heard him laughing to himself and slapping his fat thighs after I had closed his door.

When Brown came off watch he went straight to the captain, who was talking with some passengers on the boiler deck, and demanded that I be put ashore in New Orleans—and added:—

"I 'll never turn a wheel on this boat again while that cub stays."

The captain said:—

"But he need n't come round when you are on watch, Mr. Brown."

"I won't even stay on the same boat with him. *One* of us has got to go ashore."

"Very well," said the captain, "let it be yourself;" and resumed his talk with the passengers.

During the brief remainder of the trip, I knew how an emancipated slave feels; for I was an emancipated slave myself. While we lay at landings, I listened to George Ealer's flute; or to his readings from his two bibles, that is to say, Goldsmith and Shakspeare; or I played chess with him—and would have beaten him sometimes, only he always took back his last move and ran the game out differently.

XX.

A Catastrophe

WE LAY three days in New Orleans, but the captain did not succeed in finding another pilot; so he proposed that I should stand a daylight watch, and leave the night watches to George Ealer. But I was afraid; I had never stood a watch of any sort by myself, and I believed I should be sure to get into trouble in the head of some chute, or ground the boat in a near cut through some bar or other. Brown remained in his place; but he would not travel with me. So the captain gave me an order on the captain of the "A. T. Lacey," for a passage to St. Louis, and said he would find a new pilot there and my steersman's berth could then be resumed. The "Lacey" was to leave a couple of days after the "Pennsylvania."

The night before the "Pennsylvania" left, Henry and I sat chatting on a freight pile on the levee till midnight. The subject of the chat, mainly, was one which I think we had not exploited before—steamboat disasters. One was then on its way to us, little as we suspected it; the water which was to make the steam which should cause it, was washing past some point fifteen hundred miles up the river while we talked;—but it would arrive at the right time and the right place. We doubted if persons not clothed with authority were of much use in cases of disaster and attendant panic; still, they might be of *some* use; so we decided that if a disaster ever fell within our experience we would at least stick to the boat, and give such minor service as chance might throw in the way. Henry remembered this, afterward, when the disaster came, and acted accordingly.

The "Lacey" started up the river two days behind the "Pennsylvania." We touched at Greenville, Mississippi, a couple of days out, and somebody shouted:—

"The 'Pennsylvania' is blown up at Ship Island, and a hundred and fifty lives lost!"

At Napoleon, Arkansas, the same evening, we got an extra,

issued by a Memphis paper, which gave some particulars. It mentioned my brother, and said he was not hurt.

Further up the river we got a later extra. My brother was again mentioned; but this time as being hurt beyond help. We did not get full details of the catastrophe until we reached Memphis. This is the sorrowful story:—

It was six o'clock on a hot summer morning. The "Pennsylvania" was creeping along, north of Ship Island, about sixty miles below Memphis on a half-head of steam, towing a wood-flat which was fast being emptied. George Ealer was in the pilot-house—alone, I think; the second engineer and a striker had the watch in the engine room; the second mate had the watch on deck; George Black, Mr. Wood, and my brother, clerks, were asleep, as were also Brown and the head engineer, the carpenter, the chief mate, and one striker; Capt. Klinefelter was in the barber's chair, and the barber was preparing to shave him. There were a good many cabin passengers aboard, and three or four hundred deck passengers—so it was said at the time—and not very many of them were astir. The wood being nearly all out of the flat now, Ealer rang to "come ahead" full steam, and the next moment four of the eight boilers exploded with a thunderous crash, and the whole forward third of the boat was hoisted toward the sky! The main part of the mass, with the chimneys, dropped upon the boat again, a mountain of riddled and chaotic rubbish—and then, after a little, fire broke out.

Many people were flung to considerable distances, and fell in the river; among these were Mr. Wood and my brother, and the carpenter. The carpenter was still stretched upon his mattress when he struck the water seventy-five feet from the boat. Brown, the pilot, and George Black, chief clerk, were never seen or heard of after the explosion. The barber's chair, with Captain Klinefelter in it and unhurt, was left with its back overhanging vacancy—everything forward of it, floor and all, had disappeared; and the stupefied barber, who was also unhurt, stood with one toe projecting over space, still stirring his lather unconsciously, and saying not a word.

When George Ealer saw the chimneys plunging aloft in

front of him, he knew what the matter was; so he muffled his face in the lapels of his coat, and pressed both hands there tightly to keep this protection in its place so that no steam could get to his nose or mouth. He had ample time to attend to these details while he was going up and returning. He presently landed on top of the unexploded boilers, forty feet below the former pilot-house, accompanied by his wheel and a rain of other stuff, and enveloped in a cloud of scalding steam. All of the many who breathed that steam, died; none escaped. But Ealer breathed none of it. He made his way to the free air as quickly as he could; and when the steam cleared away he returned and climbed up on the boilers again, and patiently hunted out each and every one of his chessmen and the several joints of his flute.

By this time the fire was beginning to threaten. Shrieks and groans filled the air. A great many persons had been scalded, a great many crippled; the explosion had driven an iron crowbar through one man's body—I think they said he was a priest. He did not die at once, and his sufferings were very dreadful. A young French naval cadet, of fifteen, son of a French admiral, was fearfully scalded, but bore his tortures manfully. Both mates were badly scalded, but they stood to their posts, nevertheless. They drew the wood-boat aft, and they and the captain fought back the frantic herd of frightened immigrants till the wounded could be brought there and placed in safety first.

When Mr. Wood and Henry fell in the water, they struck out for shore, which was only a few hundred yards away; but Henry presently said he believed he was not hurt, (what an unaccountable error!) and therefore would swim back to the boat and help save the wounded. So they parted, and Henry returned.

By this time the fire was making fierce headway, and several persons who were imprisoned under the ruins were begging piteously for help. All efforts to conquer the fire proved fruitless; so the buckets were presently thrown aside and the officers fell-to with axes and tried to cut the prisoners out. A striker was one of the captives; he said he was not injured, but could not free himself; and when he saw that the fire was likely to drive away the workers, he begged that some one would shoot him, and thus save him from the more dreadful death. The fire did drive the axemen away, and they had to listen, helpless, to this poor fellow's supplications till the flames ended his miseries.

The fire drove all into the wood-flat that could be accommodated there; it was cut adrift, then, and it and the burning steamer floated down the river toward Ship Island. They moored the flat at the head of the island, and there, unsheltered from the blazing sun, the half-naked occupants had to remain, without food or stimulants, or help for their hurts, during the rest of the day. A steamer came along, finally, and carried the unfortunates to Memphis, and there the most lavish assistance was at once forthcoming. By this time Henry was insensible. The physicians examined his injuries and saw that they were fatal, and naturally turned their main attention to patients who could be saved.

Forty of the wounded were placed upon pallets on the floor of a great public hall, and among these was Henry. There the ladies of Memphis came every day, with flowers, fruits, and dainties and delicacies of all kinds, and there they remained and nursed the wounded. All the physicians stood watches there, and all the medical students; and the rest of the town furnished money, or whatever else was wanted. And Memphis knew how to do all these things well; for many a disaster like the "Pennsylvania's" had happened near her doors, and she was experienced, above all other cities on the river, in the gracious office of the Good Samaritan.

The sight I saw when I entered that large hall was new and strange to me. Two long rows of prostrate forms—more than forty, in all—and every face and head a shapeless wad of loose raw cotton. It was a grewsome spectacle. I watched there six days and nights, and a very melancholy experience it was. There was one daily incident which was peculiarly depressing: this was the removal of the doomed to a chamber apart. It was done in order that the *morale* of the other patients might not be injuriously affected by seeing one of their number in the death-agony. The fated one was always carried out with as little stir as possible, and the stretcher was always hidden from sight by a wall of assistants; but no matter: everybody knew what that cluster of bent forms, with its muffled step and its slow movement meant; and all eyes watched it wistfully, and a shudder went abreast of it like a wave.

I saw many poor fellows removed to the "death-room," and saw them no more afterward. But I saw our chief mate carried thither more than once. His hurts were frightful, especially his scalds. He was clothed in linseed oil and raw cotton to his waist, and resembled nothing human. He was often out of his mind; and then his pains would make him rave and shout and sometimes shriek. Then, after a period of dumb exhaustion, his disordered imagination would suddenly transform the great apartment into a forecastle, and the hurrying throng of nurses into the crew; and he would come to a sitting posture and shout, "Hump yourselves, *hump* yourselves, you petrifactions, snail-bellies, pall-bearers! going to be all *day* getting that hatful of freight out?" and supplement this explosion with a firmament-obliterating irruption of profanity which nothing could stay or stop till his crater was empty. And now and then while these frenzies possessed him, he would tear off handfuls of the cotton and expose his cooked flesh to view. It was horrible. It was bad for the others, of course— this noise and these exhibitions; so the doctors tried to give him morphine to quiet him. But, in his mind or out of it, he would not take it. He said his wife had been killed by that treacherous drug, and he would die before he would take it. He suspected that the doctors were concealing it in his ordinary medicines and in his water—so he ceased from putting either to his lips. Once, when he had been without water during two sweltering days, he took the dipper in his hand, and the sight of the limpid fluid, and the misery of his thirst, tempted him almost beyond his strength; but he mastered himself and threw it away, and after that he allowed no more to be brought near him. Three times I saw him carried to the death-room, insensible and supposed to be dying; but each time he revived, cursed his attendants, and demanded to be taken back. He lived to be mate of a steamboat again.

But he was the only one who went to the death-room and returned alive. Dr. Peyton, a principal physician, and rich in all the attributes that go to constitute high and flawless character, did all that educated judgment and trained skill could do for Henry; but, as the newspapers had said in the beginning, his hurts were past help. On the evening of the sixth day his wandering mind busied itself with matters far away, and his nerveless fingers "picked at his coverlet." His hour had struck; we bore him to the death-room, poor boy.

XXI.

A Section in My Biography

IN DUE COURSE I got my license. I was a pilot now, full
fledged. I dropped into casual employments; no misfor-
tunes resulting, intermittent work gave place to steady and
protracted engagements. Time drifted smoothly and prosper-
ously on, and I supposed—and hoped—that I was going to
follow the river the rest of my days, and die at the wheel
when my mission was ended. But by and by the war came,
commerce was suspended, my occupation was gone.

I had to seek another livelihood. So I became a silver miner
in Nevada; next, a newspaper reporter; next, a gold miner, in
California; next, a reporter in San Francisco; next, a special
correspondent in the Sandwich Islands; next, a roving correspondent in Europe and the East; next, an instructional
torch-bearer on the lecture platform; and, finally, I became a
scribbler of books, and an immovable fixture among the other
rocks of New England.

In so few words have I disposed of the twenty-one slow-
drifting years that have come and gone since I last looked
from the windows of a pilot-house.

Let us resume, now.

XXII.

I Return to My Muttons

AFTER TWENTY-ONE years' absence, I felt a very strong desire to see the river again, and the steamboats, and such of the boys as might be left; so I resolved to go out there. I enlisted a poet for company, and a stenographer to "take him down," and started westward about the middle of April.

As I proposed to make notes, with a view to printing, I took some thought as to methods of procedure. I reflected that if I were recognized, on the river, I should not be as free to go and come, talk, inquire, and spy around, as I should be if unknown; I remembered that it was the custom of steamboatmen in the old times to load up the confiding stranger with the most picturesque and admirable lies, and put the sophisticated friend off with dull and ineffectual facts: so I concluded, that, from a business point of view, it would be an advantage to disguise our party with fictitious names. The idea was certainly good, but it bred infinite bother; for although Smith, Jones, and Johnson are easy names to remember when there is no occasion to remember them, it is next to impossible to recollect them when they are wanted. How do criminals manage to keep a brand-new *alias* in mind? This is a great mystery. I was innocent; and yet was seldom able to lay my hand on my new name when it was needed; and it seemed to me that if I had had a crime on my conscience to further confuse me, I could never have kept the name by me at all.

We left per Pennsylvania Railroad, at 8 A.M. April 18.

"*Evening*. Speaking of dress. Grace and picturesqueness drop gradually out of it as one travels away from New York."

I find that among my notes. It makes no difference which direction you take, the fact remains the same. Whether you move north, south, east, or west, no matter: you can get up in the morning and guess how far you have come, by noting what degree of grace and picturesqueness is by that time lacking in the costumes of the new passengers;—I do not mean of the women alone, but of both sexes. It may be that *carriage* is at the bottom of this thing; and I think it is; for there are plenty of ladies and gentlemen in the provincial cities whose garments are all made by the best tailors and dressmakers of New York; yet this has no perceptible effect upon the grand fact: the educated eye never mistakes those people for New-Yorkers. No, there is a godless grace, and snap, and style about a born and bred New-Yorker which mere clothing cannot effect.

"*April* 19. This morning, struck into the region of full goatees—sometimes accompanied by a moustache, but only occasionally."

It was odd to come upon this thick crop of an obsolete and uncomely fashion; it was like running suddenly across a forgotten acquaintance whom you had supposed dead for a generation. The goatee extends over a wide extent of country; and is accompanied by an iron-clad belief in Adam and the biblical history of creation, which has not suffered from the assaults of the scientists.

"*Afternoon.* At the railway stations the loafers carry *both* hands in their breeches pockets; it was observable, heretofore, that one hand was sometimes out of doors,—here, never. This is an important fact in geography."

If the loafers determined the character of a country, it would be still more important, of course.

"Heretofore, all along, the station-loafer has been often observed to scratch one shin with the other foot; here, these remains of activity are wanting. This has an ominous look."

By and by, we entered the tobacco-chewing region. Fifty years ago, the tobacco-chewing region covered the Union. It is greatly restricted now.

Next, boots began to appear. Not in strong force, however. Later—away down the Mississippi—they became the rule. They disappeared from other sections of the Union with the mud; no doubt they will disappear from the river villages, also, when proper pavements come in.

We reached St. Louis at ten o'clock at night. At the counter of the hotel I tendered a hurriedly-invented fictitious name, with a miserable attempt at careless ease. The clerk paused, and inspected me in the compassionate way in which one inspects a respectable person who is found in doubtful circumstances; then he said, —

"It 's all right; I know what sort of a room you want. Used to clerk at the St. James, in New York."

An unpromising beginning for a fraudulent career. We started to the supper room, and met two other men whom I had known elsewhere. How odd and unfair it is: wicked impostors go around lecturing under my *nom de guerre*, and nobody suspects them; but when an honest man attempts an imposture, he is exposed at once.

One thing seemed plain: we must start down the river the next day, if people who could not be deceived were going to crop up at this rate: an unpalatable disappointment, for we had hoped to have a week in St. Louis. The Southern was a good hotel, and we could have had a comfortable time there. It is large, and well conducted, and its decorations do not make one cry, as do those of the vast Palmer House, in Chicago. True, the billiard-tables were of the Old Silurian Period, and the cues and balls of the Post-Pliocene; but there was refreshment in this, not discomfort; for there is rest and healing in the contemplation of antiquities.

The most notable absence observable in the billiard room, was the absence of the river man. If he was there he had taken in his sign, he was in disguise. I saw there none of the swell airs and graces, and ostentatious displays of money, and pompous squanderings of it, which used to distinguish the steamboat crowd from the dry-land crowd in the bygone days, in the thronged billiard-rooms of St. Louis. In those times, the principal saloons were always populous with river men; given fifty players present, thirty or thirty-five were likely to be from the river. But I suspected that the ranks were thin now, and the steamboatmen no longer an aristocracy. Why, in my time they used to call the "barkeep" Bill, or Joe, or Tom, and slap him on the shoulder; I watched for that.

But none of these people did it. Manifestly a glory that once was had dissolved and vanished away in these twenty-one years.

When I went up to my room, I found there the young man called Rogers, crying. Rogers was not his name; neither was Jones, Brown, Dexter, Ferguson, Bascom, nor Thompson; but he answered to either of these that a body found handy in an emergency; or to any other name, in fact, if he perceived that you meant him. He said:—

"What is a person to do here when he wants a drink of water?—drink this slush?"

"Can't you drink it?"

"I could if I had some other water to wash it with."

Here was a thing which had not changed; a score of years had not affected this water's mulatto complexion in the least; a score of centuries would succeed no better, perhaps. It comes out of the turbulent, bank-caving Missouri, and every tumblerful of it holds nearly an acre of land in solution. I got this fact from the bishop of the diocese. If you will let your glass stand half an hour, you can separate the land from the water as easy as Genesis; and then you will find them both good: the one good to eat, the other good to drink. The land is very nourishing, the water is thoroughly wholesome. The one appeases hunger; the other, thirst. But the natives do not take them separately, but together, as nature mixed them. When they find an inch of mud in the bottom of a glass, they stir it up, and then take the draught as they would gruel. It is difficult for a stranger to get used to this batter, but once used to it he will prefer it to water. This is really the case. It is good for steamboating, and good to drink; but it is worthless for all other purposes, except baptizing.

Next morning, we drove around town in the rain. The city seemed but little changed. It *was* greatly changed, but it did not seem so; because in St. Louis, as in London and Pittsburgh, you can't persuade a new thing to look new; the coal smoke turns it into an antiquity the moment you take your hand off it. The place had just about doubled its size, since I was a resident of it, and was now become a city of 400,000 inhabitants; still, in the solid business parts, it looked about as it had looked formerly. Yet I am sure there is not as much smoke in St. Louis now as there used to be. The smoke used to bank itself in a dense billowy black canopy over the town, and hide the sky from view. This shelter is very much thinner now; still, there is a sufficiency of smoke there, I think. I heard no complaint.

However, on the outskirts changes were apparent enough; notably in dwelling-house architecture. The fine new homes are noble and beautiful and modern. They stand by themselves, too, with green lawns around them; whereas the dwellings of a former day are packed together in blocks, and are all of one pattern, with windows all alike, set in an arched frame-work of twisted stone; a sort of house which was handsome enough when it was rarer.

There was another change—the Forest Park. This was new to me. It is beautiful and very extensive, and has the excellent merit of having been made mainly by nature. There are other parks, and fine ones, notably Tower Grove and the Botanical Gardens; for St. Louis interested herself in such improvements at an earlier day than did the most of our cities.

The first time I ever saw St. Louis, I could have bought it for six million dollars, and it was the mistake of my life that I did not do it. It was bitter now to look abroad over this domed and steepled metropolis, this solid expanse of bricks and mortar stretching away on every hand into dim, measure-defying distances, and remember that I had allowed that opportunity to go by. Why I should have allowed it to go by seems, of course, foolish and inexplicable to-day, at a first glance; yet there were reasons at the time to justify this course.

A Scotchman, Hon. Charles Augustus Murray, writing some forty-five or fifty years ago, said: "The streets are narrow, ill paved and ill lighted." Those streets are narrow still, of course; many of them are ill paved yet; but the reproach of ill lighting cannot be repeated, now. The "Catholic New Church" was the only notable building then, and Mr. Murray was confidently called upon to admire it, with its "species of Grecian portico, surmounted by a kind of steeple, much too diminutive in its proportions, and surmounted by sundry ornaments" which the unimaginative Scotchman found himself "quite unable to describe;" and therefore was grateful when a German tourist helped him out with the exclamation: "By—, they look exactly like bed-posts!" St. Louis is well equipped with stately and noble public buildings now, and the little church, which the people used to be so proud of, lost its importance a long time ago. Still, this would not surprise Mr. Murray, if he could come back; for he prophesied the coming greatness of St. Louis with strong confidence.

The further we drove in our inspection-tour, the more sensibly I realized how the city had grown since I had seen it last; changes in detail became steadily more apparent and frequent than at first, too: changes uniformly evidencing progress, energy, prosperity.

But the change of changes was on the "levee." This time, a departure from the rule. Half a dozen sound-asleep steamboats where I used to see a solid mile of wide-awake ones! This was melancholy, this was woful. The absence of the pervading and jocund steamboatman from the billiard-saloon was explained. He was absent because he is no more. His occupation is gone, his power has passed away, he is absorbed into the common herd, he grinds at the mill, a shorn Samson and inconspicuous. Half a dozen lifeless steamboats, a mile of empty wharves, a negro fatigued with whiskey stretched asleep, in a wide and soundless vacancy, where the serried hosts of commerce used to contend![1] Here was desolation, indeed.

> "The old, old sea, as one in tears,
>   Comes murmuring, with foamy lips,
> And knocking at the vacant piers,
>   Calls for his long-lost multitude of ships."

The towboat and the railroad had done their work, and done it well and completely. The mighty bridge, stretching along over our heads, had done its share in the slaughter and spoliation. Remains of former steamboatmen told me, with wan satisfaction, that the bridge does n't pay. Still, it can be no sufficient compensation to a corpse, to know that the dy-

[1] Capt. Marryat, writing forty-five years ago, says: "St. Louis has 20,000 inhabitants. *The river abreast of the town is crowded with steamboats, lying in two or three tiers.*"

namite that laid him out was not of as good quality as it had been supposed to be.

The pavements along the river front were bad; the sidewalks were rather out of repair; there was a rich abundance of mud. All this was familiar and satisfying; but the ancient armies of drays, and struggling throngs of men, and mountains of freight, were gone; and Sabbath reigned in their stead. The immemorial mile of cheap foul doggeries remained, but business was dull with them; the multitudes of poison-swilling Irishmen had departed, and in their places were a few scattering handfuls of ragged negroes, some drinking, some drunk, some nodding, others asleep. St. Louis is a great and prosperous and advancing city; but the river-edge of it seems dead past resurrection.

Mississippi steamboating was born about 1812; at the end of thirty years, it had grown to mighty proportions; and in less than thirty more, it was dead! A strangely short life for so majestic a creature. Of course it is not absolutely dead; neither is a crippled octogenarian who could once jump twenty-two feet on level ground; but as contrasted with what it was in its prime vigor, Mississippi steamboating may be called dead.

It killed the old-fashioned keel-boating, by reducing the freight-trip to New Orleans to less than a week. The railroads have killed the steamboat passenger traffic by doing in two or three days what the steamboats consumed a week in doing; and the towing-fleets have killed the through-freight traffic by dragging six or seven steamer-loads of stuff down the river at a time, at an expense so trivial that steamboat competition was out of the question.

Freight and passenger way-traffic remains to the steamers. This is in the hands—along the two thousand miles of river between St. Paul and New Orleans—of two or three close corporations well fortified with capital; and by able and thoroughly business-like management and system, these make a sufficiency of money out of what is left of the once prodigious steamboating industry. I suppose that St. Louis and New Orleans have not suffered materially by the change, but alas for the wood-yard man!

He used to fringe the river all the way; his close-ranked

merchandise stretched from the one city to the other, along the banks, and he sold uncountable cords of it every year for cash on the nail; but all the scattering boats that are left burn coal now, and the seldomest spectacle on the Mississippi to-day is a wood-pile. Where now is the once wood-yard man?

XXIII.

Travelling Incognito

MY IDEA was, to tarry a while in every town between St. Louis and New Orleans. To do this, it would be necessary to go from place to place by the short packet lines. It was an easy plan to make, and would have been an easy one to follow, twenty years ago—but not now. There are wide intervals between boats, these days.

I wanted to begin with the interesting old French settlements of St. Genevieve and Kaskaskia, sixty miles below St. Louis. There was only one boat advertised for that section— a Grand Tower packet. Still, one boat was enough; so we went down to look at her. She was a venerable rackheap, and a fraud to boot; for she was playing herself for personal property, whereas the good honest dirt was so thickly caked all over her that she was righteously taxable as real estate. There are places in New England where her hurricane deck would be worth a hundred and fifty dollars an acre. The soil on her forecastle was quite good—the new crop of wheat was already springing from the cracks in protected places. The companionway was of a dry sandy character, and would have been well suited for grapes, with a southern exposure and a little subsoiling. The soil of the boiler deck was thin and rocky, but good enough for grazing purposes. A colored boy was on watch here—nobody else visible. We gathered from him that this calm craft would go, as advertised, "if she got her trip;" if she did n't get it, she would wait for it.

"Has she got any of her trip?"

"Bless you, no, boss. She ain't unloadened, yit. She only come in dis mawnin'."

He was uncertain as to when she might get her trip, but thought it might be to-morrow or maybe next day. This would not answer at all; so we had to give up the novelty of sailing down the river on a farm. We had one more arrow in our quiver: a Vicksburg packet, the "Gold Dust," was to leave at 5 P.M. We took passage in her for Memphis, and gave up the idea of stopping off here and there, as being impracticable. She was neat, clean, and comfortable. We camped on the boiler deck, and bought some cheap literature to kill time with. The vender was a venerable Irishman with a benevolent face and a tongue that worked easily in the socket, and from him we learned that he had lived in St. Louis thirty-four years and had never been across the river during that period. Then he wandered into a very flowing lecture, filled with classic names and allusions, which was quite wonderful for fluency until the fact became rather apparent that this was not the first time, nor perhaps the fiftieth, that the speech had been delivered. He was a good deal of a character, and much better company than the sappy literature he was selling. A random remark, connecting Irishmen and beer, brought this nugget of information out of him:—

"They don't drink it, sir. They *can't* drink it, sir. Give an Irishman lager for a month, and he 's a dead man. An Irishman is lined with copper, and the beer corrodes it. But whiskey polishes the copper and is the saving of him, sir."

At eight o'clock, promptly, we backed out and—crossed the river. As we crept toward the shore, in the thick darkness, a blinding glory of white electric light burst suddenly from our forecastle, and lit up the water and the warehouses as with a noon-day glare. Another big change, this,—no more flickering, smoky, pitch-dripping, ineffectual torch-baskets, now: their day is past. Next, instead of calling out a score of hands to man the stage, a couple of men and a hatful of steam lowered it from the derrick where it was suspended, launched it, deposited it in just the right spot, and the whole thing was over and done-with before a mate in the olden time could have got his profanity-mill adjusted to begin the preparatory services. Why this new and simple method of handling the stages was not thought of when the first steamboat was built, is a mystery which helps one to realize what a dull-witted slug the average human being is.

We finally got away at two in the morning, and when I turned out at six, we were rounding to at a rocky point where there was an old stone warehouse—at any rate, the ruins of it; two or three decayed dwelling-houses were near by, in the shelter of the leafy hills; but there were no evidences of human or other animal life to be seen. I wondered if I had forgotten the river; for I had no recollection whatever of this place; the shape of the river, too, was unfamiliar; there was nothing in sight, anywhere, that I could remember ever having seen before. I was surprised, disappointed, and annoyed.

We put ashore a well-dressed lady and gentleman, and two well-dressed, lady-like young girls, together with sundry Russia-leather bags. A strange place for such folk! No carriage was waiting. The party moved off as if they had not expected any, and struck down a winding country road afoot.

But the mystery was explained when we got under way again; for these people were evidently bound for a large town which lay shut in behind a tow-head (*i.e.*, new island) a couple of miles below this landing. I could n't remember that town; I could n't place it, could n't call its name. So I lost part of my temper. I suspected that it might be St. Genevieve—and so it proved to be. Observe what this eccentric river had been about: it had built up this huge useless towhead directly in front of this town, cut off its river communications, fenced it away completely, and made a "country" town of it. It is a fine old place, too, and deserved a better fate. It was settled by the French, and is a relic of a time when one could travel from the mouths of the Mississippi to Quebec and be on French territory and under French rule all the way.

Presently I ascended to the hurricane deck and cast a longing glance toward the pilot-house.

XXIV.

My Incognito Is Exploded

AFTER A CLOSE STUDY of the face of the pilot on watch, I
was satisfied that I had never seen him before; so I went
up there. The pilot inspected me; I re-inspected the pilot.
These customary preliminaries over, I sat down on the high
bench, and he faced about and went on with his work. Every
detail of the pilot-house was familiar to me, with one exception,—a large-mouthed tube under the breast-board. I puzzled over that thing a considerable time; then gave up and
asked what it was for.

"To hear the engine-bells through."

It was another good contrivance which ought to have been
invented half a century sooner. So I was thinking, when the
pilot asked,—

"Do you know what this rope is for?"

I managed to get around this question, without committing myself.

"Is this the first time you were ever in a pilot-house?"

I crept under that one.

"Where are you from?"

"New England."

"First time you have ever been West?"

I climbed over this one.

"If you take an interest in such things, I can tell you what
all these things are for."

I said I should like it.

"This," putting his hand on a backing-bell rope, "is to
sound the fire-alarm; this," putting his hand on a go-a-head
bell, "is to call the texas-tender; this one," indicating the
whistle-lever, "is to call the captain"—and so he went on,
touching one object after another, and reeling off his tranquil
spool of lies.

I had never felt so like a passenger before. I thanked him,
with emotion, for each new fact, and wrote it down in my
note-book. The pilot warmed to his opportunity, and proceeded to load me up in the good old-fashioned way. At

times I was afraid he was going to rupture his invention; but it always stood the strain, and he pulled through all right. He drifted, by easy stages, into revealments of the river's marvellous eccentricities of one sort and another, and backed them up with some pretty gigantic illustrations. For instance,—

"Do you see that little bowlder sticking out of the water yonder? well, when I first came on the river, that was a solid ridge of rock, over sixty feet high and two miles long. All washed away but that." [This with a sigh.]

I had a mighty impulse to destroy him, but it seemed to me that killing, in any ordinary way, would be too good for him.

Once, when an odd-looking craft, with a vast coal-scuttle slanting aloft on the end of a beam, was steaming by in the distance, he indifferently drew attention to it, as one might to an object grown wearisome through familiarity, and observed that it was an "alligator boat."

"An alligator boat? What 's it for?"

"To dredge out alligators with."

"Are they so thick as to be troublesome?"

"Well, not now, because the government keeps them down. But they used to be. Not everywhere; but in favorite places, here and there, where the river is wide and shoal—like Plum Point, and Stack Island, and so on—places they call alligator beds."

"Did they actually impede navigation?"

"Years ago, yes, in very low water; there was hardly a trip, then, that we did n't get aground on alligators."

It seemed to me that I should certainly have to get out my tomahawk. However, I restrained myself and said,—

"It must have been dreadful."

"Yes, it was one of the main difficulties about piloting. It was so hard to tell anything about the water; the damned things shift around so—never lie still five minutes at a time. You can tell a wind-reef, straight off, by the look of it; you can tell a break; you can tell a sand-reef—that 's all easy; but an alligator reef does n't show up, worth anything. Nine times in ten you can't tell where the water is; and when you *do* see where it is, like as not it ain't there when *you* get there, the devils have swapped around so, meantime. Of course there were some few pilots that could judge of alligator water nearly as well as they could of any other kind, but they had to have natural talent for it; it was n't a thing a body could *learn*, you had to be born with it. Let me see: there was Ben Thornburg, and Beck Jolly, and Squire Bell, and Horace Bixby, and Major Downing, and John Stevenson, and Billy Gordon, and Jim Brady, and George Ealer, and Billy Young-blood—all A 1 alligator pilots. *They* could tell alligator water as far as another Christian could tell whiskey. Read it?—Ah, *could n't* they, though! I only wish I had as many dollars as they could read alligator water a mile and a half off. Yes, and it paid them to do it, too. A good alligator pilot could always get fifteen hundred dollars a month. Nights, other people had to lay up for alligators, but those fellows never laid up for alligators; they never laid up for anything but fog. They could *smell* the best alligator water—so it was said; I don't know whether it was so or not, and I think a body 's got his hands full enough if he sticks to just what he knows himself, without going around backing up other people's say-so's, though there 's a plenty that ain't backward about doing it, as long as they can roust out something wonderful to tell. Which is not the style of Robert Styles, by as much as three fathom—maybe quarter-*less*."

[My! Was this Rob Styles?—This moustached and stately figure?—A slim enough cub, in my time. How he has improved in comeliness in five and twenty years—and in the noble art of inflating his facts.] After these musings, I said aloud,—

"I should think that dredging out the alligators would n't have done much good, because they could come back again right away."

"If you had had as much experience of alligators as I have, you would n't talk like that. You dredge an alligator once and he 's *convinced*. It 's the last you hear of *him*. He would n't come back for pie. If there 's one thing that an alligator is more down on than another, it 's being dredged. Besides, they were not simply shoved out of the way; the most of the scoopful were scooped aboard; they emptied them into the hold; and when they had got a trip, they took them to Orleans to the Government works."

"What for?"

"Why, to make soldier-shoes out of their hides. All the Government shoes are made of alligator hide. It makes the best shoes in the world. They last five years, and they won't absorb water. The alligator fishery is a Government monopoly. All the alligators are Government property—just like the live-oaks. You cut down a live-oak, and Government fines you fifty dollars; you kill an alligator, and up you go for misprision of treason—lucky duck if they don't hang you, too. And they will, if you 're a Democrat. The buzzard is the sacred bird of the South, and you can't touch him; the alligator is the sacred bird of the Government, and you 've got to let him alone."

"Do you ever get aground on the alligators now?"

"Oh, no! it has n't happened for years."

"Well, then, why do they still keep the alligator boats in service?"

"Just for police duty—nothing more. They merely go up and down now and then. The present generation of alligators know them as easy as a burglar knows a roundsman; when they see one coming, they break camp and go for the woods."

After rounding-out and finishing-up and polishing-off the alligator business, he dropped easily and comfortably into the historical vein, and told of some tremendous feats of half a dozen old-time steamboats of his acquaintance, dwelling at special length upon a certain extraordinary performance of his chief favorite among this distinguished fleet—and then adding:—

"That boat was the 'Cyclone,'—last trip she ever made— she sunk, that very trip—captain was Tom Ballou, the most immortal liar that ever I struck. He could n't ever seem to tell the truth, in *any* kind of weather. Why, he would make you fairly shudder. He *was* the most scandalous liar! I left him, finally; I could n't stand it. The proverb says, 'like master, like man;' and if you stay with that kind of a man, you 'll come under suspicion by and by, just as sure as you live. He paid first-class wages; but said I, What 's wages when your reputation 's in danger? So I let the wages go, and froze to my reputation. And I 've never regretted it. Reputation 's worth everything, ain't it? That 's the way I look at it. He had more

selfish organs than any seven men in the world—all packed
in the stern-sheets of his skull, of course, where they belonged. They weighed down the back of his head so that it
made his nose tilt up in the air. People thought it was vanity,
but it was n't, it was malice. If you only saw his foot, you 'd
take him to be nineteen feet high, but he was n't; it was because his foot was out of drawing. He was intended to be
nineteen feet high, no doubt, if his foot was made first, but
he did n't get there; he was only five feet ten. That 's what he
was, and that 's what he is. You take the lies out of him, and
he 'll shrink to the size of your hat; you take the malice out
of him, and he 'll disappear. That 'Cyclone' was a rattler to
go, and the sweetest thing to steer that ever walked the waters. Set her amidships, in a big river, and just let her go; it
was all you had to do. She would hold herself on a star all
night, if you let her alone. You could n't ever feel her rudder.
It was n't any more labor to steer her than it is to count the
Republican vote in a South Carolina election. One morning,
just at daybreak, the last trip she ever made, they took her
rudder aboard to mend it; I did n't know anything about it;
I backed her out from the wood-yard and went a-weaving
down the river all serene. When I had gone about twenty-
three miles, and made four horribly crooked crossings—"

"Without any rudder?"

"Yes—old Capt. Tom appeared on the roof and began to
find fault with me for running such a dark night—"

"Such a *dark night*?—Why, you said—"

"Never mind what I said,—'t was as dark as Egypt *now*,
though pretty soon the moon began to rise, and—"

"You mean the *sun*—because you started out just at break
of—look here! Was this *before* you quitted the captain on
account of his lying, or—"

"It was before—oh, a long time before. And as I was saying, he—"

"But was this the trip she sunk, or was—"

"Oh, no!—months afterward. And so the old man, he—"

"Then she made *two* last trips, because you said—"

He stepped back from the wheel, swabbing away his perspiration, and said—

"Here!" (calling me by name), "*you* take her and lie a

while—you 're handier at it than I am. Trying to play your-self for a stranger and an innocent!—why, I knew you before you had spoken seven words; and I made up my mind to find out what was your little game. It was to *draw me out*. Well, I let you, did n't I? Now take the wheel and finish the watch; and next time play fair, and you won't have to work your passage."

Thus ended the fictitious-name business. And not six hours out from St. Louis! but I had gained a privilege, anyway, for I had been itching to get my hands on the wheel, from the beginning. I seemed to have forgotten the river, but I had n't forgotten how to steer a steamboat, nor how to enjoy it, either.

XXV.

From Cairo to Hickman

THE SCENERY, from St. Louis to Cairo—two hundred miles—is varied and beautiful. The hills were clothed in the fresh foliage of spring now, and were a gracious and worthy setting for the broad river flowing between. Our trip began auspiciously, with a perfect day, as to breeze and sunshine, and our boat threw the miles out behind her with satisfactory despatch.

We found a railway intruding at Chester, Illinois; Chester has also a penitentiary now, and is otherwise marching on. At Grand Tower, too, there was a railway; and another at Cape Girardeau. The former town gets its name from a huge, squat pillar of rock, which stands up out of the water on the Missouri side of the river—a piece of nature's fanciful handiwork—and is one of the most picturesque features of the scenery of that region. For nearer or remoter neighbors, the Tower has the Devil's Bake Oven—so called, perhaps, because it does not powerfully resemble anybody else's bake oven; and the Devil's Tea Table—this latter a great smooth-surfaced mass of rock, with diminishing wine-glass stem, perched some fifty or sixty feet above the river, beside a be-flowered and garlanded precipice, and sufficiently like a tea-table to answer for anybody, Devil or Christian. Away down the river we have the Devil's Elbow and the Devil's Race-course, and lots of other property of his which I cannot now call to mind.

The town of Grand Tower was evidently a busier place than it had been in old times, but it seemed to need some repairs here and there, and a new coat of whitewash all over. Still, it was pleasant to me to see the old coat once more. "Uncle" Mumford, our second officer, said the place had been suffering from high water and consequently was not looking its best now. But he said it was not strange that it did n't waste whitewash on itself, for more lime was made there, and of a better quality, than anywhere in the West; and added,—"On a dairy farm you never can get any milk for your coffee, nor any sugar for it on a sugar plantation; and it is against sense to go to a lime town to hunt for whitewash." In my own experience I knew the first two items to be true; and also that people who sell candy don't care for candy; therefore there was plausibility in Uncle Mumford's final observation that "people who make lime run more to religion than white-wash." Uncle Mumford said, further, that Grand Tower was a great coaling centre and a prospering place.

Cape Girardeau is situated on a hillside, and makes a hand-some appearance. There is a great Jesuit school for boys at the foot of the town by the river. Uncle Mumford said it had as high a reputation for thoroughness as any similar institu-tion in Missouri. There was another college higher up on an airy summit,—a bright new edifice, picturesquely and pecu-liarly towered and pinnacled—a sort of gigantic casters, with the cruets all complete. Uncle Mumford said that Cape Gir-ardeau was the Athens of Missouri, and contained several col-leges besides those already mentioned; and all of them on a religious basis of one kind or another. He directed my atten-tion to what he called the "strong and pervasive religious look of the town," but I could not see that it looked more religious than the other hill towns with the same slope and built of the same kind of bricks. Partialities often make people see more than really exists.

Uncle Mumford has been thirty years a mate on the river. He is a man of practical sense and a level head; has observed; has had much experience of one sort and another; has opin-ions; has, also, just a perceptible dash of poetry in his com-position, an easy gift of speech, a thick growl in his voice, and an oath or two where he can get at them when the exi-gencies of his office require a spiritual lift. He is a mate of the blessed old-time kind; and goes gravely damning around, when there is work to the fore, in a way to mellow the ex-steamboatman's heart with sweet soft longings for the van-ished days that shall come no more. "*Git* up, there,—— — you! Going to be all day? Why d'n't you *say* you was petrified in your hind legs, before you shipped!"

He is a steady man with his crew; kind and just, but firm; so they like him, and stay with him. He is still in the slouchy garb of the old generation of mates; but next trip the Anchor

Line will have him in uniform—a natty blue naval uniform, with brass buttons, along with all the officers of the line— and then he will be a totally different style of scenery from what he is now.

Uniforms on the Mississippi! It beats all the other changes put together, for surprise. Still, there is another surprise— that it was not made fifty years ago. It is so manifestly sensible, that it might have been thought of earlier, one would suppose. During fifty years, out there, the innocent passenger in need of help and information, has been mistaking the mate for the cook, and the captain for the barber—and being roughly entertained for it, too. But his troubles are ended now. And the greatly improved aspect of the boat's staff is another advantage achieved by the dress-reform period.

Steered down the bend below Cape Girardeau. They used to call it "Steersman's Bend;" plain sailing and plenty of water in it, always; about the only place in the Upper River that a new cub was allowed to take a boat through, in low water.

Thebes, at the head of the Grand Chain, and Commerce at the foot of it, were towns easily rememberable, as they had not undergone conspicuous alteration. Nor the Chain, either—in the nature of things; for it is a chain of sunken rocks admirably arranged to capture and kill steamboats on bad nights. A good many steamboat corpses lie buried there, out of sight; among the rest my first friend the "Paul Jones;" she knocked her bottom out, and went down like a pot, so the historian told me—Uncle Mumford. He said she had a gray mare aboard, and a preacher. To me, this sufficiently accounted for the disaster; as it did, of course, to Mumford, who added,—

"But there are many ignorant people who would scoff at such a matter, and call it superstition. But you will always notice that they are people who have never travelled with a gray mare and a preacher. I went down the river once in such company. We grounded at Bloody Island; we grounded at Hanging Dog; we grounded just below this same Commerce; we jolted Beaver Dam Rock; we hit one of the worst breaks in the 'Graveyard' behind Goose Island; we had a roustabout killed in a fight; we burnt a boiler; broke a shaft; collapsed a flue; and went into Cairo with nine feet of water in the hold—may have been more, may have been less. I remember it as if it were yesterday. The men lost their heads with terror. They painted the mare blue, in sight of town, and threw the preacher overboard, or we should not have arrived at all. The preacher was fished out and saved. He acknowledged, himself, that he had been to blame. I remember it all, as if it were yesterday."

That this combination—of preacher and gray mare—should breed calamity, seems strange, and at first glance unbelievable; but the fact is fortified by so much unassailable proof that to doubt is to dishonor reason. I myself remember a case where a captain was warned by numerous friends against taking a gray mare and a preacher with him, but persisted in his purpose in spite of all that could be said; and the same day,—it may have been the next, and some say it was, though I think it was the same day,—he got drunk and fell down the hatchway and was borne to his home a corpse. This is literally true.

No vestige of Hat Island is left now; every shred of it is washed away. I do not even remember what part of the river it used to be in, except that it was between St. Louis and Cairo somewhere. It was a bad region—all around and about Hat Island, in early days. A farmer who lived on the Illinois shore there, said that twenty-nine steamboats had left their bones strung along within sight from his house. Between St. Louis and Cairo the steamboat wrecks average one to the mile;—two hundred wrecks, altogether.

I could recognize big changes from Commerce down. Beaver Dam Rock was out in the middle of the river now, and throwing a prodigious "break;" it used to be close to the shore, and boats went down outside of it. A big island that used to be away out in mid-river, has retired to the Missouri shore, and boats do not go near it any more. The island called Jacket Pattern is whittled down to a wedge now, and is booked for early destruction. Goose Island is all gone but a little dab the size of a steamboat. The perilous "Graveyard," among whose numberless wrecks we used to pick our way so slowly and gingerly, is far away from the channel now, and a terror to nobody. One of the islands formerly called the Two Sisters is gone entirely; the other, which used to lie close to the Illinois shore, is now on the Missouri side, a mile away; it is joined solidly to the shore, and it takes a sharp eye to see where the seam is—but it is Illinois ground yet, and the people who live on it have to ferry themselves over and work the Illinois roads and pay Illinois taxes: singular state of things!

Near the mouth of the river several islands were missing—washed away. Cairo was still there—easily visible across the long, flat point upon whose further verge it stands; but we had to steam a long way around to get to it. Night fell as we were going out of the "Upper River" and meeting the floods of the Ohio. We dashed along without anxiety; for the hidden rock which used to lie right in the way has moved up stream a long distance out of the channel; or rather, about one county has gone into the river from the Missouri point, and the Cairo point has "made down" and added to its long tongue of territory correspondingly. The Mississippi is a just and equitable river; it never tumbles one man's farm overboard without building a new farm just like it for that man's neighbor. This keeps down hard feelings.

Going into Cairo, we came near killing a steamboat which paid no attention to our whistle and then tried to cross our bows. By doing some strong backing, we saved him; which was a great loss, for he would have made good literature.

Cairo is a brisk town now; and is substantially built, and has a city look about it which is in noticeable contrast to its former estate, as per Mr. Dickens's portrait of it. However, it was already building with bricks when I had seen it last—which was when Colonel (now General) Grant was drilling his first command there. Uncle Mumford says the libraries and Sunday-schools have done a good work in Cairo, as well as the brick masons. Cairo has a heavy railroad and river trade, and her situation at the junction of the two great rivers is so advantageous that she cannot well help prospering.

When I turned out, in the morning, we had passed Columbus, Kentucky, and were approaching Hickman, a pretty town, perched on a handsome hill. Hickman is in a rich tobacco region, and formerly enjoyed a great and lucrative trade in that staple, collecting it there in her warehouses from a large area of country and shipping it by boat; but Uncle Mumford says she built a railway to facilitate this commerce a little more, and he thinks it facilitated it the wrong way—took the bulk of the trade out of her hands by "collaring it along the line without gathering it at her doors."

XXVI.

Under Fire

TALK BEGAN to run upon the war now, for we were getting down into the upper edge of the former battle-stretch by this time. Columbus was just behind us, so there was a good deal said about the famous battle of Belmont. Several of the boat's officers had seen active service in the Mississippi war-fleet. I gathered that they found themselves sadly out of their element in that kind of business at first, but afterward got accustomed to it, reconciled to it, and more or less at home in it. One of our pilots had his first war experience in the Belmont fight, as a pilot on a boat in the Confederate service. I had often had a curiosity to know how a green hand might feel, in his maiden battle, perched all solitary and alone on high in a pilot house, a target for Tom, Dick and Harry, and nobody at his elbow to shame him from showing the white feather when matters grew hot and perilous around him; so, to me his story was valuable—it filled a gap for me which all histories had left till that time empty.

THE PILOT'S FIRST BATTLE

He said:—

It was the 7th of November. The fight began at seven in the morning. I was on the "R. H. W. Hill." Took over a load of troops from Columbus. Came back, and took over a battery of artillery. My partner said he was going to see the fight; wanted me to go along. I said, no, I was n't anxious, I would look at it from the pilot-house. He said I was a coward, and left.

That fight was an awful sight. General Cheatham made his men strip their coats off and throw them in a pile, and said, "Now follow me to hell or victory!" I heard him say that from the pilot-house; and then he galloped in, at the head of his troops. Old General Pillow, with his white hair, mounted on a white horse, sailed in, too, leading his troops as lively as a boy. By and by the Federals chased the rebels back, and here they came! tearing along, everybody for himself and Devil take the hindmost! and down under the bank they scrambled, and took shelter. I was sitting with my legs hanging out of the pilot-house window. All at once I noticed a whizzing sound passing my ear. Judged it was a bullet. I did n't stop to think about anything, I just tilted over backwards and landed on the floor, and staid there. The balls came booming around. Three cannon-balls went through the chimney; one ball took off the corner of the pilot-house; shells were screaming and bursting all around. Mighty warm times—I wished I had n't come. I lay there on the pilot-house floor, while the shots came faster and faster. I crept in behind the big stove, in the middle of the pilot-house. Presently a minie-ball came through the stove, and just grazed my head, and cut my hat. I judged it was time to go away from there. The captain was on the roof with a red-headed major from Memphis—a fine-looking man. I heard him say he wanted to leave here, but "that pilot is killed." I crept over to the starboard side to pull the bell to set her back; raised up and took a look, and I saw about fifteen shot holes through the window panes; had come so lively I had n't noticed them. I glanced out on the water, and the spattering shot were like a hail-storm. I thought best to get out of that place. I went down the pilot-house guy, head first—not feet first but head first—slid down—before I struck the deck, the captain said we must leave there. So I climbed up the guy and got on the floor again. About that time, they collared my partner and were bringing him up to the pilot-house between two soldiers. Somebody had said I was killed. He put his head in and saw me on the floor reaching for the backing bells. He said, "Oh, hell, he ain't shot," and jerked away from the men who had him by the collar, and ran below. We were there until three o'clock in the afternoon, and then got away all right.

The next time I saw my partner, I said, "Now, come out, be honest, and tell me the truth. Where did you go when you went to see that battle?" He says, "I went down in the hold."

All through that fight I was scared nearly to death. I hardly knew anything, I was so frightened; but you see, nobody knew that but me. Next day General Polk sent for me, and praised me for my bravery and gallant conduct.

I never said anything, I let it go at that. I judged it was n't so, but it was not for me to contradict a general officer.

Pretty soon after that I was sick, and used up, and had to go off to the Hot Springs. When there, I got a good many letters from commanders saying they wanted me to come back. I declined, because I was n't well enough or strong enough; but I kept still, and kept the reputation I had made.

A plain story, straightforwardly told; but Mumford told me that that pilot had "gilded that scare of his, in spots;" that his subsequent career in the war was proof of it.

We struck down through the chute of Island No. 8, and I went below and fell into conversation with a passenger, a handsome man, with easy carriage and an intelligent face. We were approaching Island No. 10, a place so celebrated during the war. This gentleman's home was on the main shore in its neighborhood. I had some talk with him about the war times; but presently the discourse fell upon "feuds," for in no part of the South has the vendetta flourished more briskly, or held out longer between warring families, than in this particular region. This gentleman said: —

"There 's been more than one feud around here, in old times, but I reckon the worst one was between the Darnells and the Watsons. Nobody don't know now what the first quarrel was about, it 's so long ago; the Darnells and the Watsons don't know, if there 's any of them living, which I don't think there is. Some says it was about a horse or a cow—anyway, it was a little matter; the money in it was n't of no consequence—none in the world—both families was rich. The thing could have been fixed up, easy enough; but no, that would n't do. Rough words had been passed; and so, nothing but blood could fix it up after that. That horse or cow, whichever it was, cost sixty years of killing and crippling! Every year or so somebody was shot, on one side or the other; and as fast as one generation was laid out, their sons took up the feud and kept it a-going. And it 's just as I say; they went on shooting each other, year in and year out—

making a kind of a religion of it, you see—till they 'd done forgot, long ago, what it was all about. Wherever a Darnell caught a Watson, or a Watson caught a Darnell, one of 'em was going to get hurt—only question was, which of them got the drop on the other. They 'd shoot one another down, right in the presence of the family. They did n't *hunt* for each other, but when they happened to meet, they pulled and begun. Men would shoot boys, boys would shoot men. A man shot a boy twelve years old—happened on him in the woods, and did n't give him no chance. If he *had* 'a' given him a chance, the boy 'd 'a' shot *him*. Both families belonged to the same church (everybody around here is religious); through all this fifty or sixty years' fuss, both tribes was there every Sunday, to worship. They lived each side of the line, and the church was at a landing called Compromise. Half the church and half the aisle was in Kentucky, the other half in Tennessee. Sundays you 'd see the families drive up, all in their Sunday clothes, men, women, and children, and file up the aisle, and set down, quiet and orderly, one lot on the Tennessee side of the church and the other on the Kentucky side; and the men and boys would lean their guns up against the wall, handy, and then all hands would join in with the prayer and praise; though they say the man next the aisle did n't kneel down, along with the rest of the family; kind of stood guard. I don't know; never was at that church in my life; but I remember that that 's what used to be said.

"Twenty or twenty-five years ago, one of the feud families caught a young man of nineteen out and killed him. Don't remember whether it was the Darnells and Watsons, or one of the other feuds; but anyway, this young man rode up—steamboat laying there at the time—and the first thing he saw was a whole gang of the enemy. He jumped down behind a wood-pile, but they rode around and begun on him, he firing back, and they galloping and cavorting and yelling and banging away with all their might. Think he wounded a couple of them; but they closed in on him and chased him into the river; and as he swum along down stream, they followed along the bank and kept on shooting at him; and when he struck shore he was dead. Windy Marshall told me about it. He saw it. He was captain of the boat.

"Years ago, the Darnells was so thinned out that the old man and his two sons concluded they 'd leave the country. They started to take steamboat just above No. 10; but the Watsons got wind of it; and they arrived just as the two young Darnells was walking up the companion-way with their wives on their arms. The fight begun then, and they never got no further—both of them killed. After that, old Darnell got into trouble with the man that run the ferry, and the ferry-man got the worst of it—and died. But his friends shot old Darnell through and through—filled him full of bullets, and ended him."

The country gentleman who told me these things had been reared in ease and comfort, was a man of good parts, and was college bred. His loose grammar was the fruit of careless habit, not ignorance. This habit among educated men in the West is not universal, but it is prevalent—prevalent in the towns, certainly, if not in the cities; and to a degree which one cannot help noticing, and marvelling at. I heard a Westerner who would be accounted a highly educated man in any country, say "never mind, it *don't make no difference*, anyway." A life-long resident who was present heard it, but it made no impression upon her. She was able to recall the fact afterward, when reminded of it; but she confessed that the words had not grated upon her ear at the time—a confession which suggests that if educated people can hear such blasphemous grammar, from such a source, and be unconscious of the deed, the crime must be tolerably common—so common that the general ear has become dulled by familiarity with it, and is no longer alert, no longer sensitive to such affronts.

No one in the world speaks blemishless grammar; no one has ever written it—*no* one, either in the world or out of it (taking the Scriptures for evidence on the latter point); therefore it would not be fair to exact grammatical perfection from the peoples of the Valley; but they and all other peoples may justly be required to refrain from *knowingly* and *purposely* debauching their grammar.

I found the river greatly changed at Island No. 10. The island which I remembered was some three miles long and a quarter of a mile wide, heavily timbered, and lay near the

Kentucky shore—within two hundred yards of it, I should say. Now, however, one had to hunt for it with a spy-glass. Nothing was left of it but an insignificant little tuft, and this was no longer near the Kentucky shore; it was clear over against the opposite shore, a mile away. In war times the island had been an important place, for it commanded the situation; and, being heavily fortified, there was no getting by it. It lay between the upper and lower divisions of the Union forces, and kept them separate, until a junction was finally effected across the Missouri neck of land; but the island being itself joined to that neck now, the wide river is without obstruction.

In this region the river passes from Kentucky into Tennessee, back into Missouri, then back into Kentucky, and thence into Tennessee again. So a mile or two of Missouri sticks over into Tennessee.

The town of New Madrid was looking very unwell; but otherwise unchanged from its former condition and aspect. Its blocks of frame-houses were still grouped in the same old flat plain, and environed by the same old forests. It was as tranquil as formerly, and apparently had neither grown nor diminished in size. It was said that the recent high water had invaded it and damaged its looks. This was surprising news; for in low water the river bank is very high there (fifty feet), and in my day an overflow had always been considered an impossibility. This present flood of 1882 will doubtless be celebrated in the river's history for several generations before a deluge of like magnitude shall be seen. It put all the unprotected low lands under water, from Cairo to the mouth; it broke down the levees in a great many places, on both sides of the river; and in some regions south, when the flood was at its highest, the Mississippi was *seventy miles* wide! A number of lives were lost, and the destruction of property was fearful. The crops were destroyed, houses washed away, and shelterless men and cattle forced to take refuge on scattering elevations here and there in field and forest, and wait in peril and suffering until the boats put in commission by the national and local governments and by newspaper enterprise could come and rescue them. The properties of multitudes of people were under water for months, and the poorer ones must have starved by the hundred if succor had not been promptly afforded.[1] The water had been falling during a considerable time now, yet as a rule we found the banks still under water.

[1]For a detailed and interesting description of the great flood, written on board of the New Orleans "Times-Democrat's" relief-boat, see Appendix A.

XXVII.

Some Imported Articles

WE MET TWO STEAMBOATS at New Madrid. Two steamboats in sight at once! an infrequent spectacle now in
the lonesome Mississippi. The loneliness of this solemn, stupendous flood is impressive—and depressing. League after
league, and still league after league, it pours its chocolate tide
along, between its solid forest walls, its almost untenanted
shores, with seldom a sail or a moving object of any kind to
disturb the surface and break the monotony of the blank, watery solitude; and so the day goes, the night comes, and again
the day—and still the same, night after night and day after
day,—majestic, unchanging sameness of serenity, repose,
tranquillity, lethargy, vacancy,—symbol of eternity, realization of the heaven pictured by priest and prophet, and longed
for by the good and thoughtless!

Immediately after the war of 1812, tourists began to come
to America, from England; scattering ones at first, then a sort
of procession of them—a procession which kept up its plodding, patient march through the land during many, many
years. Each tourist took notes, and went home and published
a book—a book which was usually calm, truthful, reasonable,
kind; but which seemed just the reverse to our tender-footed
progenitors. A glance at these tourist-books shows us that in
certain of its aspects the Mississippi has undergone no change
since those strangers visited it, but remains to-day about as it
was then. The emotions produced in those foreign breasts by
these aspects were not all formed on one pattern, of course;
they *had* to be various, along at first, because the earlier tourists were obliged to originate their emotions, whereas in older
countries one can always borrow emotions from one's prede-
cessors. And, mind you, emotions are among the toughest
things in the world to manufacture out of whole cloth; it is
easier to manufacture seven facts than one emotion. Captain
Basil Hall, R. N., writing fifty-five years ago, says:—

"Here I caught the first glimpse of the object I had so

long wished to behold, and felt myself amply repaid at that moment for all the trouble I had experienced in coming so far; and stood looking at the river flowing past till it was too dark to distinguish anything. But it was not till I had visited the same spot a dozen times, that I came to a right comprehension of the grandeur of the scene."

Following are Mrs. Trollope's emotions. She is writing a few months later in the same year, 1827, and is coming in at the mouth of the Mississippi: —

"The first indication of our approach to land was the appearance of this mighty river pouring forth its muddy mass of waters, and mingling with the deep blue of the Mexican Gulf. I never beheld a scene so utterly desolate as this entrance of the Mississippi. Had Dante seen it, he might have drawn images of another Bolgia from its horrors. One only object rears itself above the eddying waters; this is the mast of a vessel long since wrecked in attempting to cross the bar, and it still stands, a dismal witness of the destruction that has been, and a boding prophet of that which is to come."

Emotions of Hon. Charles Augustus Murray (near St. Louis), seven years later: —

"It is only when you ascend the mighty current for fifty or a hundred miles, and use the eye of imagination as well as that of nature, that you begin to understand all his might and majesty. You see him fertilizing a boundless valley, bearing along in his course the trophies of his thousand victories over the shattered forest—here carrying away large masses of soil with all their growth, and there forming islands, destined at some future period to be the residence of man; and while indulging in this prospect, it is then time for reflection to suggest that the current before you has flowed through two or three thousand miles, and has yet to travel one thousand three hundred more before reaching its ocean destination."

Receive, now, the emotions of Captain Marryat, R. N., author of the sea tales, writing in 1837, three years after Mr. Murray: —

"Never, perhaps, in the records of nations, was there an instance of a century of such unvarying and unmitigated crime as is to be collected from the history of the turbulent and blood-stained Mississippi. The stream itself appears as if appropriate for the deeds which have been committed. It is not like most rivers, beautiful to the sight, bestowing fertility in its course; not one that the eye loves to dwell upon as it sweeps along, nor can you wander upon its bank, or trust yourself without danger to its stream. It is a furious, rapid, desolating torrent, loaded with alluvial soil; and few of those who are received into its waters ever rise again,[1] or can support themselves long upon its surface without assistance from some friendly log. It contains the coarsest and most uneatable of fish, such as the cat-fish and such genus, and as you descend, its banks are occupied with the fetid alligator, while the panther basks at its edge in the cane-brakes, almost impervious to man. Pouring its impetuous waters through wild tracks covered with trees of little value except for firewood, it sweeps down whole for-ests in its course, which disappear in tumultuous confusion, whirled away by the stream now loaded with the masses of soil which nourished their roots, often blocking up and changing for a time the channel of the river, which, as if in anger at its being opposed, inundates and devastates the whole country round; and as soon as it forces its way through its former channel, plants in every direction the uprooted monarchs of the forest (upon whose branches the bird will never again perch, or the raccoon, the opossum, or the squirrel climb) as traps to the adventurous naviga-tors of its waters by steam, who, borne down upon these concealed dangers which pierce through the planks, very often have not time to steer for and gain the shore before they sink to the bottom. There are no pleasing associations connected with the great common sewer of the Western America, which pours out its mud into the Mexican Gulf, polluting the clear blue sea for many miles beyond its mouth. It is a river of desolation; and instead of reminding

[1]There was a foolish superstition of some little prevalence in that day, that the Mississippi would neither buoy up a swimmer, nor permit a drowned person's body to rise to the surface.

you, like other beautiful rivers, of an angel which has descended for the benefit of man, you imagine it a devil, whose energies have been only overcome by the wonderful power of steam."

It is pretty crude literature for a man accustomed to handling a pen; still, as a panorama of the emotions sent weltering through this noted visitor's breast by the aspect and traditions of the "great common sewer," it has a value. A value, though marred in the matter of statistics by inaccuracies; for the catfish is a plenty good enough fish for anybody, and there are no panthers that are "impervious to man."

Later still comes Alexander Mackay, of the Middle Temple, Barrister at Law, with a better digestion, and no catfish dinner aboard, and feels as follows: —

"The Mississippi! It was with indescribable emotions that I first felt myself afloat upon its waters. How often in my school-boy dreams, and in my waking visions afterwards, had my imagination pictured to itself the lordly stream, rolling with tumultuous current through the boundless region to which it has given its name, and gathering into itself, in its course to the ocean, the tributary waters of almost every latitude in the temperate zone! Here it was then in its reality, and I, at length, steaming against its tide. I looked upon it with that reverence with which every one must regard a great feature of external nature."

So much for the emotions. The tourists, one and all, remark upon the deep, brooding loneliness and desolation of the vast river. Captain Basil Hall, who saw it at flood-stage, says: —

"Sometimes we passed along distances of twenty or thirty miles without seeing a single habitation. An artist, in search of hints for a painting of the deluge, would here have found them in abundance."

The first shall be last, etc. Just two hundred years ago, the old original first and gallantest of all the foreign tourists, pioneer, head of the procession, ended his weary and tedious discovery-voyage down the solemn stretches of the great river—La Salle, whose name will last as long as the river itself shall last. We quote from Mr. Parkman:—

"And now they neared their journey's end. On the sixth of April, the river divided itself into three broad channels. La Salle followed that of the west, and D'Autray that of the east; while Tonty took the middle passage. As he drifted down the turbid current, between the low and marshy shores, the brackish water changed to brine, and the breeze grew fresh with the salt breath of the sea. Then the broad bosom of the great Gulf opened on his sight, tossing its restless billows, limitless, voiceless, lonely as when born of chaos, without a sail, without a sign of life."

Then, on a spot of solid ground, La Salle reared a column "bearing the arms of France; the Frenchmen were mustered under arms; and while the New England Indians and their squaws looked on in wondering silence, they chanted the *Te Deum*, the *Exaudiat*, and the *Domine salvum fac regem*."

Then, whilst the musketry volleyed and rejoicing shouts burst forth, the victorious discoverer planted the column, and made proclamation in a loud voice, taking formal possession of the river and the vast countries watered by it, in the name of the King. The column bore this inscription:—

LOUIS LE GRAND, ROY DE FRANCE ET DE NAVARRE, REGNE;
LE NEUVIEME AVRIL, 1682.

New Orleans intended to fittingly celebrate, this present year, the bicentennial anniversary of this illustrious event; but when the time came, all her energies and surplus money were required in other directions, for the flood was upon the land then, making havoc and devastation everywhere.

XXVIII.

Uncle Mumford Unloads

ALL DAY we swung along down the river, and had the stream almost wholly to ourselves. Formerly, at such a stage of the water, we should have passed acres of lumber rafts, and dozens of big coal barges; also occasional little trading-scows, peddling along from farm to farm, with the pedler's family on board; possibly, a random scow, bearing a humble Hamlet and Co. on an itinerant dramatic trip. But these were all absent. Far along in the day, we saw one steamboat; just one, and no more. She was lying at rest in the shade, within the wooded mouth of the Obion River. The spy-glass revealed the fact that she was named for me—or *he* was named for me, whichever you prefer. As this was the first time I had ever encountered this species of honor, it seems excusable to mention it, and at the same time call the attention of the authorities to the tardiness of my recognition of it.

Noted a big change in the river, at Island 21. It was a very large island, and used to lie out toward mid-stream; but it is joined fast to the main shore now, and has retired from business as an island.

As we approached famous and formidable Plum Point, darkness fell, but that was nothing to shudder about—in these modern times. For now the national government has turned the Mississippi into a sort of two-thousand-mile torchlight procession. In the head of every crossing, and in the foot of every crossing, the government has set up a clear-burning lamp. You are never entirely in the dark, now; there is always a beacon in sight, either before you, or behind you, or abreast. One might almost say that lamps have been squandered there. Dozens of crossings are lighted which were not shoal when they were created, and have never been shoal since; crossings so plain, too, and also so straight, that a steamboat can take herself through them without any help, after she has been through once. Lamps in such places are of course not wasted; it is much more convenient and comfortable for a pilot to hold on them than on a spread of formless blackness that won't stay still; and money is saved to the boat, at the same time, for she can of course make more miles with her rudder amidships than she can with it squared across her stern and holding her back.

But this thing has knocked the romance out of piloting, to a large extent. It and some other things together, have knocked all the romance out of it. For instance, the peril from snags is not now what it once was. The government's snagboats go patrolling up and down, in these matter-of-fact days, pulling the river's teeth; they have rooted out all the old clusters which made many localities so formidable; and they allow no new ones to collect. Formerly, if your boat got away from you, on a black night, and broke for the woods, it was an anxious time with you; so was it also, when you were groping your way through solidified darkness in a narrow chute; but all that is changed now,—you flash out your electric light, transform night into day in the twinkling of an eye, and your perils and anxieties are at an end. Horace Bixby and George Ritchie have charted the crossings and laid out the courses by compass; they have invented a lamp to go with the chart, and have patented the whole. With these helps, one may run in the fog now, with considerable security, and with a confidence unknown in the old days.

With these abundant beacons, the banishment of snags, plenty of daylight in a box and ready to be turned on whenever needed, and a chart and compass to fight the fog with, piloting, at a good stage of water, is now nearly as safe and simple as driving stage, and is hardly more than three times as romantic.

And now in these new days, these days of infinite change, the Anchor Line have raised the captain above the pilot by giving him the bigger wages of the two. This was going far, but they have not stopped there. They have decreed that the pilot shall remain at his post, and stand his watch clear through, whether the boat be under way or tied up to the shore. We, that were once the aristocrats of the river, can't go to bed now, as we used to do, and sleep while a hundred tons of freight are lugged aboard; no, we must sit in the pilot-house; and keep awake, too. Verily we are being treated like a parcel of mates and engineers. The Government has taken away the romance of our calling; the Company has taken away its state and dignity.

Plum Point looked as it had always looked by night, with the exception that now there were beacons to mark the crossings, and also a lot of other lights on the Point and along its shore; these latter glinting from the fleet of the United States River Commission, and from a village which the officials have built on the land for offices and for the employés of the service. The military engineers of the Commission have taken upon their shoulders the job of making the Mississippi over again,—a job transcended in size by only the original job of creating it. They are building wing-dams here and there, to deflect the current; and dikes to confine it in narrower bounds; and other dikes to make it stay there; and for unnumbered miles along the Mississippi, they are felling the timber-front for fifty yards back, with the purpose of shaving the bank down to low-water mark with the slant of a house-roof, and ballasting it with stones; and in many places they have protected the wasting shores with rows of piles. One who knows the Mississippi will promptly aver—not aloud, but to himself—that ten thousand River Commissions, with the mines of the world at their back, cannot tame that lawless stream, cannot curb it or confine it, cannot say to it, Go here, or Go there, and make it obey; cannot save a shore which it has sentenced; cannot bar its path with an obstruction which it will not tear down, dance over, and laugh at. But a discreet man will not put these things into spoken words; for the West Point engineers have not their superiors anywhere; they know all that can be known of their abstruse science; and so, since they conceive that they can fetter and handcuff that river and boss him, it is but wisdom for the unscientific man to keep still, lie low, and wait till they do it. Captain Eads, with his jetties, has done a work at the mouth of the Mississippi which seemed clearly impossible; so we do not feel full confidence now to prophesy against like impossibilities. Otherwise one would pipe out and say the Commission might as well bully the comets in their courses and undertake to make them behave, as try to bully the Mississippi into right and reasonable conduct.

I consulted Uncle Mumford concerning this and cognate matters; and I give here the result, stenographically reported, and therefore to be relied on as being full and correct; except that I have here and there left out remarks which were addressed to the men, such as "*where* in blazes are you going with that barrel now?" and which seemed to me to break the flow of the written statement, without compensating by adding to its information or its clearness. Not that I have ventured to strike out all such interjections; I have removed only those which were obviously irrelevant; wherever one occurred which I felt any question about, I have judged it safest to let it remain.

UNCLE MUMFORD'S IMPRESSIONS

Uncle Mumford said:—

"As long as I have been mate of a steamboat,—thirty years—I have watched this river and studied it. Maybe I could have learnt more about it at West Point, but if I believe it I wish I may be WHAT *are you sucking your fingers there for?— Collar that kag of nails!* Four years at West Point, and plenty of books and schooling, will learn a man a good deal, I reckon, but it won't learn him the river. You turn one of those little European rivers over to this Commission, with its hard bottom and clear water, and it would just be a holiday job for them to wall it, and pile it, and dike it, and tame it down, and boss it around, and make it go wherever they wanted it to, and stay where they put it, and do just as they said, every time. But this ain't that kind of a river. They have started in here with big confidence, and the best intentions in the world; but they are going to get left. What does Ecclesiastes vii. 13 say? Says enough to knock *their* little game galley-west, don't it? Now you look at their methods once. There at Devil's Island, in the Upper River, they wanted the water to go one way, the water wanted to go another. So they put up a stone wall. But what does the river care for a stone wall? When it got ready, it just bulged through it. Maybe they can build another that will stay; that is, up there—but not down here they can't. Down here in the Lower River, they drive some pegs to turn the water away from the shore and stop it from slicing off the bank; very well, don't it go straight over and cut somebody else's bank? Certainly. Are they going to peg *all* the banks? Why, they could buy ground and build a new Mississippi cheaper. They are pegging Bulletin Tow-head now. It won't do any good. If the river has got a mortgage on that island, it will foreclose, sure, pegs or no pegs. Away down yonder, they have driven two rows of piles straight through the middle of a dry bar half a mile long, which is forty foot out of the water when the river is low. What do you reckon that is for? If I know, I wish I may land in—HUMP *yourself, you son of an undertaker!*—*out with that coal-oil, now, lively,* LIVELY! And just look at what they are trying to do down there at Milliken's Bend. There 's been a cut-off in that section, and Vicksburg is left out in the cold. It 's a country town now. The river strikes in below it; and a boat can't go up to the town except in high water. Well, they are going to build wing-dams in the bend opposite the foot of 103, and throw the water over and cut off the foot of the island and plow down into an old ditch where the river used to be in ancient times; and they think they can persuade the water around that way, and get it to strike in above Vicksburg, as it used to do, and fetch the town back into the world again. That is, they are going to take this whole Mississippi, and twist it around and make it run several miles *up stream*. Well, you 've got to admire men that deal in ideas of that size and can tote them around without crutches; but you have n't got to believe they can *do* such miracles, have you? And yet you ain't absolutely obliged to believe they can't. I reckon the safe way, where a man can afford it, is to *copper* the operation, and at the same time buy enough property in Vicksburg to square you up in case they win. Government is doing a deal for the Mississippi, now—spending loads of money on her. When there used to be four thousand steamboats and ten thousand acres of coal-barges, and rafts and trading scows, there was n't a lantern from St. Paul to New Orleans, and the snags were thicker than bristles on a hog's back; and now when there 's three dozen steamboats and nary barge or raft, Government has snatched out all the snags, and lit up the shores like Broadway, and a boat 's as safe on the river as she 'd be in heaven. And I reckon that by

the time there ain't any boats left at all, the Commission will
have the old thing all reorganized, and dredged out, and
fenced in, and tidied up, to a degree that will make navigation
just simply perfect, and absolutely safe and profitable; and all
the days will be Sundays, and all the mates will be Sunday-
school su WHAT-*in-the-nation-you-fooling-around-there-for, you
sons of unrighteousness, heirs of perdition! Going to be a* YEAR
getting that hogshead ashore?"

During our trip to New Orleans and back, we had many
conversations with river men, planters, journalists, and officers of the River Commission—with conflicting and confusing results. To wit:—

1. Some believed in the Commission's scheme to arbitrarily
and permanently confine (and thus deepen) the channel, preserve threatened shores, etc.

2. Some believed that the Commission's money ought to
be spent only on building and repairing the great system of
levees.

3. Some believed that the higher you build your levee, the
higher the river's bottom will rise; and that consequently the
levee system is a mistake.

4. Some believed in the scheme to relieve the river, in
flood-time, by turning its surplus waters off into Lake
Borgne, etc.

5. Some believed in the scheme of northern lake-reservoirs
to replenish the Mississippi in low-water seasons.

Wherever you find a man down there who believes in one
of these theories you may turn to the next man and frame
your talk upon the hypothesis that he does *not* believe in that
theory; and after you have had experience, you do not take
this course doubtfully, or hesitatingly, but with the confidence of a dying murderer—converted one, I mean. For you
will have come to know, with a deep and restful certainty,
that you are not going to meet two people sick of the same
theory, one right after the other. No, there will always be one
or two with the other diseases along between. And as you
proceed, you will find out one or two other things. You will
find out that there is no distemper of the lot but is conta-

gious; and you cannot go where it is without catching it. You may vaccinate yourself with deterrent facts as much as you please—it will do no good; it will seem to "take," but it does n't; the moment you rub against any one of those theorists, make up your mind that it is time to hang out your yellow flag.

Yes, you are his sure victim: yet his work is not all to your hurt—only part of it; for he is like your family physician, who comes and cures the mumps, and leaves the scarlet-fever behind. If your man is a Lake-Borgne-relief theorist, for instance, he will exhale a cloud of deadly facts and statistics which will lay you out with that disease, sure; but at the same time he will cure you of any other of the five theories that may have previously got into your system.

I have had all the five; and had them "bad;" but ask me not, in mournful numbers, which one racked me hardest, or which one numbered the biggest sick list, for I do not know. In truth, no one can answer the latter question. Mississippi Improvement is a mighty topic, down yonder. Every man on the river banks, south of Cairo, talks about it every day, during such moments as he is able to spare from talking about the war; and each of the several chief theories has its host of zealous partisans; but, as I have said, it is not possible to determine which cause numbers the most recruits.

All were agreed upon one point, however: if Congress would make a sufficient appropriation, a colossal benefit would result. Very well; since then the appropriation has been made—possibly a sufficient one, certainly not too large a one. Let us hope that the prophecy will be amply fulfilled.

One thing will be easily granted by the reader; that an opinion from Mr. Edward Atkinson, upon any vast national commercial matter, comes as near ranking as authority, as can the opinion of any individual in the Union. What he has to say about Mississippi River Improvement will be found in the Appendix.[1]

Sometimes, half a dozen figures will reveal, as with a lightning-flash, the importance of a subject which ten thousand labored words, with the same purpose in view, had left at last

[1] See Appendix B.

but dim and uncertain. Here is a case of the sort—paragraph from the "Cincinnati Commercial:"—

"The towboat 'Jos. B. Williams' is on her way to New Orleans with a tow of thirty-two barges, containing six hundred thousand bushels (seventy-six pounds to the bushel) of coal exclusive of her own fuel, being the largest tow ever taken to New Orleans or anywhere else in the world. Her freight bill, at 3 cents a bushel, amounts to $18,000. It would take eighteen hundred cars, of three hundred and thirty-three bushels to the car, to transport this amount of coal. At $10 per ton, or $100 per car, which would be a fair price for the distance by rail, the freight bill would amount to $180,000, or $162,000 more by rail than by river. The tow will be taken from Pittsburg to New Orleans in fourteen or fifteen days. It would take one hundred trains of eighteen cars to the train to transport this one tow of six hundred thousand bushels of coal, and even if it made the usual speed of fast freight lines, it would take one whole summer to put it through by rail."

When a river in good condition can enable one to save $162,000 and a whole summer's time, on a single cargo, the wisdom of taking measures to keep the river in good condition is made plain to even the uncommercial mind.

XXIX.

A Few Specimen Bricks

WE PASSED through the Plum Point region, turned Craighead's Point, and glided unchallenged by what was once the formidable Fort Pillow, memorable because of the massacre perpetrated there during the war. Massacres are sprinkled with some frequency through the histories of several Christian nations, but this is almost the only one that can be found in American history; perhaps it is the only one which rises to a size correspondent to that huge and sombre title. We have the "Boston Massacre," where two or three people were killed; but we must bunch Anglo-Saxon history together to find the fellow to the Fort Pillow tragedy; and doubtless even then we must travel back to the days and the performances of Cœur de Lion, that fine "hero," before we accomplish it.

More of the river's freaks. In times past, the channel used to strike above Island 37, by Brandywine Bar, and down towards Island 39. Afterward, changed its course and went from Brandywine down through Vogelman's chute in the Devil's Elbow, to Island 39—part of this course reversing the old order; the river running *up* four or five miles, instead of down, and cutting off, throughout, some fifteen miles of distance. This in 1876. All that region is now called Centennial Island.

There is a tradition that Island 37 was one of the principal abiding places of the once celebrated "Murel's Gang." This was a colossal combination of robbers, horse-thieves, negro-stealers, and counterfeiters, engaged in business along the river some fifty or sixty years ago. While our journey across the country towards St. Louis was in progress we had had no end of Jesse James and his stirring history; for he had just been assassinated by an agent of the Governor of Missouri, and was in consequence occupying a good deal of space in the newspapers. Cheap histories of him were for sale by train boys. According to these, he was the most marvellous creature of his kind that had ever existed. It was a mistake. Murel was his equal in boldness; in pluck; in rapacity; in cruelty, brutality, heartlessness, treachery, and in general and comprehensive vileness and shamelessness; and very much his superior in some larger aspects. James was a retail rascal; Murel, wholesale. James's modest genius dreamed of no loftier flight than the planning of raids upon cars, coaches, and country banks; Murel projected negro insurrections and the capture of New Orleans; and furthermore, on occasion, this Murel could go into a pulpit and edify the congregation. What are James and his half-dozen vulgar rascals compared with this stately old-time criminal, with his sermons, his meditated insurrections and city-captures, and his majestic following of ten hundred men, sworn to do his evil will!

Here is a paragraph or two concerning this big operator, from a now forgotten book which was published half a century ago: —

He appears to have been a most dexterous as well as consummate villain. When he travelled, his usual disguise was that of an itinerant preacher; and it is said that his discourses were very "soul-moving"—interesting the hearers so much that they forgot to look after their horses, which were carried away by his confederates while he was preaching. But the stealing of horses in one State, and selling them in another, was but a small portion of their business; the most lucrative was the enticing slaves to run away from their masters, that they might sell them in another quarter. This was arranged as follows; they would tell a negro that if he would run away from his master, and allow them to sell him, he should receive a portion of the money paid for him, and that upon his return to them a second time they would send him to a free State, where he would be safe. The poor wretches complied with this request, hoping to obtain money and freedom; they would be sold to another master, and run away again to their employers; sometimes they would be sold in this manner three or four times, until they had realized three or four thousand dollars by them; but as, after this, there was fear of detection, the usual custom was to get rid of the only witness that could be produced against them, which was the negro himself, by murdering him, and throwing his body into the Mississippi. Even if it was established that they had stolen a negro, before he was murdered, they were always prepared to evade punishment; for they concealed the negro who had run away, until he was advertised, and a reward offered to any man who would catch him. An advertisement of this kind warrants the person to take the property, if found. And then the negro becomes a property in trust, when, therefore, they sold the negro, it only became a breach of trust, not stealing; and for a breach of trust, the owner of the property can only have redress by a civil action, which was useless, as the damages were never paid. It may be inquired, how it was that Murel escaped Lynch law under such circumstances? This will be easily understood when it is stated that he had *more than a thousand sworn confederates*, all ready at a moment's notice to support any of the gang who might be in trouble. The names of all the principal confederates of Murel were obtained from himself, in a manner which I shall presently explain. The gang was composed of two classes: the Heads or Council, as they were called, who planned and concerted, but seldom acted; they amounted to about four hundred. The other class were the active agents, and were termed strikers, and amounted to about six hundred and fifty. These were the tools in the hands of the others; they ran all the risk, and received but a small portion of the money; they were in the power of the leaders of the gang, who would sacrifice them at any time by handing them over to justice, or sinking their bodies in the Mississippi. The general rendezvous of this gang of miscreants was on the Arkansas side of the river, where they concealed their negroes in the morasses and canebrakes.

The depredations of this extensive combination were severely felt; but so well were their plans arranged, that although Murel, who was always active, was everywhere suspected, there was no proof to be obtained. It so happened, however, that a young man of the name of Stewart, who was looking after two slaves which Murel had decoyed away, fell in with him and obtained his confidence, took the oath, and was admitted into the gang as one of the

General Council. By this means all was discovered; for Stewart turned traitor, although he had taken the oath, and having obtained every information, exposed the whole concern, the names of all the parties, and finally succeeded in bringing home sufficient evidence against Murel, to procure his conviction and sentence to the Penitentiary (Murel was sentenced to fourteen years' imprisonment); so many people who were supposed to be honest, and bore a respectable name in the different States, were found to be among the list of the Grand Council as published by Stewart, that every attempt was made to throw discredit upon his assertions—his character was vilified, and more than one attempt was made to assassinate him. He was obliged to quit the Southern States in consequence. It is, however, now well ascertained to have been all true; and although some blame Mr. Stewart for having violated his oath, they no longer attempt to deny that his revelations were correct. I will quote one or two portions of Murel's confessions to Mr. Stewart, made to him when they were journeying together. I ought to have observed, that the ultimate intentions of Murel and his associates were, by his own account, on a very extended scale; having no less an object in view than *raising the blacks against the whites, taking possession of, and plundering New Orleans, and making themselves possessors of the territory.* The following are a few extracts:—

"I collected all my friends about New Orleans at one of our friends' houses in that place, and we sat in council three days before we got all our plans to our notion; we then determined to undertake the rebellion at every hazard, and make as many friends as we could for that purpose. Every man's business being assigned him, I started to Natchez on foot, having sold my horse in New Orleans,—with the intention of stealing another after I started. I walked four days, and no opportunity offered for me to get a horse. The fifth day, about twelve, I had become tired, and stopped at a creek to get some water and rest a little. While I was sitting on a log, looking down the road the way that I had come, a man came in sight riding on a good-looking horse. The very moment I saw him, I was determined to have his horse, if he was in the garb of a traveller. He rode up, and I saw from his equipage that he was a traveller. I arose and drew an elegant rifle pistol on him and ordered him to dismount. He did so, and I took his horse by the bridle and pointed down the creek, and ordered him to walk before me. He went a few hundred yards and stopped. I hitched his horse, and then made him undress himself, all to his shirt and drawers, and ordered him to turn his back to me. He said, 'If you are determined to kill me, let me have time to pray before I die.' I told him I had no time to hear him pray. He turned around and dropped on his knees, and I shot him through the back of the head. I ripped open his belly and took out his entrails, and sunk him in the creek. I then searched his pockets, and found four hundred dollars and thirty seven cents, and a number of papers that I did not take time to examine. I sunk the pocket-book and papers and his hat, in the creek. His boots were bran-new, and fitted me genteelly; and I put them on and sunk my old shoes in the creek, to atone for them. I rolled up his clothes and put them into his portmanteau, as they were bran-new cloth of the best quality. I mounted as fine a horse as ever I straddled, and directed my course for Natchez in much better style than I had been for the last five days.

"Myself and a fellow by the name of Crenshaw gathered four good horses and started for Georgia. We got in company with a young South Carolinian just before we got to Cumberland Mountain, and Crenshaw soon knew all about his business. He had been to Tennessee to buy a drove of hogs, but when he got there pork was dearer than he calculated, and he declined purchasing. We concluded he was a prize. Crenshaw winked at me; I understood his idea. Crenshaw had travelled the road before, but I never had; we had travelled several miles on the mountain, when he passed near a great precipice; just before we passed it Crenshaw asked me for my whip, which had a pound of lead in the butt; I handed it to him, and he rode up by the side of the South Carolinian, and gave him a blow on the side of the head and tumbled him from his horse; we lit from our horses and fingered his pockets; we got twelve hundred and sixty-two dollars. Crenshaw said he knew a place to hide him, and he gathered him under his arms, and I by his feet, and conveyed him to a deep crevice in the brow of the precipice, and tumbled him into it, and he went out of sight; we then tumbled in his saddle, and took his horse with us, which was worth two hundred dollars.

"We were detained a few days, and during that time our friend went to a little village in the neighborhood and saw the negro advertised (a negro in our possession), and a description of the two men of whom he had been purchased, and giving his suspicions of the men. It was rather squally times, but any port in a storm: we took the negro that night on the bank of a creek which runs by the farm of our friend, and Crenshaw shot him through the head. We took out his entrails and sunk him in the creek.

"He had sold the other negro the third time on Arkansaw River for upwards of five hundred dollars; and then stole him and delivered him into the hand of his friend, who conducted him to a swamp, and veiled the tragic scene, and got the last gleanings and sacred pledge of secrecy; as a game of that kind will not do unless it ends in a mystery to all but the fraternity. He sold the negro, first and last, for nearly two thousand dollars, and then put him forever out of the reach of all pursuers; and they can never graze him unless they can find the negro; and that they cannot do, for his carcass has fed many a tortoise and catfish before this time, and the frogs have sung this many a long day to the silent repose of his skeleton."

We were approaching Memphis, in front of which city, and witnessed by its people, was fought the most famous of the river battles of the Civil War. Two men whom I had served under, in my river days, took part in that fight: Mr. Bixby, head pilot of the Union fleet, and Montgomery, Commodore of the Confederate fleet. Both saw a great deal of active service during the war, and achieved high reputations for pluck and capacity.

As we neared Memphis, we began to cast about for an excuse to stay with the "Gold Dust" to the end of her course—Vicksburg. We were so pleasantly situated, that we did not wish to make a change. I had an errand of considerable importance to do at Napoleon, Arkansas, but perhaps I could manage it without quitting the "Gold Dust." I said as much; so we decided to stick to present quarters.

The boat was to tarry at Memphis till ten the next morning. It is a beautiful city, nobly situated on a commanding bluff overlooking the river. The streets are straight and spacious, though not paved in a way to incite distempered admiration. No, the admiration must be reserved for the town's sewerage system, which is called perfect; a recent reform, however, for it was just the other way, up to a few years ago—a reform resulting from the lesson taught by a desolating visitation of the yellow-fever. In those awful days the people were swept off by hundreds, by thousands; and so great was the reduction caused by flight and by death together, that the population was diminished three-fourths, and so remained for a time. Business stood nearly still, and the streets bore an empty Sunday aspect.

Here is a picture of Memphis, at that disastrous time, drawn by a German tourist who seems to have been an eyewitness of the scenes which he describes. It is from Chapter VII., of his book, just published, in Leipzig, "Mississippi-Fahrten, von Ernst von Hesse-Wartegg:"—

"In August the yellow-fever had reached its extremest height. Daily, hundreds fell a sacrifice to the terrible epidemic. The city was become a mighty graveyard, two-thirds of the population had deserted the place, and only the poor, the aged and the sick, remained behind, a sure prey for the insidious enemy. The houses were closed: little lamps burned in front of many—a sign that here death had entered. Often, several lay dead in a single house; from the windows hung black crape. The stores were shut up, for their owners were gone away or dead.

"Fearful evil! In the briefest space it struck down and swept away even the most vigorous victim. A slight indisposition, then an hour of fever, then the hideous delirium, then—the Yellow Death! On the street corners, and in the squares, lay sick men, suddenly overtaken by the disease; and even corpses, distorted and rigid. Food failed. Meat spoiled in a few hours in the fetid and pestiferous air, and turned black.

"Fearful clamors issue from many houses; then after a season they cease, and all is still: noble, self-sacrificing men come with the coffin, nail it up, and carry it away, to the graveyard. In the night stillness reigns. Only the physicians and the hearses hurry through the streets; and out of the distance, at intervals, comes the muffled thunder of the railway train, which with the speed of the wind, and as if hunted by furies, flies by the pest-ridden city without halting."

But there is life enough there now. The population exceeds forty thousand and is augmenting, and trade is in a flourishing condition. We drove about the city; visited the park and the sociable horde of squirrels there; saw the fine residences, rose-clad and in other ways enticing to the eye; and got a good breakfast at the hotel.

A thriving place is the Good Samaritan City of the Mississippi: has a great wholesale jobbing trade; foundries, machine shops; and manufactories of wagons, carriages, and cotton-seed oil; and is shortly to have cotton mills and elevators.

Her cotton receipts reached five hundred thousand bales last year—an increase of sixty thousand over the year before. Out from her healthy commercial heart issue five trunk lines of railway; and a sixth is being added.

This is a very different Memphis from the one which the vanished and unremembered procession of foreign tourists used to put into their books long time ago. In the days of the now forgotten but once renowned and vigorously hated Mrs. Trollope, Memphis seems to have consisted mainly of one long street of log-houses, with some outlying cabins sprinkled around rearward toward the woods; and now and then a pig, and no end of mud. That was fifty-five years ago. She stopped at the hotel. Plainly it was not the one which gave us our breakfast. She says:—

"The table was laid for fifty persons, and was nearly full. They ate in perfect silence, and with such astonishing rapidity that their dinner was over literally before ours was begun; the only sounds heard were those produced by the knives and forks, with the unceasing chorus of coughing, *etc.*"

"Coughing, *etc.*" The "etc." stands for an unpleasant word there, a word which she does not always charitably cover up, but sometimes prints. You will find it in the following description of a steamboat dinner which she ate in company with a lot of aristocratic planters; wealthy, well-born, ignorant swells they were, tinselled with the usual harmless military and judicial titles of that old day of cheap shams and windy pretence: —

"The total want of all the usual courtesies of the table; the voracious rapidity with which the viands were seized and devoured; the strange uncouth phrases and pronunciation; the loathsome spitting, from the contamination of which it was absolutely impossible to protect our dresses; the frightful manner of feeding with their knives, till the whole blade seemed to enter into the mouth; and the still more frightful manner of cleaning the teeth afterward with a pocket knife, soon forced us to feel that we were not surrounded by the generals, colonels, and majors of the old world; and that the dinner hour was to be anything rather than an hour of enjoyment."

XXX.

Sketches by the Way

IT WAS a big river, below Memphis; banks brimming full, everywhere, and very frequently more than full, the waters pouring out over the land, flooding the woods and fields for miles into the interior; and in places, to a depth of fifteen feet; signs, all about, of men's hard work gone to ruin, and all to be done over again, with straitened means and a weakened courage. A melancholy picture, and a continuous one;—hundreds of miles of it. Sometimes the beacon lights stood in water three feet deep, in the edge of dense forests which extended for miles without farm, wood-yard, clearing, or break of any kind; which meant that the keeper of the light must come in a skiff a great distance to discharge his trust,—and often in desperate weather. Yet I was told that the work is faithfully performed, in all weathers; and not always by men, sometimes by women, if the man is sick or absent. The Government furnishes oil, and pays ten or fifteen dollars a month for the lighting and tending. A Government boat distributes oil and pays wages once a month.

The Ship Island region was as woodsy and tenantless as ever. The island has ceased to be an island; has joined itself compactly to the main shore, and wagons travel, now, where the steamboats used to navigate. No signs left of the wreck of the "Pennsylvania." Some farmer will turn up her bones with his plow one day, no doubt, and be surprised.

We were getting down now into the migrating negro region. These poor people could never travel when they were slaves; so they make up for the privation now. They stay on a plantation till the desire to travel seizes them; then they pack up, hail a steamboat, and clear out. Not for any particular place; no, nearly any place will answer; they only want to be moving. The amount of money on hand will answer the rest of the conundrum for them. If it will take them fifty miles, very well; let it be fifty. If not, a shorter flight will do.

During a couple of days, we frequently answered these hails. Sometimes there was a group of high-water-stained, tumble-down cabins, populous with colored folk, and no whites visible; with grassless patches of dry ground here and there; a few felled trees, with skeleton cattle, mules, and horses, eating the leaves and gnawing the bark—no other food for them in the flood-wasted land. Sometimes there was a single lonely landing-cabin; near it the colored family that had hailed us; little and big, old and young, roosting on the scant pile of household goods; these consisting of a rusty gun, some bedticks, chests, tinware, stools, a crippled looking-glass, a venerable arm-chair, and six or eight base-born and spiritless yellow curs, attached to the family by strings. They must have their dogs; can't go without their dogs. Yet the dogs are never willing; they always object; so, one after another, in ridiculous procession, they are dragged aboard; all four feet braced and sliding along the stage, head likely to be pulled off; but the tugger marching determinedly forward, bending to his work, with the rope over his shoulder for better purchase. Sometimes a child is forgotten and left on the bank; but never a dog.

The usual river-gossip going on in the pilot-house. Island No. 63—an island with a lovely "chute," or passage, behind it in the former times. They said Jesse Jamieson, in the "Skylark," had a visiting pilot with him one trip—a poor old broken-down, superannuated fellow—left him at the wheel, at the foot of 63, to run off the watch. The ancient mariner went up through the chute, and down the river outside; and up the chute and down the river again; and yet again and again; and handed the boat over to the relieving pilot, at the end of three hours of honest endeavor, at the same old foot of the island where he had originally taken the wheel! A darkey on shore who had observed the boat go by, about thirteen times, said, " 'clar to gracious, I would n't be s'prised if dey 's a whole line o' dem Sk'ylarks!"

Anecdote illustrative of influence of reputation in the changing of opinion. The "Eclipse" was renowned for her swiftness. One day she passed along; an old darkey on shore, absorbed in his own matters, did not notice what steamer it was. Presently some one asked:—

"Any boat gone up?"

"Yes, sah."

"Was she going fast?"

"Oh, so-so—loafin' along."

"Now, do you know what boat that was?"

"No, sah."

"Why, uncle, that was the 'Eclipse.' "

"No! Is dat so? Well, I bet it was—cause she jes' went by here a-*sparklin'*!"

Piece of history illustrative of the violent style of some of the people down along here. During the early weeks of high water, A's fence rails washed down on B's ground, and B's rails washed up in the eddy and landed on A's ground. A said, "Let the thing remain so; I will use your rails, and you use mine." But B objected—would n't have it so. One day, A came down on B's ground to get his rails. B said, "I 'll kill you!" and proceeded for him with his revolver. A said, "I 'm not armed." So B, who wished to do only what was right, threw down his revolver; then pulled a knife, and cut A's throat all around, but gave his principal attention to the front, and so failed to sever the jugular. Struggling around, A managed to get his hands on the discarded revolver, and shot B dead with it—and recovered from his own injuries.

Further gossip;—after which, everybody went below to get afternoon coffee, and left me at the wheel, alone. Something presently reminded me of our last hour in St. Louis, part of which I spent on this boat's hurricane deck, aft. I was joined there by a stranger, who dropped into conversation with me—a brisk young fellow, who said he was born in a town in the interior of Wisconsin, and had never seen a steamboat until a week before. Also said that on the way down from La Crosse he had inspected and examined his boat so diligently and with such passionate interest that he had mastered the whole thing from stem to rudder-blade. Asked me where I was from. I answered, New England. "Oh, a Yank!" said he; and went chatting straight along, without waiting for assent or denial. He immediately proposed to take me all over the boat and tell me the names of her different parts, and teach me their uses. Before I could enter protest or excuse, he was already rattling glibly away at his benevolent work; and when I perceived that he was misnaming the things, and inhospitably amusing himself at the expense of an innocent stranger from a far country, I held my peace, and let him have his way. He gave me a world of misinformation; and the further he went, the wider his imagination expanded, and the more he enjoyed his cruel work of deceit. Sometimes, after palming off a particularly fantastic and outrageous lie upon me, he was so "full of laugh" that he had to step aside for a minute, upon one pretext or another, to keep me from suspecting. I staid faithfully by him until his comedy was finished. Then he remarked that he had undertaken to "learn" me all about a steamboat, and had done it; but that if he had overlooked anything, just ask him and he would supply the lack. "Anything about this boat that you don't know the name of or the purpose of, you come to me and I 'll tell you." I said I would, and took my departure; disappeared, and approached him from another quarter, whence he could not see me. There he sat, all alone, doubling himself up and writhing this way and that, in the throes of unappeasable laughter. He must have made himself sick; for he was not publicly visible afterward for several days. Meantime, the episode dropped out of my mind.

The thing that reminded me of it now, when I was alone at the wheel, was the spectacle of this young fellow standing in the pilot-house door, with the knob in his hand, silently and severely inspecting me. I don't know when I have seen anybody look so injured as he did. He did not say anything— simply stood there and looked; reproachfully looked and pondered. Finally he shut the door, and started away; halted on the texas a minute; came slowly back and stood in the door again, with that grieved look in his face; gazed upon me a while in meek rebuke, then said:—

"You let me learn you all about a steamboat, *did n't* you?"

"Yes," I confessed.

"Yes, you did— *did n't* you?"

"Yes."

"*You* are the feller that—that—"

Language failed. Pause—impotent struggle for further words—then he gave it up, choked out a deep, strong oath, and departed for good. Afterward I saw him several times below during the trip; but he was cold—would not look at me. Idiot, if he had not been in such a sweat to play his

witless practical joke upon me, in the beginning, I would
have persuaded his thoughts into some other direction, and
saved him from committing that wanton and silly impolite-
ness.

I had myself called with the four o'clock watch, mornings,
for one cannot see too many summer sunrises on the Mississippi. They are enchanting. First, there is the eloquence of
silence; for a deep hush broods everywhere. Next, there is the
haunting sense of loneliness, isolation, remoteness from the
worry and bustle of the world. The dawn creeps in stealthily;
the solid walls of black forest soften to gray, and vast stretches
of the river open up and reveal themselves; the water is glass-
smooth, gives off spectral little wreaths of white mist, there is
not the faintest breath of wind, nor stir of leaf; the tranquillity is profound and infinitely satisfying. Then a bird pipes
up, another follows, and soon the pipings develop into a ju-
bilant riot of music. You see none of the birds; you simply
move through an atmosphere of song which seems to sing
itself. When the light has become a little stronger, you have
one of the fairest and softest pictures imaginable. You have
the intense green of the massed and crowded foliage near by;
you see it paling shade by shade in front of you; upon the
next projecting cape, a mile off or more, the tint has lightened
to the tender young green of spring; the cape beyond that
one has almost lost color, and the furthest one, miles away
under the horizon, sleeps upon the water a mere dim vapor,
and hardly separable from the sky above it and about it. And
all this stretch of river is a mirror, and you have the shadowy
reflections of the leafage and the curving shores and the receding capes pictured in it. Well, that is all beautiful; soft and
rich and beautiful; and when the sun gets well up, and distributes a pink flush here and a powder of gold yonder and a
purple haze where it will yield the best effect, you grant that
you have seen something that is worth remembering.

We had the Kentucky Bend country in the early morning—
scene of a strange and tragic accident in the old times. Captain Poe had a small stern-wheel boat, for years the home of
himself and his wife. One night the boat struck a snag in the
head of Kentucky Bend, and sank with astonishing suddenness; water already well above the cabin floor when the cap-

tain got aft. So he cut into his wife's stateroom from above with an axe; she was asleep in the upper berth, the roof a flimsier one than was supposed; the first blow crashed down through the rotten boards and clove her skull.

This bend is all filled up now—result of a cut-off; and the same agent has taken the great and once much-frequented Walnut Bend, and set it away back in a solitude far from the accustomed track of passing steamers.

Helena we visited, and also a town I had not heard of before, it being of recent birth—Arkansas City. It was born of a railway; the Little Rock, Mississippi River and Texas Railroad touches the river there. We asked a passenger who belonged there what sort of a place it was. "Well," said he, after considering, and with the air of one who wishes to take time and be accurate, "It 's a hell of a place." A description which was photographic for exactness. There were several rows and clusters of shabby frame-houses, and a supply of mud sufficient to insure the town against a famine in that article for a hundred years; for the overflow had but lately subsided. There were stagnant ponds in the streets, here and there, and a dozen rude scows were scattered about, lying aground wherever they happened to have been when the waters drained off and people could do their visiting and shopping on foot once more. Still, it is a thriving place, with a rich country behind it, an elevator in front of it, and also a fine big mill for the manufacture of cotton-seed oil. I had never seen this kind of a mill before.

Cotton-seed was comparatively valueless in my time; but it is worth $12 or $13 a ton now, and none of it is thrown away. The oil made from it is colorless, tasteless, and almost if not entirely odorless. It is claimed that it can, by proper manipulation, be made to resemble and perform the office of any and all oils, and be produced at a cheaper rate than the cheapest of the originals. Sagacious people shipped it to Italy, doctored it, labelled it, and brought it back as olive oil. This trade grew to be so formidable that Italy was obliged to put a prohibitory impost upon it to keep it from working serious injury to her oil industry.

Helena occupies one of the prettiest situations on the Mississippi. Her perch is the last, the southernmost group of hills

which one sees on that side of the river. In its normal condition it is a pretty town; but the flood (or possibly the seep-
age) had lately been ravaging it; whole streets of houses had
been invaded by the muddy water, and the outsides of the
buildings were still belted with a broad stain extending upwards from the foundations. Stranded and discarded scows
lay all about; plank sidewalks on stilts four feet high were still
standing; the board sidewalks on the ground level were loose
and ruinous,—a couple of men trotting along them could
make a blind man think a cavalry charge was coming; everywhere the mud was black and deep, and in many places ma-
larious pools of stagnant water were standing. A Mississippi
inundation is the next most wasting and desolating infliction
to a fire.

We had an enjoyable time here, on this sunny Sunday: two
full hours' liberty ashore while the boat discharged freight. In
the back streets but few white people were visible, but there
were plenty of colored folk—mainly women and girls; and
almost without exception upholstered in bright new clothes
of swell and elaborate style and cut—a glaring and hilarious
contrast to the mournful mud and the pensive puddles.

Helena is the second town in Arkansas, in point of population—which is placed at five thousand. The country about
it is exceptionally productive. Helena has a good cotton trade;
handles from forty to sixty thousand bales annually; she has
a large lumber and grain commerce; has a foundry, oil mills,
machine shops and wagon factories—in brief has $1,000,000
invested in manufacturing industries. She has two railways,
and is the commercial centre of a broad and prosperous region. Her gross receipts of money, annually, from all sources,
are placed by the New Orleans "Times-Democrat" at
$4,000,000.

XXXI.

A Thumb-Print and What Came of It

WE WERE approaching Napoleon, Arkansas. So I began to think about my errand there. Time, noonday; and bright and sunny. This was bad—not best, anyway; for mine was not (preferably) a noonday kind of errand. The more I thought, the more that fact pushed itself upon me— now in one form, now in another. Finally, it took the form of a distinct question: is it good common sense to do the errand in daytime, when, by a little sacrifice of comfort and inclination, you can have night for it, and no inquisitive eyes around? This settled it. Plain question and plain answer make the shortest road out of most perplexities.

I got my friends into my stateroom, and said I was sorry to create annoyance and disappointment, but that upon reflection it really seemed best that we put our luggage ashore and stop over at Napoleon. Their disapproval was prompt and loud; their language mutinous. Their main argument was one which has always been the first to come to the surface, in such cases, since the beginning of time: "But you decided and *agreed* to stick to this boat, etc.;" as if, having determined to do an unwise thing, one is thereby bound to go ahead and make *two* unwise things of it, by carrying out that determination.

I tried various mollifying tactics upon them, with reasonably good success: under which encouragement, I increased my efforts; and, to show them that *I* had not created this annoying errand, and was in no way to blame for it, I presently drifted into its history—substantially as follows:

Toward the end of last year, I spent a few months in Munich, Bavaria. In November I was living in Fräulein Dahlweiner's *pension*, 1*a*, Karlstrasse; but my working quarters were a mile from there, in the house of a widow who supported herself by taking lodgers. She and her two young children used to drop in every morning and talk German to me— by request. One day, during a ramble about the city, I visited one of the two establishments where the Government keeps and watches corpses until the doctors decide that they are permanently dead, and not in a trance state. It was a grisly place, that spacious room. There were thirty-six corpses of adults in sight, stretched on their backs on slightly slanted boards, in three long rows—all of them with wax-white, rigid faces, and all of them wrapped in white shrouds. Along the sides of the room were deep alcoves, like bay windows; and in each of these lay several marble-visaged babes, utterly hidden and buried under banks of fresh flowers, all but their faces and crossed hands. Around a finger of each of these fifty still forms, both great and small, was a ring; and from the ring a wire led to the ceiling, and thence to a bell in a watch-room yonder, where, day and night, a watchman sits always alert and ready to spring to the aid of any of that pallid company who, waking out of death, shall make a movement— for any even the slightest movement will twitch the wire and ring that fearful bell. I imagined myself a death-sentinel drowsing there alone, far in the dragging watches of some wailing, gusty night, and having in a twinkling all my body stricken to quivering jelly by the sudden clamor of that awful summons! So I inquired about this thing; asked what resulted usually? if the watchman died, and the restored corpse came and did what it could to make his last moments easy? But I was rebuked for trying to feed an idle and frivolous curiosity in so solemn and so mournful a place; and went my way with a humbled crest.

Next morning I was telling the widow my adventure, when she exclaimed—

"Come with me! I have a lodger who shall tell you all you want to know. He has been a night watchman there."

He was a living man, but he did not look it. He was abed, and had his head propped high on pillows; his face was wasted and colorless, his deep-sunken eyes were shut; his hand, lying on his breast, was talon-like, it was so bony and long-fingered. The widow began her introduction of me. The man's eyes opened slowly, and glittered wickedly out from the twilight of their caverns; he frowned a black frown; he lifted his lean hand and waved us peremptorily away. But the widow kept straight on, till she had got out the fact that I was a stranger and an American. The man's face changed at

once; brightened, became even eager—and the next moment
he and I were alone together.

I opened up in cast-iron German; he responded in quite
flexible English; thereafter we gave the German language a
permanent rest.

This consumptive and I became good friends. I visited him
every day, and we talked about everything. At least, about
everything but wives and children. Let anybody's wife or anybody's child be mentioned, and three things always followed:
the most gracious and loving and tender light glimmered in
the man's eyes for a moment; faded out the next, and in its
place came that deadly look which had flamed there the first
time I ever saw his lids unclose; thirdly, he ceased from
speech, there and then for that day; lay silent, abstracted, and
absorbed; apparently heard nothing that I said; took no notice of my good-byes, and plainly did not know, by either
sight or hearing, when I left the room.

When I had been this Karl Ritter's daily and sole intimate
during two months, he one day said, abruptly,—

"I will tell you my story."

A DYING MAN'S CONFESSION

Then he went on as follows:—

I have never given up, until now. But now I have given up.
I am going to die. I made up my mind last night that it must
be, and very soon, too. You say you are going to revisit your
river, by and by, when you find opportunity. Very well; that,
together with a certain strange experience which fell to my lot
last night, determines me to tell you my history—for you will
see Napoleon, Arkansas; and for my sake you will stop there,
and do a certain thing for me—a thing which you will will-
ingly undertake after you shall have heard my narrative.

Let us shorten the story wherever we can, for it will need
it, being long. You already know how I came to go to America, and how I came to settle in that lonely region in the
South. But you do not know that I had a wife. My wife was
young, beautiful, loving, and oh, so divinely good and blameless and gentle! And our little girl was her mother in miniature. It was the happiest of happy households.

One night—it was toward the close of the war—I woke up out of a sodden lethargy, and found myself bound and gagged, and the air tainted with chloroform! I saw two men in the room, and one was saying to the other, in a hoarse whisper, "I *told* her I would, if she made a noise, and as for the child—"

The other man interrupted in a low, half-crying voice—

"You said we'd only gag them and rob them, not hurt them; or I would n't have come."

"Shut up your whining; *had* to change the plan when they waked up; you done all *you* could to protect them, now let that satisfy you; come, help rummage."

Both men were masked, and wore coarse, ragged "nigger" clothes; they had a bull's-eye lantern, and by its light I noticed that the gentler robber had no thumb on his right hand. They rummaged around my poor cabin for a moment; the head bandit then said, in his stage whisper,—

"It 's a waste of time—*he* shall tell where it 's hid. Undo his gag, and revive him up."

The other said—

"All right—provided no clubbing."

"No clubbing it is, then—provided he keeps still."

They approached me; just then there was a sound outside; a sound of voices and trampling hoofs; the robbers held their breath and listened; the sounds came slowly nearer and nearer; then came a shout—

"*Hello*, the house! Show a light, we want water."

"The captain's voice, by G—!" said the stage-whispering ruffian, and both robbers fled by the way of the back door, shutting off their bull's-eye as they ran.

The strangers shouted several times more, then rode by—there seemed to be a dozen of the horses—and I heard nothing more.

I struggled, but could not free myself from my bonds. I tried to speak, but the gag was effective; I could not make a sound. I listened for my wife's voice and my child's—listened long and intently, but no sound came from the other end of the room where their bed was. This silence became more and more awful, more and more ominous, every moment. Could you have endured an hour of it, do you think? Pity me, then, who had to endure three. Three hours?—it was three ages! Whenever the clock struck, it seemed as if years had gone by since I had heard it last. All this time I was struggling in my bonds; and at last, about dawn, I got myself free, and rose up and stretched my stiff limbs. I was able to distinguish details pretty well. The floor was littered with things thrown there by the robbers during their search for my savings. The first object that caught my particular attention was a document of mine which I had seen the rougher of the two ruffians glance at and then cast away. It had blood on it! I staggered to the other end of the room. Oh, poor unoffending, helpless ones, there they lay, their troubles ended, mine begun!

Did I appeal to the law—I? Does it quench the pauper's thirst if the King drink for him? Oh, no, no, no—I wanted no impertinent interference of the law. Laws and the gallows could not pay the debt that was owing to me! Let the laws leave the matter in my hands, and have no fears: I would find the debtor and collect the debt. How accomplish this, do you say? How accomplish it, and feel so sure about it, when I had neither seen the robbers' faces, nor heard their natural voices, nor had any idea who they might be? Nevertheless, I *was* sure—quite sure, quite confident. I had a clue—a clue which you would not have valued—a clue which would not have greatly helped even a detective, since he would lack the secret of how to apply it. I shall come to that, presently—you shall see. Let us go on, now, taking things in their due order. There was one circumstance which gave me a slant in a definite direction to begin with: Those two robbers were manifestly soldiers in tramp disguise; and not new to military service, but old in it—regulars, perhaps; they did not acquire their soldierly attitude, gestures, carriage, in a day, nor a month, nor yet in a year. So I thought, but said nothing. And one of them had said, "the captain's voice, by G—!"—the one whose life I would have. Two miles away, several regiments were in camp, and two companies of U. S. cavalry. When I learned that Captain Blakely, of Company C had passed our way, that night, with an escort, I said nothing, but in that company I resolved to seek my man. In conversation I studiously and persistently described the robbers as tramps, camp followers; and among this class the people made useless search, none suspecting the soldiers but me.

Working patiently, by night, in my desolated home, I made a disguise for myself out of various odds and ends of clothing; in the nearest village I bought a pair of blue goggles. By and by, when the military camp broke up, and Company C was ordered a hundred miles north, to Napoleon, I secreted my small hoard of money in my belt, and took my departure in the night. When Company C arrived in Napoleon, I was already there. Yes, I was there, with a new trade—fortune-teller. Not to seem partial, I made friends and told fortunes among all the companies garrisoned there; but I gave Company C the great bulk of my attentions. I made myself limitlessly obliging to these particular men; they could ask me no favor, put upon me no risk, which I would decline. I became the willing butt of their jokes; this perfected my popularity; I became a favorite.

I early found a private who lacked a thumb—what joy it was to me! And when I found that he alone, of all the company, had lost a thumb, my last misgiving vanished; I was *sure* I was on the right track. This man's name was Kruger, a German. There were nine Germans in the company. I watched, to see who might be his intimates; but he seemed to have no especial intimates. But *I* was his intimate; and I took care to make the intimacy grow. Sometimes I so hungered for my revenge that I could hardly restrain myself from going on my knees and begging him to point out the man who had murdered my wife and child; but I managed to bridle my tongue. I bided my time, and went on telling fortunes, as opportunity offered.

My apparatus was simple: a little red paint and a bit of white paper. I painted the ball of the client's thumb, took a print of it on the paper, studied it that night, and revealed his fortune to him next day. What was my idea in this nonsense? It was this: When I was a youth, I knew an old Frenchman who had been a prison-keeper for thirty years, and he told me that there was one thing about a person which never changed, from the cradle to the grave—the lines in the ball of the thumb; and he said that these lines were never exactly alike in

the thumbs of any two human beings. In these days, we photograph the new criminal, and hang his picture in the Rogues'
Gallery for future reference; but that Frenchman, in his day,
used to take a print of the ball of a new prisoner's thumb and
put that away for future reference. He always said that pictures were no good—future disguises could make them useless; "The thumb's the only sure thing," said he; "you can't
disguise that." And he used to prove his theory, too, on my
friends and acquaintances; it always succeeded.

I went on telling fortunes. Every night I shut myself in, all
alone, and studied the day's thumb-prints with a magnifying-
glass. Imagine the devouring eagerness with which I pored
over those mazy red spirals, with that document by my side
which bore the right-hand thumb- and finger-marks of that
unknown murderer, printed with the dearest blood—to
me—that was ever shed on this earth! And many and many
a time I had to repeat the same old disappointed remark,
"will they *never* correspond!"

But my reward came at last. It was the print of the thumb
of the forty-third man of Company C whom I had experi-
mented on—private Franz Adler. An hour before, I did not
know the murderer's name, or voice, or figure, or face, or
nationality; but now I knew all these things! I believed I
might feel sure; the Frenchman's repeated demonstrations
being so good a warranty. Still, there was a way to *make* sure.
I had an impression of Kruger's left thumb. In the morning
I took him aside when he was off duty; and when we were
out of sight and hearing of witnesses, I said, impressively:—

"A part of your fortune is so grave, that I thought it would
be better for you if I did not tell it in public. You and another
man, whose fortune I was studying last night,—private Adler,—have been murdering a woman and a child! You are
being dogged: within five days both of you will be assassinated."

He dropped on his knees, frightened out of his wits; and
for five minutes he kept pouring out the same set of words,
like a demented person, and in the same half-crying way
which was one of my memories of that murderous night in
my cabin:—

"I did n't do it; upon my soul I did n't do it; and I tried to keep *him* from doing it; I did, as God is my witness. He did it alone."

This was all I wanted. And I tried to get rid of the fool; but no, he clung to me, imploring me to save him from the assassin. He said,—

"I have money—ten thousand dollars—hid away, the fruit of loot and thievery; save me—tell me what to do, and you shall have it, every penny. Two thirds of it is my cousin Adler's; but you can take it all. We hid it when we first came here. But I hid it in a new place yesterday, and have not told him—shall not tell him. I was going to desert, and get away with it all. It is gold, and too heavy to carry when one is running and dodging; but a woman who has been gone over the river two days to prepare my way for me is going to follow me with it; and if I got no chance to describe the hiding-place to her I was going to slip my silver watch into her hand, or send it to her, and she would understand. There's a piece of paper in the back of the case, which tells it all. Here, take the watch—tell me what to do!"

He was trying to press his watch upon me, and was exposing the paper and explaining it to me, when Adler appeared on the scene, about a dozen yards away. I said to poor Kruger:—

"Put up your watch, I don't want it. You shan't come to any harm. Go, now; I must tell Adler his fortune. Presently I will tell you how to escape the assassin; meantime shall have to examine your thumb-mark again. Say nothing to Adler about this thing—say nothing to anybody."

He went away filled with fright and gratitude, poor devil. I told Adler a long fortune,—purposely so long that I could not finish it; promised to come to him on guard, that night, and tell him the really important part of it—the tragical part of it, I said,—so must be out of reach of eavesdroppers. They always kept a picket-watch outside the town,—mere discipline and ceremony,—no occasion for it, no enemy around.

Toward midnight I set out, equipped with the countersign, and picked my way toward the lonely region where Adler was to keep his watch. It was so dark that I stumbled right on a dim figure almost before I could get out a protecting word. The sentinel hailed and I answered, both at the same moment. I added, "It 's only me—the fortune-teller." Then I slipped to the poor devil's side, and without a word I drove my dirk into his heart! *Ja wohl*, laughed I, it *was* the tragedy part of his fortune, indeed! As he fell from his horse, he clutched at me, and my blue goggles remained in his hand; and away plunged the beast dragging him, with his foot in the stirrup.

I fled through the woods, and made good my escape, leaving the accusing goggles behind me in that dead man's hand.

This was fifteen or sixteen years ago. Since then I have wandered aimlessly about the earth, sometimes at work, sometimes idle; sometimes with money, sometimes with none; but always tired of life, and wishing it was done, for my mission here was finished, with the act of that night; and the only pleasure, solace, satisfaction I had, in all those tedious years, was in the daily reflection, "I have killed him!"

Four years ago, my health began to fail. I had wandered into Munich, in my purposeless way. Being out of money, I sought work, and got it; did my duty faithfully about a year, and was then given the berth of night watchman yonder in that dead-house which you visited lately. The place suited my mood. I liked it. I liked being with the dead—liked being alone with them. I used to wander among those rigid corpses, and peer into their austere faces, by the hour. The later the time, the more impressive it was; I preferred the late time. Sometimes I turned the lights low: this gave perspective, you see; and the imagination could play; always, the dim receding ranks of the dead inspired one with weird and fascinating fancies. Two years ago—I had been there a year then—I was sitting all alone in the watch-room, one gusty winter's night, chilled, numb, comfortless; drowsing gradually into unconsciousness; the sobbing of the wind and the slamming of distant shutters falling fainter and fainter upon my dulling ear each moment, when sharp and suddenly that dead-bell rang out a blood-curdling alarum over my head! The shock of it nearly paralyzed me; for it was the first time I had ever heard it.

I gathered myself together and flew to the corpse-room. About midway down the outside rank, a shrouded figure was sitting upright, wagging its head slowly from one side to the other—a grisly spectacle! Its side was toward me. I hurried to it and peered into its face. Heavens, it was Adler!

Can you divine what my first thought was? Put into words, it was this: "It seems, then, you escaped me once: there will be a different result this time!"

Evidently this creature was suffering unimaginable terrors. Think what it must have been to wake up in the midst of that voiceless hush, and look out over that grim congregation of the dead! What gratitude shone in his skinny white face when he saw a living form before him! And how the fervency of this mute gratitude was augmented when his eyes fell upon the life-giving cordials which I carried in my hands! Then imagine the horror which came into this pinched face when I put the cordials behind me, and said mockingly,—

"Speak up, Franz Adler—call upon these dead. Doubtless they will listen and have pity; but here there is none else that will."

He tried to speak, but that part of the shroud which bound his jaws, held firm and would not let him. He tried to lift imploring hands, but they were crossed upon his breast and tied. I said—

"Shout, Franz Adler; make the sleepers in the distant streets hear you and bring help. Shout—and lose no time, for there is little to lose. What, you cannot? That is a pity; but it is no matter—it does not always bring help. When you and your cousin murdered a helpless woman and child in a cabin in Arkansas—my wife, it was, and my child!—they shrieked for help, you remember; but it did no good; you remember that it did no good, is it not so? Your teeth chatter—then why cannot you shout? Loosen the bandages with your hands—then you can. Ah, I see—your hands are tied, they cannot aid you. How strangely things repeat themselves, after long years; for *my* hands were tied, that night, you remember? Yes, tied much as yours are now—how odd that is. I could not pull free. It did not occur to you to untie me; it does not occur to me to untie you. Sh——! there 's a late footstep. It is coming this way. Hark, how near it is! One can count the footfalls—one—two—three. There—it is just outside. Now is the time! Shout, man, shout!—it is the one sole chance between you and eternity! Ah, you see you have delayed too long—it is gone by. There—it is dying out. It is gone! Think of it—reflect upon it—you have heard a human footstep for the last time. How curious it must be, to listen to so common a sound as that, and know that one will never hear the fellow to it again."

Oh, my friend, the agony in that shrouded face was ecstasy to see! I thought of a new torture, and applied it—assisting myself with a trifle of lying invention:—

"That poor Kruger tried to save my wife and child, and I did him a grateful good turn for it when the time came. I persuaded him to rob you; and I and a woman helped him to desert, and got him away in safety."

A look as of surprise and triumph shone out dimly through the anguish in my victim's face. I was disturbed, disquieted. I said—

"What, then,—did n't he escape?"

A negative shake of the head.

"No? What happened, then?"

The satisfaction in the shrouded face was still plainer. The man tried to mumble out some words—could not succeed; tried to express something with his obstructed hands—failed; paused a moment, then feebly tilted his head, in a meaning way, toward the corpse that lay nearest him.

"Dead?" I asked. "Failed to escape?—caught in the act and shot?"

Negative shake of the head.

"How, then?"

Again the man tried to do something with his hands. I watched closely, but could not guess the intent. I bent over and watched still more intently. He had twisted a thumb around and was weakly punching at his breast with it.

"Ah—stabbed, do you mean?"

Affirmative nod, accompanied by a spectral smile of such peculiar devilishness, that it struck an awakening light through my dull brain, and I cried—

"Did *I* stab him, mistaking him for you?—for that stroke was meant for none but you."

The affirmative nod of the re-dying rascal was as joyous as his failing strength was able to put into its expression.

"O, miserable, miserable me, to slaughter the pitying soul

that stood a friend to my darlings when they were helpless, and would have saved them if he could! miserable, oh, miserable, miserable me!"

I fancied I heard the muffled gurgle of a mocking laugh. I took my face out of my hands, and saw my enemy sinking back upon his inclined board.

He was a satisfactory long time dying. He had a wonderful vitality, an astonishing constitution. Yes, he was a pleasant long time at it. I got a chair and a newspaper, and sat down by him and read. Occasionally I took a sip of brandy. This was necessary, on account of the cold. But I did it partly because I saw, that along at first, whenever I reached for the bottle, he thought I was going to give him some. I read aloud: mainly imaginary accounts of people snatched from the grave's threshold and restored to life and vigor by a few spoonsful of liquor and a warm bath. Yes, he had a long, hard death of it—three hours and six minutes, from the time he rang his bell.

It is believed that in all these eighteen years that have elapsed since the institution of the corpse-watch, no shrouded occupant of the Bavarian dead-houses has ever rung its bell. Well, it is a harmless belief. Let it stand at that.

The chill of that death-room had penetrated my bones. It revived and fastened upon me the disease which had been afflicting me, but which, up to that night, had been steadily disappearing. That man murdered my wife and my child; and in three days hence he will have added me to his list. No matter—God! how delicious the memory of it!—I caught him escaping from his grave, and thrust him back into it!

After that night, I was confined to my bed for a week; but as soon as I could get about, I went to the dead-house books and got the number of the house which Adler had died in. A wretched lodging-house, it was. It was my idea that he would naturally have gotten hold of Kruger's effects, being his cousin; and I wanted to get Kruger's watch, if I could. But while I was sick, Adler's things had been sold and scattered, all except a few old letters, and some odds and ends of no value. However, through those letters, I traced out a son of Kruger's, the only relative he left. He is a man of thirty, now, a shoemaker by trade, and living at No. 14 Königstrasse,

Mannheim—widower, with several small children. Without explaining to him why, I have furnished two thirds of his support, ever since.

Now, as to that watch—see how strangely things happen! I traced it around and about Germany for more than a year, at considerable cost in money and vexation; and at last I got it. Got it, and was unspeakably glad; opened it, and found nothing in it! Why, I might have known that that bit of paper was not going to stay there all this time. Of course I gave up that ten thousand dollars then; gave it up, and dropped it out of my mind: and most sorrowfully, for I had wanted it for Kruger's son.

Last night, when I consented at last that I must die, I began to make ready. I proceeded to burn all useless papers; and sure enough, from a batch of Adler's, not previously examined with thoroughness, out dropped that long-desired scrap! I recognized it in a moment. Here it is—I will translate it:

> "Brick livery stable, stone foundation, middle of town, corner of Orleans and Market. Corner toward Court-house. Third stone, fourth row. Stick notice there, saying how many are to come."

There—take it, and preserve it. Kruger explained that that stone was removable; and that it was in the north wall of the foundation, fourth row from the top, and third stone from the west. The money is secreted behind it. He said the closing sentence was a blind, to mislead in case the paper should fall into wrong hands. It probably performed that office for Adler.

Now I want to beg that when you make your intended journey down the river, you will hunt out that hidden money, and send it to Adam Kruger, care of the Mannheim address which I have mentioned. It will make a rich man of him, and I shall sleep the sounder in my grave for knowing that I have done what I could for the son of the man who tried to save my wife and child—albeit my hand ignorantly struck him down, whereas the impulse of my heart would have been to shield and serve him.

XXXII.

The Disposal of a Bonanza

S UCH WAS Ritter's narrative," said I to my two friends. There was a profound and impressive silence, which lasted a considerable time; then both men broke into a fusillade of excited and admiring ejaculations over the strange incidents of the tale; and this, along with a rattling fire of questions, was kept up until all hands were about out of breath. Then my friends began to cool down, and draw off, under shelter of occasional volleys, into silence and abysmal reverie. For ten minutes now, there was stillness. Then Rogers said dreamily: —

"Ten thousand dollars."

Adding, after a considerable pause, —

"Ten thousand. It is a heap of money."

Presently the poet inquired, —

"Are you going to send it to him right away?"

"Yes," I said. "It is a queer question."

No reply. After a little, Rogers asked, hesitatingly:

"*All* of it? — That is — I mean — "

"*Certainly*, all of it."

I was going to say more, but stopped, — was stopped by a train of thought which started up in me. Thompson spoke, but my mind was absent and I did not catch what he said. But I heard Rogers answer, —

"Yes, it seems so to me. It ought to be quite sufficient; for I don't see that *he* has done anything."

Presently the poet said, —

"When you come to look at it, it is *more* than sufficient. Just look at it — five thousand dollars! Why, he could n't spend it in a lifetime! And it would injure him, too; perhaps ruin him — you want to look at that. In a little while he would throw his last away, shut up his shop, maybe take to drinking, maltreat his motherless children, drift into other evil courses, go steadily from bad to worse — "

"Yes, that 's it," interrupted Rogers, fervently, "I 've seen it a hundred times — yes, more than a hundred. You put money into the hands of a man like that, if you want to destroy him, that's all; just put money into his hands, it's all you've got to do; and if it don't pull him down, and take all the usefulness out of him, and all the self-respect and everything, then I don't know human nature—ain't that so, Thompson? And even if we were to give him a *third* of it; why, in less than six months—"

"Less than six *weeks*, you'd better say!" said I, warming up and breaking in. "Unless he had that three thousand dollars in safe hands where he could n't touch it, he would no more last you six weeks than—"

"Of *course* he would n't," said Thompson; "I 've edited books for that kind of people; and the moment they get their hands on the royalty—maybe it's three thousand, maybe it 's two thousand—"

"What business has that shoemaker with two thousand dollars, I should like to know?" broke in Rogers, earnestly. "A man perhaps perfectly contented now, there in Mannheim, surrounded by his own class, eating his bread with the appetite which laborious industry alone can give, enjoying his humble life, honest, upright, pure in heart; and *blest!*—yes, I say blest! blest above all the myriads that go in silk attire and walk the empty artificial round of social folly—but just you put *that* temptation before him once! just you lay fifteen hundred dollars before a man like that, and say—"

"Fifteen hundred devils!" cried I, "*five* hundred would rot his principles, paralyze his industry, drag him to the rumshop, thence to the gutter, thence to the almshouse, thence to—"

"*Why* put upon ourselves this crime, gentlemen?" interrupted the poet earnestly and appealingly. "He is happy where he is, and *as* he is. Every sentiment of honor, every sentiment of charity, every sentiment of high and sacred benevolence warns us, beseeches us, commands us to leave him undisturbed. That is real friendship, that is true friendship. We could follow other courses that would be more showy; but none that would be so truly kind and wise, depend upon it."

After some further talk, it became evident that each of us, down in his heart, felt some misgivings over this settlement of the matter. It was manifest that we all felt that we ought to send the poor shoemaker *something*. There was long and thoughtful discussion of this point; and we finally decided to send him a chromo.

Well, now that everything seemed to be arranged satisfactorily to everybody concerned, a new trouble broke out: it transpired that these two men were expecting to share equally in the money with me. That was not my idea. I said that if they got half of it between them they might consider themselves lucky. Rogers said:—

"Who would have had *any* if it had n't been for me? I flung out the first hint—but for that it would all have gone to the shoemaker."

Thompson said that he was thinking of the thing himself at the very moment that Rogers had originally spoken.

I retorted that the idea would have occurred to me plenty soon enough, and without anybody's help. I was slow about thinking, maybe, but I was sure.

This matter warmed up into a quarrel; then into a fight; and each man got pretty badly battered. As soon as I had got myself mended up after a fashion, I ascended to the hurricane deck in a pretty sour humor. I found Captain McCord there, and said, as pleasantly as my humor would permit:—

"I have come to say good-bye, captain. I wish to go ashore at Napoleon."

"Go ashore where?"

"Napoleon."

The captain laughed; but seeing that I was not in a jovial mood, stopped that and said,—

"But are you serious?"

"Serious? I certainly am."

The captain glanced up at the pilot-house and said,—

"He wants to get off at Napoleon!"

"*Napoleon?*"

"That's what he says."

"Great Cæsar's ghost!"

Uncle Mumford approached along the deck. The captain said,—

"Uncle, here 's a friend of yours wants to get off at Napoleon!"

"Well, by—!"

I said,—

"Come, what is all this about? Can't a man go ashore at Napoleon if he wants to?"

"Why, hang it, don't you know? There is n't any Napoleon any more. Has n't been for years and years. The Arkansas River burst through it, tore it all to rags, and emptied it into the Mississippi!"

"Carried the *whole* town away?—banks, churches, jails, newspaper-offices, court-house, theatre, fire department, livery stable,— *everything*?"

"Everything. Just a fifteen-minute job, or such a matter. Did n't leave hide nor hair, shred nor shingle of it, except the fag-end of a shanty and one brick chimney. This boat is paddling along right now, where the dead-centre of that town used to be; yonder is the brick chimney,—all that 's left of Napoleon. These dense woods on the right used to be a mile back of the town. Take a look behind you—up-stream—now you begin to recognize this country, don't you?"

"Yes, I do recognize it now. It is the most wonderful thing I ever heard of; by a long shot the most wonderful—and unexpected."

Mr. Thompson and Mr. Rogers had arrived, meantime, with satchels and umbrellas, and had silently listened to the captain's news. Thompson put a half-dollar in my hand and said softly:—

"For my share of the chromo."

Rogers followed suit.

Yes, it was an astonishing thing to see the Mississippi rolling between unpeopled shores and straight over the spot where I used to see a good big self-complacent town twenty years ago. Town that was county-seat of a great and important county; town with a big United States marine hospital; town of innumerable fights—an inquest every day; town where I had used to know the prettiest girl, and the most accomplished in the whole Mississippi Valley; town where we were handed the first printed news of the "Pennsylvania's" mournful disaster a quarter of a century ago; a town no more—swallowed up, vanished, gone to feed the fishes; nothing left but a fragment of a shanty and a crumbling brick chimney!

XXXIII.

Refreshments and Ethics

IN REGARD to Island 74, which is situated not far from the former Napoleon, a freak of the river here has sorely perplexed the laws of men and made them a vanity and a jest. When the State of Arkansas was chartered, she controlled "to the centre of the river"—a most unstable line. The State of Mississippi claimed "to the channel"—another shifty and unstable line. No. 74 belonged to Arkansas. By and by a cut-off threw this big island out of Arkansas, and yet not *within* Mississippi. "Middle of the river" on one side of it, "channel" on the other. That is as I understand the problem. Whether I have got the details right or wrong, this *fact* remains: that here is this big and exceedingly valuable island of four thousand acres, thrust out in the cold, and belonging to neither the one State nor the other; paying taxes to neither, owing allegiance to neither. One man owns the whole island, and of right is "the man without a country."

Island 92 belongs to Arkansas. The river moved it over and joined it to Mississippi. A chap established a whiskey shop there, without a Mississippi license, and enriched himself upon Mississippi custom under Arkansas protection (where no license was in those days required).

We glided steadily down the river in the usual privacy—steamboat or other moving thing seldom seen. Scenery as always: stretch upon stretch of almost unbroken forest, on both sides of the river; soundless solitude. Here and there a cabin or two, standing in small openings on the gray and grassless banks—cabins which had formerly stood a quarter or half-mile farther to the front, and gradually been pulled farther and farther back as the shores caved in. As at Pilcher's Point, for instance, where the cabins had been moved back three hundred yards in three months, so we were told; but the caving banks had already caught up with them, and they were being conveyed rearward once more.

Napoleon had but small opinion of Greenville, Mississippi, in the old times; but behold, Napoleon is gone to the catfishes, and here is Greenville full of life and activity, and making a considerable flourish in the Valley; having three thousand inhabitants, it is said, and doing a gross trade of $2,500,000 annually. A growing town.

There was much talk on the boat about the Calhoun Land Company, an enterprise which is expected to work wholesome results. Colonel Calhoun, a grandson of the statesman, went to Boston and formed a syndicate which purchased a large tract of land on the river, in Chicot County, Arkansas,—some ten thousand acres—for cotton-growing. The purpose is to work on a cash basis: buy at first hands, and handle their own product; supply their negro laborers with provisions and necessaries at a trifling profit, say 8 or 10 per cent; furnish them comfortable quarters, etc., and encourage them to save money and remain on the place. If this proves a financial success, as seems quite certain, they propose to establish a banking-house in Greenville, and lend money at an unburdensome rate of interest—6 per cent is spoken of.

The trouble heretofore has been—I am quoting remarks of planters and steamboatmen—that the planters, although owning the land, were without cash capital; had to hypothecate both land and crop to carry on the business. Consequently, the commission dealer who furnishes the money takes some risk and demands big interest—usually 10 per cent, and $2\frac{1}{2}$ per cent for negotiating the loan. The planter has also to buy his supplies through the same dealer, paying commissions and profits. Then when he ships his crop, the dealer adds his commissions, insurance, etc. So, taking it by and large, and first and last, the dealer's share of that crop is about 25 per cent.[1]

A cotton-planter's estimate of the average margin of profit on planting, in his section: One man and mule will raise ten acres of cotton, giving ten bales cotton, worth, say, $500; cost of producing, say $350; net profit, $150, or $15 per acre. There is also a profit now from the cotton-seed, which formerly had

[1] "But what can the State do where the people are under subjection to rates of interest ranging from 18 to 30 per cent, and are also under the necessity of purchasing their crops in advance even of planting, at these rates, for the privilege of purchasing all their supplies at 100 per cent profit?"—*Edward Atkinson.*

little value—none where much transportation was necessary. In sixteen hundred pounds crude cotton, four hundred are lint, worth, say, ten cents a pound; and twelve hundred pounds of seed, worth $12 or $13 per ton. Maybe in future even the *stems* will not be thrown away. Mr. Edward Atkinson says that for each bale of cotton there are fifteen hundred pounds of stems, and that these are very rich in phosphate of lime and potash; that when ground and mixed with ensilage or cotton-seed meal (which is too rich for use as fodder in large quantities), the stem mixture makes a superior food, rich in all the elements needed for the production of milk, meat, and bone. Heretofore the stems have been considered a nuisance.

Complaint is made that the planter remains grouty toward the former slave, since the war; will have nothing but a chill business relation with him, no sentiment permitted to intrude; will not keep a "store" himself, and supply the negro's wants and thus protect the negro's pocket and make him able and willing to stay on the place and an advantage to him to do it, but lets that privilege to some thrifty Israelite, who encourages the thoughtless negro and wife to buy all sorts of things which they could do without,—buy on credit, at big prices, month after month, credit based on the negro's share of the growing crop; and at the end of the season, the negro's share belongs to the Israelite, the negro is in debt besides, is discouraged, dissatisfied, restless, and both he and the planter are injured; for he will take steamboat and migrate, and the planter must get a stranger in his place who does not know him, does not care for him, will fatten the Israelite a season, and follow his predecessor per steamboat.

It is hoped that the Calhoun Company will show, by its humane and protective treatment of its laborers, that its method is the most profitable for both planter and negro; and it is believed that a general adoption of that method will then follow.

And where so many are saying their say, shall not the barkeeper testify? He is thoughtful, observant, never drinks; endeavors to earn his salary, and *would* earn it if there were custom enough. He says the people along here in Mississippi and Louisiana will send up the river to buy vegetables rather

than raise them, and they will come aboard at the landings
and buy fruits of the barkeeper. Thinks they "don't know anything but cotton;" believes they don't know how to raise vegetables and fruit—"at least the most of them." Says "a nigger
will go to H for a watermelon" ("H" is all I find in the stenographer's report—means Halifax probably, though that
seems a good way to go for a watermelon). Barkeeper buys
watermelons for five cents up the river, brings them down
and sells them for fifty. "Why does he mix such elaborate and
picturesque drinks for the nigger hands on the boat?" Because
they won't have any other. "They want a *big* drink; don't
make any difference what you make it of, they want the worth
of their money. You give a nigger a plain gill of half-a-dollar
brandy for five cents—will he touch it? No. Ain't size enough
to it. But you put up a pint of all kinds of worthless rubbish,
and heave in some red stuff to make it beautiful—red 's the
main thing—and he would n't put down that glass to go to
a circus." All the bars on this Anchor Line are rented and
owned by one firm. They furnish the liquors from their own
establishment, and hire the barkeepers "on salary." Good liquors? Yes, on some of the boats, where there are the kind of
passengers that want it and can pay for it. On the other boats?
No. Nobody but the deck hands and firemen to drink it.
"Brandy? Yes, I 've got brandy, plenty of it; but you don't
want any of it unless you 've made your will." It is n't as it
used to be in the old times. Then everybody travelled by
steamboat, everybody drank, and everybody treated everybody else. "Now most everybody goes by railroad, and the
rest don't drink." In the old times, the barkeeper owned the
bar himself, "and was gay and smarty and talky and all jew-
elled up, and was the toniest aristocrat on the boat; used to
make $2,000 on a trip. A father who left his son a steamboat
bar, left him a fortune. Now he leaves him board and lodg-
ing; yes, and washing, if a shirt a trip will do. Yes, indeedy,
times are changed. Why, do you know, on the principal line
of boats on the Upper Mississippi, they don't have any bar at
all! Sounds like poetry, but it 's the petrified truth."

XXXIV.

Tough Yarns

S TACK ISLAND. I remembered Stack Island; also Lake
Providence, Louisiana—which is the first distinctly
Southern-looking town you come to, downward-bound; lies
level and low, shade-trees hung with venerable gray beards of
Spanish moss; "restful, pensive, Sunday aspect about the
place," comments Uncle Mumford, with feeling—also with
truth.

A Mr. H. furnished some minor details of fact concerning
this region which I would have hesitated to believe if I had
not known him to be a steamboat mate. He was a passenger
of ours, a resident of Arkansas City, and bound to Vicksburg
to join his boat, a little Sunflower packet. He was an austere
man, and had the reputation of being singularly unworldly,
for a river man. Among other things, he said that Arkansas
had been injured and kept back by generations of exaggera-
tions concerning the mosquitoes there. One may smile, said
he, and turn the matter off as being a small thing; but when
you come to look at the effects produced, in the way of discouragement of immigration, and diminished values of property, it was quite the opposite of a small thing, or thing in
any wise to be coughed down or sneered at. These mosquitoes had been persistently represented as being formidable
and lawless; whereas "the truth is, they are feeble, insignificant in size, diffident to a fault, sensitive"—and so on, and so
on; you would have supposed he was talking about his family. But if he was soft on the Arkansas mosquitoes, he was
hard enough on the mosquitoes of Lake Providence to make
up for it—"those Lake Providence colossi," as he finely called
them. He said that two of them could whip a dog, and that
four of them could hold a man down; and except help come,
they would kill him—"butcher him," as he expressed it. Referred in a sort of casual way—and yet significant way—to
"the fact that the life policy in its simplest form is unknown
in Lake Providence—they take out a mosquito policy besides." He told many remarkable things about those lawless

insects. Among others, said he had seen them try to *vote*. Noticing that this statement seemed to be a good deal of a strain on us, he modified it a little: said he might have been mistaken, as to that particular, but knew he had seen them around the polls "canvassing."

There was another passenger—friend of H.'s—who backed up the harsh evidence against those mosquitoes, and detailed some stirring adventures which he had had with them. The stories were pretty sizable, merely pretty sizable; yet Mr. H. was continually interrupting with a cold, inexorable "Wait—knock off twenty-five per cent of that; now go on;" or, "Wait—you are getting that too strong; cut it down, cut it down—you get a leetle too much costumery on to your statements: always dress a fact in tights, never in an ulster;" or, "Pardon, once more: if you are going to load anything more on to that statement, you want to get a couple of lighters and tow the rest, because it 's drawing all the water there is in the river already; stick to facts—just stick to the cold facts; what these gentlemen want for a book is the frozen truth—ain't that so, gentlemen?" He explained privately that it was necessary to watch this man all the time, and keep him within bounds; it would not do to neglect this precaution, as he, Mr. H., "knew to his sorrow." Said he, "I will not deceive you; he told me such a monstrous lie once, that it swelled my left ear up, and spread it so that I was actually not able to see out around it; it remained so for months, and people came miles to see me fan myself with it."

XXXV.

Vicksburg during the Trouble

WE USED to plough past the lofty hill-city, Vicksburg, down-stream; but we cannot do that now. A cut-off has made a country town of it, like Osceola, St. Genevieve, and several others. There is currentless water—also a big island—in front of Vicksburg now. You come down the river the other side of the island, then turn and come up to the town; that is, in high water: in low water you can't come up, but must land some distance below it.

Signs and scars still remain, as reminders of Vicksburg's tremendous war-experiences; earthworks, trees crippled by the cannon balls, cave-refuges in the clay precipices, etc. The caves did good service during the six weeks' bombardment of the city—May 18 to July 4, 1863. They were used by the non-combatants—mainly by the women and children; not to live in constantly, but to fly to for safety on occasion. They were mere holes, tunnels, driven into the perpendicular clay bank, then branched Y shape, within the hill. Life in Vicksburg, during the six weeks was perhaps—but wait; here are some materials out of which to reproduce it:—

Population, twenty-seven thousand soldiers and three thousand non-combatants; the city utterly cut off from the world—walled solidly in, the frontage by gunboats, the rear by soldiers and batteries; hence, no buying and selling with the outside; no passing to and fro; no God-speeding a parting guest, no welcoming a coming one; no printed acres of world-wide news to be read at breakfast, mornings—a tedious dull absence of such matter, instead; hence, also, no running to see steamboats smoking into view in the distance up or down, and ploughing toward the town—for none came, the river lay vacant and undisturbed; no rush and turmoil around the railway station, no struggling over bewildered swarms of passengers by noisy mobs of hackmen—all quiet there; flour two hundred dollars a barrel, sugar thirty, corn ten dollars a bushel, bacon five dollars a pound, rum a hundred dollars a gallon; other things in proportion: consequently, no roar and racket of drays and carriages tearing along the streets; nothing for them to do, among that handful of non-combatants of exhausted means; at three o'clock in the morning, silence; silence so dead that the measured tramp of a sentinel can be heard a seemingly impossible distance; out of hearing of this lonely sound, perhaps the stillness is absolute: all in a moment come ground-shaking thunder-crashes of artillery, the sky is cobwebbed with the criss-crossing red lines streaming from soaring bomb-shells, and a rain of iron fragments descends upon the city; descends upon the empty streets: streets which are not empty a moment later, but mottled with dim figures of frantic women and children skurrying from home and bed toward the cave dungeons—encouraged by the humorous grim soldiery, who shout "Rats, to your holes!" and laugh.

The cannon-thunder rages, shells scream and crash overhead, the iron rain pours down, one hour, two hours, three, possibly six, then stops; silence follows, but the streets are still empty; the silence continues; by and by a head projects from a cave here and there and yonder, and reconnoitres, cautiously; the silence still continuing, bodies follow heads, and jaded, half-smothered creatures group themselves about, stretch their cramped limbs, draw in deep draughts of the grateful fresh air, gossip with the neighbors from the next cave; maybe straggle off home presently, or take a lounge through the town, if the stillness continues; and will skurry to the holes again, by and by, when the war-tempest breaks forth once more.

There being but three thousand of these cave-dwellers—merely the population of a village—would they not come to know each other, after a week or two, and familiarly; insomuch that the fortunate or unfortunate experiences of one would be of interest to all?

Those are the materials furnished by history. From them might not almost anybody reproduce for himself the life of that time in Vicksburg? Could you, who did not experience it, come nearer to reproducing it to the imagination of another non-participant than could a Vicksburger who *did* experience it? It seems impossible; and yet there are reasons why it might not really be. When one makes his first voyage in a ship, it is an experience which multitudinously bristles with striking novelties; novelties which are in such sharp contrast with all this person's former experiences that they take a seemingly deathless grip upon his imagination and memory. By tongue or pen he can make a landsman live that strange and stirring voyage over with him; make him see it all and feel it all. But if he wait? If he make ten voyages in succession—what then? Why, the thing has lost color, snap, surprise; and has become commonplace. The man would have nothing to tell that would quicken a landsman's pulse.

Years ago, I talked with a couple of the Vicksburg noncombatants—a man and his wife. Left to tell their story in their own way, those people told it without fire, almost without interest.

A week of their wonderful life there would have made their tongues eloquent forever perhaps; but they had six weeks of it, and that wore the novelty all out; they got used to being bomb-shelled out of home and into the ground; the matter became commonplace. After that, the possibility of their ever being startlingly interesting in their talks about it was gone. What the man said was to this effect:—

"It got to be Sunday all the time. Seven Sundays in the week—to us, anyway. We had n't anything to do, and time hung heavy. Seven Sundays, and all of them broken up at one time or another, in the day or in the night, by a few hours of the awful storm of fire and thunder and iron. At first we used to shin for the holes a good deal faster than we did afterwards. The first time, I forgot the children, and Maria fetched them both along. When she was all safe in the cave she fainted. Two or three weeks afterwards, when she was running for the holes, one morning, through a shell-shower, a big shell burst near her and covered her all over with dirt, and a piece of the iron carried away her game-bag of false hair from the back of her head. Well, she stopped to get that game-bag before she shoved along again! Was getting used to things already, you see. We all got so that we could tell a good deal about shells; and after that we did n't always go under shelter if it was a light shower. Us men would loaf around and talk; and a man would say, 'There she goes!' and name the kind of shell it was from the sound of it, and go on talking—if there was n't any danger from it. If a shell was bursting close over us, we stopped talking and stood still;—uncomfortable, yes, but it was n't safe to move. When it let go, we went on talking again, if nobody hurt—maybe saying, 'That was a ripper!' or some such commonplace comment before we resumed; or, maybe, we would see a shell poising itself away high in the air overhead. In that case, every fellow just whipped out a sudden, 'See you again, gents!' and shoved. Often and often I saw gangs of ladies promenading the streets, looking as cheerful as you please, and keeping an eye canted up watching the shells; and I 've seen them stop still when they were uncertain about what a shell was going to do, and wait and make certain; and after that they s'antered along again, or lit out for shelter, according to the verdict. Streets in some towns have a litter of pieces of paper, and odds and ends of one sort or another lying around. Ours had n't; they had *iron* litter. Sometimes a man would gather up all the iron fragments and unbursted shells in his neighborhood, and pile them into a kind of monument in his front yard—a ton of it, sometimes. No glass left; glass could n't stand such a bombardment; it was all shivered out. Windows of the houses vacant—looked like eye-holes in a skull. *Whole* panes were as scarce as news.

"We had church Sundays. Not many there, along at first; but by and by pretty good turnouts. I 've seen service stop a minute, and everybody sit quiet—no voice heard, pretty funeral-like then—and all the more so on account of the awful boom and crash going on outside and overhead; and pretty soon, when a body could be heard, service would go on again. Organs and church-music mixed up with a bombardment is a powerful queer combination—along at first. Coming out of church, one morning, we had an accident— the only one that happened around me on a Sunday. I was just having a hearty hand-shake with a friend I had n't seen for a while, and saying, 'Drop into our cave to-night, after bombardment; we 've got hold of a pint of prime wh—.' Whiskey, I was going to say, you know, but a shell interrupted. A chunk of it cut the man's arm off, and left it dangling in my hand. And do you know the thing that is going to stick the longest in my memory, and outlast everything else, little and big, I reckon, is the mean thought I had then? It was 'the whiskey *is saved*.' And yet, don't you know, it was kind of excusable; because it was as scarce as diamonds, and we had only just that little; never had another taste during the siege.

"Sometimes the caves were desperately crowded, and always hot and close. Sometimes a cave had twenty or twenty-five people packed into it; no turning-room for anybody; air so foul, sometimes, you could n't have made a candle burn in it. A child was born in one of those caves one night. Think of that; why, it was like having it born in a trunk.

"Twice we had sixteen people in our cave; and a number of times we had a dozen. Pretty suffocating in there. We always had eight; eight belonged there. Hunger and misery and sickness and fright and sorrow, and I don't know what all, got so loaded into them that none of them were ever rightly their old selves after the siege. They all died but three of us within a couple of years. One night a shell burst in front of the hole and caved it in and stopped it up. It was lively times, for a while, digging out. Some of us came near smothering. After that we made two openings— ought to have thought of it at first.

"Mule meat? No, we only got down to that the last day or two. Of course it was good; anything is good when you are starving."

This man had kept a diary during—six weeks? No, only the first six days. The first day, eight close pages; the second, five; the third, one—loosely written; the fourth, three or four lines; a line or two the fifth and sixth days; seventh day, diary abandoned; life in terrific Vicksburg having now become commonplace and matter of course.

The war history of Vicksburg has more about it to interest the general reader than that of any other of the river-towns. It is full of variety, full of incident, full of the picturesque. Vicksburg held out longer than any other important river-town, and saw warfare in all its phases, both land and water—the siege, the mine, the assault, the repulse, the bombardment, sickness, captivity, famine.

The most beautiful of all the national cemeteries is here. Over the great gateway is this inscription:—

> "HERE REST IN PEACE 16,600 WHO DIED FOR THEIR
> COUNTRY IN THE YEARS 1861 TO 1865."

The grounds are nobly situated; being very high and commanding a wide prospect of land and river. They are tastefully laid out in broad terraces, with winding roads and paths; and there is profuse adornment in the way of semi-tropical shrubs and flowers; and in one part is a piece of native wild-wood, left just as it grew, and, therefore, perfect in its charm. Everything about this cemetery suggests the hand of the national Government. The Government's work is always conspicuous for excellence, solidity, thoroughness, neatness. The Government does its work well in the first place, and then takes care of it.

By winding-roads—which were often cut to so great a depth between perpendicular walls that they were mere roofless tunnels—we drove out a mile or two and visited the monument which stands upon the scene of the surrender of Vicksburg to General Grant by General Pemberton. Its metal will preserve it from the hackings and chippings which so defaced its predecessor, which was of marble; but the brick foundations are crumbling, and it will tumble down by and by. It overlooks a picturesque region of wooded hills and ravines; and is not unpicturesque itself, being well smothered in flowering weeds. The battered remnant of the marble monument has been removed to the National Cemetery.

On the road, a quarter of a mile townward, an aged colored man showed us, with pride, an unexploded bomb-shell which has lain in his yard since the day it fell there during the siege. "I was a-stannin' heah, an' de dog was a-stannin' heah; de dog he went for de shell, gwine to pick a fuss wid it; but I did n't; I says, 'Jes' make youseff at home heah; lay still whah you is, or bust up de place, jes' as you 's a mind to, but I 's got business out in de woods, I has!' "

Vicksburg is a town of substantial business streets and pleasant residences; it commands the commerce of the Yazoo and Sunflower Rivers; is pushing railways in several directions, through rich agricultural regions, and has a promising future of prosperity and importance.

Apparently, nearly all the river towns, big and little, have made up their minds that they must look mainly to railroads for wealth and upbuilding, henceforth. They are acting upon this idea. The signs are, that the next twenty years will bring about some noteworthy changes in the Valley, in the direction of increased population and wealth, and in the intellectual advancement and the liberalizing of opinion which go naturally with these. And yet, if one may judge by the past, the river towns will manage to find and use a chance, here and there, to cripple and retard their progress. They kept themselves back in the days of steamboating supremacy, by a system of wharfage-dues so stupidly graded as to prohibit what may be called small *retail* traffic in freights and passengers. Boats were charged such heavy wharfage that they could not afford to land for one or two passengers or a light lot of freight. Instead of encouraging the bringing of trade to their doors, the towns diligently and effectively discouraged it. They could have had many boats and low rates; but their policy rendered few boats and high rates compulsory. It was a policy which extended—and extends—from New Orleans to St. Paul.

We had a strong desire to make a trip up the Yazoo and the Sunflower—an interesting region at any time, but additionally interesting at this time, because up there the great inundation was still to be seen in force,—but we were nearly sure to have to wait a day or more for a New Orleans boat on our return; so we were obliged to give up the project.

Here is a story which I picked up on board the boat that night. I insert it in this place merely because it is a good story, not because it belongs here—for it does n't. It was told by a passenger—a college professor—and was called to the surface in the course of a general conversation which began with talk about horses, drifted into talk about astronomy, then into talk about the lynching of the gamblers in Vicksburg half a century ago, then into talk about dreams and superstitions; and ended, after midnight, in a dispute over free trade and protection.

XXXVI.

The Professor's Yarn

IT WAS in the early days. I was not a college professor then. I was a humble-minded young land-surveyor, with the world before me—to survey, in case anybody wanted it done. I had a contract to survey a route for a great mining-ditch in California, and I was on my way thither, by sea—a three or four weeks' voyage. There were a good many passengers, but I had very little to say to them; reading and dreaming were my passions, and I avoided conversation in order to indulge these appetites. There were three professional gamblers on board—rough, repulsive fellows. I never had any talk with them, yet I could not help seeing them with some frequency, for they gambled in an upper-deck state-room every day and night, and in my promenades I often had glimpses of them through their door, which stood a little ajar to let out the surplus tobacco smoke and profanity. They were an evil and hateful presence, but I had to put up with it, of course.

There was one other passenger who fell under my eye a good deal, for he seemed determined to be friendly with me, and I could not have gotten rid of him without running some chance of hurting his feelings, and I was far from wishing to do that. Besides, there was something engaging in his coun-trified simplicity and his beaming good-nature. The first time I saw this Mr. John Backus, I guessed, from his clothes and his looks, that he was a grazier or farmer from the back woods of some western State—doubtless Ohio—and after-ward when he dropped into his personal history and I discov-ered that he *was* a cattle-raiser from interior Ohio, I was so pleased with my own penetration that I warmed toward him for verifying my instinct.

He got to dropping alongside me every day, after breakfast, to help me make my promenade; and so, in the course of time, his easy-working jaw had told me everything about his business, his prospects, his family, his relatives, his politics—in fact everything that concerned a Backus, living or dead. And meantime I think he had managed to get out of me everything I knew about my trade, my tribe, my purposes, my prospects, and myself. He was a gentle and persuasive genius, and this thing showed it; for I was not given to talking about my matters. I said something about triangulation, once; the stately word pleased his ear; he inquired what it meant; I explained; after that he quietly and inoffensively ignored my name, and always called me Triangle.

What an enthusiast he was in cattle! At the bare name of a bull or a cow, his eye would light and his eloquent tongue would turn itself loose. As long as I would walk and listen, he would walk and talk; he knew all breeds, he loved all breeds, he caressed them all with his affectionate tongue. I tramped along in voiceless misery whilst the cattle question was up; when I could endure it no longer, I used to deftly insert a scientific topic into the conversation; then my eye fired and his faded; my tongue fluttered, his stopped; life was a joy to me, and a sadness to him.

One day he said, a little hesitatingly, and with somewhat of diffidence: —

"Triangle, would you mind coming down to my state-room a minute, and have a little talk on a certain matter?"

I went with him at once. Arrived there, he put his head out, glanced up and down the saloon warily, then closed the door and locked it. We sat down on the sofa, and he said: —

"I 'm a-going to make a little proposition to you, and if it strikes you favorable, it 'll be a middling good thing for both of us. You ain't a-going out to Californy for fun, nuther am I—it 's *business*, ain't that so? Well, you can do me a good turn, and so can I you, if we see fit. I 've raked and scraped and saved, a considerable many years, and I 've got it all here." He unlocked an old hair trunk, tumbled a chaos of shabby clothes aside, and drew a short stout bag into view for a moment, then buried it again and relocked the trunk. Dropping his voice to a cautious low tone, he continued, "She 's all there—a round ten thousand dollars in yellow-boys; now this is my little idea: What I don't know about raising cattle, ain't worth knowing. There 's mints of money in it, in Californy. Well, I know, and you know, that all along a line that 's being surveyed, there 's little dabs of land that they call 'gores,' that fall to the surveyor free gratis for nothing. All you 've got to do, on your side, is to survey in such a way that the 'gores' will fall on good fat land, then you turn 'em over to me, I stock 'em with cattle, *in* rolls the cash, I plank out your share of the dollars regular, right along, and—"

I was sorry to wither his blooming enthusiasm, but it could not be helped. I interrupted, and said severely,—

"I am not that kind of a surveyor. Let us change the subject, Mr. Backus."

It was pitiful to see his confusion and hear his awkward and shamefaced apologies. I was as much distressed as he was—especially as he seemed so far from having suspected that there was anything improper in his proposition. So I hastened to console him and lead him on to forget his mishap in a conversational orgy about cattle and butchery. We were lying at Acapulco; and, as we went on deck, it happened luckily that the crew were just beginning to hoist some beeves aboard in slings. Backus's melancholy vanished instantly, and with it the memory of his late mistake.

"Now only look at that!" cried he; "My goodness, Triangle, what *would* they say to it in *Ohio*? Would n't their eyes bug out, to see 'em handled like that?—would n't they, though?"

All the passengers were on deck to look—even the gamblers—and Backus knew them all, and had afflicted them all with his pet topic. As I moved away, I saw one of the gamblers approach and accost him; then another of them; then the third. I halted; waited; watched; the conversation continued between the four men; it grew earnest; Backus drew gradually away; the gamblers followed, and kept at his elbow. I was uncomfortable. However, as they passed me presently, I heard Backus say, with a tone of persecuted annoyance:—

"But it ain't any use, gentlemen; I tell you again, as I 've told you a half a dozen times before, I war n't raised to it, and I ain't a-going to resk it."

I felt relieved. "His level head will be his sufficient protection," I said to myself.

During the fortnight's run from Acapulco to San Francisco I several times saw the gamblers talking earnestly with Backus, and once I threw out a gentle warning to him. He chuckled comfortably and said,—

"Oh, yes! they tag around after me considerable—want me

to play a little, just for amusement, they say—but laws-a-me, if my folks have told me once to look out for that sort of live-stock, they 've told me a thousand times, I reckon."

By and by, in due course, we were approaching San Fran-cisco. It was an ugly black night, with a strong wind blowing, but there was not much sea. I was on deck, alone. Toward ten I started below. A figure issued from the gamblers' den, and disappeared in the darkness. I experienced a shock, for I was sure it was Backus. I flew down the companion-way, looked about for him, could not find him, then returned to the deck just in time to catch a glimpse of him as he re-entered that confounded nest of rascality. Had he yielded at last? I feared it. What had he gone below for?—His bag of coin? Possibly. I drew near the door, full of bodings. It was a-crack, and I glanced in and saw a sight that made me bit-terly wish I had given my attention to saving my poor cattle-friend, instead of reading and dreaming my foolish time away. He was gambling. Worse still, he was being plied with champagne, and was already showing some effect from it. He praised the "cider," as he called it, and said now that he had got a taste of it he almost believed he would drink it if it was spirits, it was so good and so ahead of anything he had ever run across before. Surreptitious smiles, at this, passed from one rascal to another, and they filled all the glasses, and whilst Backus honestly drained his to the bottom they pretended to do the same, but threw the wine over their shoulders.

I could not bear the scene, so I wandered forward and tried to interest myself in the sea and the voices of the wind. But no, my uneasy spirit kept dragging me back at quarter-hour intervals; and always I saw Backus drinking his wine—fairly and squarely, and the others throwing theirs away. It was the painfulest night I ever spent.

The only hope I had was that we might reach our anchor-age with speed—that would break up the game. I helped the ship along all I could with my prayers. At last we went boom-ing through the Golden Gate, and my pulses leaped for joy. I hurried back to that door and glanced in. Alas, there was small room for hope—Backus's eyes were heavy and blood-shot, his sweaty face was crimson, his speech maudlin and thick, his body sawed drunkenly about with the weaving motion of the ship. He drained another glass to the dregs, whilst the cards were being dealt.

He took his hand, glanced at it, and his dull eyes lit up for a moment. The gamblers observed it, and showed their gratification by hardly perceptible signs.

"How many cards?"

"None!" said Backus.

One villain—named Hank Wiley—discarded one card, the others three each. The betting began. Heretofore the bets had been trifling—a dollar or two; but Backus started off with an eagle now, Wiley hesitated a moment, then "saw it" and "went ten dollars better." The other two threw up their hands.

Backus went twenty better. Wiley said,—

"I see that, and go you a *hundred* better!" then smiled and reached for the money.

"Let it alone," said Backus, with drunken gravity.

"What! you mean to say you 're going to cover it?"

"Cover it? Well I reckon I am—and lay another hundred on top of it, too."

He reached down inside his overcoat and produced the required sum.

"Oh, that 's your little game, is it? I see your raise, and raise it five hundred!" said Wiley.

"Five hundred *better!*" said the foolish bull-driver, and pulled out the amount and showered it on the pile. The three conspirators hardly tried to conceal their exultation.

All diplomacy and pretence were dropped now, and the sharp exclamations came thick and fast, and the yellow pyramid grew higher and higher. At last ten thousand dollars lay in view. Wiley cast a bag of coin on the table, and said with mocking gentleness,—

"Five thousand dollars better, my friend from the rural districts—what do you say *now?*"

"I *call* you!" said Backus, heaving his golden shot-bag on the pile. "What have you got?"

"Four kings, you d—d fool!" and Wiley threw down his cards and surrounded the stakes with his arms.

"Four *aces*, you ass!" thundered Backus, covering his man

with a cocked revolver. "*I 'm a professional gambler myself, and I 've been laying for you duffers all this voyage!*"

Down went the anchor, rumbledy-dum-dum! and the long trip was ended.

Well—well, it is a sad world. One of the three gamblers was Backus's "pal." It was he that dealt the fateful hands. According to an understanding with the two victims, he was to have given Backus four queens, but alas, he did n't.

A week later, I stumbled upon Backus—arrayed in the height of fashion—in Montgomery Street. He said, cheerily, as we were parting,—

"Ah, by-the-way, you need n't mind about those gores. I don't really know anything about cattle, except what I was able to pick up in a week's apprenticeship over in Jersey just before we sailed. My cattle-culture and cattle-enthusiasm have served their turn—I shan't need them any more."

Next day we reluctantly parted from the "Gold Dust" and her officers, hoping to see that boat and all those officers again, some day. A thing which the fates were to render tragically impossible!

XXXVII.

The End of the "Gold Dust"

For, three months later, August 8, while I was writing one of these foregoing chapters, the New York papers brought this telegram:—

A TERRIBLE DISASTER

Seventeen Persons Killed by an Explosion on the Steamer "Gold Dust."

"Nashville, Aug. 7.—A despatch from Hickman, Ky., says:—

"The steamer 'Gold Dust' exploded her boilers at three o'clock to-day, just after leaving Hickman. Forty-seven persons were scalded and seventeen are missing. The boat was landed in the eddy just above the town, and through the exertions of the citizens the cabin passengers, officers, and part of the crew and deck passengers were taken ashore and removed to the hotels and residences. Twenty-four of the injured were lying in Holcomb's dry-goods store at one time, where they received every attention before being removed to more comfortable places."

A list of the names followed, whereby it appeared that of the seventeen dead, one was the barkeeper; and among the forty-seven wounded, were the captain, chief mate, second mate, and second and third clerks; also Mr. Lem. S. Gray, pilot, and several members of the crew.

In answer to a private telegram, we learned that none of these was severely hurt, except Mr. Gray. Letters received afterward confirmed this news, and said that Mr. Gray was improving and would get well. Later letters spoke less hopefully of his case; and finally came one announcing his death. A good man, a most companionable and manly man, and worthy of a kindlier fate.

XXXVIII.

The House Beautiful

W E TOOK PASSAGE in a Cincinnati boat for New Orleans; or on a Cincinnati boat—either is correct; the former is the eastern form of putting it, the latter the western.

Mr. Dickens declined to agree that the Mississippi steamboats were "magnificent," or that they were "floating palaces,"—terms which had always been applied to them; terms which did not over-express the admiration with which the people viewed them.

Mr. Dickens's position was unassailable, possibly; the people's position was certainly unassailable. If Mr. Dickens was comparing these boats with the crown jewels; or with the Taj, or with the Matterhorn; or with some other priceless or wonderful thing which he had seen, they were not magnificent—he was right. The people compared them with what *they* had seen; and, thus measured, thus judged, the boats were magnificent—the term was the correct one, it was not at all too strong. The people were as right as was Mr. Dickens. The steamboats were finer than anything on shore. Compared with superior dwelling-houses and first class hotels in the Valley, they were indubitably magnificent, they were "palaces." To a few people living in New Orleans and St. Louis, they were not magnificent, perhaps; not palaces; but to the great majority of those populations, and to the entire populations spread over both banks between Baton Rouge and St. Louis, they were palaces; they tallied with the citizen's dream of what magnificence was, and satisfied it.

Every town and village along that vast stretch of double river-frontage had a best dwelling, finest dwelling, mansion,—the home of its wealthiest and most conspicuous citizen. It is easy to describe it: large grassy yard, with paling fence painted white—in fair repair; brick walk from gate to door; big, square, two-story "frame" house, painted white and porticoed like a Grecian temple—with this difference, that the imposing fluted columns and Corinthian capitals were a pathetic sham, being made of white pine, and painted;

241

iron knocker; brass door knob—discolored, for lack of polishing. Within, an uncarpeted hall, of planed boards; opening out of it, a parlor, fifteen feet by fifteen—in some instances five or ten feet larger; ingrain carpet; mahogany centre-table; lamp on it, with green-paper shade—standing on a gridiron, so to speak, made of high-colored yarns, by the young ladies of the house, and called a lamp-mat; several books, piled and disposed, with cast-iron exactness, according to an inherited and unchangeable plan; among them, Tupper, much pencilled; also, "Friendship's Offering," and "Affection's Wreath," with their sappy inanities illustrated in die-away mezzotints; also, Ossian; "Alonzo and Melissa;" maybe "Ivanhoe;" also "Album," full of original "poetry" of the Thou-hast-wounded-the-spirit-that-loved-thee breed; two or three goody-goody works—"Shepherd of Salisbury Plain," etc.; current number of the chaste and innocuous Godey's "Lady's Book," with painted fashion-plate of wax-figure women with mouths all alike—lips and eyelids the same size—each five-foot woman with a two-inch wedge sticking from under her dress and letting-on to be half of her foot. Polished air-tight stove (new and deadly invention), with pipe passing through a board which closes up the discarded good old fireplace. On each end of the wooden mantel, over the fireplace, a large basket of peaches and other fruits, natural size, all done in plaster, rudely, or in wax, and painted to resemble the originals—which they don't. Over middle of mantel, engraving—Washington Crossing the Delaware; on the wall by the door, copy of it done in thunder-and-lightning crewels by one of the young ladies—work of art which would have made Washington hesitate about crossing, if he could have foreseen what advantage was going to be taken of it. Piano—kettle in disguise—with music, bound and unbound, piled on it, and on a stand near by: Battle of Prague; Bird Waltz; Arkansas Traveller; Rosin the Bow; Marseilles Hymn; On a Lone Barren Isle (St. Helena); The Last Link is Broken; She wore a Wreath of Roses the Night when last we met; Go, forget me, Why should Sorrow o'er that Brow a Shadow fling; Hours there were to Memory Dearer; Long, Long Ago; Days of Absence; A Life on the Ocean Wave, a Home on the Rolling Deep; Bird at Sea; and spread open on the rack, where the plaintive singer has left it, *Ro*-holl on, silver *moo*-hoon, guide the *trav*-el-lerr his *way*, etc. Tilted pensively against the piano, a guitar—guitar capable of playing the Spanish Fandango by itself, if you give it a start. Frantic work of art on the wall—pious motto, done on the premises, sometimes in colored yarns, sometimes in faded grasses: progenitor of the "God Bless Our Home" of modern commerce. Framed in black mouldings on the wall, other works of art, conceived and committed on the premises, by the young ladies; being grim black-and-white crayons; landscapes, mostly: lake, solitary sail-boat, petrified clouds, pre-geological trees on shore, anthracite precipice; name of criminal conspicuous in the corner. Lithograph, Napoleon Crossing the Alps. Lithograph, The Grave at St. Helena. Steel-plates, Trumbull's Battle of Bunker Hill, and the Sally from Gibraltar. Copper-plates, Moses Smiting the Rock, and Return of the Prodigal Son. In big gilt frame, slander of the family in oil: papa holding a book ("Constitution of the United States"); guitar leaning against mamma, blue ribbons fluttering from its neck; the young ladies, as children, in slippers and scalloped pantelettes, one embracing toy horse, the other beguiling kitten with ball of yarn, and both simpering up at mamma, who simpers back. These persons all fresh, raw, and red—apparently skinned. Opposite, in gilt frame, grandpa and grandma, at thirty and twenty-two, stiff, old-fashioned, high-collared, puff-sleeved, glaring pallidly out from a background of solid Egyptian night. Under a glass French clock dome, large bouquet of stiff flowers done in corpsy white wax. Pyramidal what-not in the corner, the shelves occupied chiefly with bric-a-brac of the period, disposed with an eye to best effect: shell, with the Lord's Prayer carved on it; another shell—of the long-oval sort, narrow, straight orifice, three inches long, running from end to end—portrait of Washington carved on it; not well done; the shell had Washington's mouth, originally—artist should have built to that. These two are memorials of the long-ago bridal trip to New Orleans and the French Market. Other bric-a-brac: Californian "specimens"—quartz, with gold wart adhering; old Guinea-gold locket, with circlet of ancestral hair in it; Indian arrow-heads, of flint; pair of bead moccasins, from uncle who crossed the Plains;

three "alum" baskets of various colors—being skeleton-frame of wire, clothed-on with cubes of crystallized alum in the rock-candy style—works of art which were achieved by the young ladies; their doubles and duplicates to be found upon all what-nots in the land; convention of desiccated bugs and butterflies pinned to a card; painted toy-dog, seated upon bellows-attachment—drops its under jaw and squeaks when pressed upon; sugar-candy rabbit—limbs and features merged together, not strongly defined; pewter presidential-campaign medal; miniature card-board wood-sawyer, to be attached to the stove-pipe and operated by the heat; small Napoleon, done in wax; spread-open daguerreotypes of dim children, parents, cousins, aunts, and friends, in all attitudes but customary ones; no templed portico at back, and manu-factured landscape stretching away in the distance—that came in later, with the photograph; all these vague figures lavishly chained and ringed—metal indicated and secured from doubt by stripes and splashes of vivid gold bronze; all of them too much combed, too much fixed up; and all of them uncom-fortable in inflexible Sunday-clothes of a pattern which the spectator cannot realize could ever have been in fashion; hus-band and wife generally grouped together—husband sitting, wife standing, with hand on his shoulder—and both preserv-ing, all these fading years, some traceable effect of the da-guerreotypist's brisk "Now smile, if you please!" Bracketed over what-not—place of special sacredness—an outrage in water-color, done by the young niece that came on a visit long ago, and died. Pity, too; for she might have repented of this in time. Horse-hair chairs, horse-hair sofa which keeps sliding from under you. Window shades, of oil stuff, with milk-maids and ruined castles stencilled on them in fierce col-ors. Lambrequins dependent from gaudy boxings of beaten tin, gilded. Bedrooms with rag carpets; bedsteads of the "corded" sort, with a sag in the middle, the cords needing tightening; snuffy feather-bed—not aired often enough; cane-seat chairs, splint-bottomed rocker; looking-glass on wall, school-slate size, veneered frame; inherited bureau; wash-bowl and pitcher, possibly—but not certainly; brass candlestick, tallow candle, snuffers. Nothing else in the room.

Not a bathroom in the house; and no visitor likely to come along who has ever seen one.

That was the residence of the principal citizen, all the way from the suburbs of New Orleans to the edge of St. Louis. When he stepped aboard a big fine steamboat, he entered a new and marvellous world: chimney-tops cut to counterfeit a spraying crown of plumes—and maybe painted red; pilot-house, hurricane deck, boiler-deck guards, all garnished with white wooden filagree work of fanciful patterns; gilt acorns topping the derricks; gilt deer-horns over the big bell; gaudy symbolical picture on the paddle-box, possibly; big roomy boiler-deck, painted blue, and furnished with Windsor arm-chairs; inside, a far receding snow-white "cabin;" porcelain knob and oil-picture on every state-room door; curving patterns of filagree-work touched up with gilding, stretching overhead all down the converging vista; big chandeliers every little way, each an April shower of glittering glass-drops; lovely rainbow-light falling everywhere from the colored glazing of the skylights; the whole a long-drawn, resplendent tunnel, a bewildering and soul-satisfying spectacle! in the ladies' cabin a pink and white Wilton carpet, as soft as mush, and glorified with a ravishing pattern of gigantic flowers. Then the Bridal Chamber—the animal that invented that idea was still alive and unhanged, at that day—Bridal Chamber whose pretentious flummery was necessarily overawing to the now tottering intellect of that hosannahing citizen. Every state-room had its couple of cosy clean bunks, and perhaps a look-ing-glass and a snug closet; and sometimes there was even a wash-bowl and pitcher, and part of a towel which could be told from mosquito netting by an expert—though generally these things were absent, and the shirt-sleeved passengers cleansed themselves at a long row of stationary bowls in the barber shop, where were also public towels, public combs, and public soap.

Take the steamboat which I have just described, and you have her in her highest and finest, and most pleasing, and comfortable, and satisfactory estate. Now cake her over with a layer of ancient and obdurate dirt, and you have the Cincin-nati steamer awhile ago referred to. Not all over—only inside; for she was ably officered in all departments except the steward's.

But wash that boat and repaint her, and she would be about the counterpart of the most complimented boat of the old flush times: for the steamboat architecture of the West has undergone no change; neither has steamboat furniture and ornamentation undergone any.

XXXIX.

Manufactures and Miscreants

WHERE THE RIVER, in the Vicksburg region, used to be corkscrewed, it is now comparatively straight—made so by cut-off; a former distance of seventy miles is reduced to thirty-five. It is a change which threw Vicksburg's neighbor, Delta, Louisiana, out into the country and ended its career as a river town. Its whole river-frontage is now occupied by a vast sand-bar, thickly covered with young trees—a growth which will magnify itself into a dense forest, by and by, and completely hide the exiled town.

In due time we passed Grand Gulf and Rodney, of war fame, and reached Natchez, the last of the beautiful hill-cities—for Baton Rouge, yet to come, is not on a hill, but only on high ground. Famous Natchez-under-the-hill has not changed notably in twenty years; in outward aspect—judging by the descriptions of the ancient procession of foreign tourists—it has not changed in sixty; for it is still small, straggling, and shabby. It had a desperate reputation, morally, in the old keel-boating and early steamboating times—plenty of drinking, carousing, fisticuffing, and killing there, among the riff-raff of the river, in those days. But Natchez-on-top-of-the-hill is attractive; has always been attractive. Even Mrs. Trollope (1827) had to confess its charms:

"At one or two points the wearisome level line is relieved by *bluffs*, as they call the short intervals of high ground. The town of Natchez is beautifully situated on one of those high spots. The contrast that its bright green hill forms with the dismal line of black forest that stretches on every side, the abundant growth of the paw-paw, palmetto and orange, the copious variety of sweet-scented flowers that flourish there, all make it appear like an oasis in the desert. Natchez is the furthest point to the north at which oranges ripen in the open air, or endure the winter without shelter. With the exception of this sweet spot, I thought all the little towns and villages we passed wretched-looking in the extreme."

Natchez, like her near and far river neighbors, has railways now, and is adding to them—pushing them hither and thither into all rich outlying regions that are naturally tributary to her. And like Vicksburg and New Orleans, she has her ice-factory; she makes thirty tons of ice a day. In Vicksburg and Natchez, in my time, ice was jewelry; none but the rich could wear it. But anybody and everybody can have it now. I visited one of the ice-factories in New Orleans, to see what the polar regions might look like when lugged into the edge of the tropics. But there was nothing striking in the aspect of the place. It was merely a spacious house, with some innocent steam machinery in one end of it and some big porcelain pipes running here and there. No, not porcelain—they merely seemed to be; they were iron, but the ammonia which was being breathed through them had coated them to the thickness of your hand with solid milk-white ice. It ought to have melted; for one did not require winter clothing in that atmosphere: but it did not melt; the inside of the pipe was too cold.

Sunk into the floor were numberless tin boxes, a foot square and two feet long, and open at the top end. These were full of clear water; and around each box, salt and other proper stuff was packed; also, the ammonia gases were applied to the water in some way which will always remain a secret to me, because I was not able to understand the process. While the water in the boxes gradually froze, men gave it a stir or two with a stick occasionally—to liberate the air-bubbles, I think. Other men were continually lifting out boxes whose contents had become hard frozen. They gave the box a single dip into a vat of boiling water, to melt the block of ice free from its tin coffin, then they shot the block out upon a platform car, and it was ready for market. These big blocks were hard, solid, and crystal-clear. In certain of them, big bouquets of fresh and brilliant tropical flowers had been frozen-in; in others, beautiful silken-clad French dolls, and other pretty objects. These blocks were to be set on end in a platter, in the centre of dinner-tables, to cool the tropical air;

and also to be ornamental, for the flowers and things imprisoned in them could be seen as through plate glass. I was told
that this factory could retail its ice, by wagon, throughout
New Orleans, in the humblest dwelling house quantities, at
six or seven dollars a ton, and make a sufficient profit. This
being the case, there is business for ice factories in the North;
for we get ice on no such terms there, if one take less than
three hundred and fifty pounds at a delivery.

The Rosalie Yarn Mill, of Natchez, has a capacity of 6,000
spindles and 160 looms, and employs 100 hands. The Natchez
Cotton Mills Company began operations four years ago in a
two-story building of 50 × 190 feet, with 4,000 spindles and
128 looms; capital $105,000, all subscribed in the town. Two
years later, the same stockholders increased their capital to
$225,000; added a third story to the mill, increased its length
to 317 feet; added machinery to increase the capacity to 10,300
spindles and 304 looms. The company now employ 250 op-
eratives, many of whom are citizens of Natchez. "The mill
works 5,000 bales of cotton annually and manufactures the
best standard quality of brown shirtings and sheetings and
drills, turning out 5,000,000 yards of these goods per year."[1]
A close corporation—stock held at $5,000 per share, but
none in the market.

The changes in the Mississippi River are great and strange,
yet were to be expected; but I was not expecting to live to
see Natchez and these other river towns become manufacturing strongholds and railway centres.

Speaking of manufactures reminds me of a talk upon that
topic which I heard—which I overheard—on board the Cincinnati boat. I awoke out of a fretted sleep, with a dull
confusion of voices in my ears. I listened—two men were
talking; subject, apparently, the great inundation. I looked
out through the open transom. The two men were eating a
late breakfast; sitting opposite each other; nobody else
around. They closed up the inundation with a few words—
having used it, evidently, as a mere ice-breaker and acquaint-
anceship-breeder—then they dropped into business. It soon
transpired that they were drummers—one belonging in Cincinnati, the other in New Orleans. Brisk men, energetic of

[1] "New Orleans Times-Democrat," Aug. 26, 1882.

movement and speech; the dollar their god, how to get it their religion.

"Now as to this article," said Cincinnati, slashing into the ostensible butter and holding forward a slab of it on his knife-blade, "it 's from our house; look at it—smell of it—taste it. Put any test on it you want to. Take your own time—no hurry—make it thorough. There now—what do you say? butter, ain't it? Not by a thundering sight—it's oleomarga-rine! Yes, sir, that 's what it is—oleomargarine. You can't tell it from butter; by George, an *expert* can't. It 's from our house. We supply most of the boats in the West; there 's hardly a pound of butter on one of them. We are crawling right along—*jumping* right along is the word. We are going to have that entire trade. Yes, and the hotel trade, too. You are going to see the day, pretty soon, when you can't find an ounce of butter to bless yourself with, in any hotel in the Mississippi and Ohio Valleys, outside of the biggest cities. Why, we are turning out oleomargarine *now* by the thousands of tons. And we can sell it so dirt-cheap that the whole coun-try has *got* to take it—can't get around it you see. Butter don't stand any show—there ain't any chance for competi-tion. Butter 's had its *day*—and from this out, butter goes to the wall. There 's more money in oleomargarine than—why, you can't imagine the business we do. I 've stopped in every town, from Cincinnati to Natchez; and I 've sent home big orders from every one of them."

And so-forth and so-on, for ten minutes longer, in the same fervid strain. Then New Orleans piped up and said:—

"Yes, it 's a first-rate imitation, that 's a certainty; but it ain't the only one around that 's first-rate. For instance, they make olive-oil out of cotton-seed oil, now-a-days, so that you can't tell them apart."

"Yes, that 's so," responded Cincinnati, "and it was a tip-top business for a while. They sent it over and brought it back from France and Italy, with the United States custom-house mark on it to indorse it for genuine, and there was no end of cash in it; but France and Italy broke up the game— of course they naturally would. Cracked on such a rattling impost that cotton-seed olive-oil could n't stand the raise; had to hang up and quit."

"Oh, it *did*, did it? You wait here a minute."

Goes to his state-room, brings back a couple of long bottles, and takes out the corks—says:—

"There now, smell them, taste them, examine the bottles, inspect the labels. One of 'm 's from Europe, the other 's never been out of this country. One 's European olive-oil, the other 's American cotton-seed olive-oil. Tell 'm apart? 'Course you can't. Nobody can. People that want to, can go to the expense and trouble of shipping their oils to Europe and back—it 's their privilege; but our firm knows a trick worth six of that. We turn out the whole thing—clean from the word go—in our factory in New Orleans: labels, bottles, oil, everything. Well, no, not labels: been buying *them* abroad—get them dirt-cheap there. You see, there 's just one little wee speck, essence, or whatever it is, in a gallon of cotton-seed oil, that gives it a smell, or a flavor, or something—get that out, and you 're all right—perfectly easy then to turn the oil into any kind of oil you want to, and there ain't anybody that can detect the true from the false. Well, we know how to get that one little particle out—and we 're the only firm that does. And we turn out an olive-oil that is just simply perfect—undetectable! We are doing a ripping trade, too—as I could easily show you by my order-book for this trip. Maybe you 'll butter everybody's bread pretty soon, but we 'll cotton-seed his salad for him from the Gulf to Canada, and that 's a dead-certain thing."

Cincinnati glowed and flashed with admiration. The two scoundrels exchanged business-cards, and rose. As they left the table, Cincinnati said,—

"But you have to have custom-house marks, don't you? How do you manage that?"

I did not catch the answer.

We passed Port Hudson, scene of two of the most terrific episodes of the war—the night-battle there between Farragut's fleet and the Confederate land batteries, April 14th, 1863; and the memorable land battle, two months later, which lasted eight hours—eight hours of exceptionally fierce and stubborn fighting—and ended, finally, in the repulse of the Union forces with great slaughter.

XL.

Castles and Culture

BATON ROUGE was clothed in flowers, like a bride—no, much more so; like a greenhouse. For we were in the absolute South now—no modifications, no compromises, no half-way measures. The magnolia-trees in the Capitol grounds were lovely and fragrant, with their dense rich foliage and huge snow-ball blossoms. The scent of the flower is very sweet, but you want distance on it, because it is so powerful. They are not good bedroom blossoms—they might suffocate one in his sleep. We were certainly in the South at last; for here the sugar region begins, and the plantations—vast green levels, with sugar-mill and negro quarters clustered together in the middle distance—were in view. And there was a tropical sun overhead and a tropical swelter in the air.

And at this point, also, begins the pilot's paradise: a wide river hence to New Orleans, abundance of water from shore to shore, and no bars, snags, sawyers, or wrecks in his road.

Sir Walter Scott is probably responsible for the Capitol building; for it is not conceivable that this little sham castle would ever have been built if he had not run the people mad, a couple of generations ago, with his mediæval romances. The South has not yet recovered from the debilitating influence of his books. Admiration of his fantastic heroes and their grotesque "chivalry" doings and romantic juvenilities still survives here, in an atmosphere in which is already perceptible the wholesome and practical nineteenth-century smell of cotton-factories and locomotives; and traces of its inflated language and other windy humbuggeries survive along with it. It is pathetic enough, that a whitewashed castle, with turrets and things—materials all ungenuine within and without, pretending to be what they are not—should ever have been built in this otherwise honorable place; but it is much more pathetic to see this architectural falsehood undergoing restoration and perpetuation in our day, when it would have been so easy to let dynamite finish what a charitable fire began, and then devote this restoration-money to the building of something genuine.

Baton Rouge has no patent on imitation castles, however, and no monopoly of them. Here is a picture from the advertisement of the "Female Institute" of Columbia, Tennessee. The following remark is from the same advertisement:—

> "The Institute building has long been famed as a model of striking and beautiful architecture. Visitors are charmed with its resemblance to the old castles of song and story, with its towers, turreted walls, and ivy-mantled porches."

Keeping school in a castle is a romantic thing; as romantic as keeping hotel in a castle.

By itself the imitation castle is doubtless harmless, and well enough; but as a symbol and breeder and sustainer of maudlin Middle-Age romanticism here in the midst of the plainest and sturdiest and infinitely greatest and worthiest of all the centuries the world has seen, it is necessarily a hurtful thing and a mistake.

Here is an extract from the prospectus of a Kentucky "Female College." Female college sounds well enough; but since the phrasing it in that unjustifiable way was done purely in the interest of brevity, it seems to me that she-college would have been still better—because shorter, and means the same thing: that is, if either phrase means anything at all:—

> "The president is southern by birth, by rearing, by education, and by sentiment; the teachers are all southern in sentiment, and with the exception of those born in Europe were born and raised in the south. Believing the southern to be the highest type of civilization this continent has seen,[1] the young ladies are trained according to the south-

[1] Illustrations of it thoughtlessly omitted by the advertiser:

KNOXVILLE, Tenn., October 19.—This morning a few minutes after ten o'clock, General Joseph A. Mabry, Thomas O'Connor, and Joseph A. Mabry, Jr., were killed in a shooting affray. The difficulty began yesterday afternoon by General Mabry attacking Major O'Connor and threatening to kill him. This was at the fair grounds, and O'Connor told Mabry that it was not the place to settle their difficulties. Mabry then told O'Connor he should not live. It seems that Mabry was armed and O'Connor was not. The cause of the difficulty was an old feud about the transfer of some property from Mabry to O'Connor. Later in the afternoon Mabry sent word to O'Connor that

ern ideas of delicacy, refinement, womanhood, religion, and propriety; hence we offer a first-class female college for the south and solicit southern patronage."

What, warder, ho! the man that can blow so complacent a blast as that, probably blows it from a castle.

From Baton Rouge to New Orleans, the great sugar plantations border both sides of the river all the way, and stretch their league-wide levels back to the dim forest-walls of bearded cypress in the rear. Shores lonely no longer. Plenty of dwellings all the way, on both banks—standing so close together, for long distances, that the broad river lying be-

---

he would kill him on sight. This morning Major O'Connor was standing in the door of the Mechanics' National Bank, of which he was president. General Mabry and another gentleman walked down Gay Street on the opposite side from the bank. O'Connor stepped into the bank, got a shot gun, took deliberate aim at General Mabry and fired. Mabry fell dead, being shot in the left side. As he fell O'Connor fired again, the shot taking effect in Mabry's thigh. O'Connor then reached into the bank and got another shot gun. About this time Joseph A. Mabry, Jr., son of General Mabry, came rushing down the street, unseen by O'Connor until within forty feet, when the young man fired a pistol, the shot taking effect in O'Connor's right breast, passing through the body near the heart. The instant Mabry shot, O'Connor turned and fired, the load taking effect in young Mabry's right breast and side. Mabry fell pierced with twenty buckshot, and almost instantly O'Connor fell dead without a struggle. Mabry tried to rise, but fell back dead. The whole tragedy occurred within two minutes, and neither of the three spoke after he was shot. General Mabry had about thirty buckshot in his body. A bystander was painfully wounded in the thigh with a buckshot, and another was wounded in the arm. Four other men had their clothing pierced by buckshot. The affair caused great excitement, and Gay Street was thronged with thousands of people. General Mabry and his son Joe were acquitted only a few days ago of the murder of Moses Lusby and Don Lusby, father and son, whom they killed a few weeks ago. Will Mabry was killed by Don Lusby last Christmas. Major Thomas O'Connor was President of the Mechanics' National Bank here, and was the wealthiest man in the State.—*Associated Press Telegram.*

One day last month, Professor Sharpe, of the Somerville, Tenn., Female College, "a quiet and gentlemanly man," was told that his brother-in-law, a Captain Burton, had threatened to kill him. Burton, it seems, had already killed one man and driven his knife into another. The Professor armed himself with a double-barrelled shot gun, started out in search of his brother-in-law, found him playing billiards in a saloon, and blew his brains out. The tween the two rows, becomes a sort of spacious street. A most home-like and happy-looking region. And now and then you see a pillared and porticoed great manor-house, embowered in trees. Here is testimony of one or two of the procession of foreign tourists that filed along here half a century ago. Mrs. Trollope says: —

"The unbroken flatness of the banks of the Mississippi continued unvaried for many miles above New Orleans; but the graceful and luxuriant palmetto, the dark and noble ilex, and the bright orange, were everywhere to be seen, and it was many days before we were weary of looking at them."

Captain Basil Hall: —

"The district of country which lies adjacent to the Mississippi, in the lower parts of Louisiana, is everywhere thickly peopled by sugar planters, whose showy houses, gay piazzas, trig gardens, and numerous slave-villages, all clean and neat, gave an exceedingly thriving air to the river scenery."

"Memphis Avalanche" reports that the Professor's course met with pretty general approval in the community; knowing that the law was powerless, in the actual condition of public sentiment, to protect him, he protected himself.

About the same time, two young men in North Carolina quarrelled about a girl, and "hostile messages" were exchanged. Friends tried to reconcile them, but had their labor for their pains. On the 24th the young men met in the public highway. One of them had a heavy club in his hand, the other an axe. The man with the club fought desperately for his life, but it was a hopeless fight from the first. A well-directed blow sent his club whirling out of his grasp, and the next moment he was a dead man.

About the same time, two "highly connected" young Virginians, clerks in a hardware store at Charlottesville, while "skylarking," came to blows. Peter Dick threw pepper in Charles Roads's eyes; Roads demanded an apology; Dick refused to give it, and it was agreed that a duel was inevitable, but a difficulty arose; the parties had no pistols, and it was too late at night to procure them. One of them suggested that butcher-knives would answer the purpose, and the other accepted the suggestion; the result was that Roads fell to the floor with a gash in his abdomen that may or may not prove fatal. If Dick has been arrested, the news has not reached us. He "expressed deep regret," and we are told by a Staunton correspondent of the "Philadelphia Press" that "every effort has been made to hush the matter up."—*Extracts from the Public Journals.*

All the procession paint the attractive picture in the same way. The descriptions of fifty years ago do not need to have a word changed in order to exactly describe the same region as it appears to-day—except as to the "trigness" of the houses. The whitewash is gone from the negro cabins now; and many, possibly most, of the big mansions, once so shining white, have worn out their paint and have a decayed, neglected look. It is the blight of the war. Twenty-one years ago everything was trim and trig and bright along the "coast," just as it had been in 1827, as described by those tourists.

Unfortunate tourists! People humbugged them with stupid and silly lies, and then laughed at them for believing and printing the same. They told Mrs. Trollope that the alligators—or crocodiles, as she calls them—were terrible creatures; and backed up the statement with a blood-curdling account of how one of these slandered reptiles crept into a squatter cabin one night, and ate up a woman and five children. The woman, by herself, would have satisfied any ordinarily-impossible alligator; but no, these liars must make him gorge the five children besides. One would not imagine that jokers of this robust breed would be sensitive—but they were. It is difficult, at this day, to understand, and impossible to justify, the reception which the book of the grave, honest, intelligent, gentle, manly, charitable, well-meaning Capt. Basil Hall got. Mrs. Trollope's account of it may perhaps entertain the reader; therefore I have put it in the Appendix.[1]

[1]See Appendix C.

XLI.

The Metropolis of the South

THE APPROACHES to New Orleans were familiar; general
aspects were unchanged. When one goes flying through
London along a railway propped in the air on tall arches, he
may inspect miles of upper bedrooms through the open windows, but the lower half of the houses is under his level and
out of sight. Similarly, in high-river stage, in the New Orleans region, the water is up to the top of the enclosing levee-
rim, the flat country behind it lies low—representing the bottom of a dish—and as the boat swims along, high on the
flood, one looks down upon the houses and into the upper
windows. There is nothing but that frail breastwork of earth
between the people and destruction.

The old brick salt-warehouses clustered at the upper end of
the city looked as they had always looked; warehouses which
had had a kind of Aladdin's lamp experience, however, since
I had seen them; for when the war broke out the proprietor
went to bed one night leaving them packed with thousands
of sacks of vulgar salt, worth a couple of dollars a sack, and
got up in the morning and found his mountain of salt turned
into a mountain of gold, so to speak, so suddenly and to so
dizzy a height had the war news sent up the price of the article.

The vast reach of plank wharves remained unchanged, and
there were as many ships as ever: but the long array of steamboats had vanished; not altogether, of course, but not much
of it was left.

The city itself had not changed—to the eye. It had greatly
increased in spread and population, but the look of the town
was not altered. The dust, waste-paper-littered, was still deep
in the streets; the deep, trough-like gutters alongside the
curb-stones were still half full of reposeful water with a dusty
surface; the sidewalks were still—in the sugar and bacon region—incumbered by casks and barrels and hogsheads; the
great blocks of austerely plain commercial houses were as
dusty-looking as ever.

Canal Street was finer, and more attractive and stirring than formerly, with its drifting crowds of people, its several processions of hurrying street-cars, and—toward evening—its broad second-story verandas crowded with gentlemen and ladies clothed according to the latest mode.

Not that there is any "architecture" in Canal Street: to speak in broad, general terms, there is no architecture in New Orleans, except in the cemeteries. It seems a strange thing to say of a wealthy, far-seeing, and energetic city of a quarter of a million inhabitants, but it is true. There is a huge granite U. S. Custom-house—costly enough, genuine enough, but as a decoration it is inferior to a gasometer. It looks like a state prison. But it was built before the war. Architecture in America may be said to have been born since the war. New Orleans, I believe, has had the good luck—and in a sense the bad luck—to have had no great fire in late years. It must be so. If the opposite had been the case, I think one would be able to tell the "burnt district" by the radical improvement in its architecture over the old forms. One can do this in Boston and Chicago. The "burnt district" of Boston was commonplace before the fire; but now there is no commercial district in any city in the world that can surpass it—or perhaps even rival it—in beauty, elegance, and tastefulness.

However, New Orleans has begun—just this moment, as one may say. When completed, the new Cotton Exchange will be a stately and beautiful building; massive, substantial, full of architectural graces; no shams or false pretenses or uglinesses about it anywhere. To the city, it will be worth many times its cost, for it will breed its species. What has been lacking hitherto, was a model to build toward; something to educate eye and taste; a *suggester*, so to speak.

The city is well outfitted with progressive men—thinking, sagacious, long-headed men. The contrast between the spirit of the city and the city's architecture is like the contrast between waking and sleep. Apparently there is a "boom" in everything but that one dead feature. The water in the gutters used to be stagnant and slimy, and a potent disease-breeder; but the gutters are flushed now, two or three times a day, by powerful machinery; in many of the gutters the water never stands still, but has a steady current. Other sanitary improvements have been made; and with such effect that New Orleans claims to be (during the long intervals between the occasional yellow-fever assaults) one of the healthiest cities in the Union. There's plenty of ice now for everybody, manufactured in the town. It is a driving place commercially, and has a great river, ocean, and railway business. At the date of our visit, it was the best lighted city in the Union, electrically speaking. The New Orleans electric lights were more numerous than those of New York, and very much better. One had this modified noonday not only in Canal and some neighboring chief streets, but all along a stretch of five miles of river frontage. There are good clubs in the city now—several of them but recently organized—and inviting modern-style pleasure resorts at West End and Spanish Fort. The telephone is everywhere. One of the most notable advances is in journalism. The newspapers, as I remember them, were not a striking feature. Now they are. Money is spent upon them with a free hand. They get the news, let it cost what it may. The editorial work is not hack-grinding, but literature. As an example of New Orleans journalistic achievement, it may be mentioned that the "Times-Democrat" of August 26, 1882, contained a report of the year's business of the towns of the Mississippi Valley, from New Orleans all the way to St. Paul—two thousand miles. That issue of the paper consisted of *forty* pages; seven columns to the page; two hundred and eighty columns in all; fifteen hundred words to the column; an aggregate of four hundred and twenty thousand words. That is to say, not much short of three times as many words as there are in this book. One may with sorrow contrast this with the architecture of New Orleans.

I have been speaking of public architecture only. The domestic article in New Orleans is reproachless, notwithstanding it remains as it always was. All the dwellings are of wood—in the American part of the town, I mean—and all have a comfortable look. Those in the wealthy quarter are spacious; painted snow-white usually, and generally have wide verandas, or double-verandas, supported by ornamental columns. These mansions stand in the centre of large grounds, and rise, garlanded with roses, out of the midst of swelling masses of shining green foliage and many-colored blossoms. No houses could well be in better harmony with their surroundings, or more pleasing to the eye, or more home-like and comfortable-looking.

One even becomes reconciled to the cistern presently; this is a mighty cask, painted green, and sometimes a couple of stories high, which is propped against the house-corner on stilts. There is a mansion-and-brewery suggestion about the combination which seems very incongruous at first. But the people cannot have wells, and so they take rain-water. Neither can they conveniently have cellars, or graves;[1] the town being built upon "made" ground; so they do without both, and few of the living complain, and none of the others.

[1] The Israelites are buried in graves—by permission, I take it, not requirement; but none else, except the destitute, who are buried at public expense. The graves are but three or four feet deep.

XLII.

Hygiene and Sentiment

T HEY BURY their dead in vaults, above the ground.
These vaults have a resemblance to houses—sometimes to temples; are built of marble, generally; are architecturally graceful and shapely; they face the walks and driveways of the cemetery; and when one moves through the midst of a thousand or so of them and sees their white roofs and gables stretching into the distance on every hand, the phrase "city of the dead" has all at once a meaning to him. Many of the cemeteries are beautiful, and are kept in perfect order. When one goes from the levee or the business streets near it, to a cemetery, he observes to himself that if those people down there would live as neatly while they are alive as they do after they are dead, they would find many advantages in it; and besides, their quarter would be the wonder and admiration of the business world. Fresh flowers, in vases of water, are to be seen at the portals of many of the vaults: placed there by the pious hands of bereaved parents and children, husbands and wives, and renewed daily. A milder form of sorrow finds its inexpensive and lasting remembrancer in the coarse and ugly but indestructible "immortelle"—which is a wreath or cross or some such emblem, made of rosettes of black linen, with sometimes a yellow rosette at the conjunction of the cross's bars,—kind of sorrowful breast-pin, so to say. The immortelle requires no attention: you just hang it up, and there you are; just leave it alone, it will take care of your grief for you, and keep it in mind better than you can; stands weather first-rate, and lasts like boiler-iron.

On sunny days, pretty little chameleons—gracefullest of leggéd reptiles—creep along the marble fronts of the vaults, and catch flies. Their changes of color—as to variety—are not up to the creature's reputation. They change color when a person comes along and hangs up an immortelle; but that is nothing: any right-feeling reptile would do that.

I will gradually drop this subject of graveyards. I have been trying all I could to get down to the sentimental part of it, but I cannot accomplish it. I think there is no genuinely sentimental part to it. It is all grotesque, ghastly, horrible. Graveyards may have been justifiable in the bygone ages, when nobody knew that for every dead body put into the ground, to glut the earth and the plant-roots and the air with disease-germs, five or fifty, or maybe a hundred, persons must die before their proper time; but they are hardly justifiable now, when even the children know that a dead saint enters upon a century-long career of assassination the moment the earth closes over his corpse. It is a grim sort of a thought. The relics of St. Anne, up in Canada, have now, after nineteen hundred years, gone to curing the sick by the dozen. But it is merest matter-of-course that these same relics, within a generation after St. Anne's death and burial, *made* several thousand people sick. Therefore these miracle-performances are simply compensation, nothing more. St. Anne is somewhat slow pay, for a Saint, it is true; but better a debt paid after nineteen hundred years, and outlawed by the statute of limitations, than not paid at all; and most of the knights of the halo do not pay at all. Where you find one that pays—like St. Anne—you find a hundred and fifty that take the benefit of the statute. And none of them pay any more than the principal of what they owe—they pay none of the interest either simple or compound. A Saint can never *quite* return the principal, however; for his dead body *kills* people, whereas his relics *heal* only—they never restore the dead to life. That part of the account is always left unsettled.

"Dr. F. Julius Le Moyne, after fifty years of medical practice, wrote: 'The inhumation of human bodies, dead from infectious diseases, results in constantly loading the atmosphere, and polluting the waters, with not only the germs that rise from simply putrefaction, but also with the *specific* germs of the diseases from which death resulted.'

"The gases (from buried corpses) will rise to the surface through eight or ten feet of gravel, just as coal-gas will do, and there is practically no limit to their power of escape.

"During the epidemic in New Orleans in 1853, Dr. E. H. Barton reported that in the Fourth District the mortality was four hundred and fifty-two per thousand—more than double that of any other. In this district were three large cemeteries, in which during the previous year more than three thousand bodies had been buried. In other districts the proximity of cemeteries seemed to aggravate the disease.

"In 1828 Professor Bianchi demonstrated how the fearful reappearance of the plague at Modena was caused by excavations in ground where, *three hundred years previously* the victims of the pestilence had been buried. Mr. Cooper, in explaining the causes of some epidemics, remarks that the opening of the plague burial-grounds at Eyam resulted in an immediate outbreak of disease."—*North American Review, No. 3, Vol.* 135.

In an address before the Chicago Medical Society, in advocacy of cremation, Dr. Charles W. Purdy made some striking comparisons to show what a burden is laid upon society by the burial of the dead:—

"One and one-fourth times more money is expended annually in funerals in the United States than the Government expends for public-school purposes. Funerals cost this country in 1880 enough money to pay the liabilities of all the commercial failures in the United States during the same year, and give each bankrupt a capital of $8,630 with which to resume business. Funerals cost annually more money than the value of the combined gold and silver yield of the United States in the year 1880! These figures do not include the sums invested in burial-grounds and expended in tombs and monuments, nor the loss from depreciation of property in the vicinity of cemeteries."

For the rich, cremation would answer as well as burial; for the ceremonies connected with it could be made as costly and ostentatious as a Hindoo *suttee*; while for the poor, cremation would be better than burial, because so cheap[1]—so cheap until the poor got to imitating the rich, which they would do by and by. The adoption of cremation would relieve us of a muck of threadbare burial-witticisms; but, on the other hand, it would resurrect a lot of mildewed old cremation-jokes that have had a rest for two thousand years.

[1] Four or five dollars is the minimum cost.

I have a colored acquaintance who earns his living by odd jobs and heavy manual labor. He never earns above four hundred dollars in a year, and as he has a wife and several young children, the closest scrimping is necessary to get him through to the end of the twelve months debtless. To such a man a funeral is a colossal financial disaster. While I was writing one of the preceding chapters, this man lost a little child. He walked the town over with a friend, trying to find a coffin that was within his means. He bought the very cheapest one he could find, plain wood, stained. It cost him *twenty-six dollars*. It would have cost less than four, probably, if it had been built to put something useful into. He and his family will feel that outlay a good many months.

XLIII.

The Art of Inhumation

ABOUT THE SAME TIME, I encountered a man in the street, whom I had not seen for six or seven years; and something like this talk followed. I said,—

"But you used to look sad and oldish; you don't now. Where did you get all this youth and bubbling cheerfulness? Give me the address."

He chuckled blithely, took off his shining tile, pointed to a notched pink circlet of paper pasted into its crown, with something lettered on it, and went on chuckling while I read, "J. B——, UNDERTAKER." Then he clapped his hat on, gave it an irreverent tilt to leeward, and cried out,—

"That's what's the matter! It used to be rough times with me when you knew me—insurance-agency business, you know; mighty irregular. Big fire, all right—brisk trade for ten days while people scared; after that, dull policy-business till next fire. Town like this don't have fires often enough—a fellow strikes so many dull weeks in a row that he gets discouraged. But you bet you, *this* is the business! People don't wait for examples to *die*. No, sir, they drop off right along—there ain't any dull spots in the undertaker line. I just started in with two or three little old coffins and a hired hearse, and *now* look at the thing! I've worked up a business here that would satisfy any man, don't care who he is. Five years ago, lodged in an attic; live in a swell house now, with a mansard roof, and all the modern inconveniences."

"Does a coffin pay so well? Is there much profit on a coffin?"

"*Go*-way! How you talk!" Then, with a confidential wink, a dropping of the voice, and an impressive laying of his hand on my arm; "Look here; there's one thing in this world which is n't ever cheap. That's a coffin. There's one thing in this world which a person don't ever try to jew you down on. That's a coffin. There's one thing in this world which a person don't say,—'I'll look around a little, and if I find I can't do better I'll come back and take it.' That's a coffin.

There 's one thing in this world which a person won't take in pine if he can go walnut; and won't take in walnut if he can go mahogany; and won't take in mahogany if he can go an iron casket with silver door-plate and bronze handles. That 's a coffin. And there 's one thing in this world which you don't have to worry around after a person to get him to pay for. And *that* 's a coffin. Undertaking?—why it 's the dead-surest business in Christendom, and the nobbiest.

"Why, just look at it. A rich man won't have anything but your very best; and you can just pile it on, too—pile it on and sock it to him—he won't ever holler. And you take in a poor man, and if you work him right he 'll bust himself on a single lay-out. Or especially a woman. F'r instance: Mrs. O'Flaherty comes in—widow—wiping her eyes and kind of moaning. Unhandkerchiefs one eye, bats it around tearfully over the stock; says,—

"'And fhat might ye ask for that wan?'

"'Thirty-nine dollars, madam,' says I.

"'It 's a foine big price, sure, but Pat shall be buried like a gintleman, as he was, if I have to work me fingers off for it. I 'll have that wan, sor.'

"'Yes, madam,' says I, 'and it is a very good one, too; not costly, to be sure, but in this life we must cut our garment to our clothes, as the saying is.' And as she starts out, I heave in, kind of casually, 'This one with the white satin lining is a beauty, but I am afraid—well, sixty-five dollars *is* a rather—rather—but no matter, I felt obliged to say to Mrs. O'Shaughnessy,—'

"'D' ye mane to soy that Bridget O'Shaughnessy bought the mate to that joo-ul box to ship that dhrunken divil to Purgatory in?'

"'Yes, madam.'

"'Then Pat shall go to heaven in the twin to it, if it takes the last rap the O'Flaherties can raise; and moind you, stick on some extras, too, and I 'll give ye another dollar.'

"And as I lay-in with the livery stables, of course I don't forget to mention that Mrs. O'Shaughnessy hired fifty-four dollars' worth of hacks and flung as much style into Dennis's funeral as if he had been a duke or an assassin. And of course she sails in and goes the O'Shaughnessy about four hacks and an omnibus better. That *used* to be, but that 's all played now; that is, in this particular town. The Irish got to piling up hacks so, on their funerals, that a funeral left them ragged and hungry for two years afterward; so the priest pitched in and broke it all up. He don't allow them to have but two hacks now, and sometimes only one."

"Well," said I, "if you are so light-hearted and jolly in ordinary times, what *must* you be in an epidemic?"

He shook his head.

"No, you 're off, there. We don't like to see an epidemic. An epidemic don't pay. Well, of course I don't mean that, exactly; but it don't pay in proportion to the regular thing. Don't it occur to you, why?"

"No."

"Think."

"I can't imagine. What is it?"

"It 's just two things."

"Well, what *are* they?"

"One 's Embamming."

"And what 's the other?"

"Ice."

"How is that?"

"Well, in ordinary times, a person dies, and we lay him up in ice; one day, two days, maybe three, to wait for friends to come. Takes a lot of it—melts fast. We charge jewelry rates for that ice, and war-prices for attendance. Well, don't you know, when there 's an epidemic, they rush 'em to the cemetery the minute the breath 's out. No market for ice in an epidemic. Same with Embamming. You take a family that 's able to embam, and you 've got a soft thing. You can mention sixteen different ways to do it—though there *ain't* only one or two ways, when you come down to the bottom facts of it—and they 'll take the highest-priced way, every time. It 's human nature—human nature in grief. It don't reason, you see. 'Time being, it don't care a dam. All it wants is physical immortality for deceased, and they 're willing to pay for it. All you 've got to do is to just be ca'm and stack it up—they 'll stand the racket. Why, man, you can take a defunct that you could n't *give* away; and get your embamming traps around you and go to work; and in a couple of hours he is worth a cool six hundred—that 's what *he* 's worth. There ain't anything equal to it but trading rats for di'monds in time of famine. Well, don't you see, when there 's an epidemic, people don't wait to embam. No, indeed they don't; and it hurts the business like hellth, as we say—hurts it like hell-th, *health*, see?—Our little joke in the trade. Well, I must be going. Give me a call whenever you need any—I mean, when you 're going by, sometime."

In his joyful high spirits, he did the exaggerating himself, if any has been done. I have not enlarged on him.

With the above brief references to inhumation, let us leave the subject. As for me, I hope to be cremated. I made that remark to my pastor once, who said, with what he seemed to think was an impressive manner,—

"I would n't worry about that, if I had your chances."

Much he knew about it—the family all so opposed to it.

XLIV.

City Sights

T HE OLD FRENCH PART of New Orleans—anciently the Spanish part—bears no resemblance to the American end of the city: the American end which lies beyond the intervening brick business-centre. The houses are massed in blocks; are austerely plain and dignified; uniform of pattern, with here and there a departure from it with pleasant effect; all are plastered on the outside, and nearly all have long, iron-railed verandas running along the several stories. Their chief beauty is the deep, warm, varicolored stain with which time and the weather have enriched the plaster. It harmonizes with all the surroundings, and has as natural a look of belonging there as has the flush upon sunset clouds. This charming decoration cannot be successfully imitated; neither is it to be found elsewhere in America.

The iron railings are a specialty, also. The pattern is often exceedingly light and dainty, and airy and graceful—with a large cipher or monogram in the centre, a delicate cobweb of baffling, intricate forms, wrought in steel. The ancient railings are hand-made, and are now comparatively rare and proportionately valuable. They are become bric-a-brac.

The party had the privilege of idling through this ancient quarter of New Orleans with the South's finest literary genius, the author of "the Grandissimes." In him the South has found a masterly delineator of its interior life and its history. In truth, I find by experience, that the untrained eye and vacant mind can inspect it and learn of it and judge of it more clearly and profitably in his books than by personal contact with it.

With Mr. Cable along to see for you, and describe and explain and illuminate, a jog through that old quarter is a vivid pleasure. And you have a vivid *sense* as of unseen or dimly seen things—vivid, and yet fitful and darkling; you glimpse salient features, but lose the fine shades or catch them imperfectly through the vision of the imagination: a case, as it were, of ignorant near-sighted stranger traversing the rim of wide vague horizons of Alps with an inspired and enlightened long-sighted native.

We visited the old St. Louis Hotel, now occupied by municipal offices. There is nothing strikingly remarkable about it; but one can say of it as of the Academy of Music in New York, that if a broom or a shovel has ever been used in it there is no circumstantial evidence to back up the fact. It is curious that cabbages and hay and things do not grow in the Academy of Music; but no doubt it is on account of the interruption of the light by the benches, and the impossibility of hoeing the crop except in the aisles. The fact that the ushers grow their buttonhole-bouquets on the premises shows what might be done if they had the right kind of an agricultural head to the establishment.

We visited also the venerable Cathedral, and the pretty square in front of it; the one dim with religious light, the other brilliant with the worldly sort, and lovely with orange trees and blossomy shrubs; then we drove in the hot sun through the wilderness of houses and out on to the wide dead level beyond, where the villas are, and the water wheels to drain the town, and the commons populous with cows and children; passing by an old cemetery where we were told lie the ashes of an early pirate; but we took him on trust, and did not visit him. He was a pirate with a tremendous and sanguinary history; and as long as he preserved unspotted, in retirement, the dignity of his name and the grandeur of his ancient calling, homage and reverence were his from high and low; but when at last he descended into politics and became a paltry alderman, the public "shook" him, and turned aside and wept. When he died, they set up a monument over him; and little by little he has come into respect again; but it is respect for the pirate, not the alderman. To-day the loyal and generous remember only what he was, and charitably forget what he became.

Thence, we drove a few miles across a swamp, along a raised shell road, with a canal on one hand and a dense wood on the other; and here and there, in the distance, a ragged and angular-limbed and moss-bearded cypress, top standing out, clear cut against the sky, and as quaint of form as the apple-trees in Japanese pictures—such was our course and the surroundings of it. There was an occasional alligator swimming comfortably along in the canal, and an occasional picturesque colored person on the bank, flinging his statue-rigid reflection upon the still water and watching for a bite.

And by and by we reached the West End, a collection of hotels of the usual light summer-resort pattern, with broad verandas all around, and the waves of the wide and blue Lake Pontchartrain lapping the thresholds. We had dinner on a ground-veranda over the water—the chief dish the renowned fish called the pompano, delicious as the less criminal forms of sin.

Thousands of people come by rail and carriage to West End and to Spanish Fort every evening, and dine, listen to the bands, take strolls in the open air under the electric lights, go sailing on the lake, and entertain themselves in various and sundry other ways.

We had opportunities on other days and in other places to test the pompano. Notably, at an editorial dinner at one of the clubs in the city. He was in his last possible perfection there, and justified his fame. In his suite was a tall pyramid of scarlet cray-fish—large ones; as large as one's thumb; delicate, palatable, appetizing. Also devilled whitebait; also shrimps of choice quality; and a platter of small soft-shell crabs of a most superior breed. The other dishes were what one might get at Delmonico's, or Buckingham Palace; those I have spoken of can be had in similar perfection in New Orleans only, I suppose.

In the West and South they have a new institution,—the Broom Brigade. It is composed of young ladies who dress in a uniform costume, and go through the infantry drill, with broom in place of musket. It is a very pretty sight, on private view. When they perform on the stage of a theatre, in the blaze of colored fires, it must be a fine and fascinating spectacle. I saw them go through their complex manual with grace, spirit, and admirable precision. I saw them do everything which a human being can possibly do with a broom, except sweep. I did not see them sweep. But I know they could learn. What they have already learned proves that. And if they ever should learn, and should go on the war-path down Tchoupitoulas or some of those other streets around there, those thoroughfares would bear a greatly improved aspect in a very few minutes. But the girls themselves would n't; so nothing would be really gained, after all.

The drill was in the Washington Artillery building. In this building we saw many interesting relics of the war. Also a fine oil-painting representing Stonewall Jackson's last interview with General Lee. Both men are on horseback. Jackson has just ridden up, and is accosting Lee. The picture is very valuable, on account of the portraits, which are authentic. But, like many another historical picture, it means nothing without its label. And one label will fit it as well as another: —

First Interview between Lee and Jackson.

Last Interview between Lee and Jackson.

Jackson Introducing Himself to Lee.

Jackson Accepting Lee's Invitation to Dinner.

Jackson Declining Lee's Invitation to Dinner—with Thanks.

Jackson Apologizing for a Heavy Defeat.

Jackson Reporting a Great Victory.

Jackson Asking Lee for a Match.

It tells *one* story, and a sufficient one; for it says quite plainly and satisfactorily, "Here are Lee and Jackson together." The artist would have made it tell that this is Lee and Jackson's last interview if he could have done it. But he could n't, for there was n't any way to do it. A good legible label is usually worth, for information, a ton of significant attitude and expression in a historical picture. In Rome, people with fine sympathetic natures stand up and weep in front of the celebrated "Beatrice Cenci the Day before her Execution." It shows what a label can do. If they did not know the picture, they would inspect it unmoved, and say, "Young girl with hay fever; young girl with her head in a bag."

I found the half-forgotten Southern intonations and elisions as pleasing to my ear as they had formerly been. A Southerner talks music. At least it is music to me, but then I was born in the South. The educated Southerner has no use for an *r*, except at the beginning of a word. He says "honah," and "dinnah," and "Gove'nuh," and "befo' the waw," and so on. The words may lack charm to the eye, in print, but they have it to the ear. When did the *r* disappear from Southern speech, and how did it come to disappear? The custom of dropping it was not borrowed from the North, nor inherited from England. Many Southerners—most Southerners—put a *y* into occasional words that begin with the *k* sound. For instance, they say Mr. K'yahtah (Carter) and speak of playing k'yahds or of riding in the k'yahs. And they have the pleasant custom—long ago fallen into decay in the North—of frequently employing the respectful "Sir." Instead of the curt Yes, and the abrupt No, they say "Yes, Suh"; "No, Suh."

But there are some infelicities. Such as "like" for "as," and the addition of an "at" where it is n't needed. I heard an educated gentleman say, "Like the flag-officer did." His cook or his butler would have said, "Like the flag-officer done." You hear gentlemen say, "Where have you been at?" And here is the aggravated form—heard a ragged street Arab say it to a comrade: "I was a-ask'n' Tom whah you was a-sett'n' at." The very elect carelessly say "will" when they mean "shall"; and many of them say, "I did n't go to do it," meaning "I did n't mean to do it." The Northern word "guess"— imported from England, where it used to be common, and now regarded by satirical Englishmen as a Yankee original— is but little used among Southerners. They say "reckon." They have n't any "does n't" in their language; they say "don't" instead. The unpolished often use "went" for "gone." It is nearly as bad as the Northern "had n't ought." This reminds me that a remark of a very peculiar nature was made here in my neighborhood (in the North) a few days ago: "He had n't ought to have went." How is that? Is n't that a good deal of a triumph? One knows the orders combined in this half-breed's architecture without inquiring: one parent Northern, the other Southern. To-day I heard a school-mistress ask, "Where is John gone?" This form is so common—so nearly universal, in fact—that if she had used "whither" instead of "where," I think it would have sounded like an affectation.

We picked up one excellent word—a word worth travelling to New Orleans to get; a nice limber, expressive, handy word—"Lagniappe." They pronounce it lanny-*yap*. It is Spanish—so they said. We discovered it at the head of a column of odds and ends in the Picayune, the first day; heard twenty people use it the second; inquired what it meant the third; adopted it and got facility in swinging it the fourth. It has a restricted meaning, but I think the people spread it out a little when they choose. It is the equivalent of the thirteenth roll in a "baker's dozen." It is something thrown in, gratis, for good measure. The custom originated in the Spanish quarter of the city. When a child or a servant buys something in a shop—or even the mayor or the governor, for aught I know—he finishes the operation by saying,—

"Give me something for lagniappe."

The shopman always responds; gives the child a bit of li-quorice-root, gives the servant a cheap cigar or a spool of thread, gives the governor—I don't know what he gives the governor; support, likely.

When you are invited to drink,—and this does occur now and then in New Orleans,—and you say, "What, again?—no, I 've had enough;" the other party says, "But just this one time more,—this is for lagniappe." When the beau perceives that he is stacking his compliments a trifle too high, and sees by the young lady's countenance that the edifice would have been better with the top compliment left off, he puts his "I beg pardon,—no harm intended," into the briefer form of "Oh, that 's for lagniappe." If the waiter in the restaurant stumbles and spills a gill of coffee down the back of your neck, he says, "For lagniappe, sah," and gets you another cup without extra charge.

XLV.

Southern Sports

IN THE NORTH one hears the war mentioned, in social conversation, once a month; sometimes as often as once a
week; but as a distinct subject for talk, it has long ago been
relieved of duty. There are sufficient reasons for this. Given a
dinner company of six gentlemen to-day, it can easily happen
that four of them—and possibly five—were not in the field
at all. So the chances are four to two, or five to one, that the
war will at no time during the evening become the topic of
conversation; and the chances are still greater that if it become the topic it will remain so but a little while. If you add
six ladies to the company, you have added six people who
saw so little of the dread realities of the war that they ran out
of talk concerning them years ago, and now would soon
weary of the war topic if you brought it up.

The case is very different in the South. There, every man
you meet was in the war; and every lady you meet saw the
war. The war is the great chief topic of conversation. The
interest in it is vivid and constant; the interest in other topics
is fleeting. Mention of the war will wake up a dull company
and set their tongues going, when nearly any other topic
would fail. In the South, the war is what A.D. is elsewhere:
they date from it. All day long you hear things "placed" as
having happened since the waw; or du'in' the waw; or befo'
the waw; or right aftah the waw; or 'bout two yeahs or five
yeahs or ten yeahs befo' the waw or aftah the waw. It shows
how intimately every individual was visited, in his own person, by that tremendous episode. It gives the inexperienced
stranger a better idea of what a vast and comprehensive calamity invasion is than he can ever get by reading books at
the fireside.

At a club one evening, a gentleman turned to me and said,
in an aside:—

"You notice, of course, that we are nearly always talking
about the war. It is n't because we have n't anything else to
talk about, but because nothing else has so strong an interest

for us. And there is another reason: In the war, each of us, in his own person, seems to have sampled all the different varieties of human experience; as a consequence, you can't mention an outside matter of any sort but it will certainly remind some listener of something that happened during the war,— and out he comes with it. Of course that brings the talk back to the war. You may try all you want to, to keep other subjects before the house, and we may all join in and help, but there can be but one result: the most random topic would load every man up with war reminiscences, and *shut* him up, too; and talk would be likely to stop presently, because you can't talk pale inconsequentialities when you 've got a crimson fact or fancy in your head that you are burning to fetch out."

The poet was sitting some little distance away; and presently he began to speak—about the moon.

The gentleman who had been talking to me remarked in an "aside:" "There, the moon is far enough from the seat of war, but you will see that it will suggest something to somebody about the war; in ten minutes from now the moon, as a topic, will be shelved."

The poet was saying he had noticed something which was a surprise to him; had had the impression that down here, toward the equator, the moonlight was much stronger and brighter than up North; had had the impression that when he visited New Orleans, many years ago, the moon—

Interruption from the other end of the room:—

"Let me explain that. Reminds me of an anecdote. Everything is changed since the war, for better or for worse; but you 'll find people down here born grumblers, who see no change except the change for the worse. There was an old negro woman of this sort. A young New-Yorker said in her presence, 'What a wonderful moon you have down here!' She sighed and said, 'Ah, bless yo' heart, honey, you ought to seen dat moon befo' de waw!' "

The new topic was dead already. But the poet resurrected it, and gave it a new start.

A brief dispute followed, as to whether the difference between Northern and Southern moonlight really existed or was only imagined. Moonlight talk drifted easily into talk about artificial methods of dispelling darkness. Then somebody remembered that when Farragut advanced upon Port Hudson on a dark night—and did not wish to assist the aim of the Confederate gunners—he carried no battle-lanterns, but painted the decks of his ships white, and thus created a dim but valuable light, which enabled his own men to grope their way around with considerable facility. At this point the war got the floor again—the ten minutes not quite up yet.

I was not sorry, for war talk by men who have been in a war is always interesting; whereas moon talk by a poet who has not been in the moon is likely to be dull.

We went to a cockpit in New Orleans on a Saturday afternoon. I had never seen a cock-fight before. There were men and boys there of all ages and all colors, and of many languages and nationalities. But I noticed one quite conspicuous and surprising absence: the traditional brutal faces. There were no brutal faces. With no cock-fighting going on, you could have played the gathering on a stranger for a prayer-meeting; and after it began, for a revival,—provided you blindfolded your stranger,—for the shouting was something prodigious.

A negro and a white man were in the ring; everybody else outside. The cocks were brought in in sacks; and when time was called, they were taken out by the two bottle-holders, stroked, caressed, poked toward each other, and finally liberated. The big black cock plunged instantly at the little gray one and struck him on the head with his spur. The gray responded with spirit. Then the Babel of many-tongued shoutings broke out, and ceased not thenceforth. When the cocks had been fighting some little time, I was expecting them momently to drop dead, for both were blind, red with blood, and so exhausted that they frequently fell down. Yet they would not give up, neither would they die. The negro and the white man would pick them up every few seconds, wipe them off, blow cold water on them in a fine spray, and take their heads in their mouths and hold them there a moment— to warm back the perishing life perhaps; I do not know. Then, being set down again, the dying creatures would totter gropingly about, with dragging wings, find each other, strike a guess-work blow or two, and fall exhausted once more.

I did not see the end of the battle. I forced myself to endure it as long as I could, but it was too pitiful a sight; so I made frank confession to that effect, and we retired. We heard afterward that the black cock died in the ring, and fighting to the last.

Evidently there is abundant fascination about this "sport" for such as have had a degree of familiarity with it. I never saw people enjoy anything more than this gathering enjoyed this fight. The case was the same with old gray-heads and with boys of ten. They lost themselves in frenzies of delight. The "cocking-main" is an inhuman sort of entertainment, there is no question about that; still, it seems a much more respectable and far less cruel sport than fox-hunting—for the cocks like it; they experience, as well as confer enjoyment; which is not the fox's case.

We assisted—in the French sense—at a mule race, one day. I believe I enjoyed this contest more than any other mule there. I enjoyed it more than I remember having enjoyed any other animal race I ever saw. The grand stand was well filled with the beauty and the chivalry of New Orleans. That phrase is not original with me. It is the Southern reporter's. He has used it for two generations. He uses it twenty times a day, or twenty thousand times a day; or a million times a day—according to the exigencies. He is obliged to use it a million times a day, if he have occasion to speak of respectable men and women that often; for he has no other phrase for such service except that single one. He never tires of it; it always has a fine sound to him. There is a kind of swell mediæval bulliness and tinsel about it that pleases his gaudy barbaric soul. If he had been in Palestine in the early times, we should have had no references to "much people" out of him. No, he would have said "the beauty and the chivalry of Galilee" assembled to hear the Sermon on the Mount. It is likely that the men and women of the South are sick enough of that phrase by this time, and would like a change, but there is no immediate prospect of their getting it.

The New Orleans editor has a strong, compact, direct, un-flowery style; wastes no words, and does not gush. Not so with his average correspondent. In the Appendix I have quoted a good letter, penned by a trained hand; but the average correspondent hurls a style which differs from that. For instance:—

The "Times-Democrat" sent a relief-steamer up one of the bayous, last April. This steamer landed at a village, up there somewhere, and the Captain invited some of the ladies of the village to make a short trip with him. They accepted and came aboard, and the steamboat shoved out up the creek. That was all there was "to it." And that is all that the editor of the "Times-Democrat" would have got out of it. There was nothing in the thing but statistics, and he would have got nothing else out of it. He would probably have even tabulated them, partly to secure perfect clearness of statement, and partly to save space. But his special correspondent knows other methods of handling statistics. He just throws off all restraint and wallows in them:—

"On Saturday, early in the morning, the beauty of the place graced our cabin, and proud of her fair freight the gallant little boat glided up the bayou."

Twenty-two words to say the ladies came aboard and the boat shoved out up the creek, is a clean waste of ten good words, and is also destructive of compactness of statement.

The trouble with the Southern reporter is—Women. They unsettle him; they throw him off his balance. He is plain, and sensible, and satisfactory, until a woman heaves in sight. Then he goes all to pieces; his mind totters, he becomes flowery and idiotic. From reading the above extract, you would imagine that this student of Sir Walter Scott is an apprentice, and knows next to nothing about handling a pen. On the contrary, he furnishes plenty of proofs, in his long letter, that he knows well enough how to handle it when the women are not around to give him the artificial-flower complaint. For instance:—

"At 4 o'clock ominous clouds began to gather in the southeast, and presently from the Gulf there came a blow which increased in severity every moment. It was not safe to leave the landing then, and there was a delay. The oaks shook off long tresses of their mossy beards to the tugging

of the wind, and the bayou in its ambition put on miniature waves in mocking of much larger bodies of water. A
lull permitted a start, and homewards we steamed, an inky
sky overhead and a heavy wind blowing. As darkness crept
on, there were few on board who did not wish themselves
nearer home."

There is nothing the matter with that. It is good description, compactly put. Yet there was great temptation, there, to
drop into lurid writing.

But let us return to the mule. Since I left him, I have rummaged around and found a full report of the race. In it I find
confirmation of the theory which I broached just now —
namely, that the trouble with the Southern reporter is
Women: Women, supplemented by Walter Scott and his
knights and beauty and chivalry, and so on. This is an excellent report, as long as the women stay out of it. But when
they intrude, we have this frantic result: —

"It will be probably a long time before the ladies' stand
presents such a sea of foam-like loveliness as it did yesterday. The New Orleans women are always charming, but
never so much so as at this time of the year, when in their
dainty spring costumes they bring with them a breath of
balmy freshness and an odor of sanctity unspeakable. The
stand was so crowded with them that, walking at their feet
and seeing no possibility of approach, many a man appreciated as he never did before the Peri's feeling at the Gates
of Paradise, and wondered what was the priceless boon that
would admit him to their sacred presence. Sparkling on
their white-robed breasts or shoulders were the colors of
their favorite knights, and were it not for the fact that the
doughty heroes appeared on unromantic mules, it would
have been easy to imagine one of King Arthur's gala-days."

There were thirteen mules in the first heat; all sorts of
mules, they were; all sorts of complexions, gaits, dispositions,
aspects. Some were handsome creatures, some were not;
some were sleek, some had n't had their fur brushed lately;
some were innocently gay and frisky; some were full of malice
and all unrighteousness; guessing from looks, some of them

thought the matter on hand was war, some thought it was a lark, the rest took it for a religious occasion. And each mule acted according to his convictions. The result was an absence of harmony well compensated by a conspicuous presence of variety—variety of a picturesque and entertaining sort.

All the riders were young gentlemen in fashionable society. If the reader has been wondering why it is that the ladies of New Orleans attend so humble an orgy as a mule-race, the thing is explained now. It is a fashion-freak; all connected with it are people of fashion.

It is great fun, and cordially liked. The mule-race is one of the marked occasions of the year. It has brought some pretty fast mules to the front. One of these had to be ruled out, because he was so fast that he turned the thing into a one-mule contest, and robbed it of one of its best features—variety. But every now and then somebody disguises him with a new name and a new complexion, and rings him in again.

The riders dress in full jockey costumes of bright-colored silks, satins, and velvets.

The thirteen mules got away in a body, after a couple of false starts, and scampered off with prodigious spirit. As each mule and each rider had a distinct opinion of his own as to how the race ought to be run, and which side of the track was best in certain circumstances, and how often the track ought to be crossed, and when a collision ought to be accomplished, and when it ought to be avoided, these twenty-six conflicting opinions created a most fantastic and picturesque confusion, and the resulting spectacle was killingly comical.

Mile heat; time, 2:22. Eight of the thirteen mules distanced. I had a bet on a mule which would have won if the procession had been reversed. The second heat was good fun; and so was the "consolation race for beaten mules," which followed later; but the first heat was the best in that respect.

I think that much the most enjoyable of all races is a steamboat race; but, next to that, I prefer the gay and joyous mulerush. Two red-hot steamboats raging along, neck-and-neck, straining every nerve—that is to say, every rivet in the boilers—quaking and shaking and groaning from stem to stern, spouting white steam from the pipes, pouring black smoke from the chimneys, raining down sparks, parting the river into long breaks of hissing foam—this is sport that makes a body's very liver curl with enjoyment. A horse-race is pretty tame and colorless in comparison. Still, a horse-race might be well enough, in its way, perhaps, if it were not for the tiresome false starts. But then, nobody is ever killed. At least, nobody was ever killed when I was at a horse-race. They have been crippled, it is true; but this is little to the purpose.

XLVI.

Enchantments and Enchanters

THE LARGEST ANNUAL EVENT in New Orleans is a something which we arrived too late to sample—the Mardi-Gras festivities. I saw the procession of the Mystic Crew of Comus there, twenty-four years ago—with knights and nobles and so on, clothed in silken and golden Paris-made gorgeousnesses, planned and bought for that single night's use; and in their train all manner of giants, dwarfs, monstrosities, and other diverting grotesquerie—a startling and wonderful sort of show, as it filed solemnly and silently down the street in the light of its smoking and flickering torches; but it is said that in these latter days the spectacle is mightily augmented, as to cost, splendor, and variety. There is a chief personage—"Rex;" and if I remember rightly, neither this king nor any of his great following of subordinates is known to any outsider. All these people are gentlemen of position and consequence; and it is a proud thing to belong to the organization; so the mystery in which they hide their personality is merely for romance's sake, and not on account of the police.

Mardi-Gras is of course a relic of the French and Spanish occupation; but I judge that the religious feature has been pretty well knocked out of it now. Sir Walter has got the advantage of the gentlemen of the cowl and rosary, and he will stay. His mediæval business, supplemented by the monsters and the oddities, and the pleasant creatures from fairyland, is finer to look at than the poor fantastic inventions and performances of the revelling rabble of the priest's day, and serves quite as well, perhaps, to emphasize the day and admonish men that the grace-line between the worldly season and the holy one is reached.

This Mardi-Gras pageant was the exclusive possession of New Orleans until recently. But now it has spread to Memphis and St. Louis and Baltimore. It has probably reached its limit. It is a thing which could hardly exist in the practical North; would certainly last but a very brief time; as brief a time as it would last in London. For the soul of it is the romantic, not the funny and the grotesque. Take away the romantic mysteries, the kings and knights and big-sounding titles, and Mardi-Gras would die, down there in the South. The very feature that keeps it alive in the South—girly-girly romance—would kill it in the North or in London. Puck and Punch, and the press universal, would fall upon it and make merciless fun of it, and its first exhibition would be also its last.

Against the crimes of the French Revolution and of Bonaparte may be set two compensating benefactions: the Revolution broke the chains of the *ancien régime* and of the Church, and made of a nation of abject slaves a nation of freemen; and Bonaparte instituted the setting of merit above birth, and also so completely stripped the divinity from royalty, that whereas crowned heads in Europe were gods before, they are only men, since, and can never be gods again, but only figure-heads, and answerable for their acts like common clay. Such benefactions as these compensate the temporary harm which Bonaparte and the Revolution did, and leave the world in debt to them for these great and permanent services to liberty, humanity, and progress.

Then comes Sir Walter Scott with his enchantments, and by his single might checks this wave of progress, and even turns it back; sets the world in love with dreams and phantoms; with decayed and swinish forms of religion; with decayed and degraded systems of government; with the sillinesses and emptinesses, sham grandeurs, sham gauds, and sham chivalries of a brainless and worthless long-vanished society. He did measureless harm; more real and lasting harm, perhaps, than any other individual that ever wrote. Most of the world has now outlived good part of these harms, though by no means all of them; but in our South they flourish pretty forcefully still. Not so forcefully as half a generation ago, perhaps, but still forcefully. There, the genuine and wholesome civilization of the nineteenth century is curiously confused and commingled with the Walter Scott Middle-Age sham civilization and so you have practical, common-sense, progressive ideas, and progressive works, mixed up with the duel, the inflated speech, and the jejune romanticism of an absurd past that is dead, and out of charity ought to be buried. But for the Sir Walter disease, the character of the Southerner—or Southron, according to Sir Walter's starchier way of phrasing it—would be wholly modern, in place of modern and mediæval mixed, and the South would be fully a generation further advanced than it is. It was Sir Walter that made every gentleman in the South a Major or a Colonel, or a General or a Judge, before the war; and it was he, also, that made these gentlemen value these bogus decorations. For it was he that created rank and caste down there, and also reverence for rank and caste, and pride and pleasure in them. Enough is laid on slavery, without fathering upon it these creations and contributions of Sir Walter.

Sir Walter had so large a hand in making Southern character, as it existed before the war, that he is in great measure responsible for the war. It seems a little harsh toward a dead man to say that we never should have had any war but for Sir Walter; and yet something of a plausible argument might, perhaps, be made in support of that wild proposition. The Southerner of the American revolution owned slaves; so did the Southerner of the Civil War: but the former resembles the latter as an Englishman resembles a Frenchman. The change of character can be traced rather more easily to Sir Walter's influence than to that of any other thing or person.

One may observe, by one or two signs, how deeply that influence penetrated, and how strongly it holds. If one take up a Northern or Southern literary periodical of forty or fifty years ago, he will find it filled with wordy, windy, flowery "eloquence," romanticism, sentimentality—all imitated from Sir Walter, and sufficiently badly done, too—innocent travesties of his style and methods, in fact. This sort of literature being the fashion in both sections of the country, there was opportunity for the fairest competition; and as a consequence, the South was able to show as many well-known literary names, proportioned to population, as the North could.

But a change has come, and there is no opportunity now for a fair competition between North and South. For the North has thrown out that old inflated style, whereas the Southern writer still clings to it—clings to it and has a restricted market for his wares, as a consequence. There is as much literary talent in the South, now, as ever there was, of course; but its work can gain but slight currency under present conditions; the authors write for the past, not the present; they use obsolete forms, and a dead language. But when a Southerner of genius writes modern English, his book goes upon crutches no longer, but upon wings; and they carry it swiftly all about America and England, and through the great English reprint publishing houses of Germany—as witness the experience of Mr. Cable and Uncle Remus, two of the very few Southern authors who do not write in the southern style. Instead of three or four widely-known literary names, the South ought to have a dozen or two—and will have them when Sir Walter's time is out.

A curious exemplification of the power of a single book for good or harm is shown in the effects wrought by Don Quixote and those wrought by Ivanhoe. The first swept the world's admiration for the mediæval chivalry-silliness out of existence; and the other restored it. As far as our South is concerned, the good work done by Cervantes is pretty nearly a dead letter, so effectually has Scott's pernicious work undermined it.

XLVII.

Uncle Remus and Mr. Cable

M R. JOEL CHANDLER HARRIS ("Uncle Remus") was to arrive from Atlanta at seven o'clock Sunday morning; so we got up and received him. We were able to detect him among the crowd of arrivals at the hotel-counter by his correspondence with a description of him which had been furnished us from a trustworthy source. He was said to be undersized, red-haired, and somewhat freckled. He was the only man in the party whose outside tallied with this bill of particulars. He was said to be very shy. He is a shy man. Of this there is no doubt. It may not show on the surface, but the shyness is there. After days of intimacy one wonders to see that it is still in about as strong force as ever. There is a fine and beautiful nature hidden behind it, as all know who have read the Uncle Remus book; and a fine genius, too, as all know by the same sign. I seem to be talking quite freely about this neighbor; but in talking to the public I am but talking to his personal friends, and these things are permissible among friends.

He deeply disappointed a number of children who had flocked eagerly to Mr. Cable's house to get a glimpse of the illustrious sage and oracle of the nation's nurseries. They said:—

"Why, he 's white!"

They were grieved about it. So, to console them, the book was brought, that they might hear Uncle Remus's Tar-Baby story from the lips of Uncle Remus himself—or what, in their outraged eyes, was left of him. But it turned out that he had never read aloud to people, and was too shy to venture the attempt now. Mr. Cable and I read from books of ours, to show him what an easy trick it was; but his immortal shyness was proof against even this sagacious strategy, so we had to read about Brer Rabbit ourselves.

Mr. Harris ought to be able to read the negro dialect better than anybody else, for in the matter of writing it he is the only master the country has produced. Mr. Cable is the only master in the writing of French dialects that the country has produced; and he reads them in perfection. It was a great treat to hear him read about Jean-ah Poquelin, and about Innerarity and his famous "pigshoo" representing "Louisihanna *Rif*-fusing to Hanter the Union," along with passages of nicely-shaded German dialect from a novel which was still in manuscript.

It came out in conversation, that in two different instances Mr. Cable got into grotesque trouble by using, in his books, next-to-impossible French names which nevertheless happened to be borne by living and sensitive citizens of New-Orleans. His names were either inventions or were borrowed from the ancient and obsolete past, I do not now remember which; but at any rate living bearers of them turned up, and were a good deal hurt at having attention directed to themselves and their affairs in so excessively public a manner.

Mr. Warner and I had an experience of the same sort when we wrote the book called "The Gilded Age." There is a character in it called "Sellers." I do not remember what his first name was, in the beginning; but anyway, Mr. Warner did not like it, and wanted it improved. He asked me if I was able to imagine a person named "Eschol Sellers." Of course I said I could not, without stimulants. He said that away out West, once, he had met, and contemplated, and actually shaken hands with a man bearing that impossible name—"Eschol Sellers." He added,—

"It was twenty years ago; his name has probably carried him off before this; and if it has n't, he will never see the book anyhow. We will confiscate his name. The name you are using is common, and therefore dangerous; there are probably a thousand Sellerses bearing it, and the whole horde will come after us; but Eschol Sellers is a safe name—it is a rock."

So we borrowed that name; and when the book had been out about a week, one of the stateliest and handsomest and most aristocratic looking white men that ever lived, called around, with the most formidable libel suit in his pocket that ever—well, in brief, we got his permission to suppress an edition of ten million[1] copies of the book and change that name to "Mulberry Sellers" in future editions.

[1]Figures taken from memory, and probably incorrect. Think it was more.

XLVIII.

Sugar and Postage

ONE DAY, on the street, I encountered the man whom, of all men, I most wished to see—Horace Bixby; formerly pilot under me—or rather, over me—now captain of the great steamer "City of Baton Rouge," the latest and swiftest addition to the Anchor Line. The same slender figure, the same tight curls, the same springy step, the same alertness, the same decision of eye and answering decision of hand, the same erect military bearing; not an inch gained or lost in girth, not an ounce gained or lost in weight, not a hair turned. It is a curious thing, to leave a man thirty-five years old, and come back at the end of twenty-one years and find him still only thirty-five. I have not had an experience of this kind before, I believe. There were some crow's-feet, but they counted for next to nothing, since they were inconspicuous.

His boat was just in. I had been waiting several days for her, purposing to return to St. Louis in her. The captain and I joined a party of ladies and gentlemen, guests of Major Wood, and went down the river fifty-four miles, in a swift tug, to ex-Governor Warmouth's sugar plantation. Strung along below the city, were a number of decayed, ram-shackly, superannuated old steamboats, not one of which had I ever seen before. They had all been built, and worn out, and thrown aside, since I was here last. This gives one a realizing sense of the frailness of a Mississippi boat and the briefness of its life.

Six miles below town a fat and battered brick chimney, sticking above the magnolias and live-oaks, was pointed out as the monument erected by an appreciative nation to celebrate the battle of New Orleans—Jackson's victory over the British, January 8, 1815. The war had ended, the two nations were at peace, but the news had not yet reached New Orleans. If we had had the cable telegraph in those days, this blood would not have been spilt, those lives would not have been wasted; and better still, Jackson would probably never have been president. We have gotten over the harms done us by the war of 1812, but not over some of those done us by Jackson's presidency.

The Warmouth plantation covers a vast deal of ground, and the hospitality of the Warmouth mansion is graduated to the same large scale. We saw steam-plows at work, here, for the first time. The traction engine travels about on its own wheels, till it reaches the required spot; then it stands still and by means of a wire rope pulls the huge plow toward itself two or three hundred yards across the field, between the rows of cane. The thing cuts down into the black mould a foot and a half deep. The plow looks like a fore-and-aft brace of a Hudson river steamer, inverted. When the negro steersman sits on one end of it, that end tilts down near the ground, while the other sticks up high in air. This great see-saw goes rolling and pitching like a ship at sea, and it is not every circus rider that could stay on it.

The plantation contains two thousand six hundred acres; six hundred and fifty are in cane; and there is a fruitful orange grove of five thousand trees. The cane is cultivated after a modern and intricate scientific fashion, too elaborate and complex for me to attempt to describe; but it lost $40,000 last year. I forget the other details. However, this year's crop will reach ten or twelve hundred tons of sugar, consequently last year's loss will not matter. These troublesome and expensive scientific methods achieve a yield of a ton and a half, and from that to two tons, to the acre; which is three or four times what the yield of an acre was in my time.

The drainage-ditches were everywhere alive with little crabs—"fiddlers." One saw them scampering sidewise in every direction whenever they heard a disturbing noise. Expensive pests, these crabs; for they bore into the levees, and ruin them.

The great sugar-house was a wilderness of tubs and tanks and vats and filters, pumps, pipes, and machinery. The process of making sugar is exceedingly interesting. First, you heave your cane into the centrifugals and grind out the juice; then run it through the evaporating pan to extract the fibre; then through the bone-filter to remove the alcohol; then through the clarifying tanks to discharge the molasses; then through the granulating pipe to condense it; then through the vacuum pan to extract the vacuum. It is now ready for market. I have jotted these particulars down from memory. The thing looks simple and easy. Do not deceive yourself. To make sugar is really one of the most difficult things in the world. And to make it right, is next to impossible. If you will examine your own supply every now and then for a term of years, and tabulate the result, you will find that not two men in twenty can make sugar without getting sand into it.

We could have gone down to the mouth of the river and visited Captain Eads' great work, the "jetties," where the river has been compressed between walls, and thus deepened to twenty-six feet; but it was voted useless to go, since at this stage of the water everything would be covered up and invisible.

We could have visited that ancient and singular burg, "Pilot-town," which stands on stilts in the water—so they say; where nearly all communication is by skiff and canoe, even to the attending of weddings and funerals; and where the littlest boys and girls are as handy with the oar as unamphibious children are with the velocipede.

We could have done a number of other things; but on account of limited time, we went back home. The sail up the breezy and sparkling river was a charming experience, and would have been satisfyingly sentimental and romantic but for the interruptions of the tug's pet parrot, whose tireless comments upon the scenery and the guests were always this-worldly, and often profane. He had also a superabundance of the discordant, ear-splitting, metallic laugh common to his breed,—a machine-made laugh, a Frankenstein laugh, with the soul left out of it. He applied it to every sentimental remark, and to every pathetic song. He cackled it out with hideous energy after "Home again, home again, from a foreign shore," and said he "wouldn't give a damn for a tug-load of such rot." Romance and sentiment cannot long survive this sort of discouragement; so the singing and talking presently ceased; which so delighted the parrot that he cursed himself hoarse for joy.

Then the male members of the party moved to the forecastle, to smoke and gossip. There were several old steamboat-men along, and I learned from them a great deal of what had been happening to my former river friends during my long absence. I learned that a pilot whom I used to steer for is become a spiritualist, and for more than fifteen years has been receiving a letter every week from a deceased relative, through a New York spiritualistic medium named Manchester—postage graduated by distance: from the local post-office in Paradise to New York, five dollars; from New York to St. Louis, three cents. I remember Mr. Manchester very well. I called on him once, ten years ago, with a couple of friends, one of whom wished to inquire after a deceased uncle. This uncle had lost his life in a peculiarly violent and unusual way, half a dozen years before: a cyclone blew him some three miles and knocked a tree down with him which was four feet through at the butt and sixty-five feet high. He did not survive this triumph. At the *séance* just referred to, my friend questioned his late uncle, through Mr. Manchester, and the late uncle wrote down his replies, using Mr. Manchester's hand and pencil for that purpose. The following is a fair example of the questions asked, and also of the sloppy twaddle in the way of answers, furnished by Manchester under the pretence that it came from the spectre. If this man is not the paltriest fraud that lives, I owe him an apology:—

Question. Where are you?

Answer. In the spirit world.

Q. Are you happy?

A. Very happy. Perfectly happy.

Q. How do you amuse yourself?

A. Conversation with friends, and other spirits.

Q. What else?

A. Nothing else. Nothing else is necessary.

Q. What do you talk about?

A. About how happy we are; and about friends left behind in the earth, and how to influence them for their good.

Q. When your friends in the earth all get to the spirit land, what shall you have to talk about then?—nothing but about how happy you all are?

No reply. It is explained that spirits will not answer frivolous questions.

Q. How is it that spirits that are content to spend an eternity in frivolous employments, and accept it as happiness, are so fastidious about frivolous questions upon the subject?

No reply.

Q. Would you like to come back?

A. No.

Q. Would you say that under oath?

A. Yes.

Q. What do you eat there?

A. We do not eat.

Q. What do you drink?

A. We do not drink.

Q. What do you smoke?

A. We do not smoke.

Q. What do you read?

A. We do not read.

Q. Do all the good people go to your place?

A. Yes.

Q. You know my present way of life. Can you suggest any additions to it, in the way of crime, that will reasonably insure my going to some other place?

A. No reply.

Q. When did you die?

A. I did not die, I passed away.

Q. Very well, then, when did you pass away? How long have you been in the spirit land?

A. We have no measurements of time here.

Q. Though you may be indifferent and uncertain as to dates and times in your present condition and environment, this has nothing to do with your former condition. You had dates then. One of these is what I ask for. You departed on a certain day in a certain year. Is not this true?

A. Yes.

Q. Then name the day of the month.

(Much fumbling with pencil, on the part of the medium, accompanied by violent spasmodic jerkings of his head and body, for some little time. Finally, explanation to the effect that spirits often forget dates, such things being without importance to them.)

Q. Then this one has actually forgotten the date of its translation to the spirit land?

This was granted to be the case.

Q. This is very curious. Well, then, what year was it?

(More fumbling, jerking, idiotic spasms, on the part of the medium. Finally, explanation to the effect that the spirit has forgotten the year.)

Q. This is indeed stupendous. Let me put one more question, one last question, to you, before we part to meet no more;—for even if I fail to avoid your asylum, a meeting there will go for nothing *as* a meeting, since by that time you will easily have forgotten me and my name: did you die a natural death, or were you cut off by a catastrophe?

A. (After long hesitation and many throes and spasms.) *Natural death.*

This ended the interview. My friend told the medium that when his relative was in this poor world, he was endowed with an extraordinary intellect and an absolutely defectless memory, and it seemed a great pity that he had not been allowed to keep some shred of these for his amusement in the realms of everlasting contentment, and for the amazement and admiration of the rest of the population there.

This man had plenty of clients—has plenty yet. He receives letters from spirits located in every part of the spirit world, and delivers them all over this country through the United States mail. These letters are filled with advice—advice from "spirits" who don't know as much as a tadpole—and this advice is religiously followed by the receivers. One of these clients was a man whom the spirits (if one may thus plurally describe the ingenious Manchester) were teaching how to contrive an improved railway car-wheel. It is coarse employment for a spirit, but it is higher and wholesomer activity than talking forever about "how happy we are."

XLIX.

Episodes in Pilot Life

IN THE COURSE of the tug-boat gossip, it came out that out of every five of my former friends who had quitted the river, four had chosen farming as an occupation. Of course this was not because they were peculiarly gifted, agriculturally, and thus more likely to succeed as farmers than in other industries: the reason for their choice must be traced to some other source. Doubtless they chose farming because that life is private and secluded from irruptions of undesirable strangers,—like the pilot-house hermitage. And doubtless they also chose it because on a thousand nights of black storm and danger they had noted the twinkling lights of solitary farmhouses, as the boat swung by, and pictured to themselves the serenity and security and cosiness of such refuges at such times, and so had by and by come to dream of that retired and peaceful life as the one desirable thing to long for, anticipate, earn, and at last enjoy.

But I did not learn that any of these pilot-farmers had astonished anybody with their successes. Their farms do not support them: they support their farms. The pilot-farmer disappears from the river annually, about the breaking of spring, and is seen no more till next frost. Then he appears again, in damaged homespun, combs the hay-seed out of his hair, and takes a pilot-house berth for the winter. In this way he pays the debts which his farming has achieved during the agricultural season. So his river bondage is but half broken; he is still the river's slave the hardest half of the year.

One of these men bought a farm, but did not retire to it. He knew a trick worth two of that. He did not propose to pauperize his farm by applying his personal ignorance to working it. No, he put the farm into the hands of an agricultural expert to be worked on shares—out of every three loads of corn the expert to have two and the pilot the third. But at the end of the season the pilot received no corn. The expert explained that *his* share was not reached. The farm produced only two loads.

Some of the pilots whom I had known had had adventures;—the outcome fortunate, sometimes, but not in all cases. Captain Montgomery, whom I had steered for when he was a pilot, commanded the Confederate fleet in the great battle before Memphis; when his vessel went down, he swam ashore, fought his way through a squad of soldiers, and made a gallant and narrow escape. He was always a cool man; nothing could disturb his serenity. Once when he was captain of the "Crescent City," I was bringing the boat into port at New Orleans, and momently expecting orders from the hurricane deck, but received none. I had stopped the wheels, and there my authority and responsibility ceased. It was evening—dim twilight—the captain's hat was perched upon the big bell, and I supposed the intellectual end of the captain was in it, but such was not the case. The captain was very strict; therefore I knew better than to touch a bell without orders. My duty was to hold the boat steadily on her calamitous course, and leave the consequences to take care of themselves—which I did. So we went plowing past the sterns of steamboats and getting closer and closer—the crash was bound to come very soon—and still that hat never budged; for alas, the captain was napping in the texas. . . . Things were becoming exceedingly nervous and uncomfortable. It seemed to me that the captain was not going to appear in time to see the entertainment. But he did. Just as we were walking into the stern of a steamboat, he stepped out on deck, and said, with heavenly serenity, "Set her back on both"—which I did; but a trifle late, however, for the next moment we went smashing through that other boat's flimsy outer works with a most prodigious racket. The captain never said a word to me about the matter afterwards, except to remark that I had done right, and that he hoped I would not hesitate to act in the same way again in like circumstances.

One of the pilots whom I had known when I was on the river had died a very honorable death. His boat caught fire, and he remained at the wheel until he got her safe to land. Then he went out over the breast-board with his clothing in flames, and was the last person to get ashore. He died from his injuries in the course of two or three hours, and his was the only life lost.

The history of Mississippi piloting affords six or seven instances of this sort of martyrdom, and half a hundred instances of escapes from a like fate which came within a second or two of being fatally too late; *but there is no instance of a pilot deserting his post to save his life while by remaining and sacrificing it he might secure other lives from destruction.* It is well worth while to set down this noble fact, and well worth while to put it in italics, too.

The "cub" pilot is early admonished to despise all perils connected with a pilot's calling, and to prefer any sort of death to the deep dishonor of deserting his post while there is any possibility of his being useful in it. And so effectively are these admonitions inculcated, that even young and but half-tried pilots can be depended upon to stick to the wheel, and die there when occasion requires. In a Memphis graveyard is buried a young fellow who perished at the wheel a great many years ago, in White River, to save the lives of other men. He said to the captain that if the fire would give him time to reach a sand bar, some distance away, all could be saved, but that to land against the bluff bank of the river would be to insure the loss of many lives. He reached the bar and grounded the boat in shallow water; but by that time the flames had closed around him, and in escaping through them he was fatally burned. He had been urged to fly sooner, but had replied as became a pilot to reply:—

"I will not go. If I go, nobody will be saved; if I stay, no one will be lost but me. I will stay."

There were two hundred persons on board, and no life was lost but the pilot's. There used to be a monument to this young fellow, in that Memphis graveyard. While we tarried in Memphis on our down trip, I started out to look for it, but our time was so brief that I was obliged to turn back before my object was accomplished.

The tug-boat gossip informed me that Dick Kennet was dead—blown up, near Memphis, and killed; that several others whom I had known had fallen in the war—one or two of them shot down at the wheel; that another and very particular friend, whom I had steered many trips for, had stepped out of his house in New Orleans, one night years ago, to collect some money in a remote part of the city, and had never been seen again,—was murdered and thrown into the river, it was thought; that Ben Thornburgh was dead long ago; also his wild "cub" whom I used to quarrel with, all through every daylight watch. A heedless, reckless creature he was, and always in hot water, always in mischief. An Arkansas passenger brought an enormous bear aboard, one day, and chained him to a life-boat on the hurricane deck. Thornburgh's "cub" could not rest till he had gone there and unchained the bear, to "see what he would do." He was promptly gratified. The bear chased him around and around the deck, for miles and miles, with two hundred eager faces grinning through the railings for audience, and finally snatched off the lad's coat-tail and went into the texas to chew it. The off-watch turned out with alacrity, and left the bear in sole possession. He presently grew lonesome, and started out for recreation. He ranged the whole boat—visited every part of it, with an advance guard of fleeing people in front of him and a voiceless vacancy behind him; and when his owner captured him at last, those two were the only visible beings anywhere; everybody else was in hiding, and the boat was a solitude.

I was told that one of my pilot friends fell dead at the wheel, from heart disease, in 1869. The captain was on the roof at the time. He saw the boat breaking for the shore; shouted, and got no answer; ran up, and found the pilot lying dead on the floor.

Mr. Bixby had been blown up, in Madrid bend; was not injured, but the other pilot was lost.

George Ritchie had been blown up near Memphis—blown into the river from the wheel, and disabled. The water was very cold; he clung to a cotton bale—mainly with his teeth—and floated until nearly exhausted, when he was rescued by some deck hands who were on a piece of the wreck. They tore open the bale and packed him in the cotton, and warmed the life back into him, and got him safe to Memphis. He is one of Bixby's pilots on the "Baton Rouge" now.

Into the life of a steamboat clerk, now dead, had dropped a bit of romance,—somewhat grotesque romance, but romance nevertheless. When I knew him he was a shiftless young spendthrift, boisterous, good-hearted, full of careless generosities, and pretty conspicuously promising to fool his possibilities away early, and come to nothing. In a Western city lived a rich and childless old foreigner and his wife; and in their family was a comely young girl—sort of friend, sort of servant. The young clerk of whom I have been speaking,— whose name was not George Johnson, but who shall be called George Johnson for the purposes of this narrative,— got acquainted with this young girl, and they sinned; and the old foreigner found them out, and rebuked them. Being ashamed, they lied, and said they were married; that they had been privately married. Then the old foreigner's hurt was healed, and he forgave and blessed them. After that, they were able to continue their sin without concealment. By and by the foreigner's wife died; and presently he followed after her. Friends of the family assembled to mourn; and among the mourners sat the two young sinners. The will was opened and solemnly read. It bequeathed every penny of that old man's great wealth to *Mrs. George Johnson!*

And there was no such person. The young sinners fled forth then, and did a very foolish thing: married themselves before an obscure Justice of the Peace, and got him to ante-date the thing. That did no sort of good. The distant relatives flocked in and exposed the fraudful date with extreme suddenness and surprising ease, and carried off the fortune, leaving the Johnsons very legitimately, and legally, and irre-vocably chained together in honorable marriage, but with not so much as a penny to bless themselves withal. Such are the actual facts; and not all novels have for a base so telling a situation.

L.

The "Original Jacobs"

WE HAD SOME TALK about Captain Isaiah Sellers, now many years dead. He was a fine man, a high-minded man, and greatly respected both ashore and on the river. He was very tall, well built, and handsome; and in his old age—as I remember him—his hair was as black as an Indian's, and his eye and hand were as strong and steady and his nerve and judgment as firm and clear as anybody's, young or old, among the fraternity of pilots. He was the patriarch of the craft; he had been a keelboat pilot before the day of steamboats; and a steamboat pilot before any other steamboat pilot, still surviving at the time I speak of, had ever turned a wheel. Consequently his brethren held him in the sort of awe in which illustrious survivors of a bygone age are always held by their associates. He knew how he was regarded, and perhaps this fact added some trifle of stiffening to his natural dignity, which had been sufficiently stiff in its original state.

He left a diary behind him; but apparently it did not date back to his first steamboat trip, which was said to be 1811, the year the first steamboat disturbed the waters of the Mississippi. At the time of his death a correspondent of the "St. Louis Republican" culled the following items from the diary:—

"In February, 1825, he shipped on board the steamer 'Rambler,' at Florence, Ala., and made during that year three trips to New Orleans and back,—this on the 'Gen. Carrol,' between Nashville and New Orleans. It was during his stay on this boat that Captain Sellers introduced the tap of the bell as a signal to heave the lead, previous to which time it was the custom for the pilot to speak to the men below when soundings were wanted. The proximity of the forecastle to the pilot-house, no doubt, rendered this an easy matter; but how different on one of our palaces of the present day.

"In 1827 we find him on board the 'President,' a boat of

two hundred and eighty-five tons burden, and plying between Smithland and New Orleans. Thence he joined the 'Jubilee' in 1828, and on this boat he did his first piloting in the St. Louis trade; his first watch extending from Herculaneum to St. Genevieve. On May 26, 1836, he completed and left Pittsburg in charge of the steamer 'Prairie,' a boat of four hundred tons, and the first steamer with a *state-room cabin* ever seen at St. Louis. In 1857 he introduced the signal for meeting boats, and which has, with some slight change, been the universal custom of this day; in fact, is rendered obligatory by act of Congress.

"As general items of river history, we quote the following marginal notes from his general log: —

"In March, 1825, Gen. Lafayette left New Orleans for St. Louis on the low-pressure steamer 'Natchez.'

"In January, 1828, twenty-one steamers left the New Orleans wharf to celebrate the occasion of Gen. Jackson's visit to that city.

"In 1830 the 'North American' made the run from New Orleans to Memphis in six days—best time on record to that date. It has since been made in two days and ten hours.

"In 1831 the Red River cut-off formed.

"In 1832 steamer 'Hudson' made the run from White River to Helena, a distance of seventy-five miles, in twelve hours. This was the source of much talk and speculation among parties directly interested.

"In 1839 Great Horseshoe cut-off formed.

"Up to the present time, a term of thirty-five years, we ascertain, by reference to the diary, he has made four hundred and sixty round trips to New Orleans, which gives a distance of one million one hundred and four thousand miles, or an average of eighty-six miles a day."

Whenever Captain Sellers approached a body of gossiping pilots, a chill fell there, and talking ceased. For this reason: whenever six pilots were gathered together, there would always be one or two newly fledged ones in the lot, and the elder ones would be always "showing off" before these poor fellows; making them sorrowfully feel how callow they were, how recent their nobility, and how humble their degree, by talking largely and vaporously of old-time experiences on the river; always making it a point to date everything back as far as they could, so as to make the new men feel their newness to the sharpest degree possible, and envy the old stagers in the like degree. And how these complacent bald-heads *would* swell, and brag, and lie, and date back—ten, fifteen, twenty years,—and how they did enjoy the effect produced upon the marvelling and envying youngsters!

And perhaps just at this happy stage of the proceedings, the stately figure of Captain Isaiah Sellers, that real and only genuine Son of Antiquity, would drift solemnly into the midst. Imagine the size of the silence that would result on the instant. And imagine the feelings of those bald-heads, and the exultation of their recent audience when the ancient captain would begin to drop casual and indifferent remarks of a reminiscent nature,—about islands that had disappeared, and cut-offs that had been made, a generation before the oldest bald-head in the company had ever set his foot in a pilot-house!

Many and many a time did this ancient mariner appear on the scene in the above fashion, and spread disaster and humiliation around him. If one might believe the pilots, he always dated his islands back to the misty dawn of river history; and he never used the same island twice; and never did he employ an island that still existed, or give one a name which anybody present was old enough to have heard of before. If you might believe the pilots, he was always conscientiously particular about little details; never spoke of "the State of Mississippi," for instance,—no, he would say, "When the State of Mississippi was where Arkansas now is;" and would never speak of Louisiana or Missouri in a general way, and leave an incorrect impression on your mind,—no, he would say, "When Louisiana was up the river farther," or "When Missouri was on the Illinois side."

The old gentleman was not of literary turn or capacity, but he used to jot down brief paragraphs of plain practical information about the river, and sign them "MARK TWAIN," and give them to the "New Orleans Picayune." They related to the stage and condition of the river, and were accurate and valuable; and thus far, they contained no poison. But in speaking of the stage of the river to-day, at a given point, the captain was pretty apt to drop in a little remark about this being the first time he had seen the water so high or so low at that particular point for forty-nine years; and now and then he would mention Island so and so, and follow it, in parentheses, with some such observation as "disappeared in 1807, if I remember rightly." In these antique interjections lay poison and bitterness for the other old pilots, and they used to chaff the "Mark Twain" paragraphs with unsparing mockery.

It so chanced that one of these paragraphs[1] became the text for my first newspaper article. I burlesqued it broadly, very broadly, stringing my fantastics out to the extent of eight hundred or a thousand words. I was a "cub" at the time. I showed my performance to some pilots, and they eagerly rushed it into print in the "New Orleans True Delta." It was a great pity; for it did nobody any worthy service, and it sent a pang deep into a good man's heart. There was no malice in my rubbish; but it laughed at the captain. It laughed at a man to whom such a thing was new and strange and dreadful. I did not know then, though I do now, that there is no suffering comparable with that which a private person feels when he is for the first time pilloried in print.

Captain Sellers did me the honor to profoundly detest me from that day forth. When I say he did me the honor, I am not using empty words. It was a very real honor to be in the thoughts of so great a man as Captain Sellers, and I had wit enough to appreciate it and be proud of it. It was distinction to be loved by such a man; but it was a much greater distinction to be hated by him, because he loved scores of people; but he did n't sit up nights to hate anybody but me.

He never printed another paragraph while he lived, and he

[1]The original MS. of it, in the captain's own hand, has been sent to me from New Orleans. It reads as follows: —

"VICKSBURG, May 4, 1859.

"My opinion for the benefit of the citizens of New Orleans: The water is higher this far up than it has been since 1815. My opinion is that the water will be 4 feet deep in Canal street before the first of next June. Mrs. Turner's plantation at the head of Big Black Island is all under water, and it has not been since 1815.

"I. SELLERS."

never again signed "Mark Twain" to anything. At the time that the telegraph brought the news of his death, I was on the Pacific coast. I was a fresh new journalist, and needed a *nom de guerre*; so I confiscated the ancient mariner's discarded one, and have done my best to make it remain what it was in his hands—a sign and symbol and warrant that whatever is found in its company may be gambled on as being the petrified truth; how I have succeeded, it would not be modest in me to say.

The captain had an honorable pride in his profession and an abiding love for it. He ordered his monument before he died, and kept it near him until he did die. It stands over his grave now, in Bellefontaine cemetery, St. Louis. It is his image, in marble, standing on duty at the pilot wheel; and worthy to stand and confront criticism, for it represents a man who in life would have staid there till he burned to a cinder, if duty required it.

The finest thing we saw on our whole Mississippi trip, we saw as we approached New Orleans in the steam-tug. This was the curving frontage of the crescent city lit up with the white glare of five miles of electric lights. It was a wonderful sight, and very beautiful.

LI.

Reminiscences

W E LEFT for St. Louis in the "City of Baton Rouge," on a delightfully hot day, but with the main purpose of my visit but lamely accomplished. I had hoped to hunt up and talk with a hundred steamboatmen, but got so pleasantly involved in the social life of the town that I got nothing more than mere five-minute talks with a couple of dozen of the craft.

I was on the bench of the pilot-house when we backed out and "straightened up" for the start—the boat pausing for a "good ready," in the old-fashioned way, and the black smoke piling out of the chimneys equally in the old-fashioned way. Then we began to gather momentum, and presently were fairly under way and booming along. It was all as natural and familiar—and so were the shoreward sights—as if there had been no break in my river life. There was a "cub," and I judged that he would take the wheel now; and he did. Captain Bixby stepped into the pilot-house. Presently the cub closed up on the rank of steamships. He made me nervous, for he allowed too much water to show between our boat and the ships. I knew quite well what was going to happen, because I could date back in my own life and inspect the record. The captain looked on, during a silent half-minute, then took the wheel himself, and crowded the boat in, till she went scraping along within a hand-breadth of the ships. It was exactly the favor which he had done me, about a quarter of a century before, in that same spot, the first time I ever steamed out of the port of New Orleans. It was a very great and sincere pleasure to me to see the thing repeated—with somebody else as victim.

We made Natchez (three hundred miles) in twenty-two hours and a half,—much the swiftest passage I have ever made over that piece of water.

The next morning I came on with the four o'clock watch, and saw Ritchie successfully run half a dozen crossings in a fog, using for his guidance the marked chart devised and pat-

305

ented by Bixby and himself. This sufficiently evidenced the great value of the chart.

By and by, when the fog began to clear off, I noticed that the reflection of a tree in the smooth water of an overflowed bank, six hundred yards away, was stronger and blacker than the ghostly tree itself. The faint spectral trees, dimly glimpsed through the shredding fog, were very pretty things to see.

We had a heavy thunder-storm at Natchez, another at Vicksburg, and still another about fifty miles below Memphis. They had an old-fashioned energy which had long been unfamiliar to me. This third storm was accompanied by a raging wind. We tied up to the bank when we saw the tempest coming, and everybody left the pilot-house but me. The wind bent the young trees down, exposing the pale underside of the leaves; and gust after gust followed, in quick succession, thrashing the branches violently up and down, and to this side and that, and creating swift waves of alternating green and white according to the side of the leaf that was exposed, and these waves raced after each other as do their kind over a wind-tossed field of oats. No color that was visible anywhere was quite natural,—all tints were charged with a leaden tinge from the solid cloud-bank overhead. The river was leaden; all distances the same; and even the far-reaching ranks of combing white-caps were dully shaded by the dark, rich atmosphere through which their swarming legions marched. The thunder-peals were constant and deafening; explosion followed explosion with but inconsequential intervals between, and the reports grew steadily sharper and higher-keyed, and more trying to the ear; the lightning was as diligent as the thunder, and produced effects which enchanted the eye and sent electric ecstasies of mixed delight and apprehension shivering along every nerve in the body in unintermittent procession. The rain poured down in amazing volume; the ear-splitting thunder-peals broke nearer and nearer; the wind increased in fury and began to wrench off boughs and tree-tops and send them sailing away through space; the pilot-house fell to rocking and straining and cracking and surging, and I went down in the hold to see what time it was.

People boast a good deal about Alpine thunder-storms; but

the storms which I have had the luck to see in the Alps were
not the equals of some which I have seen in the Mississippi
Valley. I may not have seen the Alps do their best, of course,
and if they can beat the Mississippi, I don't wish to.

On this up trip I saw a little towhead (infant island) half a
mile long, which had been formed during the past nineteen
years. Since there was so much time to spare that nineteen
years of it could be devoted to the construction of a mere
towhead, where was the use, originally, in rushing this whole
globe through in six days? It is likely that if more time had
been taken, in the first place, the world would have been
made right, and this ceaseless improving and repairing would
not be necessary now. But if you hurry a world or a house,
you are nearly sure to find out by and by, that you have left
out a towhead, or a broom-closet, or some other little convenience, here and there, which has got to be supplied, no
matter how much expense and vexation it may cost.

We had a succession of black nights, going up the river,
and it was observable that whenever we landed, and suddenly
inundated the trees with the intense sunburst of the electric
light, a certain curious effect was always produced: hundreds
of birds flocked instantly out from the masses of shining
green foliage, and went careering hither and thither through
the white rays, and often a song-bird tuned up and fell to
singing. We judged that they mistook this superb artificial day
for the genuine article.

We had a delightful trip in that thoroughly well-ordered
steamer, and regretted that it was accomplished so speedily.
By means of diligence and activity, we managed to hunt out
nearly all the old friends. One was missing, however; he went
to his reward, whatever it was, two years ago. But I found
out all about him. His case helped me to realize how lasting
can be the effect of a very trifling occurrence. When he was
an apprentice-blacksmith in our village, and I a schoolboy, a
couple of young Englishmen came to the town and sojourned
a while; and one day they got themselves up in cheap royal
finery and did the Richard III. sword-fight with maniac energy and prodigious powwow, in the presence of the village
boys. This blacksmith cub was there, and the histrionic poison entered his bones. This vast, lumbering, ignorant, dull-

witted lout was stage-struck, and irrecoverably. He disappeared, and presently turned up in St. Louis. I ran across him there, by and by. He was standing musing on a street corner, with his right hand on his hip, the thumb of his left supporting his chin, face bowed and frowning, slouch hat pulled down over his forehead—imagining himself to be Othello or some such character, and imagining that the passing crowd marked his tragic bearing and were awestruck.

I joined him, and tried to get him down out of the clouds, but did not succeed. However, he casually informed me, presently, that he was a member of the Walnut Street theatre company,—and he tried to say it with indifference, but the indifference was thin, and a mighty exultation showed through it. He said he was cast for a part in Julius Cæsar, for that night, and if I should come I would see him. *If* I should come! I said I would n't miss it if I were dead.

I went away stupefied with astonishment, and saying to myself, "How strange it is! *we* always thought this fellow a fool; yet the moment he comes to a great city, where intelligence and appreciation abound, the talent concealed in this shabby napkin is at once discovered, and promptly welcomed and honored."

But I came away from the theatre that night disappointed and offended; for I had had no glimpse of my hero, and his name was not in the bills. I met him on the street the next morning, and before I could speak, he asked:—

"Did you see me?"

"No, you were n't there."

He looked surprised and disappointed. He said:—

"Yes, I was. Indeed I was. I was a Roman soldier."

"Which one?"

"Why, did n't you see them Roman soldiers that stood back there in a rank, and sometimes marched in procession around the stage?"

"Do you mean the Roman army?—those six sandalled roustabouts in nightshirts, with tin shields and helmets, that marched around treading on each other's heels, in charge of a spider-legged consumptive dressed like themselves?"

"That 's it! that 's it! I was one of them Roman soldiers. I was the next to the last one. A half a year ago I used to always be the last one; but I 've been promoted."

Well, they told me that that poor fellow remained a Roman soldier to the last—a matter of thirty-four years. Sometimes they cast him for a "speaking part," but not an elaborate one. He could be trusted to go and say, "My lord, the carriage waits," but if they ventured to add a sentence or two to this, his memory felt the strain and he was likely to miss fire. Yet, poor devil, he had been patiently studying the part of Hamlet for more than thirty years, and he lived and died in the belief that some day he would be invited to play it!

And this is what came of that fleeting visit of those young Englishmen to our village such ages and ages ago! What noble horseshoes this man might have made, but for those Englishmen; and what an inadequate Roman soldier he *did* make!

A day or two after we reached St. Louis, I was walking along Fourth Street when a grizzly-headed man gave a sort of start as he passed me, then stopped, came back, inspected me narrowly, with a clouding brow, and finally said with deep asperity:—

"Look here, *have you got that drink yet?*"

A maniac, I judged, at first. But all in a flash I recognized him. I made an effort to blush that strained every muscle in me, and answered as sweetly and winningly as ever I knew how:—

"Been a little slow, but am just this minute closing in on the place where they keep it. Come in and help."

He softened, and said make it a bottle of champagne and he was agreeable. He said he had seen my name in the papers, and had put all his affairs aside and turned out, resolved to find me or die; and make me answer that question satisfactorily, or kill me; though the most of his late asperity had been rather counterfeit than otherwise.

This meeting brought back to me the St. Louis riots of about thirty years ago. I spent a week there, at that time, in a boarding-house, and had this young fellow for a neighbor across the hall. We saw some of the fightings and killings; and by and by we went one night to an armory where two hundred young men had met, upon call, to be armed and go forth against the rioters, under command of a military man. We drilled till about ten o'clock at night; then news came that the mob were in great force in the lower end of the town, and were sweeping everything before them. Our column moved at once. It was a very hot night, and my musket was very heavy. We marched and marched; and the nearer we approached the seat of war, the hotter I grew and the thirstier I got. I was behind my friend; so, finally, I asked him to hold my musket while I dropped out and got a drink. Then I branched off and went home. I was not feeling any solicitude about *him* of course, because I knew he was so well armed, now, that he could take care of himself without any trouble. If I had had any doubts about that, I would have borrowed another musket for him. I left the city pretty early the next morning, and if this grizzled man had not happened to encounter my name in the papers the other day in St. Louis, and felt moved to seek me out, I should have carried to my grave a heart-torturing uncertainty as to whether he ever got out of the riots all right or not. I ought to have inquired, thirty years ago; I know that. And I would have inquired, if I had had the muskets; but, in the circumstances, he seemed better fixed to conduct the investigations than I was.

One Monday, near the time of our visit to St. Louis, the "Globe-Democrat" came out with a couple of pages of Sunday statistics, whereby it appeared that 119,448 St. Louis people attended the morning and evening church services the day before, and 23,102 children attended Sunday-school. Thus 142,550 persons, out of the city's total of 400,000 population, respected the day religious-wise. I found these statistics, in a condensed form, in a telegram of the Associated Press, and preserved them. They made it apparent that St. Louis was in a higher state of grace than she could have claimed to be in my time. But now that I canvass the figures narrowly, I suspect that the telegraph mutilated them. It cannot be that there are more than 150,000 Catholics in the town; the other 250,000 must be classified as Protestants. Out of these 250,000, according to this questionable telegram, only 26,362 attended church and Sunday-school, while out of the 150,000 Catholics, 116,118 went to church and Sunday-school.

LII.

A Burning Brand

ALL AT ONCE the thought came into my mind, "I have not
sought out Mr. Brown."

Upon that text I desire to depart from the direct line of my
subject, and make a little excursion. I wish to reveal a secret
which I have carried with me nine years, and which has become burdensome.

Upon a certain occasion, nine years ago, I had said, with
strong feeling, "If ever I see St. Louis again, I will seek out
Mr. Brown, the great grain merchant, and ask of him the
privilege of shaking him by the hand."

The occasion and the circumstances were as follows. A
friend of mine, a clergyman, came one evening and said: —

"I have a most remarkable letter here, which I want to read
to you, if I can do it without breaking down. I must preface
it with some explanations, however. The letter is written by
an ex-thief and ex-vagabond of the lowest origin and basest
rearing, a man all stained with crime and steeped in ignorance; but, thank God, with a mine of pure gold hidden away
in him, as you shall see. His letter is written to a burglar
named Williams, who is serving a nine-year term in a certain
State prison, for burglary. Williams was a particularly daring
burglar, and plied that trade during a number of years; but
he was caught at last and jailed, to await trial in a town where
he had broken into a house at night, pistol in hand, and
forced the owner to hand over to him $8,000 in government
bonds. Williams was not a common sort of person, by any
means; he was a graduate of Harvard College, and came of
good New England stock. His father was a clergyman. While
lying in jail, his health began to fail, and he was threatened
with consumption. This fact, together with the opportunity
for reflection afforded by solitary confinement, had its
effect—its natural effect. He fell into serious thought; his
early training asserted itself with power, and wrought with
strong influence upon his mind and heart. He put his old life
behind him, and became an earnest Christian. Some ladies in

the town heard of this, visited him, and by their encouraging words supported him in his good resolutions and strengthened him to continue in his new life. The trial ended in his conviction and sentence to the State prison for the term of nine years, as I have before said. In the prison he became acquainted with the poor wretch referred to in the beginning of my talk, Jack Hunt, the writer of the letter which I am going to read. You will see that the acquaintanceship bore fruit for Hunt. When Hunt's time was out, he wandered to St. Louis; and from that place he wrote his letter to Williams. The letter got no further than the office of the prison warden, of course; prisoners are not often allowed to receive letters from outside. The prison authorities read this letter, but did not destroy it. They had not the heart to do it. They read it to several persons, and eventually it fell into the hands of those ladies of whom I spoke a while ago. The other day I came across an old friend of mine—a clergyman—who had seen this letter, and was full of it. The mere remembrance of it so moved him that he could not talk of it without his voice breaking. He promised to get a copy of it for me; and here it is,—an exact copy, with all the imperfections of the original preserved. It has many slang expressions in it—thieves' *argot*—but their meaning has been interlined, in parentheses, by the prison authorities:"—

ST. LOUIS, JUNE 9th, 1872.

MR. W——friend Charlie if i may call you so: i no you are surprised to get a letter from me, but i hope you won't be mad at my writing to you. i want to tell you my thanks for the way you talked to me when i was in prison—it has led me to try and be a better man; i guess you thought i did not cair for what you said, & at the first go off I did n't, but i noed you was a man who had don big work with good men & want no sucker, nor want gasing & all the boys knod it.

I used to think at nite what you said, & for it i nocked off swearing 5 months before my time was up, for i saw it want no good, nohow—the day my time was up you told me if i would shake the cross, *(quit stealing)* & live on the square for 3 months, it would be the best job i ever done in my life. The state agent give me a ticket to here, & on the car i thought more of what you said to me, but didn't make up my mind. When we got to Chicago on the cars from there to here, I pulled off an old woman's leather; *(robbed her of her pocketbook)* i had n't no more than got it off when i wished i had n't done it, for awhile before that i made up my mind to be a square bloke, for 3 months on your word, but forgot it when i saw the leather was a grip *(easy to get)*—but i kept clos to her & when she got out of the cars at a way place i said, marm have you lost anything? & she tumbled *(discovered)* her leather was off *(gone)*—is this it says i, giving it to her—well if you aint honest, says she, but i had nt got cheak enough to stand that sort of talk, so i left her in a hurry. When i got here i had $1 and 25 cents left & i did n't get no work for 3 days as i aint strong enough for roust about on a steam bote *(for a deck hand)*—The afternoon of the 3rd day I spent my last 10 cts for 2 moons *(large, round sea-biscuit)* & cheese & i felt pretty rough & was thinking i would have to go on the dipe *(picking pockets)* again, when i thought of what you once said about a fellows calling on the Lord when he was in hard luck, & i thought i would try it once anyhow, but when i tryed it i got stuck on the start, & all i could get off wos, Lord give a poor fellow a chance to square it for 3 months for Christ's sake, amen; & i kept a thinking, of it over and over as i went along—about an hour after that i was in 4th St. & this is what happened & is the cause of my being where i am now & about which i will tell you before i get done writing. As i was walking along i herd a big noise & saw a horse running away with a carriage with 2 children in it, & I grabed up a peace of box cover from the side walk & run in the middle of the street, & when the horse came up i smashed him over the head as hard as i could drive—the bord split to peces & the horse checked up a little & i grabbed the reigns & pulled his head down until he stopped—the gentleman what owned him came running up & soon as he saw the children were all rite, he shook hands with me & gave me a $50 green back, & my asking the Lord to help me come into my head, & i was so thunderstruck i could n't drop the reigns nor say nothing—

he saw something was up, & coming back to me said, my boy are you hurt? & the thought come into my head just then to ask him for work; & i asked him to take back the bill and give me a job—says he, jump in here & lets talk about it, but keep the money—he asked me if i could take care of horses & i said yes, for i used to hang round livery stables & often would help clean & drive horses, he told me he wanted a man for that work, & would give me $16. a month & bord me. You bet i took that chance at once. that nite in my little room over the stable i sat a long time thinking over my past life & of what had just happened & i just got down on my nees & thanked the Lord for the job & to help me to square it, & to bless you for putting me up to it, & the next morning i done it again & got me some new togs *(clothes)* & a bible for i *made up my mind* after what the Lord had done for me i would read the bible every nite and morning, & ask him to keep an eye on me. When I had been there about a week Mr Brown (that's his name) came in my room one nite & saw me reading the bible—he asked me if i was a Christian & i told him no— he asked me how it was i read the bible instead of papers & books—Well Charlie i thought i had better give him a square deal in the start, so i told him all about my being in prison & about you, & how i had almost done give up looking for work & how the Lord got me the job when i asked him; & the only way i had to pay him back was to read the bible & square it, & i asked him to give me a chance for 3 months—he talked to me like a father for a long time, & told me i could stay & then i felt better than ever i had done in my life, for i had given Mr. Brown a fair start with me & now i did n't fear no one giving me a back cap *(exposing his past life)* & running me off the job—the next morning he called me into the library & gave me an-other square talk, & advised me to study some every day, & he would help me one or 2 hours every nite, & he gave me a Arithmetic, a spelling book, a Geography & a writing book, & he hers me every nite—he lets me come into the house to prayers every morning, & got me put in a bible class in the Sunday School which i likes very much for it helps me to understand my bible better.

Now, Charlie the 3 months on the square are up 2 months ago, & as you said, it is the best job i ever did in my life, & i commenced another of the same sort right away, only it is to God helping me to last a lifetime Charlie—i wrote this letter to tell you I do think God has forgiven my sins & herd your prayers, for you told me you should pray for me—i no i love to read his word & tell him all my troubles & he helps me i know for i have plenty of chances to steal but i don't feel to as i once did & now i take more pleasure in going to church than to the theatre & that wasnt so once—our minister and others often talk with me & a month ago they wanted me to join the church, but I said no, not now, i may be mistaken in my feelings, i will wait awhile, but now i feel that God has called me & on the first Sunday in July i will join the church—dear friend i wish i could write to you as i feel, but i cant do it yet—you no i learned to read and write while in prisons & i aint got well enough along to write as i would talk; i no i aint spelled all the words rite in this & lots of other mistakes but you will excuse it i no, for you no i was brought up in a poor house until i run away, & that i never new who my father and mother was & i dont no my rite name, & i hope you wont be mad at me, but i have as much rite to one name as another & i have taken your name, for you wont use it when you get out i no, & you are the man i think most of in the world; so i hope you wont be mad—I am doing well, i put $10 a month in bank with $25 of the $50—if you ever want any or all of it let me know, & it is yours. i wish you would let me send you some now. I send you with this a receipt for a year of Littles Living Age, i did n't know what you would like & i told Mr Brown & he said he thought you would like it— i wish i was nere you so i could send you chuck *(refreshments)* on holidays; it would spoil this weather from here, but i will send you a box next thanksgiving any way—next week Mr Brown takes me into his store as lite porter & will advance me as soon as i know a little more—he keeps a big granary store, wholesale—i forgot to tell you of my mission school, sunday school class—the school is in the sunday afternoon, i went out two sunday afternoons, and picked up seven kids *(little boys)* & got them to come in. two of them new as much as i did & i had them put in a class where they could learn something. i dont no much myself, but as these kids cant read i get on nicely with them. i make sure of them by going after them every Sunday ½ hour before school time, i also got 4 girls to come. tell Mack and Harry about me, if they will come out here when their time is up i will get them jobs at once. i hope you will excuse this long letter & all mistakes, i wish i could see you for i cant write as i would talk—i hope the warm weather is doing your lungs good—i was afraid when you was bleeding you would die—give my respects to all the boys and tell them how i am doing—i am doing well and every one here treats me as kind as they can—Mr Brown is going to write to you sometime—i hope some day you will write to me, this letter is from your very true friend

C——W——

who you know as Jack Hunt.

I send you Mr Brown's card. Send my letter to him.

Here was true eloquence; irresistible eloquence; and without a single grace or ornament to help it out. I have seldom been so deeply stirred by any piece of writing. The reader of it halted, all the way through, on a lame and broken voice; yet he had tried to fortify his feelings by several private readings of the letter before venturing into company with it. He was practising upon me to see if there was any hope of his being able to read the document to his prayer-meeting with anything like a decent command over his feelings. The result was not promising. However, he determined to risk it; and did. He got through tolerably well; but his audience broke down early, and stayed in that condition to the end.

The fame of the letter spread through the town. A brother minister came and borrowed the manuscript, put it bodily into a sermon, preached the sermon to twelve hundred people on a Sunday morning, and the letter drowned them in their own tears. Then my friend put it into a sermon and went before his Sunday morning congregation with it. It scored another triumph. The house wept as one individual.

My friend went on summer vacation up into the fishing

regions of our northern British neighbors, and carried this sermon with him, since he might possibly chance to need a sermon. He was asked to preach, one day. The little church was full. Among the people present were the late Dr. J. G. Holland, the late Mr. Seymour of the "New York Times," Mr. Page, the philantropist and temperance advocate, and, I think, Senator Frye, of Maine. The marvellous letter did its wonted work; all the people were moved, all the people wept; the tears flowed in a steady stream down Dr. Holland's cheeks, and nearly the same can be said with regard to all who were there. Mr. Page was so full of enthusiasm over the letter that he said he would not rest until he made pilgrimage to that prison, and had speech with the man who had been able to inspire a fellow-unfortunate to write so priceless a tract.

Ah, that unlucky Page!—and another man. If they had only been in Jericho, that letter would have rung through the world and stirred all the hearts of all the nations for a thousand years to come, and nobody might ever have found out that it was the confoundedest, brazenest, ingeniousest piece of fraud and humbuggery that was ever concocted to fool poor confiding mortals with!

The letter was a pure swindle, and that is the truth. And take it by and large, it was without a compeer among swindles. It was perfect, it was rounded, symmetrical, complete, colossal!

The reader learns it at this point; but we did n't learn it till some miles and weeks beyond this stage of the affair. My friend came back from the woods, and he and other clergymen and lay missionaries began once more to inundate audiences with their tears and the tears of said audiences; I begged hard for permission to print the letter in a magazine and tell the watery story of its triumphs; numbers of people got copies of the letter, with permission to circulate them in writing, but not in print; copies were sent to the Sandwich Islands and other far regions.

Charles Dudley Warner was at church, one day, when the worn letter was read and wept over. At the church door, afterward, he dropped a peculiarly cold iceberg down the clergyman's back with the question,—

"Do you know that letter to be genuine?"

It was the first suspicion that had ever been voiced; but it had that sickening effect which first-uttered suspicions against one's idol always have. Some talk followed:—

"Why—what should make you suspect that it is n't genuine?"

"Nothing that I know of, except that it is too neat, and compact, and fluent, and nicely put together for an ignorant person, an unpractised hand. I think it was done by an educated man."

The literary artist had detected the literary machinery. If you will look at the letter now, you will detect it yourself—it is observable in every line.

Straightway the clergyman went off, with this seed of suspicion sprouting in him, and wrote to a minister residing in that town where Williams had been jailed and converted; asked for light; and also asked if a person in the literary line (meaning me) might be allowed to print the letter and tell its history. He presently received this answer:—

Rev. —— ——.

My Dear Friend,—In regard to that "convict's letter" there can be no doubt as to its genuineness. "Williams," to whom it was written, lay in our jail and professed to have been converted, and Rev. Mr.——, the chaplain, had great faith in the genuineness of the change—as much as one can have in any such case.

The letter was sent to one of our ladies, who is a Sunday-school teacher,—sent either by Williams himself, or the chaplain of the State's prison, probably. She has been greatly annoyed in having so much publicity, lest it might seem a breach of confidence, or be an injury to Williams. In regard to its publication, I can give no permission; though if the names and places were omitted, and especially if sent out of the country, I think you might take the responsibility and do it.

It is a wonderful letter, which no Christian genius, much less one unsanctified, could ever have written. As showing the work of grace in a human heart, and in a very degraded and wicked one, it proves its own origin and reproves our weak faith in its power to cope with any form of wicked-ness.

"Mr. Brown" of St. Louis, some one said, was a Hart-ford man. Do all whom you send from Hartford serve their Master as well?

P. S. Williams is still in the State's prison, serving out a long sentence—of nine years, I think. He has been sick and threatened with consumption, but I have not inquired after him lately. This lady that I speak of corresponds with him, I presume, and will be quite sure to look after him.

This letter arrived a few days after it was written—and up went Mr. Williams's stock again. Mr. Warner's low-down suspicion was laid in the cold, cold grave, where it apparently belonged. It was a suspicion based upon mere internal evi-dence, anyway; and when you come to internal evidence, it 's a big field and a game that two can play at: as witness this other internal evidence, discovered by the writer of the note above quoted, that "it is a wonderful letter—which no Chris-tian genius, much less one unsanctified, could ever have written."

I had permission now to print—provided I suppressed names and places and sent my narrative out of the country. So I chose an Australian magazine for vehicle, as being far enough out of the country, and set myself to work on my article. And the ministers set the pumps going again, with the letter to work the handles.

But meantime Brother Page had been agitating. He had not visited the penitentiary, but he had sent a copy of the illustrious letter to the chaplain of that institution, and ac-companied it with—apparently—inquiries. He got an an-swer, dated four days later than that other Brother's reassur-ing epistle; and before my article was complete, it wandered into my hands. The original is before me, now, and I here append it. It is pretty well loaded with internal evidence of the most solid description:—

STATE'S PRISON, CHAPLAIN'S OFFICE, July 11, 1873.

DEAR BRO. PAGE,—Herewith please find the letter kindly loaned me. I am afraid its genuineness cannot be established. It purports to be addressed to some prisoner here. No such letter ever came to a prisoner here. All letters received are carefully read by officers of the prison before they go into the hands of the convicts, and any such letter could not be forgotten. Again, Charles Williams is not a Christian man, but a dissolute, cunning prodigal, whose father is a minister of the gospel. His name is an assumed one. I am glad to have made your acquaintance. I am preparing a lecture upon life seen through prison bars, and should like to deliver the same in your vicinity.

And so ended that little drama. My poor article went into the fire; for whereas the materials for it were now more abundant and infinitely richer than they had previously been, there were parties all around me, who, although longing for the publication before, were a unit for suppression at this stage and complexion of the game. They said,—"Wait—the wound is too fresh, yet." All the copies of the famous letter except mine, disappeared suddenly; and from that time onward, the aforetime same old drought set in in the churches. As a rule, the town was on a spacious grin for a while, but there were places in it where the grin did not appear, and where it was dangerous to refer to the ex-convict's letter.

A word of explanation. "Jack Hunt," the professed writer of the letter, was an imaginary person. The burglar Williams—Harvard graduate, son of a minister—wrote the letter himself, *to* himself: got it smuggled out of the prison; got it conveyed to persons who had supported and encouraged him in his conversion—where he knew two things would happen: the genuineness of the letter would not be doubted or inquired into; and the nub of it would be noticed, and would have valuable effect—the effect, indeed, of starting a movement to get Mr. Williams pardoned out of prison.

That "nub" is so ingeniously, so casually, flung in, and immediately left there in the tail of the letter, undwelt upon, that an indifferent reader would never suspect that it was the heart and core of the epistle, if he even took note of it at all. This is the "nub":—

"i hope the warm weather is doing your lungs good—*i was afraid when you was bleeding you would die*—give my respects," etc.

That is all there is of it—simply touch and go—no dwelling upon it. Nevertheless it was intended for an eye that would be swift to see it; and it was meant to move a kind heart to try to effect the liberation of a poor reformed and purified fellow lying in the fell grip of consumption.

When I for the first time heard that letter read, nine years ago, I felt that it was the most remarkable one I had ever encountered. And it so warmed me toward Mr. Brown of St. Louis that I said that if ever I visited that city again, I would seek out that excellent man and kiss the hem of his garment if it was a new one. Well, I visited St. Louis, but I did not hunt for Mr. Brown; for, alas! the investigations of long ago had proved that the benevolent Brown, like "Jack Hunt," was not a real person, but a sheer invention of that gifted rascal, Williams—burglar, Harvard graduate, son of a clergyman.

LIII.

My Boyhood's Home

WE TOOK PASSAGE in one of the fast boats of the St. Louis and St. Paul Packet Company, and started up the river.

When I, as a boy, first saw the mouth of the Missouri River, it was twenty-two or twenty-three miles above St. Louis, according to the estimate of pilots; the wear and tear of the banks has moved it down eight miles since then; and the pilots say that within five years the river will cut through and move the mouth down five miles more, which will bring it within ten miles of St. Louis.

About nightfall we passed the large and flourishing town of Alton, Illinois; and before daylight next morning the town of Louisiana, Missouri, a sleepy village in my day, but a brisk railway centre now; however, all the towns out there are railway centres now. I could not clearly recognize the place. This seemed odd to me, for when I retired from the rebel army in '61 I retired upon Louisiana in good order; at least in good enough order for a person who had not yet learned how to retreat according to the rules of war, and had to trust to native genius. It seemed to me that for a first attempt at a retreat it was not badly done. I had done no advancing in all that campaign that was at all equal to it.

There was a railway bridge across the river here well sprinkled with glowing lights, and a very beautiful sight it was.

At seven in the morning we reached Hannibal, Missouri, where my boyhood was spent. I had had a glimpse of it fifteen years ago, and another glimpse six years earlier, but both were so brief that they hardly counted. The only notion of the town that remained in my mind was the memory of it as I had known it when I first quitted it twenty-nine years ago. That picture of it was still as clear and vivid to me as a photograph. I stepped ashore with the feeling of one who returns out of a dead-and-gone generation. I had a sort of realizing sense of what the Bastille prisoners must have felt when they used to come out and look upon Paris after years of captivity, and note how curiously the familiar and the strange were mixed together before them. I saw the new houses—saw them plainly enough—but they did not affect the older picture in my mind, for through their solid bricks and mortar I saw the vanished houses, which had formerly stood there, with perfect distinctness.

It was Sunday morning, and everybody was abed yet. So I passed through the vacant streets, still seeing the town as it was, and not as it is, and recognizing and metaphorically shaking hands with a hundred familiar objects which no longer exist; and finally climbed Holiday's Hill to get a comprehensive view. The whole town lay spread out below me then, and I could mark and fix every locality, every detail. Naturally, I was a good deal moved. I said, "Many of the people I once knew in this tranquil refuge of my childhood are now in heaven; some, I trust, are in the other place."

The things about me and before me made me feel like a boy again—convinced me that I was a boy again, and that I had simply been dreaming an unusually long dream; but my reflections spoiled all that; for they forced me to say, "I see fifty old houses down yonder, into each of which I could enter and find either a man or a woman who was a baby or unborn when I noticed those houses last, or a grandmother who was a plump young bride at that time."

From this vantage ground the extensive view up and down the river, and wide over the wooded expanses of Illinois, is very beautiful,—one of the most beautiful on the Mississippi, I think; which is a hazardous remark to make, for the eight hundred miles of river between St. Louis and St. Paul afford an unbroken succession of lovely pictures. It may be that my affection for the one in question biases my judgment in its favor; I cannot say as to that. No matter, it was satisfyingly beautiful to me, and it had this advantage over all the other friends whom I was about to greet again: it had suffered no change; it was as young and fresh and comely and gracious as ever it had been; whereas, the faces of the others would be old, and scarred with the campaigns of life, and marked with their griefs and defeats, and would give me no upliftings of spirit.

An old gentleman, out on an early morning walk, came

along, and we discussed the weather, and then drifted into other matters. I could not remember his face. He said he had been living here twenty-eight years. So he had come after my time, and I had never seen him before. I asked him various questions; first about a mate of mine in Sunday school— what became of him?

"He graduated with honor in an Eastern college, wandered off into the world somewhere, succeeded at nothing, passed out of knowledge and memory years ago, and is supposed to have gone to the dogs."

"He was bright, and promised well when he was a boy."

"Yes, but the thing that happened is what became of it all."

I asked after another lad, altogether the brightest in our village school when I was a boy.

"He, too, was graduated with honors, from an Eastern college; but life whipped him in every battle, straight along, and he died in one of the Territories, years ago, a defeated man."

I asked after another of the bright boys.

"He is a success, always has been, always will be, I think."

I inquired after a young fellow who came to the town to study for one of the professions when I was a boy.

"He went at something else before he got through—went from medicine to law, or from law to medicine—then to some other new thing; went away for a year, came back with a young wife; fell to drinking, then to gambling behind the door; finally took his wife and two young children to her father's, and went off to Mexico; went from bad to worse, and finally died there, without a cent to buy a shroud, and without a friend to attend the funeral."

"Pity, for he was the best-natured, and most cheery and hopeful young fellow that ever was."

I named another boy.

"Oh, he is all right. Lives here yet; has a wife and children, and is prospering."

Same verdict concerning other boys.

I named three school-girls.

"The first two live here, are married and have children; the other is long ago dead—never married."

I named, with emotion, one of my early sweethearts.

"She is all right. Been married three times; buried two husbands, divorced from the third, and I hear she is getting ready to marry an old fellow out in Colorado somewhere. She 's got children scattered around here and there, most everywheres."

The answer to several other inquiries was brief and simple,—

"Killed in the war."

I named another boy.

"Well, now, his case *is* curious! There was n't a human being in this town but knew that that boy was a perfect chucklehead; perfect dummy; just a stupid ass, as you may say. Everybody knew it, and everybody said it. Well, if that very boy is n't the first lawyer in the State of Missouri to-day, I 'm a Democrat!"

"Is that so?"

"It 's actually so. I 'm telling you the truth."

"How do you account for it?"

"Account for it? There ain't any accounting for it, except that if you send a damned fool to St. Louis, and you don't tell them he 's a damned fool *they 'll* never find it out. There 's one thing sure—if I had a damned fool I should know what to do with him: ship him to St. Louis—it 's the noblest market in the world for that kind of property. Well, when you come to look at it all around, and chew at it and think it over, *don't* it just bang anything you ever heard of?"

"Well, yes, it does seem to. But don't you think maybe it was the Hannibal people who were mistaken about the boy, and not the St. Louis people?"

"Oh, nonsense! The people here have known him from the very cradle—they knew him a hundred times better than the St. Louis idiots *could* have known him. No, if you have got any damned fools that you want to realize on, take my advice—send them to St. Louis."

I mentioned a great number of people whom I had formerly known. Some were dead, some were gone away, some had prospered, some had come to naught; but as regarded a dozen or so of the lot, the answer was comforting:

"Prosperous—live here yet—town littered with their children."

I asked about Miss ——.

"Died in the insane asylum three or four years ago—never was out of it from the time she went in; and was always suffering, too; never got a shred of her mind back."

If he spoke the truth, here was a heavy tragedy, indeed. Thirty-six years in a madhouse, that some young fools might have some fun! I was a small boy, at the time; and I saw those giddy young ladies come tiptoeing into the room where Miss —— sat reading at midnight by a lamp. The girl at the head of the file wore a shroud and a doughface; she crept behind the victim, touched her on the shoulder, and she looked up and screamed, and then fell into convulsions. She did not recover from the fright, but went mad. In these days it seems incredible that people believed in ghosts so short a time ago. But they did.

After asking after such other folk as I could call to mind, I finally inquired about *myself*:

"Oh, he succeeded well enough—another case of damned fool. If they 'd sent him to St. Louis, he 'd have succeeded sooner."

It was with much satisfaction that I recognized the wisdom of having told this candid gentleman, in the beginning, that my name was Smith.

LIV.

Past and Present

BEING LEFT TO MYSELF, up there, I went on picking out old houses in the distant town, and calling back their former inmates out of the mouldy past. Among them I presently recognized the house of the father of Lem Hackett (fictitious name). It carried me back more than a generation in a moment, and landed me in the midst of a time when the happenings of life were not the natural and logical results of great general laws, but of special orders, and were freighted with very precise and distinct purposes—partly punitive in intent, partly admonitory; and usually local in application.

When I was a small boy, Lem Hackett was drowned—on a Sunday. He fell out of an empty flat-boat, where he was playing. Being loaded with sin, he went to the bottom like an anvil. He was the only boy in the village who slept that night. We others all lay awake, repenting. We had not needed the information, delivered from the pulpit that evening, that Lem's was a case of special judgment—we knew that, already. There was a ferocious thunder-storm, that night, and it raged continuously until near dawn. The winds blew, the windows rattled, the rain swept along the roof in pelting sheets, and at the briefest of intervals the inky blackness of the night vanished, the houses over the way glared out white and blinding for a quivering instant, then the solid darkness shut down again and a splitting peal of thunder followed which seemed to rend everything in the neighborhood to shreds and splinters. I sat up in bed quaking and shuddering, waiting for the destruction of the world, and expecting it. To me there was nothing strange or incongruous in heaven's making such an uproar about Lem Hackett. Apparently it was the right and proper thing to do. Not a doubt entered my mind that all the angels were grouped together, discussing this boy's case and observing the awful bombardment of our beggarly little village with satisfaction and approval. There was one thing which disturbed me in the most serious way; that was the thought that this centering of the celestial interest on our village could not fail to attract the attention of the observers to people among us who might otherwise have escaped notice for years. I felt that I was not only one of those people, but the very one most likely to be discovered. That discovery could have but one result: I should be in the fire with Lem before the chill of the river had been fairly warmed out of him. I knew that this would be only just and fair. I was increasing the chances against myself all the time, by feeling a secret bitterness against Lem for having attracted this fatal attention to me, but I could not help it—this sinful thought persisted in infesting my breast in spite of me. Every time the lightning glared I caught my breath, and judged I was gone. In my terror and misery, I meanly began to suggest other boys, and mention acts of theirs which were wickeder than mine, and peculiarly needed punishment—and I tried to pretend to myself that I was simply doing this in a casual way, and without intent to divert the heavenly attention to them for the purpose of getting rid of it myself. With deep sagacity I put these mentions into the form of sorrowing recollections and left-handed sham-supplications that the sins of those boys might be allowed to pass unnoticed—"Possibly they may repent." "It is true that Jim Smith broke a window and lied about it—but maybe he did not mean any harm. And although Tom Holmes says more bad words than any other boy in the village, he probably intends to repent—though he has never said he would. And whilst it is a fact that John Jones did fish a little on Sunday, once, he did n't really catch anything but only just one small useless mud-cat; and maybe that would n't have been so awful if he had thrown it back—as he says he did, but he did n't. Pity but they would repent of these dreadful things—and maybe they will yet."

But while I was shamefully trying to draw attention to these poor chaps—who were doubtless directing the celestial attention to me at the same moment, though I never once suspected that—I had heedlessly left my candle burning. It was not a time to neglect even trifling precautions. There was no occasion to add anything to the facilities for attracting notice to me—so I put the light out.

It was a long night to me, and perhaps the most distressful

one I ever spent. I endured agonies of remorse for sins which I knew I had committed, and for others which I was not certain about, yet was sure that they had been set down against me in a book by an angel who was wiser than I and did not trust such important matters to memory. It struck me, by and by, that I had been making a most foolish and calamitous mistake, in one respect: doubtless I had not only made my own destruction sure by directing attention to those other boys, but had already accomplished theirs!—Doubtless the lightning had stretched them all dead in their beds by this time! The anguish and the fright which this thought gave me made my previous sufferings seem trifling by comparison.

Things had become truly serious. I resolved to turn over a new leaf instantly; I also resolved to connect myself with the church the next day, if I survived to see its sun appear. I resolved to cease from sin in all its forms, and to lead a high and blameless life forever after. I would be punctual at church and Sunday-school; visit the sick; carry baskets of victuals to the poor (simply to fulfil the regulation conditions, although I knew we had none among us so poor but they would smash the basket over my head for my pains); I would instruct other boys in right ways, and take the resulting trouncings meekly; I would subsist entirely on tracts; I would invade the rum shop and warn the drunkard—and finally, if I escaped the fate of those who early become too good to live, I would go for a missionary.

The storm subsided toward daybreak, and I dozed gradually to sleep with a sense of obligation to Lem Hackett for going to eternal suffering in that abrupt way, and thus preventing a far more dreadful disaster—my own loss.

But when I rose refreshed, by and by, and found that those other boys were still alive, I had a dim sense that perhaps the whole thing was a false alarm; that the entire turmoil had been on Lem's account and nobody's else. The world looked so bright and safe that there did not seem to be any real occasion to turn over a new leaf. I was a little subdued, during that day, and perhaps the next; after that, my purpose of reforming slowly dropped out of my mind, and I had a peaceful, comfortable time again, until the next storm.

That storm came about three weeks later; and it was the

most unaccountable one, to me, that I had ever experienced; for on the afternoon of that day, "Dutchy" was drowned. Dutchy belonged to our Sunday-school. He was a German lad who did not know enough to come in out of the rain; but he was exasperatingly good, and had a prodigious memory. One Sunday he made himself the envy of all the youth and the talk of all the admiring village, by reciting three thousand verses of Scripture without missing a word; then he went off the very next day and got drowned.

Circumstances gave to his death a peculiar impressiveness. We were all bathing in a muddy creek which had a deep hole in it, and in this hole the coopers had sunk a pile of green hickory hoop poles to soak, some twelve feet under water. We were diving and "seeing who could stay under longest." We managed to remain down by holding on to the hoop poles. Dutchy made such a poor success of it that he was hailed with laughter and derision every time his head appeared above water. At last he seemed hurt with the taunts, and begged us to stand still on the bank and be fair with him and give him an honest count—"be friendly and kind just this once, and not miscount for the sake of having the fun of laughing at him." Treacherous winks were exchanged, and all said "All right, Dutchy—go ahead, we 'll play fair."

Dutchy plunged in, but the boys, instead of beginning to count, followed the lead of one of their number and scampered to a range of blackberry bushes close by and hid behind it. They imagined Dutchy's humiliation, when he should rise after a superhuman effort and find the place silent and vacant, nobody there to applaud. They were "so full of laugh" with the idea, that they were continually exploding into muffled cackles. Time swept on, and presently one who was peeping through the briers, said, with surprise:—

"Why, he has n't come up, yet!"

The laughing stopped.

"Boys, it 's a splendid dive," said one.

"Never mind that," said another, "the joke on him is all the better for it."

There was a remark or two more, and then a pause. Talking ceased, and all began to peer through the vines. Before long, the boys' faces began to look uneasy, then anxious, then terrified. Still there was no movement of the placid water. Hearts began to beat fast, and faces to turn pale. We all glided out, silently, and stood on the bank, our horrified eyes wandering back and forth from each other's countenances to the water.

"Somebody must go down and see!"

Yes, that was plain; but nobody wanted that grisly task.

"Draw straws!"

So we did—with hands which shook so, that we hardly knew what we were about. The lot fell to me, and I went down. The water was so muddy I could not see anything, but I felt around among the hoop poles, and presently grasped a limp wrist which gave me no response—and if it had I should not have known it, I let it go with such a frightened suddenness.

The boy had been caught among the hoop poles and entangled there, helplessly. I fled to the surface and told the awful news. Some of us knew that if the boy were dragged out at once he might possibly be resuscitated, but we never thought of that. We did not think of anything; we did not know what to do, so we did nothing—except that the smaller lads cried, piteously, and we all struggled frantically into our clothes, putting on anybody's that came handy, and getting them wrong-side-out and upside-down, as a rule. Then we scurried away and gave the alarm, but none of us went back to see the end of the tragedy. We had a more important thing to attend to: we all flew home, and lost not a moment in getting ready to lead a better life.

The night presently closed down. Then came on that tremendous and utterly unaccountable storm. I was perfectly dazed; I could not understand it. It seemed to me that there must be some mistake. The elements were turned loose, and they rattled and banged and blazed away in the most blind and frantic manner. All heart and hope went out of me, and the dismal thought kept floating through my brain, "If a boy who knows three thousand verses by heart is not satisfactory, what chance is there for anybody else?"

Of course I never questioned for a moment that the storm was on Dutchy's account, or that he or any other inconsequential animal was worthy of such a majestic demonstration from on high; the lesson of it was the only thing that troubled me; for it convinced me that if Dutchy, with all his perfections, was not a delight, it would be vain for me to turn over a new leaf, for I must infallibly fall hopelessly short of that boy, no matter how hard I might try. Nevertheless I did turn it over—a highly educated fear compelled me to do that—but succeeding days of cheerfulness and sunshine came bothering around, and within a month I had so drifted backward that again I was as lost and comfortable as ever.

Breakfast time approached while I mused these musings and called these ancient happenings back to mind; so I got me back into the present and went down the hill.

On my way through town to the hotel, I saw the house which was my home when I was a boy. At present rates, the people who now occupy it are of no more value than I am; but in my time they would have been worth not less than five hundred dollars apiece. They are colored folk.

After breakfast, I went out alone again, intending to hunt up some of the Sunday-schools and see how this generation of pupils might compare with their progenitors who had sat with me in those places and had probably taken me as a model—though I do not remember as to that now. By the public square there had been in my day a shabby little brick church called the "Old Ship of Zion," which I had attended as a Sunday-school scholar; and I found the locality easily enough, but not the old church; it was gone, and a trig and rather hilarious new edifice was in its place. The pupils were better dressed and better looking than were those of my time; consequently they did not resemble their ancestors; and consequently there was nothing familiar to me in their faces. Still, I contemplated them with a deep interest and a yearning wistfulness, and if I had been a girl I would have cried; for they were the offspring, and represented, and occupied the places, of boys and girls some of whom I had loved to love, and some of whom I had loved to hate, but all of whom were dear to me for the one reason or the other, so many years gone by—and, Lord, where be they now!

I was mightily stirred, and would have been grateful to be allowed to remain unmolested and look my fill; but a bald-summited superintendent who had been a tow-headed Sun-

day-school mate of mine on that spot in the early ages, recognized me, and I talked a flutter of wild nonsense to those
children to hide the thoughts which were in me, and which
could not have been spoken without a betrayal of feeling that
would have been recognized as out of character with me.

Making speeches without preparation is no gift of mine;
and I was resolved to shirk any new opportunity, but in the
next and larger Sunday-school I found myself in the rear of
the assemblage; so I was very willing to go on the platform a
moment for the sake of getting a good look at the scholars.
On the spur of the moment I could not recall any of the old
idiotic talks which visitors used to insult me with when I was
a pupil there; and I was sorry for this, since it would have
given me time and excuse to dawdle there and take a long
and satisfying look at what I feel at liberty to say was an array
of fresh young comeliness not matchable in another Sunday-
school of the same size. As I talked merely to get a chance to
inspect; and as I strung out the random rubbish solely to pro-
long the inspection, I judged it but decent to confess these
low motives, and I did so.

If the Model Boy was in either of these Sunday-schools, I
did not see him. The Model Boy of my time—we never had
but the one—was perfect: perfect in manners, perfect in
dress, perfect in conduct, perfect in filial piety, perfect in ex-
terior godliness; but at bottom he was a prig; and as for the
contents of his skull, they could have changed place with the
contents of a pie and nobody would have been the worse off
for it but the pie. This fellow's reproachlessness was a standing reproach to every lad in the village. He was the admiration of all the mothers, and the detestation of all their sons.
I was told what became of him, but as it was a disappointment to me, I will not enter into details. He succeeded in life.

LV.

A Vendetta and Other Things

DURING MY THREE DAYS' STAY in the town, I woke up
every morning with the impression that I was a boy—
for in my dreams the faces were all young again, and looked
as they had looked in the old times—but I went to bed a
hundred years old, every night—for meantime I had been
seeing those faces as they are now.

Of course I suffered some surprises, along at first, before I
had become adjusted to the changed state of things. I met
young ladies who did not seem to have changed at all; but
they turned out to be the daughters of the young ladies I had
in mind—sometimes their grand-daughters. When you are
told that a stranger of fifty is a grandmother, there is nothing
surprising about it; but if, on the contrary, she is a person
whom you knew as a little girl, it seems impossible. You say
to yourself, "How can a little girl be a grandmother?" It takes
some little time to accept and realize the fact that while you
have been growing old, your friends have not been standing
still, in that matter.

I noticed that the greatest changes observable were with
the women, not the men. I saw men whom thirty years had
changed but slightly; but their wives had grown old. These
were good women; it is very wearing to be good.

There was a saddler whom I wished to see; but he was
gone. Dead, these many years, they said. Once or twice a day,
the saddler used to go tearing down the street, putting on his
coat as he went; and then everybody knew a steamboat was
coming. Everybody knew, also, that John Stavely was not expecting anybody by the boat—or any freight, either; and
Stavely must have known that everybody knew this, still it
made no difference to him; he liked to seem to himself to be
expecting a hundred thousand tons of saddles by this boat,
and so he went on all his life, enjoying being faithfully on
hand to receive and receipt for those saddles, in case by any
miracle they should come. A malicious Quincy paper used
always to refer to this town, in derision as "Stavely's Land-

ing." Stavely was one of my earliest admirations; I envied him his rush of imaginary business, and the display he was able to make of it, before strangers, as he went flying down the street struggling with his fluttering coat.

But there was a carpenter who was my chiefest hero. He was a mighty liar, but I did not know that; I believed everything he said. He was a romantic, sentimental, melodramatic fraud, and his bearing impressed me with awe. I vividly remember the first time he took me into his confidence. He was planing a board, and every now and then he would pause and heave a deep sigh; and occasionally mutter broken sentences—confused and not intelligible—but out of their midst an ejaculation sometimes escaped which made me shiver and did me good: one was, "O God, it is his blood!" I sat on the tool-chest and humbly and shudderingly admired him; for I judged he was full of crime. At last he said in a low voice:—

"My little friend, can you keep a secret?"

I eagerly said I could.

"A dark and dreadful one?"

I satisfied him on that point.

"Then I will tell you some passages in my history; for oh, I *must* relieve my burdened soul, or I shall die!"

He cautioned me once more to be "as silent as the grave;" then he told me he was a "red-handed murderer." He put down his plane, held his hands out before him, contemplated them sadly, and said:—

"Look—with these hands I have taken the lives of thirty human beings!"

The effect which this had upon me was an inspiration to him, and he turned himself loose upon his subject with interest and energy. He left generalizing, and went into details,—began with his first murder; described it, told what measures he had taken to avert suspicion; then passed to his second homicide, his third, his fourth, and so on. He had always done his murders with a bowie-knife, and he made all my hairs rise by suddenly snatching it out and showing it to me.

At the end of this first *séance* I went home with six of his fearful secrets among my freightage, and found them a great help to my dreams, which had been sluggish for a while back.

I sought him again and again, on my Saturday holidays; in fact I spent the summer with him—all of it which was valuable to me. His fascinations never diminished, for he threw something fresh and stirring, in the way of horror, into each successive murder. He always gave names, dates, places— everything. This by and by enabled me to note two things: that he had killed his victims in every quarter of the globe, and that these victims were always named Lynch. The destruction of the Lynches went serenely on, Saturday after Saturday, until the original thirty had multiplied to sixty,—and more to be heard from yet; then my curiosity got the better of my timidity, and I asked how it happened that these justly punished persons all bore the same name.

My hero said he had never divulged that dark secret to any living being; but felt that he could trust me, and therefore he would lay bare before me the story of his sad and blighted life. He had loved one "too fair for earth," and she had reciprocated "with all the sweet affection of her pure and noble nature." But he had a rival, a "base hireling" named Archibald Lynch, who said the girl should be his, or he would "dye his hands in her heart's best blood." The carpenter, "innocent and happy in love's young dream," gave no weight to the threat, but led his "golden-haired darling to the altar," and there, the two were made one; there also, just as the minister's hands were stretched in blessing over their heads, the fell deed was done—with a knife—and the bride fell a corpse at her husband's feet. And what did the husband do? He plucked forth that knife, and kneeling by the body of his lost one, swore to "consecrate his life to the extermination of all the human scum that bear the hated name of Lynch."

That was it. He had been hunting down the Lynches and slaughtering them, from that day to this—twenty years. He had always used that same consecrated knife; with it he had murdered his long array of Lynches, and with it he had left upon the forehead of each victim a peculiar mark—a cross, deeply incised. Said he:—

"The cross of the Mysterious Avenger is known in Europe, in America, in China, in Siam, in the Tropics, in the Polar Seas, in the deserts of Asia, in all the earth. Wherever in the uttermost parts of the globe, a Lynch has penetrated, there has the Mysterious Cross been seen, and those who have seen it have shuddered and said, 'it is his mark, he has been here.' You have heard of the Mysterious Avenger—look upon him, for before you stands no less a person! But beware—breathe not a word to any soul. Be silent, and wait. Some morning this town will flock aghast to view a gory corpse; on its brow will be seen the awful sign, and men will tremble and whisper, 'he has been here,—it is the Mysterious Avenger's mark!' You will come here, but I shall have vanished; you will see me no more."

This ass has been reading the "Jibbenainosay," no doubt, and had had his poor romantic head turned by it; but as I had not yet seen the book then, I took his inventions for truth, and did not suspect that he was a plagiarist.

However, we had a Lynch living in the town; and the more I reflected upon his impending doom, the more I could not sleep. It seemed my plain duty to save him, and a still plainer and more important duty to get some sleep for myself, so at last I ventured to go to Mr. Lynch and tell him what was about to happen to him—under strict secrecy. I advised him to "fly," and certainly expected him to do it. But he laughed at me; and he did not stop there; he led me down to the carpenter's shop, gave the carpenter a jeering and scornful lecture upon his silly pretensions, slapped his face, made him get down on his knees and beg—then went off and left me to contemplate the cheap and pitiful ruin of what, in my eyes, had so lately been a majestic and incomparable hero. The carpenter blustered, flourished his knife, and doomed this Lynch in his usual volcanic style, the size of his fateful words undiminished; but it was all wasted upon me; he was a hero to me no longer but only a poor, foolish, exposed humbug. I was ashamed of him, and ashamed of myself; I took no further interest in him, and never went to his shop any more. He was a heavy loss to me, for he was the greatest hero I had ever known. The fellow must have had some talent; for some of his imaginary murders were so vividly and dramatically described that I remember all their details yet.

The people of Hannibal are not more changed than is the town. It is no longer a village; it is a city, with a mayor, and a council, and water-works, and probably a debt. It has fifteen thousand people, is a thriving and energetic place, and is paved like the rest of the west and south—where a well-paved street and a good sidewalk are things so seldom seen, that one doubts them when he does see them. The customary half-dozen railways centre in Hannibal now, and there is a new depot which cost a hundred thousand dollars. In my time the town had no specialty, and no commercial grandeur; the daily packet usually landed a passenger and bought a cat-fish, and took away another passenger and a hatful of freight; but now a huge commerce in lumber has grown up and a large miscellaneous commerce is one of the results. A deal of money changes hands there now.

Bear Creek—so called, perhaps, because it was always so particularly bare of bears—is hidden out of sight now, under islands and continents of piled lumber, and nobody but an expert can find it. I used to get drowned in it every summer regularly, and be drained out, and inflated and set going again by some chance enemy; but not enough of it is unoc-cupied now to drown a person in. It was a famous breeder of chills and fever in its day. I remember one summer when ev-erybody in town had this disease at once. Many chimneys were shaken down, and all the houses were so racked that the town had to be rebuilt. The chasm or gorge between Lover's Leap and the hill west of it is supposed by scientists to have been caused by glacial action. This is a mistake.

There is an interesting cave a mile or two below Hannibal, among the bluffs. I would have liked to revisit it, but had not time. In my time the person who then owned it turned it into a mausoleum for his daughter, aged fourteen. The body of this poor child was put into a copper cylinder filled with al-cohol, and this was suspended in one of the dismal avenues of the cave. The top of the cylinder was removable; and it was said to be a common thing for the baser order of tourists to drag the dead face into view and examine it and comment upon it.

LVI.

A Question of Law

THE SLAUGHTER-HOUSE is gone from the mouth of Bear Creek and so is the small jail (or "calaboose") which once stood in its neighborhood. A citizen asked, "Do you remember when Jimmy Finn, the town drunkard, was burned to death in the calaboose?"

Observe, now, how history becomes defiled, through lapse of time and the help of the bad memories of men. Jimmy Finn was not burned in the calaboose, but died a natural death in a tan vat, of a combination of delirium tremens and spontaneous combustion. When I say natural death, I mean it was a natural death for Jimmy Finn to die. The calaboose victim was not a citizen; he was a poor stranger, a harmless whiskey-sodden tramp. I know more about his case than anybody else; I knew too much of it, in that bygone day, to relish speaking of it. That tramp was wandering about the streets one chilly evening, with a pipe in his mouth, and begging for a match; he got neither matches nor courtesy; on the contrary, a troop of bad little boys followed him around and amused themselves with nagging and annoying him. I assisted; but at last, some appeal which the wayfarer made for forbearance, accompanying it with a pathetic reference to his forlorn and friendless condition, touched such sense of shame and remnant of right feeling as were left in me, and I went away and got him some matches, and then hied me home and to bed, heavily weighted as to conscience, and unbuoyant in spirit. An hour or two afterward, the man was arrested and locked up in the calaboose by the marshal—large name for a constable, but that was his title. At two in the morning, the church bells rang for fire, and everybody turned out, of course—I with the rest. The tramp had used his matches disastrously: he had set his straw bed on fire, and the oaken sheathing of the room had caught. When I reached the ground, two hundred men, women, and children stood massed together, transfixed with horror, and staring at the grated windows of the jail. Behind the iron bars, and tugging frantically at them, and screaming for help, stood the tramp; he seemed like a black object set against a sun, so white and intense was the light at his back. That marshal could not be found, and he had the only key. A battering-ram was quickly improvised, and the thunder of its blows upon the door had so encouraging a sound that the spectators broke into wild cheering, and believed the merciful battle won. But it was not so. The timbers were too strong; they did not yield. It was said that the man's death-grip still held fast to the bars after he was dead; and that in this position the fires wrapped him about and consumed him. As to this, I do not know. What was seen after I recognized the face that was pleading through the bars was seen by others, not by me.

I saw that face, so situated, every night for a long time afterward; and I believed myself as guilty of the man's death as if I had given him the matches purposely that he might burn himself up with them. I had not a doubt that I should be hanged if my connection with this tragedy were found out. The happenings and the impressions of that time are burnt into my memory, and the study of them entertains me as much now as they themselves distressed me then. If anybody spoke of that grisly matter, I was all ears in a moment, and alert to hear what might be said, for I was always dreading and expecting to find out that I was suspected; and so fine and so delicate was the perception of my guilty conscience, that it often detected suspicion in the most purposeless remarks, and in looks, gestures, glances of the eye which had no significance, but which sent me shivering away in a panic of fright, just the same. And how sick it made me when somebody dropped, howsoever carelessly and barren of intent, the remark that "murder will out!" For a boy of ten years, I was carrying a pretty weighty cargo.

All this time I was blessedly forgetting one thing—the fact that I was an inveterate talker in my sleep. But one night I awoke and found my bed-mate—my younger brother—sitting up in bed and contemplating me by the light of the moon. I said:—

"What is the matter?"

"You talk so much I can't sleep."

I came to a sitting posture in an instant, with my kidneys in my throat and my hair on end.

"What did I say? Quick—out with it—what did I say?"

"Nothing much."

"It 's a lie—you know everything."

"Everything about what?"

"You know well enough. About *that*."

"About *what*?—I don't know what you are talking about. I think you are sick or crazy or something. But anyway, you 're awake, and I 'll get to sleep while I 've got a chance."

He fell asleep and I lay there in a cold sweat, turning this new terror over in the whirling chaos which did duty as my mind. The burden of my thought was, How much did I divulge? How much does he know?—what a distress is this uncertainty! But by and by I evolved an idea—I would wake my brother and probe him with a supposititious case. I shook him up, and said—

"Suppose a man should come to you drunk—"

"This is foolish—I never get drunk."

"I don't mean you, idiot—I mean the man. Suppose a *man* should come to you drunk, and borrow a knife, or a tomahawk, or a pistol, and you forgot to tell him it was loaded, and—"

"How could you load a tomahawk?"

"I don't mean the tomahawk, and I did n't *say* the tomahawk; I said the pistol. Now don't you keep breaking in that way, because this is serious. There 's been a man killed."

"What! In this town?"

"Yes, in this town."

"Well, go on—I won't say a single word."

"Well, then, suppose you forgot to tell him to be careful with it, because it was loaded, and he went off and shot himself with that pistol,—fooling with it, you know, and probably doing it by accident, being drunk. Well, would it be murder?"

"No—suicide."

"No, no. I don't mean *his* act, I mean yours: would you be a murderer for letting him have that pistol?"

After deep thought came this answer,—

"Well, I should think I was guilty of something—maybe

murder—yes, probably murder, but I don't quite know."

This made me very uncomfortable. However, it was not a decisive verdict. I should have to set out the real case—there seemed to be no other way. But I would do it cautiously, and keep a watch out for suspicious effects. I said:—

"I was supposing a case, but I am coming to the real one now. Do you know how the man came to be burned up in the calaboose?"

"No."

"Have n't you the least idea?"

"Not the least."

"Wish you may die in your tracks if you have?"

"Yes, wish I may die in my tracks."

"Well, the way of it was this. The man wanted some matches to light his pipe. A boy got him some. The man set fire to the calaboose with those very matches, and burnt himself up."

"Is that so?"

"Yes, it is. Now, is that boy a murderer, do you think?"

"Let me see. The man was drunk?"

"Yes, he was drunk."

"Very drunk?"

"Yes."

"And the boy knew it?"

"Yes, he knew it."

There was a long pause. Then came this heavy verdict:—

"If the man was drunk, and the boy knew it, the boy murdered that man. This is certain."

Faint, sickening sensations crept along all the fibres of my body, and I seemed to know how a person feels who hears his death sentence pronounced from the bench. I waited to hear what my brother would say next. I believed I knew what it would be, and I was right. He said,—

"I know the boy."

I had nothing to say; so I said nothing. I simply shuddered. Then he added,—

"Yes, before you got half through telling about the thing, I knew perfectly well who the boy was; it was Ben Coontz!"

I came out of my collapse as one who rises from the dead. I said, with admiration:—

"Why, how in the world did you ever guess it?"

"You told it in your sleep."

I said to myself, "How splendid that is! This is a habit which must be cultivated."

My brother rattled innocently on:—

"When you were talking in your sleep, you kept mumbling something about 'matches,' which I could n't make anything out of; but just now, when you began to tell me about the man and the calaboose and the matches, I remembered that in your sleep you mentioned Ben Coontz two or three times; so I put this and that together, you see, and right away I knew it was Ben that burnt that man up."

I praised his sagacity effusively. Presently he asked,—

"Are you going to give him up to the law?"

"No," I said; "I believe that this will be a lesson to him. I shall keep an eye on him, of course, for that is but right; but if he stops where he is and reforms, it shall never be said that I betrayed him."

"How good you are!"

"Well, I try to be. It is all a person can do in a world like this."

And now, my burden being shifted to other shoulders, my terrors soon faded away.

The day before we left Hannibal, a curious thing fell under my notice,—the surprising spread which longitudinal time undergoes there. I learned it from one of the most unostentatious of men,—the colored coachman of a friend of mine, who lives three miles from town. He was to call for me at the Park Hotel at 7.30 P.M., and drive me out. But he missed it considerably,—did not arrive till ten. He excused himself by saying:—

"De time is mos' an hour en a half slower in de country en what it is in de town; you 'll be in plenty time, boss. Sometimes we shoves out early for church, Sunday, en fetches up dah right plum in de middle er de sermon. Diffunce in de time. A body can't make no calculations 'bout it."

I had lost two hours and a half; but I had learned a fact worth four.

LVII.

An Archangel

FROM ST. LOUIS northward there are all the enlivening signs of the presence of active, energetic, intelligent, prosperous, practical nineteenth-century populations. The people don't dream, they work. The happy result is manifest all around in the substantial outside aspect of things, and the suggestions of wholesome life and comfort that everywhere appear.

Quincy is a notable example,—a brisk, handsome, well-ordered city; and now, as formerly, interested in art, letters, and other high things.

But Marion City is an exception. Marion City has gone backwards in a most unaccountable way. This metropolis promised so well that the projectors tacked "city" to its name in the very beginning, with full confidence; but it was bad prophecy. When I first saw Marion City, thirty-five years ago, it contained one street, and nearly or quite six houses. It contains but one house now, and this one, in a state of ruin, is getting ready to follow the former five into the river.

Doubtless Marion City was too near to Quincy. It had another disadvantage: it was situated in a flat mud bottom, below high-water mark, whereas Quincy stands high up on the slope of a hill.

In the beginning Quincy had the aspect and ways of a model New England town: and these she has yet: broad, clean streets, trim, neat dwellings and lawns, fine mansions, stately blocks of commercial buildings. And there are ample fair-grounds, a well kept park, and many attractive drives; library, reading-rooms, a couple of colleges, some handsome and costly churches, and a grand court-house, with grounds which occupy a square. The population of the city is thirty thousand. There are some large factories here, and manufacturing, of many sorts, is done on a great scale.

La Grange and Canton are growing towns, but I missed Alexandria; was told it was under water, but would come up to blow in the summer.

Keokuk was easily recognizable. I lived there in 1857,—an extraordinary year there in real-estate matters. The "boom" was something wonderful. Everybody bought, everybody sold,—except widows and preachers; they always hold on; and when the tide ebbs, they get left. Anything in the semblance of a town lot, no matter how situated, was salable, and at a figure which would still have been high if the ground had been sodded with greenbacks.

The town has a population of fifteen thousand now, and is progressing with a healthy growth. It was night, and we could not see details, for which we were sorry, for Keokuk has the reputation of being a beautiful city. It was a pleasant one to live in long ago, and doubtless has advanced, not retrograded, in that respect.

A mighty work which was in progress there in my day is finished now. This is the canal over the Rapids. It is eight miles long, three hundred feet wide, and is in no place less than six feet deep. Its masonry is of the majestic kind which the War Department usually deals in, and will endure like a Roman aqueduct. The work cost four or five millions.

After an hour or two spent with former friends, we started up the river again. Keokuk, a long time ago, was an occasional loafing-place of that erratic genius, Henry Clay Dean. I believe I never saw him but once; but he was much talked of when I lived there. This is what was said of him:—

He began life poor and without education. But he educated himself—on the curb-stones of Keokuk. He would sit down on a curb-stone with his book, careless or unconscious of the clatter of commerce and the tramp of the passing crowds, and bury himself in his studies by the hour, never changing his position except to draw in his knees now and then to let a dray pass unobstructed; and when his book was finished, its contents, however abstruse, had been burnt into his memory, and were his permanent possession. In this way he acquired a vast hoard of all sorts of learning, and had it pigeon-holed in his head where he could put his intellectual hand on it whenever it was wanted.

His clothes differed in no respect from a "wharf-rat's," except that they were raggeder, more ill-assorted and inharmonious (and therefore more extravagantly picturesque), and several layers dirtier. Nobody could infer the master-mind in the top of that edifice from the edifice itself.

He was an orator,—by nature in the first place, and later by the training of experience and practice. When he was out on a canvass, his name was a loadstone which drew the farmers to his stump from fifty miles around. His theme was always politics. He used no notes, for a volcano does not need notes. In 1862, a son of Keokuk's late distinguished citizen, Mr. Claggett, gave me this incident concerning Dean:

The war feeling was running high in Keokuk (in '61), and a great mass meeting was to be held on a certain day in the new Athenæum. A distinguished stranger was to address the house. After the building had been packed to its utmost capacity with sweltering folk of both sexes, the stage still remained vacant,—the distinguished stranger had failed to connect. The crowd grew impatient, and by and by indignant and rebellious. About this time a distressed manager discovered Dean on a curb-stone, explained the dilemma to him, took his book away from him, rushed him into the building the back way, and told him to make for the stage and save his country.

Presently a sudden silence fell upon the grumbling audience, and everybody's eyes sought a single point,—the wide, empty, carpetless stage. A figure appeared there whose aspect was familiar to hardly a dozen persons present. It was the scarecrow Dean,—in foxy shoes, down at the heels; socks of odd colors, also "down;" damaged trousers, relics of antiquity, and a world too short, exposing some inches of naked ankle; an unbuttoned vest, also too short, and exposing a zone of soiled and wrinkled linen between it and the waistband; shirt bosom open; long black handkerchief, wound round and round the neck like a bandage; bob-tailed blue coat, reaching down to the small of the back, with sleeves which left four inches of forearm unprotected; small, stiff-brimmed soldier-cap hung on a corner of the bump of— whichever bump it was. This figure moved gravely out upon the stage and, with sedate and measured step, down to the front, where it paused, and dreamily inspected the house, saying no word. The silence of surprise held its own for a moment, then was broken by a just audible ripple of merriment which swept the sea of faces like the wash of a wave. The figure remained as before, thoughtfully inspecting. Another wave started,—laughter, this time. It was followed by another, then a third,—this last one boisterous.

And now the stranger stepped back one pace, took off his soldier-cap, tossed it into the wing, and began to speak, with deliberation, nobody listening, everybody laughing and whispering. The speaker talked on unembarrassed, and presently delivered a shot which went home, and silence and attention resulted. He followed it quick and fast, with other telling things; warmed to his work and began to pour his words out, instead of dripping them; grew hotter and hotter, and fell to discharging lightnings and thunder,—and now the house began to break into applause, to which the speaker gave no heed, but went hammering straight on; unwound his black bandage and cast it away, still thundering; presently discarded the bob-tailed coat and flung it aside, firing up higher and higher all the time; finally flung the vest after the coat; and then for an untimed period stood there, like another Vesuvius, spouting smoke and flame, lava and ashes, raining pumice-stone and cinders, shaking the moral earth with intellectual crash upon crash, explosion upon explosion, while the mad multitude stood upon their feet in a solid body, answering back with a ceaseless hurricane of cheers, through a thrashing snow-storm of waving handkerchiefs.

"When Dean came," said Claggett, "the people thought he was an escaped lunatic; but when he went, they thought he was an escaped archangel."

Burlington, home of the sparkling Burdette, is another hill city; and also a beautiful one; unquestionably so; a fine and flourishing city, with a population of twenty-five thousand, and belted with busy factories of nearly every imaginable description. It was a very sober city, too—for the moment—for a most sobering bill was pending; a bill to forbid the manufacture, exportation, importation, purchase, sale, borrowing, lending, stealing, drinking, smelling, or possession, by conquest, inheritance, intent, accident, or otherwise, in the State of Iowa, of each and every deleterious beverage known to the human race, except water. This measure was approved by all the rational people in the State; but not by the bench of Judges.

Burlington has the progressive modern city's full equipment of devices for right and intelligent government; including a paid fire department, a thing which the great city of New Orleans is without, but still employs that relic of antiquity, the independent system.

In Burlington, as in all these Upper-River towns, one breathes a go-ahead atmosphere which tastes good in the nostrils. An opera-house has lately been built there which is in strong contrast with the shabby dens which usually do duty as theatres in cities of Burlington's size.

We had not time to go ashore in Muscatine, but had a daylight view of it from the boat. I lived there awhile, many years ago, but the place, now, had a rather unfamiliar look; so I suppose it has clear outgrown the town which I used to know. In fact, I know it has; for I remember it as a small place—which it is n't now. But I remember it best for a lunatic who caught me out in the fields, one Sunday, and extracted a butcher-knife from his boot and proposed to carve me up with it, unless I acknowledged him to be the only son of the Devil. I tried to compromise on an acknowledgment that he was the only member of the family I had met; but that did not satisfy him; he would n't have any half-measures; I must say he was the sole and only son of the Devil—and he whetted his knife on his boot. It did not seem worth while to make trouble about a little thing like that; so I swung round to his view of the matter and saved my skin whole. Shortly afterward, he went to visit his father; and as he has not turned up since, I trust he is there yet.

And I remember Muscatine—still more pleasantly—for its summer sunsets. I have never seen any, on either side of the ocean, that equalled them. They used the broad smooth river as a canvas, and painted on it every imaginable dream of color, from the mottled daintinesses and delicacies of the opal, all the way up, through cumulative intensities, to blinding purple and crimson conflagrations which were enchanting to the eye, but sharply tried it at the same time. All the Upper Mississippi region has these extraordinary sunsets as a familiar spectacle. It is the true Sunset Land: I am sure no other country can show so good a right to the name. The sunrises are also said to be exceedingly fine. I do not know.

LVIII.

On the Upper River

THE BIG TOWNS drop in, thick and fast, now: and between stretch processions of thrifty farms, not desolate solitude. Hour by hour, the boat plows deeper and deeper into the great and populous Northwest; and with each successive section of it which is revealed, one's surprise and respect gather emphasis and increase. Such a people, and such achievements as theirs, compel homage. This is an independent race who think for themselves, and who are competent to do it, because they are educated and enlightened; they read, they keep abreast of the best and newest thought, they fortify every weak place in their land with a school, a college, a library, and a newspaper; and they live under law. Solicitude for the future of a race like this is not in order.

This region is new; so new that it may be said to be still in its babyhood. By what it has accomplished while still teething, one may forecast what marvels it will do in the strength of its maturity. It is so new that the foreign tourist has not heard of it yet; and has not visited it. For sixty years, the foreign tourist has steamed up and down the river between St. Louis and New Orleans, and then gone home and written his book, believing he had seen all of the river that was worth seeing or that had anything to see. In not six of all these books is there mention of these Upper-River towns— for the reason that the five or six tourists who penetrated this region did it before these towns were projected. The latest tourist of them all (1878) made the same old regulation trip— he had not heard that there was anything north of St. Louis.

Yet there was. There was this amazing region, bristling with great towns, projected day before yesterday, so to speak, and built next morning. A score of them number from fifteen hundred to five thousand people. Then we have Muscatine, ten thousand; Winona, ten thousand; Moline, ten thousand; Rock Island, twelve thousand; La Crosse, twelve thousand; Burlington, twenty-five thousand; Dubuque, twenty-five thousand; Davenport, thirty thousand; St. Paul, fifty-eight thousand; Minneapolis, sixty thousand and upward.

The foreign tourist has never heard of these; there is no note of them in his books. They have sprung up in the night, while he slept. So new is this region, that I, who am comparatively young, am yet older than it is. When I was born, St. Paul had a population of three persons, Minneapolis had just a third as many. The then population of Minneapolis died two years ago; and when he died he had seen himself undergo an increase, in forty years, of fifty-nine thousand nine hundred and ninety-nine persons. He had a frog's fertility.

I must explain that the figures set down above, as the population of St. Paul and Minneapolis, are several months old. These towns are far larger now. In fact, I have just seen a newspaper estimate which gives the former seventy-one thousand, and the latter seventy-eight thousand. This book will not reach the public for six or seven months yet; none of the figures will be worth much then.

We had a glimpse of Davenport, which is another beautiful city, crowning a hill—a phrase which applies to all these towns; for they are all comely, all well built, clean, orderly, pleasant to the eye, and cheering to the spirit; and they are all situated upon hills. Therefore we will give that phrase a rest. The Indians have a tradition that Marquette and Joliet camped where Davenport now stands, in 1673. The next white man who camped there, did it about a hundred and seventy years later—in 1834. Davenport has gathered its thirty thousand people within the past thirty years. She sends more children to her schools now, than her whole population numbered twenty-three years ago. She has the usual Upper-River quota of factories, newspapers, and institutions of learning; she has telephones, local telegraphs, an electric alarm, and an admirable paid fire department, consisting of six hook and ladder companies, four steam fire engines, and thirty churches. Davenport is the official residence of two bishops— Episcopal and Catholic.

Opposite Davenport is the flourishing town of Rock Island, which lies at the foot of the Upper Rapids. A great railroad bridge connects the two towns—one of the thirteen which fret the Mississippi and the pilots, between St. Louis and St. Paul.

The charming island of Rock Island, three miles long and half a mile wide, belongs to the United States, and the Government has turned it into a wonderful park, enhancing its natural attractions by art, and threading its fine forests with many miles of drives. Near the centre of the island one catches glimpses, through the trees, of ten vast stone four-story buildings, each of which covers an acre of ground. These are the Government workshops; for the Rock Island establishment is a national armory and arsenal.

We move up the river—always through enchanting scenery, there being no other kind on the Upper Mississippi—and pass Moline, a centre of vast manufacturing industries; and Clinton and Lyons, great lumber centres; and presently reach Dubuque, which is situated in a rich mineral region. The lead mines are very productive, and of wide extent. Dubuque has a great number of manufacturing establishments; among them a plough factory which has for customers all Christendom in general. At least so I was told by an agent of the concern who was on the boat. He said:—

"You show me any country under the sun where they really know *how* to plough, and if I don't show you our mark on the plough they use, I 'll eat that plough; and I won't ask for any Woostershyre sauce to flavor it up with, either."

All this part of the river is rich in Indian history and traditions. Black Hawk's was once a puissant name hereabouts; as was Keokuk's, further down. A few miles below Dubuque is the Tête de Mort—Death's-head rock, or bluff—to the top of which the French drove a band of Indians, in early times, and cooped them up there, with death for a certainty, and only the manner of it matter of choice—to starve, or jump off and kill themselves. Black Hawk adopted the ways of the white people, toward the end of his life; and when he died he was buried, near Des Moines, in Christian fashion, modified by Indian custom; that is to say, clothed in a Christian military uniform, and with a Christian cane in his hand, but deposited in the grave in a sitting posture. Formerly, a horse had always been buried with a chief. The substitution of the cane shows that Black Hawk's haughty nature was really humbled, and he expected to walk when he got over.

We noticed that above Dubuque the water of the Mississippi was olive-green—rich and beautiful and semi-transparent, with the sun on it. Of course the water was nowhere as clear or of as fine a complexion as it is in some other seasons of the year; for now it was at flood stage, and therefore dimmed and blurred by the mud manufactured from caving banks.

The majestic bluffs that overlook the river, along through this region, charm one with the grace and variety of their forms, and the soft beauty of their adornment. The steep verdant slope, whose base is at the water's edge, is topped by a lofty rampart of broken, turreted rocks, which are exquisitely rich and mellow in color—mainly dark browns and dull greens, but splashed with other tints. And then you have the shining river, winding here and there and yonder, its sweep interrupted at intervals by clusters of wooded islands threaded by silver channels; and you have glimpses of distant villages, asleep upon capes; and of stealthy rafts slipping along in the shade of the forest walls; and of white steamers vanishing around remote points. And it is all as tranquil and reposeful as dreamland, and has nothing this-worldly about it—nothing to hang a fret or a worry upon.

Until the unholy train comes tearing along—which it presently does, ripping the sacred solitude to rags and tatters with its devil's warwhoop and the roar and thunder of its rushing wheels—and straightway you are back in this world, and with one of its frets ready to hand for your entertainment: for you remember that this is the very road whose stock always goes down after you buy it, and always goes up again as soon as you sell it. It makes me shudder to this day, to remember that I once came near not getting rid of my stock at all. It must be an awful thing to have a railroad left on your hands.

The locomotive is in sight from the deck of the steamboat almost the whole way from St. Louis to St. Paul—eight hundred miles. These railroads have made havoc with the steamboat commerce. The clerk of our boat was a steamboat clerk before these roads were built. In that day the influx of population was so great, and the freight business so heavy, that the boats were not able to keep up with the demands made upon their carrying capacity; consequently the captains were very independent and airy—pretty "biggity," as Uncle Remus would say. The clerk nut-shelled the contrast between the former time and the present, thus:—

"Boat used to land—captain on hurricane roof—mighty stiff and straight—iron ramrod for a spine—kid gloves, plug tile, hair parted behind—man on shore takes off hat and says:—

" 'Got twenty-eight tons of wheat, cap'n—be great favor if you can take them.'

"Captain says:—

" ''ll take two of them'—and don't even condescend to look at him.

"But now-a-days the captain takes off his old slouch, and smiles all the way around to the back of his ears, and gets off a bow which he has n't got any ramrod to interfere with, and says:—

" 'Glad to see you, Smith, glad to see you—you 're looking well—have n't seen you looking so well for years—what you got for us?'

" 'Nuth'n', says Smith; and keeps his hat on, and just turns his back and goes to talking with somebody else.

"Oh, yes, eight years ago, the captain was on top; but it 's Smith's turn now. Eight years ago a boat used to go up the river with every stateroom full, and people piled five and six deep on the cabin floor; and a solid deck-load of immigrants and harvesters down below, into the bargain. To get a first-class stateroom, you 'd got to prove sixteen quarterings of nobility and four hundred years of descent, or be personally acquainted with the nigger that blacked the captain's boots. But it 's all changed now; plenty staterooms above, no harvesters below—there 's a patent self-binder now, and they don't have harvesters any more; they 've gone where the woodbine twineth—and they did n't go by steamboat, either; went by the train."

Up in this region we met massed acres of lumber rafts coming down—but not floating leisurely along, in the old-fashioned way, manned with joyous and reckless crews of fiddling, song-singing, whiskey-drinking, breakdown-dancing rapscallions; no, the whole thing was shoved swiftly along by a powerful stern-wheeler, modern fashion, and the small crews were quiet, orderly men, of a sedate business aspect, with not a suggestion of romance about them anywhere.

Along here, somewhere, on a black night, we ran some exceedingly narrow and intricate island-chutes by aid of the electric light. Behind was solid blackness—a crackless bank of it; ahead, a narrow elbow of water, curving between dense walls of foliage that almost touched our bows on both sides; and here every individual leaf, and every individual ripple stood out in its natural color, and flooded with a glare as of noonday intensified. The effect was strange, and fine, and very striking.

We passed Prairie du Chien, another of Father Marquette's camping-places; and after some hours of progress through varied and beautiful scenery, reached La Crosse. Here is a town of twelve or thirteen thousand population, with electric lighted streets, and with blocks of buildings which are stately enough, and also architecturally fine enough, to command respect in any city. It is a choice town, and we made satisfactory use of the hour allowed us, in roaming it over, though the weather was rainier than necessary.

LIX.

Legends and Scenery

WE ADDED several passengers to our list, at La Crosse; among others an old gentleman who had come to this northwestern region with the early settlers, and was familiar with every part of it. Pardonably proud of it, too. He said:—

"You 'll find scenery between here and St. Paul that can give the Hudson points. You 'll have the Queen's Bluff—seven hundred feet high, and just as imposing a spectacle as you can find anywheres; and Trempeleau Island, which is n't like any other island in America, I believe, for it is a gigantic mountain, with precipitous sides, and is full of Indian traditions, and used to be full of rattlesnakes; if you catch the sun just right there, you will have a picture that will stay with you. And above Winona you 'll have lovely prairies; and then come the Thousand Islands, too beautiful for anything; green? why you never saw foliage so green, nor packed so thick; it 's like a thousand plush cushions afloat on a looking-glass—when the water 's still; and then the monstrous bluffs on both sides of the river—ragged, rugged, dark-com-plected—just the frame that 's wanted; you always want a strong frame, you know, to throw up the nice points of a delicate picture and make them stand out."

The old gentleman also told us a touching Indian legend or two—but not very powerful ones.

After this excursion into history, he came back to the scenery, and described it, detail by detail, from the Thousand Islands to St. Paul; naming its names with such facility, tripping along his theme with such nimble and confident ease, slamming in a three-ton word, here and there, with such a complacent air of 't is n't-anything,-I-can-do-it-any-time-I-want-to, and letting off fine surprises of lurid eloquence at such judicious intervals, that I presently began to suspect—

But no matter what I began to suspect. Hear him:—

"Ten miles above Winona we come to Fountain City, nest-ling sweetly at the feet of cliffs that lift their awful fronts,

Jovelike, toward the blue depths of heaven, bathing them in
virgin atmospheres that have known no other contact save
that of angels' wings.

"And next we glide through silver waters, amid lovely and
stupendous aspects of nature that attune our hearts to adoring
admiration, about twelve miles, and strike Mount Vernon, six
hundred feet high, with romantic ruins of a once first-class
hotel perched far among the cloud shadows that mottle its
dizzy heights—sole remnant of once-flourishing Mount Vernon, town of early days, now desolate and utterly deserted.

"And so we move on. Past Chimney Rock we fly—noble
shaft of six hundred feet; then just before landing at Min-
nieska our attention is attracted by a most striking promon-
tory rising over five hundred feet—the ideal mountain
pyramid. Its conic shape—thickly-wooded surface girding its
sides, and its apex like that of a cone, cause the spectator to
wonder at nature's workings. From its dizzy heights superb
views of the forests, streams, bluffs, hills and dales below and
beyond for miles are brought within its focus. What grander
river scenery can be conceived, as we gaze upon this enchanting landscape, from the uppermost point of these bluffs upon
the valleys below? The primeval wildness and awful loneliness
of these sublime creations of nature and nature's God, excite
feelings of unbounded admiration, and the recollection of
which can never be effaced from the memory, as we view
them in any direction.

"Next we have the Lion's Head and the Lioness's Head,
carved by nature's hand, to adorn and dominate the beau-
teous stream; and then anon the river widens, and a most
charming and magnificent view of the valley before us suddenly bursts upon our vision; rugged hills, clad with verdant
forests from summit to base, level prairie lands, holding in
their lap the beautiful Wabasha, City of the Healing Waters,
puissant foe of Bright's disease, and that grandest conception
of nature's works, incomparable Lake Pepin—these constitute a picture whereon the tourist's eye may gaze uncounted
hours, with rapture unappeased and unappeasable.

"And so we glide along; in due time encountering those
majestic domes, the mighty Sugar Loaf, and the sublime
Maiden's Rock—which latter, romantic superstition has in-

vested with a voice; and oft-times as the birch canoe glides near, at twilight, the dusky paddler fancies he hears the soft sweet music of the long-departed Winona, darling of Indian song and story.

"Then Frontenac looms upon our vision, delightful resort of jaded summer tourists; then progressive Red Wing; and Diamond Bluff, impressive and preponderous in its lone sublimity; then Prescott and the St. Croix; and anon we see bursting upon us the domes and steeples of St. Paul, giant young chief of the North, marching with seven-league stride in the van of progress, banner-bearer of the highest and newest civilization, carving his beneficent way with the tomahawk of commercial enterprise, sounding the warwhoop of Christian culture, tearing off the reeking scalp of sloth and superstition to plant there the steam-plow and the school-house — ever in his front stretch arid lawlessness, ignorance, crime, despair; ever in his wake bloom the jail, the gallows, and the pulpit; and ever —"

"Have you ever travelled with a panorama?"

"I have formerly served in that capacity."

My suspicion was confirmed.

"Do you still travel with it?"

"No, she is laid up till the fall season opens. I am helping now to work up the materials for a Tourist's Guide which the St. Louis and St. Paul Packet Company are going to issue this summer for the benefit of travellers who go by that line."

"When you were talking of Maiden's Rock, you spoke of the long-departed Winona, darling of Indian song and story. Is she the maiden of the rock? — and are the two connected by legend?"

"Yes, and a very tragic and painful one. Perhaps the most celebrated, as well as the most pathetic, of all the legends of the Mississippi."

We asked him to tell it. He dropped out of his conversational vein and back into his lecture-gait without an effort, and rolled on as follows: —

"A little distance above Lake City is a famous point known as Maiden's Rock, which is not only a picturesque spot, but is full of romantic interest from the event which gave it its name. Not many years ago this locality was a favorite resort

for the Sioux Indians on account of the fine fishing and hunting to be had there, and large numbers of them were always
to be found in this locality. Among the families which used
to resort here, was one belonging to the tribe of Wabasha.
We-no-na (first-born) was the name of a maiden who had
plighted her troth to a lover belonging to the same band. But
her stern parents had promised her hand to another, a famous
warrior, and insisted on her wedding him. The day was fixed
by her parents, to her great grief. She appeared to accede to
the proposal and accompany them to the rock, for the purpose of gathering flowers for the feast. On reaching the rock,
We-no-na ran to its summit and standing on its edge up-
braided her parents who were below, for their cruelty, and
then singing a death-dirge, threw herself from the precipice
and dashed them in pieces on the rock below."

"Dashed who in pieces—her parents?"

"Yes."

"Well, it certainly was a tragic business, as you say. And
moreover, there is a startling kind of dramatic surprise about
it which I was not looking for. It is a distinct improvement
upon the threadbare form of Indian legend. There are fifty
Lover's Leaps along the Mississippi from whose summit disappointed Indian girls have jumped, but this is the only jump
in the lot that turned out in the right and satisfactory way.
What became of Winona?"

"She was a good deal jarred up and jolted: but she got
herself together and disappeared before the coroner reached
the fatal spot; and 't is said she sought and married her true
love, and wandered with him to some distant clime, where
she lived happy ever after, her gentle spirit mellowed and
chastened by the romantic incident which had so early de-
prived her of the sweet guidance of a mother's love and a
father's protecting arm, and thrown her, all unfriended, upon
the cold charity of a censorious world."

I was glad to hear the lecturer's description of the scenery,
for it assisted my appreciation of what I saw of it, and enabled me to imagine such of it as we lost by the intrusion of
night.

As the lecturer remarked, this whole region is blanketed
with Indian tales and traditions. But I reminded him that

people usually merely mentioned this fact—doing it in a way to make a body's mouth water—and judiciously stopped there. Why? Because the impression left, was that these tales were full of incident and imagination—a pleasant impression which would be promptly dissipated if the tales were told. I showed him a lot of this sort of literature which I had been collecting, and he confessed that it was poor stuff, exceedingly sorry rubbish; and I ventured to add that the legends which he had himself told us were of this character, with the single exception of the admirable story of Winona. He granted these facts, but said that if I would hunt up Mr. Schoolcraft's book, published near fifty years ago, and now doubtless out of print, I would find some Indian inventions in it that were very far from being barren of incident and imagination; that the tales in Hiawatha were of this sort, and they came from Schoolcraft's book; and that there were others in the same book which Mr. Longfellow could have turned into verse with good effect. For instance, there was the legend of "The Undying Head." He could not tell it, for many of the details had grown dim in his memory; but he would recommend me to find it and enlarge my respect for the Indian imagination. He said that this tale, and most of the others in the book, were current among the Indians along this part of the Mississippi when he first came here; and that the contributors to Schoolcraft's book had got them directly from Indian lips, and had written them down with strict exactness, and without embellishments of their own.

I have found the book. The lecturer was right. There are several legends in it which confirm what he said. I will offer two of them—"The Undying Head," and "Peboan and Seegwun, an Allegory of the Seasons." The latter is used in Hiawatha; but it is worth reading in the original form, if only that one may see how effective a genuine poem can be without the helps and graces of poetic measure and rhythm:—

PEBOAN AND SEEGWUN

An old man was sitting alone in his lodge, by the side of a frozen stream. It was the close of winter, and his fire was almost out. He appeared very old and very desolate. His locks were white with age, and he trembled in every joint. Day after day passed in solitude, and he heard nothing but the sound of the tempest, sweeping before it the new-fallen snow.

One day, as his fire was just dying, a handsome young man approached and entered his dwelling. His cheeks were red with the blood of youth, his eyes sparkled with animation, and a smile played upon his lips. He walked with a light and quick step. His forehead was bound with a wreath of sweet grass, in place of a warrior's frontlet, and he carried a bunch of flowers in his hand.

"Ah, my son," said the old man, "I am happy to see you. Come in. Come and tell me of your adventures, and what strange lands you have been to see. Let us pass the night together. I will tell you of my prowess and exploits, and what I can perform. You shall do the same, and we will amuse ourselves."

He then drew from his sack a curiously wrought antique pipe, and having filled it with tobacco, rendered mild by a mixture of certain leaves, handed it to his guest. When this ceremony was concluded they began to speak.

"I blow my breath," said the old man, "and the stream stands still. The water becomes stiff and hard as clear stone."

"I breathe," said the young man, "and flowers spring up over the plain."

"I shake my locks," retorted the old man, "and snow covers the land. The leaves fall from the trees at my command, and my breath blows them away. The birds get up from the water, and fly to a distant land. The animals hide themselves from my breath, and the very ground becomes as hard as flint."

"I shake my ringlets," rejoined the young man, "and warm showers of soft rain fall upon the earth. The plants lift up their heads out of the earth, like the eyes of children glistening with delight. My voice recalls the birds. The warmth of my breath unlocks the streams. Music fills the groves wherever I walk, and all nature rejoices."

At length the sun began to rise. A gentle warmth came over the place. The tongue of the old man became silent.

The robin and bluebird began to sing on the top of the lodge. The stream began to murmur by the door, and the fragrance of growing herbs and flowers came softly on the vernal breeze.

Daylight fully revealed to the young man the character of his entertainer. When he looked upon him, he had the icy visage of *Peboan*.[1] Streams began to flow from his eyes. As the sun increased, he grew less and less in stature, and anon had melted completely away. Nothing remained on the place of his lodge-fire but the *miskodeed*,[2] a small white flower, with a pink border, which is one of the earliest species of northern plants.

"The Undying Head" is a rather long tale, but it makes up in weird conceits, fairy-tale prodigies, variety of incident, and energy of movement, for what it lacks in brevity.[3]

[1] Winter.
[2] The *trailing arbutus*.
[3] See Appendix D.

LX.

Speculations and Conclusions

W E REACHED ST. PAUL, at the head of navigation of the Mississippi, and there our voyage of two thousand miles from New Orleans ended. It is about a ten-day trip by steamer. It can probably be done quicker by rail. I judge so because I know that one may go by rail from St. Louis to Hannibal—a distance of at least a hundred and twenty miles—in seven hours. This is better than walking; unless one is in a hurry.

The season being far advanced when we were in New Orleans, the roses and magnolia blossoms were falling; but here in St. Paul it was the snow. In New Orleans we had caught an occasional withering breath from over a crater, apparently; here in St. Paul we caught a frequent benumbing one from over a glacier, apparently.

I am not trying to astonish by these statistics. No, it is only natural that there should be a sharp difference between climates which lie upon parallels of latitude which are one or two thousand miles apart. I take this position, and I will hold it and maintain it in spite of the newspapers. The newspaper thinks it is n't a natural thing; and once a year, in February, it remarks, with ill-concealed exclamation points, that while we, away up here are fighting snow and ice, folks are having new strawberries and peas down South; callas are blooming out of doors, and the people are complaining of the warm weather. The newspaper never gets done being surprised about it. It is caught regularly every February. There must be a reason for this; and this reason must be change of hands at the editorial desk. You cannot surprise an individual more than twice with the same marvel—not even with the February miracles of the Southern climate; but if you keep putting new hands at the editorial desk every year or two, and forget to vaccinate them against the annual climatic surprise, that same old thing is going to occur right along. Each year one new hand will have the disease, and be safe from its recurrence; but this does not save the newspaper. No, the newspaper is in as bad case as ever; it will forever have its new hand; and so, it will break out with the strawberry surprise every February as long as it lives. The new hand is curable; the newspaper itself is incurable. An act of Congress—no, Congress could not prohibit the strawberry surprise without questionably stretching its powers. An amendment to the Constitution might fix the thing, and that is probably the best and quickest way to get at it. Under authority of such an amendment, Congress could then pass an act inflicting imprisonment for life for the first offence, and some sort of lingering death for subsequent ones; and this, no doubt, would presently give us a rest. At the same time, the amendment and the resulting act and penalties might easily be made to cover various cognate abuses, such as the Annual-Veteran-who-has-Voted-for-Every-President-from-Washington-down, -and-Walked-to-the-Polls-Yesterday-with-as-Bright-an-Eye-and-as-Firm-a-Step-as-Ever, and ten or eleven other weary yearly marvels of that sort, and of the Oldest-Freemason, and Oldest-Printer, and Oldest-Baptist-Preacher, and Oldest-Alumnus sort, and Three-Children-Born-at-a-Birth sort, and so on, and so on. And then England would take it up and pass a law prohibiting the further use of Sidney Smith's jokes, and appointing a commissioner to construct some new ones. Then life would be a sweet dream of rest and peace, and the nations would cease to long for heaven.

But I wander from my theme. St. Paul is a wonderful town. It is put together in solid blocks of honest brick and stone, and has the air of intending to stay. Its post-office was established thirty-six years ago; and by and by, when the postmaster received a letter, he carried it to Washington, horseback, to inquire what was to be done with it. Such is the legend. Two frame houses were built that year, and several persons were added to the population. A recent number of the leading St. Paul paper, the "Pioneer Press," gives some statistics which furnish a vivid contrast to that old state of things, to wit: Population, autumn of the present year (1882), 71,000; number of letters handled, first half of the year, 1,209,387; number of houses built during three-quarters of the year, 989; their cost, $3,186,000. The increase of letters over the corresponding six months of last year was fifty per cent. Last year the new buildings added to the city cost above $4,500,000. St. Paul's strength lies in her commerce—I mean his commerce. He is a manufacturing city, of course—all the cities of that region are—but he is peculiarly strong in the matter of commerce. Last year his jobbing trade amounted to upwards of $52,000,000.

He has a custom-house, and is building a costly capitol to replace the one recently burned—for he is the capital of the State. He has churches without end; and not the cheap poor kind, but the kind that the rich Protestant puts up, the kind that the poor Irish "hired-girl" delights to erect. What a passion for building majestic churches the Irish hired-girl has. It is a fine thing for our architecture; but too often we enjoy her stately fanes without giving her a grateful thought. In fact, instead of reflecting that "every brick and every stone in this beautiful edifice represents an ache or a pain, and a handful of sweat, and hours of heavy fatigue, contributed by the back and forehead and bones of poverty," it is our habit to forget these things entirely, and merely glorify the mighty temple itself, without vouchsafing one praiseful thought to its humble builder, whose rich heart and withered purse it symbolizes.

This is a land of libraries and schools. St. Paul has three public libraries, and they contain, in the aggregate, some forty thousand books. He has one hundred and sixteen schoolhouses, and pays out more than seventy thousand dollars a year in teachers' salaries.

There is an unusually fine railway station; so large is it, in fact, that it seemed somewhat overdone, in the matter of size, at first; but at the end of a few months it was perceived that the mistake was distinctly the other way. The error is to be corrected.

The town stands on high ground; it is about seven hundred feet above the sea level. It is so high that a wide view of river and lowland is offered from its streets.

It is a very wonderful town indeed, and is not finished yet. All the streets are obstructed with building material, and this is being compacted into houses as fast as possible, to make room for more—for other people are anxious to build, as soon as they can get the use of the streets to pile up their bricks and stuff in.

How solemn and beautiful is the thought, that the earliest pioneer of civilization, the van-leader of civilization, is never the steamboat, never the railroad, never the newspaper, never the Sabbath-school, never the missionary—but always whiskey! Such is the case. Look history over; you will see. The missionary comes after the whiskey—I mean he arrives after the whiskey has arrived; next comes the poor immigrant, with axe and hoe and rifle; next, the trader; next, the miscellaneous rush; next, the gambler, the desperado, the highwayman, and all their kindred in sin of both sexes; and next, the smart chap who has bought up an old grant that covers all the land; this brings the lawyer tribe; the vigilance committee brings the undertaker. All these interests bring the newspaper; the newspaper starts up politics and a railroad; all hands turn to and build a church and a jail,—and behold, civilization is established forever in the land. But whiskey, you see, was the van-leader in this beneficent work. It always is. It was like a foreigner—and excusable in a foreigner—to be ignorant of this great truth, and wander off into astronomy to borrow a symbol. But if he had been conversant with the facts, he would have said,—

Westward the Jug of Empire takes its way.

This great van-leader arrived upon the ground which St. Paul now occupies, in June, 1837. Yes, at that date, Pierre Parrant, a Canadian, built the first cabin, uncorked his jug, and began to sell whiskey to the Indians. The result is before us.

All that I have said of the newness, briskness, swift progress, wealth, intelligence, fine and substantial architecture, and general slash and go, and energy of St. Paul, will apply to his near neighbor, Minneapolis—with the addition that the latter is the bigger of the two cities.

These extraordinary towns were ten miles apart, a few months ago, but were growing so fast that they may possibly be joined now, and getting along under a single mayor. At any rate, within five years from now there will be at least such a substantial ligament of buildings stretching between them and uniting them that a stranger will not be able to tell where the one Siamese twin leaves off and the other begins. Combined, they will then number a population of two hundred and fifty thousand, if they continue to grow as they are now growing. Thus, this centre of population at the head of Mississippi navigation, will then begin a rivalry as to numbers, with that centre of population at the foot of it—New Orleans.

Minneapolis is situated at the falls of St. Anthony, which stretch across the river, fifteen hundred feet, and have a fall of eighty-two feet—a waterpower which, by art, has been made of inestimable value, business-wise, though somewhat to the damage of the Falls as a spectacle, or as a background against which to get your photograph taken.

Thirty flouring mills turn out two million barrels of the very choicest of flour every year; twenty sawmills produce two hundred million feet of lumber annually; then there are woollen mills, cotton mills, paper and oil mills; and sash, nail, furniture, barrel, and other factories, without number, so to speak. The great flouring-mills here and at St. Paul use the "new process" and mash the wheat by rolling, instead of grinding it.

Sixteen railroads meet in Minneapolis, and sixty-five passenger trains arrive and depart daily.

In this place, as in St. Paul, journalism thrives. Here there are three great dailies, ten weeklies, and three monthlies.

There is a university, with four hundred students—and, better still, its good efforts are not confined to enlightening the one sex. There are sixteen public schools, with buildings which cost $500,000; there are six thousand pupils and one hundred and twenty-eight teachers. There are also seventy churches existing, and a lot more projected. The banks aggregate a capital of $3,000,000, and the wholesale jobbing trade of the town amounts to $50,000,000 a year.

Near St. Paul and Minneapolis are several points of interest—Fort Snelling, a fortress occupying a river-bluff a hundred feet high; the falls of Minnehaha; White-bear Lake, and so forth. The beautiful falls of Minnehaha are sufficiently celebrated—they do not need a lift from me, in that direction. The White-bear Lake is less known. It is a lovely sheet of water, and is being utilized as a summer resort by the wealth and fashion of the State. It has its club-house, and its hotel, with the modern improvements and conveniences; its fine summer residences; and plenty of fishing, hunting, and pleasant drives. There are a dozen minor summer resorts around about St. Paul and Minneapolis, but the White-bear Lake is *the* resort. Connected with White-bear Lake is a most idiotic Indian legend. I would resist the temptation to print it here, if I could, but the task is beyond my strength. The guide-book names the preserver of the legend, and compliments his "facile pen." Without further comment or delay then, let us turn the said facile pen loose upon the reader:—

A LEGEND OF WHITE-BEAR LAKE

Every spring, for perhaps a century, or as long as there has been a nation of red men, an island in the middle of White-bear Lake has been visited by a band of Indians for the purpose of making maple sugar.

Tradition says that many springs ago, while upon this island, a young warrior loved and wooed the daughter of his chief, and it is said, also, the maiden loved the warrior. He had again and again been refused her hand by her parents, the old chief alleging that he was no brave, and his old consort called him a woman!

The sun had again set upon the "sugar-bush," and the bright moon rose high in the bright blue heavens, when the young warrior took down his flute and went out alone, once more to sing the story of his love, the mild breeze gently moved the two gay feathers in his head-dress, and as he mounted on the trunk of a leaning tree, the damp snow fell from his feet heavily. As he raised his flute to his lips, his blanket slipped from his well-formed shoulders, and lay partly on the snow beneath. He began his weird, wild love-song, but soon felt that he was cold, and as he reached back for his blanket, some unseen hand laid it gently on his shoulders; it was the hand of his love, his guardian angel. She took her place beside him, and for the present they were happy; for the Indian has a heart to love, and in this pride he is as noble as in his own freedom, which makes him the child of the forest. As the legend runs, a large white-bear, thinking, perhaps, that polar snows and dismal winter weather extended everywhere, took up his journey southward. He at length approached the northern shore of the lake which now bears his name, walked down the bank and made his way noiselessly through the deep heavy snow toward the island. It was the same spring ensuing that the lovers met. They had left their first retreat, and were now seated among the branches of a large elm which hung far over the lake. (The same tree is still standing, and excites universal curiosity and interest.) For fear of being detected, they talked almost in a whisper, and now, that they might get back to camp in good time and thereby avoid suspicion, they were just rising to return, when the maiden uttered a shriek which was heard at the camp, and bounding toward the young brave, she caught his blanket, but missed the direction of her foot and fell, bearing the blanket with her into the great arms of the ferocious monster. Instantly every man, woman, and child of the band were upon the bank, but all unarmed. Cries and wailings went up from every mouth. What was to be done? In the meantime this white and savage beast held the breathless maiden in his huge grasp, and fondled with his precious prey as if he were used to scenes like this. One deafening yell from the lover warrior is heard above the cries of hundreds of his tribe, and dashing away to his wigwam he grasps his faithful knife, returns almost at a single bound to the scene of fear and fright, rushes out along the leaning tree to the spot where his treasure fell, and springing with the fury of a mad panther, pounced upon his prey. The animal turned, and with one stroke of his huge paw brought the lovers heart to heart, but the next moment the warrior, with one plunge of the blade of his knife, opened the crimson sluices of death, and the dying bear relaxed his hold.

That night there was no more sleep for the band or the lovers, and as the young and the old danced about the carcass of the dead monster, the gallant warrior was presented with another plume, and ere another moon had set he had a living treasure added to his heart. Their children for many years played upon the skin of the white-bear—from which the lake derives its name—and the maiden and the brave remembered long the fearful scene and rescue that made them one, for Kis-se-me-pa and Ka-go-ka could never forget their fearful encounter with the huge monster that came so near sending them to the happy hunting-ground.

It is a perplexing business. First, she fell down out of the tree—she and the blanket; and the bear caught her and fondled her—her and the blanket; then she fell up into the tree again—leaving the blanket; meantime the lover goes war-whooping home and comes back "heeled," climbs the tree, jumps down on the bear, the girl jumps down after him—apparently, for she was up the tree—resumes her place in the bear's arms along with the blanket, the lover rams his knife into the bear, and saves—whom, the blanket? No—nothing of the sort. You get yourself all worked up and excited about that blanket, and then all of a sudden, just when a happy climax seems imminent, you are let down flat—nothing saved but the girl. Whereas, one is not interested in the girl; she is not the prominent feature of the legend. Nevertheless, there you are left, and there you must remain; for if you live a thousand years you will never know who got the blanket. A dead man could get up a better legend than this one. I don't mean a fresh dead man either; I mean a man that's been dead weeks and weeks.

We struck the home-trail now, and in a few hours were in that astonishing Chicago—a city where they are always rubbing the lamp, and fetching up the genii, and contriving and achieving new impossibilities. It is hopeless for the occasional visitor to try to keep up with Chicago—she outgrows his prophecies faster than he can make them. She is always a novelty; for she is never the Chicago you saw when you passed through the last time. The Pennsylvania road rushed us to New York without missing schedule time ten minutes anywhere on the route; and there ended one of the most enjoyable five-thousand-mile journeys I have ever had the good fortune to make.

Appendix

A.

[*From the New-Orleans Times-Democrat, of March* 29, 1882.]

VOYAGE OF THE TIMES-DEMOCRAT'S RELIEF BOAT
THROUGH THE INUNDATED REGIONS.

IT WAS NINE O'CLOCK Thursday morning when the "Susie" left the Mississippi and entered Old River, or what is now called the mouth of the Red. Ascending on the left, a flood was pouring in through and over the levees on the Chandler plantation, the most northern point in Pointe Coupée parish. The water completely covered the place, although the levees had given way but a short time before. The stock had been gathered in a large flat-boat, where, without food, as we passed, the animals were huddled together, waiting for a boat to tow them off. On the right-hand side of the river is Turnbull's Island, and on it is a large plantation which formerly was pronounced one of the most fertile in the State. The water has hitherto allowed it to go scot-free in usual floods, but now broad sheets of water told only where fields were. The top of the protecting levee could be seen here and there, but nearly all of it was submerged.

The trees have put on a greener foliage since the water has poured in, and the woods look bright and fresh, but this pleasant aspect to the eye is neutralized by the interminable waste of water. We pass mile after mile, and it is nothing but trees standing up to their branches in water. A water-turkey now and again rises and flies ahead into the long avenue of silence. A pirogue sometimes flits from the bushes and crosses the Red River on its way out to the Mississippi, but the sad-faced paddlers never turn their heads to look at our boat. The puffing of the boat is music in this gloom, which affects one most curiously. It is not the gloom of deep forests or dark caverns, but a peculiar kind of solemn silence and impressive awe that holds one perforce to its recognition. We passed two negro families on a raft tied up in the willows this morning. They were evidently of the well-to-do class, as they had a supply of meal and three or four hogs with them. Their rafts were about twenty feet square, and in front of an improvised shelter earth had been placed, on which they built their fire.

The current running down the Atchafalaya was very swift, the Mississippi showing a predilection in that direction, which needs only to be seen to enforce the opinion of that river's desperate endeavors to find a short way to the Gulf. Small boats, skiffs, pirogues, etc., are in great demand, and many have been stolen by piratical negroes, who take them where they will bring the greatest price. From what was told me by Mr. C. P. Ferguson, a planter near Red River Landing, whose place has just gone under, there is much suffering in the rear of that place. The negroes had given up all thoughts of a crevasse there, as the upper levee had stood so long, and when it did come they were at its mercy. On Thursday a number were taken out of trees and off of cabin roofs and brought in, many yet remaining.

One does not appreciate the sight of earth until he has travelled through a flood. At sea one does not expect or look for it, but here, with fluttering leaves, shadowy forest aisles, house-tops barely visible, it is expected. In fact a grave-yard, if the mounds were above water, would be appreciated. The river here is known only because there is an opening in the trees, and that is all. It is in width, from Fort Adams on the left bank of the Mississippi to the bank of Rapides Parish, a distance of about sixty miles. A large portion of this was under cultivation, particularly along the Mississippi and back of the Red. When Red River proper was entered, a strong current was running directly across it, pursuing the same direction as that of the Mississippi.

After a run of some hours, Black River was reached. Hardly was it entered before signs of suffering became visible. All the willows along the banks were stripped of their leaves. One man, whom your correspondent spoke to, said that he had had one hundred and fifty head of cattle and one hundred head of hogs. At the first appearance of water he had started to drive them to the high lands of Avoyelles, thirty-five miles off, but he lost fifty head of the beef cattle and sixty hogs. Black River is quite picturesque, even if its shores are under water. A dense growth of ash, oak, gum, and hickory make the shores almost impenetrable, and where one can get a view down some avenue in the trees, only the dim outlines of distant trunks can be barely distinguished in the gloom.

A few miles up this river, the depth of water on the banks was fully eight feet, and on all sides could be seen, still holding against the strong current, the tops of cabins. Here and there one overturned was surrounded by drift-wood, forming the nucleus of possibly some future island.

In order to save coal, as it was impossible to get that fuel at any point to be touched during the expedition, a lookout was kept for a wood-pile. On rounding a point a pirogue, skilfully paddled by a youth, shot out, and in its bow was a girl of fifteen, of fair face, beautiful black eyes, and demure manners. The boy asked for a paper, which was thrown to him, and the couple pushed their tiny craft out into the swell of the boat.

Presently a little girl, not certainly over twelve years, paddled out in the smallest little canoe and handled it with all the deftness of an old voyageur. The little one looked more like an Indian than a white child, and laughed when asked if she were afraid. She had been raised in a pirogue and could go anywhere. She was bound out to pick willow leaves for the stock, and she pointed to a house near by with water three inches deep on the floors. At its back door was moored a raft about thirty feet square, with a sort of fence built upon it, and inside of this some sixteen cows and twenty hogs were standing. The family did not complain, except on account of losing their stock, and promptly brought a supply of wood in a flat.

From this point to the Mississippi River, fifteen miles, there is not a spot of earth above water, and to the westward for thirty-five miles there is nothing but the river's flood. Black River had risen during Thursday, the 23d, $1^3/4$ inches, and was going up at night still. As we progress up the river habitations become more frequent, but are yet still miles apart. Nearly all of them are deserted, and the out-houses floated off. To add to the gloom, almost every living thing seems to have departed, and not a whistle of a bird nor the bark of the squirrel can be heard in this solitude. Sometimes a morose gar will throw his tail aloft and disappear in the river, but beyond this everything is quiet—the quiet of dissolution. Down the river floats now a neatly whitewashed hen-house, then a cluster of neatly split fence-rails, or a door and a bloated carcass, solemnly guarded by a pair of buzzards, the only bird to be seen, which feast on the carcass as it bears them along. A picture-frame in which there was a cheap lithograph of a soldier on horseback, as it floated on told of some hearth invaded by the water and despoiled of this ornament.

At dark, as it was not prudent to run, a place alongside the woods was hunted and to a tall gum-tree the boat was made fast for the night.

A pretty quarter of the moon threw a pleasant light over forest and river, making a picture that would be a delightful piece of landscape study, could an artist only hold it down to his canvas. The motion of the engines had ceased, the puffing of the escaping steam was stilled, and the enveloping silence closed upon us, and such silence it was! Usually in a forest at night one can hear the piping of frogs, the hum of insects, or the dropping of limbs; but here nature was dumb. The dark recesses, those aisles into this cathedral, gave forth no sound, and even the ripplings of the current die away.

At daylight Friday morning all hands were up, and up the Black we started. The morning was a beautiful one, and the river, which is remarkably straight, put on its loveliest garb. The blossoms of the haw perfumed the air deliciously, and a few birds whistled blithely along the banks. The trees were larger, and the forest seemed of older growth than below. More fields were passed than nearer the mouth, but the same scene presented itself—smoke-houses drifting out in the pastures, negro quarters anchored in confusion against some oak, and the modest residence just showing its eaves above water. The sun came up in a glory of carmine, and the trees were brilliant in their varied shades of green. Not a foot of soil is to be seen anywhere, and the water is apparently growing deeper and deeper, for it reaches up to the branches of the largest trees. All along, the bordering willows have been denuded of leaves, showing how long the people have been at work gathering this fodder for their animals. An old man in a pirogue was asked how the willow leaves agreed with his cattle. He stopped in his work, and with an ominous shake of his head replied: "Well, sir, it 's enough to keep warmth in their bodies and that 's all we expect, but it 's hard on the hogs, particularly the small ones. They is dropping off powerful fast. But what can you do? It 's all we 've got."

At thirty miles above the mouth of Black River the water extends from Natchez on the Mississippi across to the pine hills of Louisiana, a distance of seventy-three miles, and there is hardly a spot that is not ten feet under it. The tendency of the current up the Black is toward the west. In fact, so much is this the case, the waters of Red River have been driven down from toward the Calcasieu country, and the waters of the Black enter the Red some fifteen miles above the mouth of the former, a thing never before seen by even the oldest steamboatmen. The water now in sight of us is entirely from the Mississippi.

Up to Trinity, or rather Troy, which is but a short distance below, the people have nearly all moved out, those remaining having enough for their present personal needs. Their cattle, though, are suffering and dying off quite fast, as the confinement on rafts and the food they get breeds disease.

After a short stop we started, and soon came to a section where there were many open fields and cabins thickly scattered about. Here were seen more pictures of distress. On the inside of the houses the inmates had built on boxes a scaffold on which they placed the furniture. The bed-posts were sawed off on top, as the ceiling was not more than four feet from the improvised floor. The buildings looked very insecure, and threaten every moment to float off. Near the houses were cattle standing breast high in the water, perfectly impassive. They did not move in their places, but stood patiently waiting for help to come. The sight was a distressing one, and the poor creatures will be sure to die unless speedily rescued. Cattle differ from horses in this peculiar quality. A horse, after finding no relief comes, will swim off in search of food, whereas a beef will stand in its tracks until with exhaustion it drops in the water and drowns.

At half-past twelve o'clock a hail was given from a flat-boat inside the line of the bank. Rounding to we ran alongside, and General York stepped aboard. He was just then engaged in getting off stock, and welcomed the "Times-Democrat Boat" heartily, as he said there was much need for her. He said that the distress was not exaggerated in the least. People were in a condition it was difficult even for one to imagine. The water was so high there was great danger of their houses being swept away. It had already risen so high that it was approaching the eaves, and when it reaches this point there is always imminent risk of their being swept away. If this occurs, there will be great loss of life. The General spoke of the gallant work of many of the people in their attempts to save their stock, but thought that fully twenty-five per cent had perished. Already twenty-five hundred people had received rations from Troy, on Black River, and he had towed out a great many cattle, but a very great quantity remained and were in dire need. The water was now eighteen inches higher than in 1874, and there was no land between Vidalia and the hills of Catahoula.

At two o'clock the "Susie" reached Troy, sixty-five miles above the mouth of Black River. Here on the left comes in Little River; just beyond that the Ouachita, and on the right the Tensas. These three rivers form the Black River. Troy, or a portion of it, is situated on and around three large Indian mounds, circular in shape, which rise above the present water about twelve feet. They are about one hundred and fifty feet in diameter and are about two hundred yards apart. The houses are all built between these mounds, and hence are all flooded to a depth of eighteen inches on their floors.

These elevations, built by the aborigines hundreds of years ago, are the only points of refuge for miles. When we arrived we found them crowded with stock, all of which was thin and hardly able to stand up. They were mixed together, sheep, hogs, horses, mules, and cattle. One of these mounds has been used for many years as the grave-yard, and to-day we saw attenuated cows lying against the marble tomb-stones, chewing their cud in contentment, after a meal of corn furnished by General York. Here, as below, the remarkable skill of the women and girls in the management of the smaller pirogues was noticed. Children were paddling about in these most ticklish crafts with all the nonchalance of adepts.

General York has put into operation a perfect system in regard to furnishing relief. He makes a personal inspection of the place where it is asked, sees what is necessary to be done, and then, having two boats chartered, with flats, sends them promptly to the place, when the cattle are loaded and towed to the pine hills and uplands of Catahoula. He has made Troy his headquarters, and to this point boats come for their supply of feed for cattle. On the opposite side of Little River, which branches to the left out of Black, and between it and the Ouachita, is situated the town of Trinity, which is hourly threatened with destruction. It is much lower than Troy, and the water is eight and nine feet deep in the houses. A strong current sweeps through it, and it is remarkable that all of its houses have not gone before. The residents of both Troy and Trinity have been cared for, yet some of their stock have to be furnished with food.

As soon as the "Susie" reached Troy, she was turned over to General York and placed at his disposition to carry out the work of relief more rapidly. Nearly all her supplies were landed on one of the mounds to lighten her, and she was headed down stream to relieve those below. At Tom Hooper's place, a few miles from Troy, a large flat, with about fifty head of stock on board, was taken in tow. The animals were fed, and soon regained some strength. To-day we go on Little River, where the suffering is greatest.

DOWN BLACK RIVER.

SATURDAY EVENING, March 25.

We started down Black River quite early, under the direction of General York, to bring out what stock could be reached. Going down river a flat in tow was left in a central locality, and from there men poled her back in the rear of plantations, picking up the animals wherever found. In the loft of a gin-house there were seventeen head found, and after a gangway was built they were led down into the flat without difficulty. Taking a skiff with the General, your reporter was pulled up to a little house of two rooms, in which the water was standing two feet on the floors. In one of the large rooms were huddled the horses and cows of the place, while in the other the Widow Taylor and her son were seated on a scaffold raised on the floor. One or two dug-outs were drifting about in the room ready to be put in service at any time. When the flat was brought up, the side of the house was cut away as the only means of getting the animals out, and the cattle were driven on board the boat. General York, in this as in every case, inquired if the family desired to leave, informing them that Major Burke, of "The Times-Democrat," has sent the "Susie" up for that purpose. Mrs. Taylor said she thanked Major Burke, but she would try and hold out. The remarkable tenacity of the people here to their homes is beyond all comprehension. Just below, at a point sixteen miles from Troy, information was received that the house of Mr. Tom Ellis was in danger, and his family were all in it. We steamed there immediately, and a sad picture was presented. Looking out of the half of the window left above water was Mrs. Ellis, who is in feeble health, whilst at the door were her seven children, the oldest not fourteen years. One side of the house was given up to the work animals, some twelve head, besides hogs. In the next room the family lived, the water coming within two inches of the bed-rail. The stove was below water, and the cooking was done on a fire on top of it. The house threatened to give way at any moment: one end of it was sinking, and, in fact, the building looked a mere shell. As the boat rounded to, Mr. Ellis came out in a dug-out, and General York told him that he had come to his relief; that "The Times-Democrat" boat was at his service, and would remove his family at once to the hills, and on Monday a flat would take out his stock, as, until that time, they would be busy. Notwithstanding the deplorable situation himself and family were in, Mr. Ellis did not want to leave. He said he thought he would wait until Monday, and take the risk of his house falling. The children around the door looked perfectly contented, seeming to care little for the danger they were in.

These are but two instances of the many. After weeks of privation and suffering, people still cling to their houses and leave only when there is not room between the water and the ceiling to build a scaffold on which to stand. It seemed to be incomprehensible, yet the love for the old place was stronger than that for safety.

After leaving the Ellis place, the next spot touched at was the Oswald place. Here the flat was towed alongside the gin-house where there were fifteen head standing in water; and yet, as they stood on scaffolds, their heads were above the top of the entrance. It was found impossible to get them out without cutting away a portion of the front; and so axes were brought into requisition and a gap made. After much labor the horses and mules were securely placed on the flat.

At each place we stop there are always three, four, or more dug-outs arriving, bringing information of stock in other places in need. Notwithstanding the fact that a great many had driven a part of their stock to the hills some time ago, there yet remains a large quantity, which General York, who is working with indomitable energy, will get landed in the pine hills by Tuesday.

All along Black River the "Susie" has been visited by scores of planters, whose tales are the repetition of those already heard of suffering and loss. An old planter, who has lived on the river since 1844, said there never was such a rise, and he was satisfied more than one quarter of the stock has been lost. Luckily the people cared first for their work stock, and when they could find it horses and mules were housed in a place of safety. The rise which still continues, and was two inches last night, compels them to get them out to the hills; hence it is that the work of General York is of such a great value. From daylight to late at night he is going this way and that, cheering by his kindly words and directing with calm judgment what is to be done. One unpleasant story, of a certain merchant in New Orleans, is told all along the river. It appears for some years past the planters have been dealing with this individual, and many of them had balances in his hands. When the overflow came they wrote for coffee, for meal, and, in fact, for such little necessities as were required. No response to these letters came, and others were written, and yet

these old customers, with plantations under water, were refused even what was necessary to sustain life. It is needless to
say he is not popular now on Black River.

The hills spoken of as the place of refuge for the people
and stock on Black River are in Catahoula parish, twenty-four
miles from Black River.

After filling the flat with cattle we took on board the family
of T. S. Hooper, seven in number, who could not longer
remain in their dwelling, and we are now taking them up
Little River to the hills.

THE FLOOD STILL RISING.

TROY, March 27, 1882, noon.

The flood here is rising about three and a half inches every
twenty-four hours, and rains have set in which will increase
this. General York feels now that our efforts ought to be directed towards saving life, as the increase of the water has
jeopardized many houses. We intend to go up the Tensas in
a few minutes, and then we will return and go down Black
River to take off families. There is a lack of steam transportation here to meet the emergency. The General has three
boats chartered, with flats in tow, but the demand for these
to tow out stock is greater than they can meet with prompt-
ness. All are working night and day, and the "Susie" hardly
stops for more than an hour anywhere. The rise has placed
Trinity in a dangerous plight, and momentarily it is expected
that some of the houses will float off. Troy is a little higher,
yet all are in the water. Reports have come in that a woman
and child have been washed away below here, and two cabins
floated off. Their occupants are the same who refused to
come off day before yesterday. One would not believe the
utter passiveness of the people.

As yet no news has been received of the steamer "Delia,"
which is supposed to be the one sunk in yesterday's storm on
Lake Catahoula. She is due here now, but has not arrived.
Even the mail here is most uncertain, and this I send by skiff
to Natchez to get it to you. It is impossible to get accurate
data as to past crops, etc., as those who know much about

the matter have gone, and those who remain are not well versed in the production of this section.

General York desires me to say that the amount of rations formerly sent should be duplicated and sent at once. It is impossible to make any estimate, for the people are fleeing to the hills, so rapid is the rise. The residents here are in a state of commotion that can only be appreciated when seen, and complete demoralization has set in.

If rations are drawn for any particular section hereabouts, they would not be certain to be distributed, so everything should be sent to Troy as a centre, and the General will have it properly disposed of. He has sent for one hundred tents, and, if all go to the hills who are in motion now, two hundred will be required.

B.

The condition of this rich valley of the Lower Mississippi, immediately after and since the war, constituted one of the disastrous effects of war most to be deplored. Fictitious property in slaves was not only righteously destroyed, but very much of the work which had depended upon the slave labor was also destroyed or greatly impaired, especially the levee system.

It might have been expected by those who have not investigated the subject, that such important improvements as the construction and maintenance of the levees would have been assumed at once by the several States. But what can the State do where the people are under subjection to rates of interest ranging from 18 to 30 per cent, and are also under the necessity of pledging their crops in advance even of planting, at these rates, for the privilege of purchasing all of their supplies at 100 per cent profit?

It has needed but little attention to make it perfectly obvious that the control of the Mississippi River, if undertaken at all, must be undertaken by the national government, and cannot be compassed by States. The river must be treated as a unit; its control cannot be compassed under a divided or separate system of administration.

Neither are the States especially interested competent to

combine among themselves for the necessary operations. The work must begin far up the river; at least as far as Cairo, if not beyond; and must be conducted upon a consistent general plan throughout the course of the river.

It does not need technical or scientific knowledge to comprehend the elements of the case if one will give a little time and attention to the subject, and when a Mississippi River commission has been constituted, as the existing commission is, of thoroughly able men of different walks in life, may it not be suggested that their verdict in the case should be accepted as conclusive, so far as any *a priori* theory of construction or control can be considered conclusive?

It should be remembered that upon this board are General Gilmore, General Comstock, and General Suter, of the United States Engineers; Professor Henry Mitchell (the most competent authority on the question of hydrography), of the United States Coast Survey; B. B. Harrod, the State Engineer of Louisiana; Jas. B. Eads, whose success with the jetties at New Orleans is a warrant of his competency, and Judge Taylor, of Indiana.

It would be presumption on the part of any single man, however skilled, to contest the judgment of such a board as this.

The method of improvement proposed by the commission is at once in accord with the results of engineering experience and with observations of nature where meeting our wants. As in nature the growth of trees and their proneness where undermined to fall across the slope and support the bank secures at some points a fair depth of channel and some degree of permanence, so in the project of the engineer the use of timber and brush and the encouragement of forest growth are the main features. It is proposed to reduce the width where excessive by brushwood dykes, at first low, but raised higher and higher as the mud of the river settles under their shelter, and finally slope them back at the angle upon which willows will grow freely. In this work there are many details connected with the forms of these shelter dykes, their arrangements so as to present a series of settling basins, etc., a description of which would only complicate the conception. Through the larger part of the river works of contraction will not be required, but nearly all the banks on the concave side of the bends must be held against the wear of the stream, and much of the opposite banks defended at critical points. The works having in view this conservative object may be generally designated works of revetment; and these also will be largely of brushwood, woven in continuous carpets, or twined into wire-netting. This veneering process has been successfully employed on the Missouri River; and in some cases they have so covered themselves with sediments, and have become so overgrown with willows, that they may be regarded as permanent. In securing these mats rubble-stone is to be used in small quantities, and in some instances the dressed slope between high and low river will have to be more or less paved with stone.

Any one who has been on the Rhine will have observed operations not unlike those to which we have just referred; and, indeed, most of the rivers of Europe flowing among their own alluvia have required similar treatment in the interest of navigation and agriculture.

The levee is the crowning work of bank revetment, although not necessarily in immediate connection. It may be set back a short distance from the revetted bank; but it is, in effect, the requisite parapet. The flood river and the low river cannot be brought into register, and compelled to unite in the excavation of a single permanent channel, without a complete control of all the stages; and even the abnormal rise must be provided against, because this would endanger the levee, and once in force behind the works of revetment would tear them also away.

Under the general principle that the local slope of a river is the result and measure of the resistance of its bed, it is evident that a narrow and deep stream should have less slope, because it has less frictional surface in proportion to capacity; *i.e.*, less perimeter in proportion to area of cross section. The ultimate effect of levees and revetments confining the floods and bringing all the stages of the river into register is to deepen the channel and let down the slope. The first effect of the levees is to raise the surface; but this, by inducing greater velocity of flow, inevitably causes an enlargement of section, and if this enlargement is prevented from being made at the expense of the banks, the bottom must give way and the form of the waterway be so improved as to admit this flow with less rise. The actual experience with levees upon the Mississippi River, with no attempt to hold the banks, has been favorable, and no one can doubt, upon the evidence furnished in the reports of the commission, that if the earliest levees had been accompanied by revetment of banks, and made complete, we should have to-day a river navigable at low water and an adjacent country safe from inundation.

Of course it would be illogical to conclude that the constrained river can ever lower its flood slope so as to make levees unnecessary, but it is believed that, by this lateral constraint, the river as a conduit may be so improved in form that even those rare floods which result from the coincident rising of many tributaries will find vent without destroying levees of ordinary height. That the actual capacity of a channel through alluvium depends upon its service during floods has been often shown, but this capacity does not include anomalous, but recurrent, floods.

It is hardly worth while to consider the projects for relieving the Mississippi River floods by creating new outlets, since these sensational propositions have commended themselves only to unthinking minds, and have no support among engineers. Were the river bed cast-iron, a resort to openings for surplus waters might be a necessity; but as the bottom is yielding, and the best form of outlet is a single deep channel, as realizing the least ratio of perimeter to area of cross section, there could not well be a more unphilosophical method of treatment than the multiplication of avenues of escape.

In the foregoing statement the attempt has been made to condense in as limited a space as the importance of the subject would permit, the general elements of the problem, and the general features of the proposed method of improvement which has been adopted by the Mississippi River Commission.

The writer cannot help feeling that it is somewhat presumptuous on his part to attempt to present the facts relating to an enterprise which calls for the highest scientific skill; but it is a matter which interests every citizen of the United States, and is one of the methods of reconstruction which ought to be approved. It is a war claim which implies no private gain, and no compensation except for one of the cases of destruction incident to war, which may well be repaired by the people of the whole country.

EDWARD ATKINSON.

Boston, April 14, 1882.

C.

RECEPTION OF CAPTAIN BASIL HALL'S BOOK IN THE UNITED STATES.

Having now arrived nearly at the end of our travels, I am induced, ere I conclude, again to mention what I consider as one of the most remarkable traits in the national character of the Americans; namely, their exquisite sensitiveness and soreness respecting everything said or written concerning them. Of this, perhaps, the most remarkable example I can give is the effect produced on nearly every class of readers by the appearance of Captain Basil Hall's "Travels in North America." In fact, it was a sort of moral earthquake, and the vibration it occasioned through the nerves of the republic, from one corner of the Union to the other, was by no means over when I left the country in July, 1831, a couple of years after the shock.

I was in Cincinnati when these volumes came out, but it was not till July, 1830, that I procured a copy of them. One bookseller to whom I applied told me that he had had a few copies before he understood the nature of the work, but that, after becoming acquainted with it, nothing should induce him to sell another. Other persons of his profession must, however, have been less scrupulous; for the book was read in city, town, village, and hamlet, steamboat, and stage-coach, and a sort of war-whoop was sent forth perfectly unprecedented in my recollection upon any occasion whatever.

An ardent desire for approbation, and a delicate sensitiveness under censure, have always, I believe, been considered as amiable traits of character; but the condition into which the appearance of Captain Hall's work threw the republic shows plainly that these feelings, if carried to excess, produce a weakness which amounts to imbecility.

It was perfectly astonishing to hear men who, on other subjects, were of some judgment utter their opinions upon this. I never heard of any instance in which the common-sense generally found in national criticism was so overthrown by passion. I do not speak of the want of justice, and of fair and liberal interpretation: these, perhaps, were hardly to be expected. Other nations have been called thin-skinned, but the citizens of the Union have, apparently, no skins at all; they wince if a breeze blows over them, unless it be tempered with adulation. It was not, therefore, very surprising that the acute and forcible observations of a traveller they knew would be listened to should be received testily. The extraordinary features of the business were, first, the excess of the rage into which they lashed themselves; and, secondly, the puerility of the inventions by which they attempted to account for the severity with which they fancied they had been treated.

Not content with declaring that the volumes contained no word of truth from beginning to end (which is an assertion I heard made very nearly as often as they were mentioned), the whole country set to work to discover the causes why Captain Hall had visited the United States, and why he had published his book.

I have heard it said with as much precision and gravity as if the statement had been conveyed by an official report, that Captain Hall had been sent out by the British government expressly for the purpose of checking the growing admiration of England for the government of the United States,—that it was by a commission from the treasury he had come, and that it was only in obedience to orders that he had found anything to object to.

I do not give this as the gossip of a coterie; I am persuaded that it is the belief of a very considerable portion of the country. So deep is the conviction of this singular people that they cannot be seen without being admired, that they will not admit the possibility that anv one should honestly and sincerely find aught to disapprove in them or their country.

The American Reviews are, many of them, I believe, well known in England; I need not, therefore, quote them here, but I sometimes wondered that they, none of them, ever thought of translating Obadiah's curse into classic American;

if they had done so, on placing (he, Basil Hall,) between brackets, instead of (he, Obadiah,) it would have saved them a world of trouble.

I can hardly describe the curiosity with which I sat down at length to peruse these tremendous volumes; still less can I do justice to my surprise at their contents. To say that I found not one exaggerated statement throughout the work is by no means saying enough. It is impossible for any one who knows the country not to see that Captain Hall earnestly sought out things to admire and commend. When he praises, it is with evident pleasure; and when he finds fault, it is with evident reluctance and restraint, excepting where motives purely patriotic urge him to state roundly what it is for the benefit of his country should be known.

In fact, Captain Hall saw the country to the greatest possible advantage. Furnished, of course, with letters of introduction to the most distinguished individuals, and with the still more influential recommendation of his own reputation, he was received in full drawing-room style and state from one end of the Union to the other. He saw the country in full dress, and had little or no opportunity of judging of it unhouselled, unanointed, unannealed, with all its imperfections on its head, as I and my family too often had.

Captain Hall had certainly excellent opportunities of making himself acquainted with the form of the government and the laws; and of receiving, moreover, the best oral commentary upon them, in conversation with the most distinguished citizens. Of these opportunities he made excellent use; nothing important met his eye which did not receive that sort of analytical attention which an experienced and philosophical traveller alone can give. This has made his volumes highly interesting and valuable; but I am deeply persuaded, that were a man of equal penetration to visit the United States with no other means of becoming acquainted with the national character than the ordinary working-day intercourse of life, he would conceive an infinitely lower idea of the moral atmosphere of the country than Captain Hall appears to have done; and the internal conviction on my mind is strong, that if Captain Hall had not placed a firm restraint on himself, he must have given expression to far deeper indignation than any he has uttered against many points in the American character, with which he shows from other circumstances that he was well acquainted. His rule appears to have been to state just so much of the truth as would leave on the mind of his readers a correct impression, at the least cost of pain to the sensitive folks he was writing about. He states his own opinions and feelings, and leaves it to be inferred that he has good grounds for adopting them; but he spares the Americans the bitterness which a detail of the circumstances would have produced.

If any one chooses to say that some wicked antipathy to twelve millions of strangers is the origin of my opinion, I must bear it; and were the question one of mere idle speculation, I certainly would not court the abuse I must meet for stating it. But it is not so.

.   .   .   .

The candor which he expresses, and evidently feels, they mistake for irony, or totally distrust; his unwillingness to give pain to persons from whom he has received kindness, they scornfully reject as affectation, and although they must know right well, in their own secret hearts, how infinitely more they lay at his mercy than he has chosen to betray; they pretend, even to themselves, that he has exaggerated the bad points of their character and institutions; whereas, the truth is, that he has let them off with a degree of tenderness which may be quite suitable for him to exercise, however little merited; while, at the same time, he has most industriously magnified their merits, whenever he could possibly find anything favorable.

D.

THE UNDYING HEAD.

In a remote part of the North lived a man and his sister, who had never seen a human being. Seldom, if ever, had the man any cause to go from home; for, as his wants demanded food, he had only to go a little distance from the lodge, and there, in some particular spot, place his arrows, with their barbs in the ground. Telling his sister where they had been placed, every morning she would go in search, and never fail of finding each stuck through the heart of a deer. She had then only to drag them into the lodge and prepare their food. Thus she lived till she attained womanhood, when one day her brother, whose name was Iamo, said to her: "Sister, the time is at hand when you will be ill. Listen to my advice. If you do not, it will probably be the cause of my death. Take the implements with which we kindle our fires. Go some distance from our lodge and build a separate fire. When you are in want of food, I will tell you where to find it. You must cook for yourself, and I will for myself. When you are ill, do not attempt to come near the lodge, or bring any of the utensils you use. Be sure always to fasten to your belt the implements you need, for you do not know when the time will come. As for myself, I must do the best I can." His sister promised to obey him in all he had said.

Shortly after, her brother had cause to go from home. She was alone in her lodge, combing her hair. She had just untied the belt to which the implements were fastened, when suddenly the event, to which her brother had alluded, occurred. She ran out of the lodge, but in her haste forgot the belt. Afraid to return, she stood for some time thinking. Finally, she decided to enter the lodge and get it. For, thought she, my brother is not at home, and I will stay but a moment to catch hold of it. She went back. Running in suddenly, she caught hold of it, and was coming out when her brother came in sight. He knew what was the matter. "Oh," he said, "did I not tell you to take care? But now you have killed me." She was going on her way, but her brother said to her, "What can you do there now? The accident has happened. Go in, and stay where you have always stayed. And what will become of you? You have killed me."

He then laid aside his hunting-dress and accoutrements, and soon after both his feet began to turn black, so that he could not move. Still he directed his sister where to place the arrows, that she might always have food. The inflammation continued to increase, and had now reached his first rib; and he said: "Sister, my end is near. You must do as I tell you. You see my medicine-sack, and my war-club tied to it. It contains all my medicines, and my war-plumes, and my paints of all colors. As soon as the inflammation reaches my breast, you will take my war-club. It has a sharp point, and you will cut off my head. When it is free from my body, take it, place its neck in the sack, which you must open at one end. Then hang it up in its former place. Do not forget my bow and arrows. One of the last you will take to procure food. The remainder, tie in my sack, and then hang it up, so that I can look towards the door. Now and then I will speak to you, but not often." His sister again promised to obey.

In a little time his breast was affected. "Now," said he, "take the club and strike off my head." She was afraid, but he told her to muster courage. "*Strike*," said he, and a smile was on his face. Mustering all her courage, she gave the blow and cut off the head. "Now," said the head, "place me where I told you." And fearfully she obeyed it in all its commands. Retaining its animation, it looked around the lodge as usual, and it would command its sister to go in such places as it thought would procure for her the flesh of different animals she needed. One day the head said: "The time is not distant when I shall be freed from this situation, and I shall have to undergo many sore evils. So the superior manito decrees, and I must bear all patiently." In this situation we must leave the head.

In a certain part of the country was a village inhabited by a numerous and warlike band of Indians. In this village was a family of ten young men—brothers. It was in the spring of the year that the youngest of these blackened his face and fasted. His dreams were propitious. Having ended his fast, he went secretly for his brothers at night, so that none in the village could overhear or find out the direction they intended to go. Though their drum was heard, yet that was a common occurrence. Having ended the usual formalities, he told how favorable his dreams were, and that he had called them together to know if they would accompany him in a war excursion. They all answered they would. The third brother from the eldest, noted for his oddities, coming up with his war-club when his brother had ceased speaking, jumped up. "Yes," said he, "I will go, and this will be the way I will treat those I am going to fight;" and he struck the post in the centre of the lodge, and gave a yell. The others spoke to him, saying: "Slow, slow, Mudjikewis, when you are in other peo-

ple's lodges." So he sat down. Then, in turn, they took the
drum, and sang their songs, and closed with a feast. The
youngest told them not to whisper their intention to their
wives, but secretly to prepare for their journey. They all
promised obedience, and Mudjikewis was the first to say so.

The time for their departure drew near. Word was given to
assemble on a certain night, when they would depart immediately. Mudjikewis was loud in his demands for his moccasins. Several times his wife asked him the reason. "Besides,"
said she, "you have a good pair on." "Quick, quick," said he,
"since you must know, we are going on a war excursion; so
be quick." He thus revealed the secret. That night they met
and started. The snow was on the ground, and they travelled
all night, lest others should follow them. When it was daylight, the leader took snow and made a ball of it, then tossing
it into the air, he said: "It was in this way I saw snow fall in
a dream, so that I could not be tracked." And he told them
to keep close to each other for fear of losing themselves, as
the snow began to fall in very large flakes. Near as they
walked, it was with difficulty they could see each other. The
snow continued falling all that day and the following night,
so it was impossible to track them.

They had now walked for several days, and Mudjikewis was
always in the rear. One day, running suddenly forward, he
gave the *saw-saw-quan*,[1] and struck a tree with his war-club,
and it broke into pieces as if struck with lightning. "Brothers," said he, "this will be the way I will serve those we are
going to fight." The leader answered, "Slow, slow, Mudjikewis, the one I lead you to is not to be thought of so lightly."
Again he fell back and thought to himself: "What! what! who
can this be he is leading us to?" He felt fearful and was silent.
Day after day they travelled on, till they came to an extensive
plain, on the borders of which human bones were bleaching
in the sun. The leader spoke: "They are the bones of those
who have gone before us. None has ever yet returned to tell
the sad tale of their fate." Again Mudjikewis became restless,
and, running forward, gave the accustomed yell. Advancing
to a large rock which stood above the ground, he struck it,
and it fell to pieces. "See, brothers," said he, "thus will I treat

[1] War-whoop.

those whom we are going to fight." "Still, still," once more said the leader; "he to whom I am leading you is not to be compared to the rock."

Mudjikewis fell back thoughtful, saying to himself: "I wonder who this can be that he is going to attack;" and he was afraid. Still they continued to see the remains of former warriors, who had been to the place where they were now going, some of whom had retreated as far back as the place where they first saw the bones, beyond which no one had ever escaped. At last they came to a piece of rising ground, from which they plainly distinguished, sleeping on a distant mountain, a mammoth bear.

The distance between them was very great, but the size of the animal caused him to be plainly seen. "There," said the leader, "it is he to whom I am leading you; here our troubles will commence, for he is a mishemokwa and a manito. It is he who has that we prize so dearly (*i.e.* wampum), to obtain which, the warriors whose bones we saw, sacrificed their lives. You must not be fearful; be manly. We shall find him asleep." Then the leader went forward and touched the belt around the animal's neck. "This," said he, "is what we must get. It contains the wampum." Then they requested the eldest to try and slip the belt over the bear's head, who appeared to be fast asleep, as he was not in the least disturbed by the attempt to obtain the belt. All their efforts were in vain, till it came to the one next the youngest. He tried, and the belt moved nearly over the monster's head, but he could get it no farther. Then the youngest one, and the leader, made his attempt, and succeeded. Placing it on the back of the oldest, he said, "Now we must run," and off they started. When one became fatigued with its weight, another would relieve him. Thus they ran till they had passed the bones of all former warriors, and were some distance beyond, when, looking back, they saw the monster slowly rising. He stood some time before he missed his wampum. Soon they heard his tremendous howl, like distant thunder, slowly filling all the sky; and then they heard him speak and say, "Who can it be that has dared to steal my wampum? earth is not so large but that I can find them;" and he descended from the hill in pursuit. As if convulsed, the earth shook with every jump he made. Very soon he approached the party. They, however, kept the belt, exchanging it from one to another, and encouraging each other; but he gained on them fast. "Brothers," said the leader, "has never any one of you, when fasting, dreamed of some friendly spirit who would aid you as a guardian?" A dead silence followed. "Well," said he, "fasting, I dreamed of being in danger of instant death, when I saw a small lodge, with smoke curling from its top. An old man lived in it, and I dreamed he helped me; and may it be verified soon," he said, running forward and giving the peculiar yell, and a howl as if the sounds came from the depths of his stomach, and what is called *checaudum*. Getting upon a piece of rising ground, behold! a lodge, with smoke curling from its top, appeared. This gave them all new strength, and they ran forward and entered it. The leader spoke to the old man who sat in the lodge, saying, "Ne-mesho, help us; we claim your protection, for the great bear will kill us." "Sit down and eat, my grandchildren," said the old man. "Who is a great manito?" said he. "There is none but me; but let me look," and he opened the door of the lodge, when, lo! at a little distance he saw the enraged animal coming on, with slow but powerful leaps. He closed the door. "Yes," said he, "he is indeed a great manito: my grand-children, you will be the cause of my losing my life; you asked my protection, and I granted it; so now, come what may, I will protect you. When the bear arrives at the door, you must run out of the other door of the lodge." Then putting his hand to the side of the lodge where he sat, he brought out a bag which he opened. Taking out two small black dogs, he placed them before him. "These are the ones I use when I fight," said he; and he commenced patting with both hands the sides of one of them, and he began to swell out, so that he soon filled the lodge by his bulk; and he had great strong teeth. When he attained his full size he growled, and from that moment, as from instinct, he jumped out at the door and met the bear, who in another leap would have reached the lodge. A terrible combat ensued. The skies rang with the howls of the fierce monsters. The remaining dog soon took the field. The brothers, at the onset, took the advice of the old man, and escaped through the opposite side of the lodge. They had not proceeded far before they heard the dying cry of one of the dogs, and soon after of the other. "Well," said the leader, "the old man will share their fate: so run; he will soon be after us." They started with fresh vigor, for they had received food from the old man: but very soon the bear came in sight, and again was fast gaining upon them. Again the leader asked the brothers if they could do nothing for their safety. All were silent. The leader, running forward, did as before. "I dreamed," he cried, "that, being in great trouble, an old man helped me who was a manito; we shall soon see his lodge." Taking courage, they still went on. After going a short distance they saw the lodge of the old manito. They entered immediately and claimed his protection, telling him a manito was after them. The old man, setting meat before them, said: "Eat! who is a manito? there is no manito but me; there is none whom I fear;" and the earth trembled as the monster advanced. The old man opened the door and saw him coming. He shut it slowly, and said: "Yes, my grandchildren, you have brought trouble upon me." Procuring his medicine-sack, he took out his small war-clubs of black stone, and told the young men to run through the other side of the lodge. As he handled the clubs, they became very large, and the old man stepped out just as the bear reached the door. Then striking him with one of the clubs, it broke in pieces; the bear stumbled. Renewing the attempt with the other war-club, that also was broken, but the bear fell senseless. Each blow the old man gave him sounded like a clap of thunder, and the howls of the bear ran along till they filled the heavens.

The young men had now run some distance, when they looked back. They could see that the bear was recovering from the blows. First he moved his paws, and soon they saw him rise on his feet. The old man shared the fate of the first, for they now heard his cries as he was torn in pieces. Again the monster was in pursuit, and fast overtaking them. Not yet discouraged, the young men kept on their way; but the bear was now so close, that the leader once more applied to his brothers, but they could do nothing. "Well," said he, "my dreams will soon be exhausted; after this I have but one more." He advanced, invoking his guardian spirit to aid him. "Once," said he, "I dreamed that, being sorely pressed, I came to a large lake, on the shore of which was a canoe, partly out of water, having ten paddles all in readiness. Do not fear," he cried, "we shall soon get it." And so it was, even as he had said. Coming to the lake, they saw the canoe with ten paddles, and immediately they embarked. Scarcely had they reached the centre of the lake, when they saw the bear arrive at its borders. Lifting himself on his hind legs, he looked all around. Then he waded into the water; then losing his footing he turned back, and commenced making the circuit of the lake. Meantime the party remained stationary in the centre to watch his movements. He travelled all around, till at last he came to the place from whence he started. Then he commenced drinking up the water, and they saw the current fast setting in towards his open mouth. The leader encouraged them to paddle hard for the opposite shore. When only a short distance from land, the current had increased so much, that they were drawn back by it, and all their efforts to reach it were in vain.

Then the leader again spoke, telling them to meet their fates manfully. "Now is the time, Mudjikewis," said he, "to show your prowess. Take courage and sit at the bow of the canoe; and when it approaches his mouth, try what effect your club will have on his head." He obeyed, and stood ready to give the blow; while the leader, who steered, directed the canoe for the open mouth of the monster.

Rapidly advancing, they were just about to enter his mouth, when Mudjikewis struck him a tremendous blow on the head, and gave the *saw-saw-quan*. The bear's limbs doubled under him, and he fell, stunned by the blow. But before Mudjikewis could renew it, the monster disgorged all the water he had drank, with a force which sent the canoe with great velocity to the opposite shore. Instantly leaving the canoe, again they fled, and on they went till they were completely exhausted. The earth again shook, and soon they saw the monster hard after them. Their spirits drooped, and they felt discouraged. The leader exerted himself, by actions and words, to cheer them up; and once more he asked them if they thought of nothing, or could do nothing for their rescue; and, as before, all were silent. "Then," he said, "this is the last time I can apply to my guardian spirit. Now, if we do not succeed, our fates are decided." He ran forward, invoking his spirit with great earnestness, and gave the yell. "We shall soon arrive," said he to his brothers, "at the place where my last guardian spirit dwells. In him I place great confidence. Do not, do not be afraid, or your limbs will be fear-bound. We shall soon reach his lodge. Run, run," he cried.

Returning now to Iamo, he had passed all the time in the same condition we had left him, the head directing his sister, in order to procure food, where to place the magic arrows, and speaking at long intervals. One day the sister saw the eyes of the head brighten, as if with pleasure. At last it spoke. "Oh, sister," it said, "in what a pitiful situation you have been the cause of placing me! Soon, very soon, a party of young men will arrive and apply to me for aid; but alas! How can I give what I would have done with so much pleasure? Nevertheless, take two arrows, and place them where you have been in the habit of placing the others, and have meat prepared and cooked before they arrive. When you hear them coming and calling on my name, go out and say, 'Alas! it is long ago that an accident befell him. I was the cause of it.' If they still come near, ask them in, and set meat before them. And now you must follow my directions strictly. When the bear is near, go out and meet him. You will take my medicine-sack, bows and arrows, and my head. You must then untie the sack, and spread out before you my paints of all colors, my war-eagle feathers, my tufts of dried hair, and whatever else it contains. As the bear approaches, you will take all these articles, one by one, and say to him, 'This is my deceased brother's paint,' and so on with all the other articles, throwing each of them as far as you can. The virtues contained in them will cause him to totter; and, to complete his destruction, you will take my head, and that too you will cast as far off as you can, crying aloud, 'See, this is my deceased brother's head.' He will then fall senseless. By this time the young men will have eaten, and you will call them to your assistance. You must then cut the carcass into pieces, yes, into small pieces, and scatter them to the four winds; for, unless you do this, he will again revive." She promised that all should be done as he said. She had only time to prepare the meat, when the voice of the leader was heard calling upon Iamo for aid. The woman went out and said as her brother had directed. But the war party being closely pursued, came up to the lodge. She invited them in, and placed the meat before them. While they were eating, they heard the bear approaching. Untying the medicine-sack and taking the head, she had all in readiness for his approach. When he came up she did as she had been told; and, before she had expended the paints and feathers, the bear began to totter, but, still advancing, came close to the woman. Saying as she was commanded, she then took the head, and cast it as far from her as she could. As it rolled along the ground, the blood, excited by the feelings of the head in this terrible scene, gushed from the nose and mouth. The bear, tottering, soon fell with a tremendous noise. Then she cried for help, and the young men came rushing out, having partially regained their strength and spirits.

Mudjikewis, stepping up, gave a yell and struck him a blow upon the head. This he repeated, till it seemed like a mass of brains, while the others, as quick as possible, cut him into very small pieces, which they then scattered in every direction. While thus employed, happening to look around where they had thrown the meat, wonderful to behold, they saw starting up and running off in every direction small black bears, such as are seen at the present day. The country was soon overspread with these black animals. And it was from this monster that the present race of bears derived their origin.

Having thus overcome their pursuer, they returned to the lodge. In the mean time, the woman, gathering the implements she had used, and the head, placed them again in the sack. But the head did not speak again, probably from its great exertion to overcome the monster.

Having spent so much time and traversed so vast a country in their flight, the young men gave up the idea of ever returning to their own country, and game being plenty, they determined to remain where they now were. One day they moved off some distance from the lodge for the purpose of hunting, having left the wampum with the woman. They were very successful, and amused themselves, as all young men do when alone, by talking and jesting with each other. One of them spoke and said, "We have all this sport to ourselves; let us go and ask our sister if she will not let us bring the head to this place, as it is still alive. It may be pleased to hear us talk, and

be in our company. In the mean time take food to our sister."
They went and requested the head. She told them to take it,
and they took it to their hunting-grounds, and tried to amuse
it, but only at times did they see its eyes beam with pleasure.
One day, while busy in their encampment, they were unex-
pectedly attacked by unknown Indians. The skirmish was
long contested and bloody; many of their foes were slain, but
still they were thirty to one. The young men fought desperately till they were all killed. The attacking party then retreated to a height of ground, to muster their men, and to
count the number of missing and slain. One of their young
men had stayed away, and, in endeavoring to overtake them,
came to the place where the head was hung up. Seeing that
alone retain animation, he eyed it for some time with fear and
surprise. However, he took it down and opened the sack, and
was much pleased to see the beautiful feathers, one of which
he placed on his head.

Starting off, it waved gracefully over him till he reached his
party, when he threw down the head and sack, and told them
how he had found it, and that the sack was full of paints and
feathers. They all looked at the head and made sport of it.
Numbers of the young men took the paint and painted themselves, and one of the party took the head by the hair and
said: —

"Look, you ugly thing, and see your paints on the faces of
warriors."

But the feathers were so beautiful, that numbers of them
also placed them on their heads. Then again they used all
kinds of indignity to the head, for which they were in turn
repaid by the death of those who had used the feathers. Then
the chief commanded them to throw away all except the head.
"We will see," said he, "when we get home, what we can do
with it. We will try to make it shut its eyes."

When they reached their homes they took it to the council-
lodge, and hung it up before the fire, fastening it with raw
hide soaked, which would shrink and become tightened by
the action of the fire. "We will then see," they said, "if we
cannot make it shut its eyes."

Meantime, for several days, the sister had been waiting for
the young men to bring back the head; till, at last, getting

impatient, she went in search of it. The young men she found
lying within short distances of each other, dead, and covered
with wounds. Various other bodies lay scattered in different
directions around them. She searched for the head and sack,
but they were nowhere to be found. She raised her voice and
wept, and blackened her face. Then she walked in different
directions, till she came to the place from whence the head
had been taken. Then she found the magic bow and arrows,
where the young men, ignorant of their qualities, had left
them. She thought to herself that she would find her
brother's head, and came to a piece of rising ground, and
there saw some of his paints and feathers. These she carefully
put up, and hung upon the branch of a tree till her return.

At dusk she arrived at the first lodge of a very extensive
village. Here she used a charm, common among Indians
when they wish to meet with a kind reception. On applying
to the old man and woman of the lodge, she was kindly received. She made known her errand. The old man promised
to aid her, and told her the head was hung up before the
council-fire, and that the chiefs of the village, with their
young men, kept watch over it continually. The former are
considered as manitoes. She said she only wished to see it,
and would be satisfied if she could only get to the door of the
lodge. She knew she had not sufficient power to take it by
force. "Come with me," said the Indian, "I will take you
there." They went, and they took their seats near the door.
The council-lodge was filled with warriors, amusing themselves with games, and constantly keeping up a fire to smoke
the head, as they said, to make dry meat. They saw the head
move, and not knowing what to make of it, one spoke and
said: "Ha! ha! It is beginning to feel the effects of the smoke."
The sister looked up from the door, and her eyes met those
of her brother, and tears rolled down the cheeks of the head.
"Well," said the chief, "I thought we would make you do
something at last. Look! look at it—shedding tears," said he
to those around him; and they all laughed and passed their
jokes upon it. The chief, looking around, and observing the
woman, after some time said to the man who came with her:
"Who have you got there? I have never seen that woman before in our village." "Yes," replied the man, "you have seen

her; she is a relation of mine, and seldom goes out. She stays at my lodge, and asked me to allow her to come with me to this place." In the centre of the lodge sat one of those young men who are always forward, and fond of boasting and displaying themselves before others. "Why," said he, "I have seen her often, and it is to this lodge I go almost every night to court her." All the others laughed and continued their games. The young man did not know he was telling a lie to the woman's advantage, who by that means escaped.

She returned to the man's lodge, and immediately set out for her own country. Coming to the spot where the bodies of her adopted brothers lay, she placed them together, their feet toward the east. Then taking an axe which she had, she cast it up into the air, crying out, "Brothers, get up from under it, or it will fall on you." This she repeated three times, and the third time the brothers all arose and stood on their feet.

Mudjikewis commenced rubbing his eyes and stretching himself. "Why," said he, "I have overslept myself." "No, indeed," said one of the others, "do you not know we were all killed, and that it is our sister who has brought us to life?" The young men took the bodies of their enemies and burned them. Soon after, the woman went to procure wives for them, in a distant country, they knew not where; but she returned with ten young women, which she gave to the ten young men, beginning with the eldest. Mudjikewis stepped to and fro, uneasy lest he should not get the one he liked. But he was not disappointed, for she fell to his lot. And they were well matched, for she was a female magician. They then all moved into a very large lodge, and their sister told them that the women must now take turns in going to her brother's head every night, trying to untie it. They all said they would do so with pleasure. The eldest made the first attempt, and with a rushing noise she fled through the air.

Toward daylight she returned. She had been unsuccessful, as she succeeded in untying only one of the knots. All took their turns regularly, and each one succeeded in untying only one knot each time. But when the youngest went, she commenced the work as soon as she reached the lodge; although it had always been occupied, still the Indians never could see any one. For ten nights now, the smoke had not ascended, but filled the lodge and drove them out. This last night they were all driven out, and the young woman carried off the head.

The young people and the sister heard the young woman coming high through the air, and they heard her saying: "Prepare the body of our brother." And as soon as they heard it, they went to a small lodge where the black body of Iamo lay. His sister commenced cutting the neck part, from which the neck had been severed. She cut so deep as to cause it to bleed; and the others who were present, by rubbing the body and applying medicines, expelled the blackness. In the mean time the one who brought it, by cutting the neck of the head, caused that also to bleed.

As soon as she arrived, they placed that close to the body, and, by aid of medicines and various other means, succeeded in restoring Iamo to all his former beauty and manliness. All rejoiced in the happy termination of their troubles, and they had spent some time joyfully together, when Iamo said: "Now I will divide the wampum;" and getting the belt which contained it, he commenced with the eldest, giving it in equal portions. But the youngest got the most splendid and beautiful, as the bottom of the belt held the richest and rarest.

They were told that, since they had all once died, and were restored to life, they were no longer mortal, but spirits, and they were assigned different stations in the invisible world. Only Mudjikewis's place was, however, named. He was to direct the west wind, hence generally called Kebeyun, there to remain forever. They were commanded, as they had it in their power, to do good to the inhabitants of the earth, and, forgetting their sufferings in procuring the wampum, to give all things with a liberal hand. And they were also commanded that it should also be held by them sacred; those grains or shells of the pale hue to be emblematic of peace, while those of the darker hue would lead to evil and war.

The spirits then, amid songs and shouts, took their flight to their respective abodes on high; while Iamo, with his sister Iamoqua, descended into the depths below.

Chronology

1835   Samuel Langhorne Clemens born November 30 in Florida, Missouri, third of the four children of John Marshall Clemens (1798–1847) and Jane Lampton Clemens (1803–90) who survived into adulthood. The other children were: Orion (1825–97); Pamela (1827–1904); and Henry (1838–58). The Clemenses, of slaveholding but struggling Virginia farming stock, arrived about June 1 in Florida after unsuccessful efforts to establish themselves in Kentucky and Tennessee. Martha Ann Quarles, sister of Jane Clemens, and her husband, John Quarles, were already in Florida.

1839   John Clemens—austere, industrious, luckless—moves his family thirty miles from inland Florida to Hannibal, a port village about 116 miles by road (or about 130 miles by water) north of St. Louis.

1847   Unsuccessful as storekeeper, farmer, lawyer, and landowner, John Clemens dies on March 24. A few months later, Sam begins part-time work but probably receives intermittent schooling for two additional years. During the autumn is employed in the printshop of Joseph P. Ament.

1848   Works in the office of Ament's *Missouri Courier* and lives meagerly in Ament's house as an apprentice.

1851   On January 16 publishes first known sketch, the humorous anecdote "A Gallant Fireman," in the Hannibal *Western Union*. The newspaper is owned and edited by his brother Orion. Receives little or no pay as printer and editorial assistant.

1852   Writes squibs for Orion's new paper, the *Journal*, and publishes a brief example of Southwestern humor, "The Dandy Frightening the Squatter," in the Boston *Carpet Bag*, May 1. On September 9 signs a sketch "W. Epaminondas Adrastus Perkins," probably the first of his many pseudonyms.

1853–57   Leaves Hannibal at the end of May, 1853, to work as a
           printer in St. Louis, New York, Philadelphia, Keokuk, and
           Cincinnati. Publishes humorous travel letters in the Mus-
           catine, Iowa, *Journal*.

1857–61   About April, 1857, becomes a cub pilot on the Mississippi
           under tutelage of Horace Bixby. Henry Clemens, a much-
           loved brother, dies (1858) as a result of an explosion on the
           steamboat *Pennsylvania*. Publishes May 17, 1859, in the
           New Orleans *Crescent* a widely read lampoon of Captain
           Isaiah Sellers, a senior pilot, from whom Clemens later
           claimed (though unconvincingly) he borrowed the pseu-
           donym "Mark Twain." License as a pilot granted him on
           September 9, 1859. Continues on the river until approxi-
           mately April 25, 1861, when river traffic is disrupted.

1861   Member of the Marion Rangers, a small Confederate mi-
           litia group, for perhaps two weeks. Through the influence
           of Edward Bates of St. Louis, Attorney General under
           Lincoln, Orion is appointed Secretary to the Nevada Ter-
           ritory. Sam accompanies Orion with some prospect of
           assisting him. They arrive in Carson City by stage on Au-
           gust 14. Sam is clerk of the Territorial Legislature October
           1 through November 29. Enters timber claims, speculates
           in mining stock, and prospects for silver.

1862   Contributes letters and sketches to the Keokuk, Iowa,
           Gate City; the Carson City, Nevada, *Silver Age*; the Vir-
           ginia City, Nevada, *Territorial Enterprise*; and the Sacra-
           mento, California, *Union*. Probably late in September
           joins the staff of the *Enterprise* as local reporter and re-
           ports on the proceedings of the legislature when it is in
           session. Quickly masters such popular forms of newspaper
           comedy as the satirical sketch, the tall tale, the hoax, and
           the burlesque; gains a reputation with Western readers.

1863   On February 3, in a letter from Carson City to the *Enter-
           prise* reporting legislative proceedings, signs himself for
           the first time as "Mark Twain." Vacations in San Francisco
           during May and June. Becomes a correspondent for the
           San Francisco *Morning Call*. Contributes to the *Golden
           Era*, a literary weekly.

1864   Leaves Virginia City on May 29, 1864, for San Francisco. Works about four months as a local reporter for the *Morning Call* but dislikes the restraints of straight reporting. Contributes to the *Californian*, a literary weekly edited by Bret Harte. Joins storytelling prospectors in the Tuolumne hills and hears, perhaps from Ben Coon of Angel's Camp, a tale about a jumping frog.

1865   Returns to San Francisco on February 25 and remains for a year writing for newspapers and literary periodicals. Publishes "Jim Smiley and His Jumping Frog"—often called his earliest masterpiece—in the New York *Saturday Press* for November 18, 1865.

1866   Leaves San Francisco for Sacramento at the end of February, then takes five-month journey to the Sandwich Islands (Hawaii) to report in letters to the Sacramento *Union* on prospects for industry and trade. October 2 enters the lucrative business of public lecturing and reading by delivering first of many lectures on the Islands. Already he is taking on the attributes of a charismatic public figure and metaphoric Western hero. Publicized as the best of the Western humorists, he sails, with conquest in mind, for New York on December 15 as roving correspondent for the San Francisco *Alta California*.

1867   Is commissioned by the *Alta* to sail June 10 on the first cruise ship, the *Quaker City*, for Europe and the Holy Land in order to send back entertaining travel letters. Dislikes most of his affluent, religiously minded fellow passengers, but accepts from Mrs. Abel W. Fairbanks ("Mother Fairbanks") correction of his manners and purification of his prose. Young Charles Jervis Langdon (born 1849), another passenger, is said to have shown him a miniature of his sister, Olivia Lewis Langdon (born 1845). Returns to United States on November 19. Meets Olivia (Livy) in New York on December 27. Her parents, the Jervis Langdons of Elmira, New York, are newly rich from mining and marketing coal. Serves briefly in Washington as private secretary to Senator William M. Stewart of Nevada. In collaboration with Charles Henry Webb publishes *The Celebrated Jumping Frog of Calaveras County and Other Sketches*.

1868   Lectures widely. Assists in support of his mother, sister, and his always aspiring, always indigent brother, Orion. Begins courtship of the semi-invalid Livy Langdon. Reworks and expands his *Quaker City* letters. At his insistence, Livy begins her career as chief among his many editors and censors. Livy's influence, like that of the East in general, is toward the serious and genteel, away from the vulgar and comic.

1869   With a loan from Livy's father, buys a one-third interest in the Buffalo *Express*. The thoroughly reworked *Quaker City* travel letters, published as *The Innocents Abroad*, are a great financial success and set patterns for a number of his later books.

1870   Marries Livy on February 2. The next day goes with members of the bridal party by private train to Buffalo, where he and Livy are installed in the handsome house Jervis Langdon has bought and furnished for them. Langdon dies on August 16. Son, Langdon, born to Livy November 7.

1871   Hating the tedium of newspaper work, sells house and interest in the *Express*, both at losses. Begins residence of twenty-one years in Hartford, Connecticut, interspersed with periods abroad and working summers at Quarry Farm, near Elmira, home of Susan Crane (Mrs. Theodore Crane), Livy's sister-by-adoption.

1872   Susan Olivia Clemens (Susy), born March 19. First-born, sickly Langdon dies in June. Clemens publishes *Roughing It*.

1873   Takes family for the first of several stays in Europe, some of long duration. Economy in living is often the chief object, as speculations and lavish expenditures consume his and Livy's income and a substantial portion of Livy's inheritance. Publishes *The Gilded Age* with co-author Charles Dudley Warner, friend and Hartford neighbor.

1874   Clara Langdon Clemens born June 8 in Elmira. In September the family moves into their not-quite-complete, architecturally bizarre, extremely costly, luxuriously furnished mansion in the "Nook Farm" area of Hartford. Clemens increasingly in demand as a speaker at breakfasts, lunches, dinners, political rallies, reunions, fund raisings, and celebrations of all kinds.

1875   Publishes "Old Times on the Mississippi" (later part of *Life on the Mississippi*) in the *Atlantic Monthly*, then edited by his friend, admirer, and sometimes literary adviser and censor, William Dean Howells.

1876   In summer receives proofs of *The Adventures of Tom Sawyer* and begins writing *Adventures of Huckleberry Finn*. Is becoming deeply engaged in exploiting boyhood and the vernacular in a partly remembered, partly imagined Mississippi River valley, the post-frontier. Publishes *The Adventures of Tom Sawyer*.

1877   On December 17 delivers the "Whittier Birthday Speech," a burlesque treating the New Englanders Longfellow, Emerson, and Holmes in a way that shocks a number of listeners and is at times to be deeply regretted by Clemens.

1878–79   Travels in Europe, turns again to the writing of *Huckleberry Finn*.

1880   In this or the following year begins "investing" in the Paige typesetter, the most monetarily and psychically costly of his many speculations. Expends approximately $190,000 and untold hours before abandoning hope for this machine in January, 1895. Between late 1880 and early 1883 works once more on *Huckleberry Finn*. Publishes *A Tramp Abroad* and permits the private publication of the best known and most reprinted of his scatological writings, *1601. Conversation, as It Was by the Social Fireside, in the Time of the Tudors*. Jane Lampton Clemens (called Jean) born July 26.

1882   Makes trip on the Mississippi with James R. Osgood (at this time his publisher) and a stenographer to refresh his recollections, form new impressions, and collect information useful in completing *Life on the Mississippi*. Leaves New York on April 18, returns to Hartford on May 24. Publishes *The Prince and the Pauper,* a favorite with Livy and the children.

1883   Once again returns to writing *Huckleberry Finn*. Publishes *Life on the Mississippi*.

1884–85 Makes successful reading tour with George W. Cable, Louisiana writer and civil rights advocate (November 5– February 28). On December 10, 1884, publishes *Adventures of Huckleberry Finn* in England; on February 18, 1885, through his own publishing house, Charles L. Webster & Company, in the United States.

1889 Publishes *A Connecticut Yankee in King Arthur's Court*. Annoyed by its mixed reception in England.

1890 Jane Clemens (his mother) and Olivia L. Langdon (Livy's mother) both die.

1891 Sails for Europe in June and lives there for most of the next decade.

1894 Charles L. Webster & Company declares itself bankrupt in April. Clemens loses roughly $110,000 of his own money and $60,000 of Livy's. With the encouragement of Livy and the shrewd assistance of Henry H. Rogers, a vice-president of the Standard Oil Company, begins the difficult task of setting his tangled affairs in order, making his copyrights secure, and paying off his creditors. His inclination toward pessimism and determinism is heightened. Publishes *Pudd'nhead Wilson, A Tale* in the *Century Magazine*. (In book form the novel is entitled *The Tragedy of Pudd'nhead Wilson*.)

1895 In August begins a lecture trip around the world to raise money to repay creditors. Has become a public figure world-wide. Tour ends in Europe in July, 1896.

1896 Publishes *Personal Recollections of Joan of Arc*. Daughter Susy dies in Hartford of meningitis, August 18, while Clemens is in London, Livy and Clara are en route home. Clemens characteristically blames himself, then inveighs against fate and a God whom he increasingly depicts as malevolent. Jean Clemens diagnosed as epileptic; thereafter often in rest homes and clinics.

1897 Publishes *Following the Equator*.

1898   In March Henry Rogers notifies Clemens in Vienna that
            his undisputed creditors have been repaid. Within days
            Clemens attempts to engage in new, grandiose speculative
            ventures. During these last years he places increased em-
            phasis on the monetary value of his writings, which he has
            always treated as marketable products. At the same time
            he is strongly moved to write "seriously," to set down
            what he deems unprintable truths about God, religious
            institutions, man, politicians, tycoons, business associates,
            friends, and relatives.

1900   Returns to New York from England in October. Makes
            anti-missionary and anti-imperialist statements in connec-
            tion with actions of the United States in China and the
            Philippines.

1901   Receives honorary degree from Yale.

1902   Receives honorary degree from the University of Mis-
            souri. Isabel Lyon, who comes into the household to be
            secretary to Livy, becomes Clemens' secretary and general
            family factotum until forced out, April, 1909, following
            bitter quarrels, especially with Clara. Their fortunes partly
            restored, the Clemenses' combined incomes for the year
            amount to more than $100,000.

1903   Takes a villa in Florence for the benefit of Livy's health.

1904   Olivia Clemens dies in Florence on June 5, and her body
            is taken to Elmira for burial. Clara enters a sanitarium in
            July; later undergoes a number of restorative treatments.
            Clemens' pleasure in the companionship of little girls be-
            comes marked and continues until his death.

1906   Publishes *What Is Man?* privately and anonymously. In
            January accepts as his biographer Albert Bigelow Paine. A
            close association begins that lasts until Clemens' death and
            results in the publication of a massive biography and mis-
            cellaneous additional volumes.

1907   Receives honorary degree from Oxford University;
            enjoys displaying himself then and later in his crimson
            gown.

1908   John Howells (architect son of William Dean Howells) and Isabel Lyon supervise the building of a mansion called Stormfield near Redding, Connecticut. Clemens moves there from New York.

1909   Clara marries Ossip Gabrilowitsch, pianist and conductor, at Stormfield on October 6. Jean dies in bathtub, apparently during a seizure, on the morning of Christmas Eve.

1910   Clemens dies at Stormfield on April 21. Joseph Twichell of Hartford, one of Clemens' oldest friends, and Henry Van Dyck conduct services at the Presbyterian Brick Church in New York. Buried in Elmira on April 24 in the Langdon family plot, where little Langdon, Susy, Livy, and Jean had been interred before him. Left behind an enormous quantity of unpublished papers: autobiographical dictations, notebooks, letters, finished and unfinished sketches, essays, stories, polemics, and incomplete drafts of "The Mysterious Stranger," generally considered even in its unfinished state to be the most powerful of his later writings. For literary executors and editors, sifting and publishing these literary remains becomes almost at once a major, long-continuing enterprise.

Note on the Text

As early as January 1866, Clemens had contemplated writing a travel book about the Mississippi River. Five years later, he told his wife that he proposed to spend two months on the river and take notes, but the actual beginning of "the Mississippi book" did not come until William Dean Howells, editor of the *Atlantic Monthly*, pressed Clemens for a contribution to follow "A True Story" (November 1874). Clemens wrote twice to Howells on October 24, 1874, first to say "my head won't 'go,'" next to propose a topic. While walking in the woods with his friend and pastor, Joseph Twichell, he explained, he "got to telling him about old Mississippi days of steamboating glory & grandeur" as he had seen them from the pilot house. Twichell exclaimed, "What a virgin subject to hurl into a magazine!" The work that resulted went into seven issues of the *Atlantic*, January through August 1875, omitting July.

The contribution to the *Atlantic* was not nearly enough to make a subscription book, however, and only after a series of efforts to persuade Howells or some other friend to accompany him on a note-taking visit to the Mississippi did Clemens at last undertake the journey in 1882. By the terms of his contract for the book with James R. Osgood, Clemens became in effect his own publisher, Osgood—who had no experience in the publishing of subscription books—his agent.

Clemens redivided chapters, revised chapter titles, added "The Record of Some Famous Trips" (118–20), made perhaps forty-five other changes, and the *Atlantic* material became chapters IV through XVII of the book. In composing the additional forty-six chapters—a wearying task—Clemens made voluminous use of his own travel notes and padded the work with previously written but unpublished tales, such as "The Professor's Yarn" (chapter XXXVI). He also borrowed perhaps 11,000 words from other writers. Most interestingly, he took the "raft passage" from his manuscript for what later became *Adventures of Huckleberry Finn* and incorporated it in "Frescoes from the Past" (chapter III). Indeed, he crowded so many pages into his manuscript that some became superfluous; he was able to omit some 13,000 to 15,000 words and to move other material to appendices.

The first American edition (1883) is reprinted here. Ultimately, the methodically prepared text of the future will involve a comparison of the first American edition and the holograph manuscript held since 1909 by the J. Pierpont Morgan Library. The manuscript contains matter not in the book, and the book, matter not in the manuscript. Except for a few pages that Clemens called "the eighth batch" and—because of the illness of his typist—sent to Osgood in holograph form, the first American edition was set from a typescript made from the Morgan manuscript. Only a few pages of the typescript survive (at the Morgan Library and at the Houghton Library, Harvard). Clemens revised both the typescript and printer's proofs. That collating the manuscript with the first American edition will reveal errors in the book text has been shown by Willis Wager in "A Critical Edition of the Morgan Manuscript of Mark Twain's *Life on the Mississippi*," a dissertation submitted at New York University, Washington Square College, 1942. A few original manuscript readings are given in the notes that follow at 17.3, 164.14, 235.32, and 300.27–28.

The standards for American English continue to fluctuate and in some ways were different in earlier periods from what they are now. In nineteenth-century writings, for example, a word might be spelled in more than one way, even in the same work. Commas could be used expressively to suggest the movements of voice, and capitals sometimes gave significances to a word beyond those it might have in its lower-case form. Since modernization would remove these effects, this volume has preserved the spelling, punctuation, capitalization, and wording of the edition reprinted here.

The present edition is concerned only with presenting the text; it does not attempt to reproduce features of the typographic design—such as the display capitalization of chapter openings. Footnotes within the text are those supplied by Clemens. Open contractions are retained if they appeared in the original edition. Typographical errors have also been corrected. The following is a list of those errors, cited by page and line number: 49.5, What; 69.9, beeen; 173.32–33, a number; 176.36, R. N.

Notes

In the notes below, numbers refer to page and line of the present volume (line count includes chapter headings). No note is made for material included in a standard desk-reference book.

1.1   LIFE ON THE MISSISSIPPI]   Clemens considered, then rejected, titles that would relate this book to *The Innocents Abroad*, his early, successful travel volume: *Abroad on the Great River; Abroad on the Father of Waters;* and *Abroad on the Mississippi*.

14.34   burnt Fisher]   John Fisher (1459–1535), Bishop of Rochester, was convicted of treason against Henry VIII and was beheaded.

17.3   La Salle himself sued]   The manuscript reading here is: La Salle humbly sued.

19.1   rude . . . paintings]   Francis Parkman, whose *La Salle and the Discovery of the Great West* (1869; rev. ed. 1879) Clemens uses extensively in chapters I and II, mentions that the sighting of these paintings by Louis Joliet, Jacques Marquette, and their party "reminded them that the Devil was still lord paramount of this wilderness." A pair of monsters painted in red, black, and green—each as large as a calf and visible from the river—were painted on a flat rock. These paintings, later called the Piasa Bird or Thunder Bird, were destroyed during blasting operations in 1870 but were reproduced in 1934.

22.26   Natchez-under-the-hill]   The chief part of Natchez, Mississippi, was on high ground, but at the foot of the bluff there grew up around 1800 a small settlement notorious during much of the nineteenth century for its vices. Its decline began with the Civil War. For a comment by Clemens, see p. 247.

23.20–24   By . . . more.]   The "raft passage" that follows was composed in 1876 for a manuscript that later became *Adventures of Huckleberry Finn*. Clemens considered restoring the passage to chapter XVI of *Huckleberry Finn*, but he never did so.

23.33   bound for Cairo]   The Ohio river joins the Mississippi at Cairo, and the runaway slave, Jim, intended to go up the Ohio to safety.

24.22   it . . . song]   Clemens incorporated a version of this ballad in an incomplete farce that probably belongs to his San Francisco period, put it into *The Prince and the Pauper* in bowdlerized form, and sang it when he played a role in a dramatization by his children and their friends at Christmas time in 1884.

37.2   *The Boys' Ambition*]   Here begins what was called "Old Times on the Mississippi," first published in the *Atlantic Monthly*.

40.21   "mud clerks;"]   A mud-clerk, the second or third clerk of a steamer, so called because it was his duty to go ashore, often at a mere mud-bank, to receive or check off freight.

44.27   wildcat literature]   Unrealistic, unbelievable, in the same way that wildcat banks and wildcat currency were not to be depended on.

48.23   "Father . . . declining,"]   From what has been published as an anonymous hymn in two stanzas. The first stanza begins: "Fading, still fading, the last beam is shining, / Father in Heaven, the day is declining" (*Plymouth Collection of Hymns, for the use of Christian Congregations*, ed. H. W. Beecher [New York: A. S. Barnes and Co., 1855], p. 822. Under the title "The Last Beam," words and music are given by Roswell Dwight Hitchcock, et al., eds., *Carmina Sanctorum: A Selection of Hymns and Songs of Praise* [New York: A. S. Barnes and Co., 1886], p. 33).

101.11−12   'Buffalo Gals,]   Minstrel show performers changed the place reference in "Lubly Fan Will You Cum Out To Night" by "Cool White"—John Hodges—copyrighted 1844) as they moved from town to town. The most popular version was known as "Buffalo Gals" (copyrighted in 1848 by the "Ethiopian Serenaders").

103.21−22   organization . . . guild]   A Louisville Pilots' Benevolent Association was organized in 1841, a Little Rock Pilots' Association in 1845−49. Soon after 1854 the St. Louis–New Orleans association was formed. In 1870 associations of pilots were active on the runs between Cincinnati and St. Louis, Cincinnati and New Orleans, and St. Louis and New Orleans. The Steamboat Inspection Act of 1852 included a stringent system for licensing engineers and pilots. (In 1842 associations of engineers were formed in Cincinnati and St. Louis.)

115.35   "doctor"]   An independent steam pump with a working beam, used on western river steamers.

118.26   *Commodore Rollingpin's Almanac*]   John Henton Carter, a reporter of river news for St. Louis newspapers and an acquaintance of Clemens', used the pseudonym "Commodore Rollingpin."

145.2   *I . . . Muttons*]   *Revenons à nos moutons*: let us get back to our subject; a line from the anonymous *La Farce de maître Pathelin* (ca. 1464).

145.6   a poet . . . stenographer]   James R. Osgood, of Boston, at this time Clemens' publisher, and not a poet; and Roswell H. Phelps, a stenographer of Hartford, who made part of the trip with Clemens and Osgood. Clemens refers to him below as "Rogers."

149.30   Charles Augustus Murray]   Author of *Travels in North America during the Years 1834, 1835 & 1836 . . .* (2 vols., 1839). Clemens made use of eighteen or more travel books in writing *Life on the Mississippi*, including at least two not identified in his text. Among the writers made use of are: Captain Basil Hall, *Travels in North America in the Years 1827 and 1828* (3 vols., 1828); Mrs. Frances Trollope, *Domestic Manners of the Americans* (1832); and Alexander Mackay, *Western World, or Travels in the United States in 1846–47* (3 vols., 1849).

164.14   dress-reform period]   Manuscript reading here is: achieved by the dress-reform. This error suggests that Clemens' typist may have had parts of the holograph manuscript read to her.

166.26   Mr. Dickens's]   In his *American Notes for General Circulation* (2 vols., 1842), Charles Dickens took a frequently condemnatory look at American towns, manners, and mores. Slavery distressed him, and he was disgusted by what he saw of semi-frontier conditions.

176.15   images . . . Bolgia]   That is, of another ditch like the ten ditches of Malebolge, the eighth circle of Dante's *Inferno*; of a place of extreme disorder.

183.29–30   Ecclesiastes vii.13]   "Consider the work of God: for who can make *that* straight, which he hath made crooked?"

186.15–16   ask . . . numbers,]   More accurately, "Tell me not, in mournful numbers," from "A Psalm of Life," by Henry Wadsworth Longfellow.

186.31   Mr. Edward Atkinson]   Atkinson (1827–1905), named here and below (222.39–40; 223.5–6; 384.5), a Bostonian, published books on such topics as labor and capital, cotton manufacturing, and railways. He recommended diversified agriculture for the South.

188.32   Jesse James]   The well-known desperado (1847–82) who served as a Confederate guerilla under William Clarke Quantrill and, in 1866, formed a band of brigands that operated for approximately fifteen years.

206.21   A . . . CONFESSION]   James R. Osgood, who at the request of Clemens helped him with revisions, suggested that this story be condensed. Clemens decided against the suggestion, but he did condense or delete other passages at the suggestion of Osgood.

235.32   short stout bag]   The manuscript reading here is: shot-bag.

242.12   "Alonzo and Melissa;"]   Clemens is almost surely referring to *Alonzo and Melissa; or The Unfeeling Father* (1811), a plagiarized version by Daniel Jackson, Jr., of Isaac Mitchell's *The Asylum; or Alonzo and Melissa* (1810), first published as "Alonzo and Melissa, A Tale," in weekly installments (1804) in the *Political Barometer* of Poughkeepsie, New York.

269.25   author . . . "The Grandissimes."]   George Washington Cable. He and Clemens made a successful joint reading tour, November 5, 1884, through February 28, 1885.

272.33–36   I . . . South.]   Florida and Hannibal, Missouri, were usually called West, but they were slaveholding communities; and upon occasion Clemens considered them to have been in the South and himself to have been, like his parents, Southern.

278.30   "much people"]   St. Mark 5:21.

288.17   Mr. Warner]   Charles Dudley Warner, a Hartford neighbor.

291.10   Captain Eads' . . . jetties,"]   James Buchanan Eads (1820–87) constructed ironclad steamers and mortar boats for the Federal Government during the Civil War, built the Eads bridge (1874) across the Mississippi at St. Louis, and, his greatest work, by means of jetties deepened and fixed the mouths of the Mississippi.

300.3   Captain Isaiah Sellers]   Clemens said and wrote repeatedly, as he does below, that he borrowed the pseudonym "Mark Twain" from Captain Sellers (who supposedly had contributed river news over that signature to a New Orleans newspaper) at the death of Sellers. It has been established, however, that Clemens first used the pseudonym on February 3, 1863, and that Sellers did not die until March 6, 1864. It is possible, moreover, that Sellers never used the pseudonym.

300.27–28   Orleans . . . Orleans.]   Apparently the copyist missed a line here. The manuscript reads: Orleans and back—this boat was 115 tons burthen. In 1826 he was engaged on the 'Gen. Carrol,' between Nashville and New Orleans.

337.11   the "Jibbenainosay,"]   Robert Montgomery Bird, *Nick of the Woods, or the Jibbenainosay, a Tale of Kentucky* (2 vols., 1837).

345.23   Henry Clay Dean]   Dean was a Methodist circuit rider, lawyer, and Chaplain of the United States Senate.

346.8–9   a son . . . Claggett,]   William H. Claggett served in both houses of the Nevada legislature, was notary public for Unionville, Nevada, and later was in the Congress from Montana. He prospected for silver with Clemens.

347.28   the sparkling Burdette]   Robert J. Burdette (1844–1914), a platform lecturer, Baptist clergyman, newspaper humorist, and acquaintance of Clemens. He worked for the Peoria *Daily Transcript*, the Burlington *Daily Hawkeye*, and contributed columns to the Brooklyn *Daily Eagle*. Known as "the Burlington Hawkeye Man," he published *The Rise and Fall of the Mustache and Other "Hawk-Eyetems"* (1877).

359.11   Mr. Schoolcraft's book]   Clemens is probably referring to Henry Rowe Schoolcraft's *Algic Researches* . . . (2 vols., 1839), the first volume of which contains "Peboan and Seegwun" and "Iamo; or, the Undying Head."

365.24   Westward . . . way.]   George Berkeley (1685–1753), bishop of

Cloyne, in "Verses, on the Prospect of Planting Arts and Learning in America" (1752), wrote, "Westward the course of empire takes its way."

385.40   Obadiah's curse] The allusion is to Obadiah, shortest book in the Old Testament. A judgment is promised on the nations, including the Edomites, who gave aid to the Babylonians and gloated over Israel when Jerusalem fell in 586 B.C.

386.21–22   unhouselled, unanointed, unannealed] *Hamlet*, I, i, 77. The "unanointed" is Pope's emendation; the line should read: "Unhousel'd, disappointed, unaneled."

The Library of America Paperback Classics Series

American Speeches: Political Oratory from Patrick Henry to Barack Obama (various authors)
With an introduction by Ted Widmer
ISBN: 978-1-59853-094-0

The Education of Henry Adams by Henry Adams
With an introduction by Leon Wieseltier
ISBN: 978-1-59853-060-5

The Red Badge of Courage by Stephen Crane
With an introduction by Robert Stone
ISBN: 978-1-59853-061-2

The Souls of Black Folk by W.E.B. Du Bois
With an introduction by John Edgar Wideman
ISBN: 978-1-59853-054-4

Essays: First and Second Series by Ralph Waldo Emerson
With an introduction by Douglas Crase
ISBN: 978-1-59853-084-1

The Autobiography by Benjamin Franklin
With an introduction by Daniel Aaron
ISBN: 978-1-59853-095-7

The Varieties of Religious Experience by William James
With an introduction by Jaroslav Pelikan
ISBN: 978-1-59853-062-9

Selected Writings by Thomas Jefferson
With an introduction by Tom Wicker
ISBN: 978-1-59853-096-4

Selected Speeches and Writings by Abraham Lincoln
With an introduction by Gore Vidal
ISBN: 978-1-59853-053-7

The Call of the Wild by Jack London
With an introduction by E. L. Doctorow
ISBN: 978-1-59853-058-2

Moby-Dick by Herman Melville
With an introduction by Edward Said
ISBN: 978-1-59853-085-8

Selected Tales, with The Narrative of Arthur Gordon Pym
by Edgar Allan Poe
With an introduction by Diane Johnson
ISBN: 978-1-59853-056-8

Uncle Tom's Cabin by Harriet Beecher Stowe
With an introduction by James M. McPherson
ISBN: 978-1-59853-086-5

Walden by Henry David Thoreau
With an introduction by Edward Hoagland
ISBN: 978-1-59853-063-6

The Adventures of Tom Sawyer by Mark Twain
With an introduction by Russell Baker
ISBN: 978-1-59853-087-2

Life on the Mississippi by Mark Twain
With an introduction by Jonathan Raban
ISBN: 978-1-59853-057-5

The House of Mirth by Edith Wharton
With an introduction by Mary Gordon
ISBN: 978-1-59853-055-1

Leaves of Grass, The Complete 1855 and 1891–92 Editions
by Walt Whitman
With an introduction by John Hollander
ISBN: 978-1-59853-097-1

≡ The Library *of* America

The contents of this Paperback Classic are drawn from *Mark Twain: Mississippi Writings*, volume #5 in the Library of America series. It is joined in the series by six companion volumes, gathering the collected works of Mark Twain.

Created with seed funding from the National Endowment for the Humanities and the Ford Foundation, The Library of America is a non-profit cultural institution that preserves our nation's literary heritage by publishing, and keeping permanently in print, authoritative editions of America's best and most significant writing. Hailed as "the most important book-publishing project in the nation's history" (*Newsweek*), this award-winning series maintains America's most treasured writers in "the finest-looking, longest-lasting edition ever made" (*The New Republic*).

Since 1982, over 190 hardcover volumes have been published in the Library of America series, each containing up to 1600 pages and including a number of works. In many cases, the complete works of a writer are collected in as few as three compact volumes. New volumes are added each year to make all the essential writings of America's foremost novelists, historians, poets, essayists, philosophers, playwrights, journalists, and statesmen part of The Library of America.

Each volume features: authoritative, unabridged texts • a chronology of the author's life, helpful notes, and a brief textual essay • a handsomely designed, easy-to-read page • high-quality, acid-free paper, bound in a cloth cover and sewn to lie flat when opened • a ribbon marker and printed end papers.

For more information, a complete list of titles, tables of contents, and to request a catalogue, please visit **www.loa.org**